Friends of the human race and of what is holiest to it! Accept what appears to you most worthy of belief after careful and sincere examination, whether of facts or rational grounds; only do not dispute that prerogative of reason which makes it the highest good on earth, the prerogative of being the final touchstone of truth.

Immanuel Kant, "What Does It Mean
to Orient Oneself in Thinking?"

A voice says, "Cry!"
And I said, "What shall I cry?"
All flesh is grass, and all its beauty is like the flower of the field. . . .
The grass withers, the flower fades; but the word of our God
will stand for ever.

Isaiah 40:6-8

The Agnostic Inquirer

Revelation from a Philosophical Standpoint

Sandra Menssen and Thomas D. Sullivan

WILLIAM B. EERDMANS PUBLISHING COMPANY

GRAND RAPIDS, MICHIGAN / CAMBRIDGE, U.K.

Published 2007 by
Wm. B. Eerdmans Publishing Co.
2140 Oak Industrial Drive N.E., Grand Rapids, Michigan 49505 /
P.O. Box 163, Cambridge CB3 9PU U.K.

Printed in the United States of America

12 11 10 09 08 07   7 6 5 4 3 2 1

Library of Congress Cataloging-in-Publication Data

Menssen, Sandra Lee.
    The agnostic inquirer: revelation from a philosophical standpoint /
    Sandra Menssen and Thomas D. Sullivan.
        p.   cm.
    ISBN 978-0-8028-0394-8 (pbk.: alk. paper)
    1. Revelation.   2. Good and evil.   3. Christianity — Philosophy.
    4. Philosophical theology.   I. Sullivan, Thomas D.   II. Title.

    BT127.3.M46   2007
    212'.6 — dc22

                                            2007016747

www.eerdmans.com

Contents

Foreword

For a generation and more, the topic of divine revelation has fallen on hard times in philosophical circles. The interest has shifted to other topics. The topic rarely shows up in introductory textbooks. Students are at a loss to know what to make of its place in debates about the rationality of Christian belief. I do not say this by way of complaint. The good news is that in the last forty years we have seen a wealth of fresh ideas and stimulating proposals that have changed the debate about the justification of religious belief from top to bottom. When I went to Oxford as a graduate student in 1973, little did I know that we were at the beginning of a golden period in the philosophy of religion. Aside from the odd article here and there, even then the topic of divine reve-lation was pretty low in the philosophical food chain.[1] It was enough to get the whole debate about the justification of religious belief back on the table. The onus at the time was clearly on those who were committed theists to take a lead and create the intellectual space in which Christian belief could be taken seriously once again. The outcome over the last forty years, as seen in the wealth of material that has been published, has been startling in its origi-nality and depth. Perhaps we have been so busy absorbing the splendid new work in the epistemology of theology that we have not noticed our failure to look at divine revelation. Or maybe we were lulled into the illusion that we could help ourselves to the full weight of Christian conviction without deal-ing with this hoary old subject.

Whatever the etiology of our condition, we now have in this volume of Sandra Menssen and Thomas Sullivan a treatment of the topic of divine reve-

---

1. I recall a brilliant article by Austin Farrer, "Revelation," in Basil Mitchell, ed., *Faith and Logic* (London: George Allen and Unwin, 1957), pp. 84-107.

lation that is long overdue. I first came across their intellectual endeavors in a conference on evangelism in St. Louis. I was immediately stunned by the lucidity and originality of their thinking. Up until now they have concentrated on first-rate essays on tough topics in ethics and epistemology. They have an amazing ability to work together, producing material that is a seamless whole. It was only a matter of time before they came through with a major piece of work, and in *The Agnostic Inquirer* they have done exactly that. Over several summers I have been privileged with a number of graduate students and other philosophers to explore these ruminations in weeklong seminars at the University of St. Thomas, St. Paul, Minnesota, where Professors Menssen and Sullivan teach, as their initial ideas were being birthed and developed. Our discussions around their work were exceptionally fruitful and stimulating. As it happened, I was working at the same time on the topic of revelation.[2] I found the proposals of Menssen and Sullivan a splendid complement and spur to my own reflections. Where I was burrowing outward from within the Christian tradition, they were tunneling from the opposite direction from within the citadel of philosophy itself. The result is a startling achievement.

This material represents the highest standards of analytical philosophy. It is clear, rigorous, scrupulously fair, succinct, brimming with intellectual virtue, and extremely well organized. Every part of this volume deserves to be pondered with care. I cannot overemphasize how original and groundbreaking this work is. Few if any in the history of philosophy have considered the possibility that divine revelation constitutes evidence for the reality of God. We first had to get to the existence of God; only then could we take up the nature and significance of divine revelation. Nobody thought to question this agreed assumption. Not only have Menssen and Sullivan opened up a fresh discussion of divine revelation; they have also called into question in an entirely proper academic way the standard way of handling the ordering of issues in philosophy of religion.

The last really good piece of work on divine revelation in North America was that of George Mavrodes in his *Revelation in Religious Belief*.[3] That book is full of profound insight and good sense, but it fails to tackle the standard supposition that governs the whole discussion, namely, there is no point in bothering with divine revelation unless theism has first been established. Menssen and Sullivan tackle this assumption head on. Hence they create fresh

---

2. This work was published in *Crossing the Threshold of Divine Revelation* (Grand Rapids: Eerdmans, 2006).

3. Philadelphia: Temple University Press, 1988. Richard Swinburne's *Revelation: From Analogy to Metaphor* (Oxford: Clarendon Press, 1992) is another fine exception to the general rule that the topic of divine revelation has been systematically neglected.

space for a totally new look at the epistemic status of claims to divine revelation. There are hints in Mavrodes that divine revelation might stand as evidence of the existence of God, but these are not articulated. The argument in favor of this revisionary strategy is splendidly laid out and executed in *The Agnostic Inquirer*. All future work, if it is to be up to speed, will have to deal with what Menssen and Sullivan have done.

There will, of course, be resistance. Philosophers and theologians will want to stay by the old assumption that revelation is a secondary topic and go back to business as usual. In time they will have to come around and either accept the case made out here or offer a substantial rebuttal. If this book receives the attention it deserves, it could be as important as Alvin Plantinga's *God and Other Minds*[4] was in 1967, and as Basil Mitchell's *The Justification of Religious Belief*[5] was in 1973. Both these books are rightly seen in retrospect as landmark texts that were the harbinger of revolution in the field because they opened up a whole new discussion on the justification of theism that continues unabated in our own day. *The Agnostic Inquirer* could well do the same for the much-neglected topic of divine revelation. I can well envisage a whole new nest of issues emerging that will be pivotal for all future debate both about divine revelation and about the justification of religious belief. We certainly need to move in this direction.

One reason why this work is so important is that it provides an integrated discussion of the relation between natural theology and divine revelation. It is fully in touch with the current discussion in and around the topic of natural theology. What is becoming increasingly clear is that current attempts to justify robust forms of theism without drawing on divine revelation, most notably in the work of Alvin Plantinga and the wonderful arguments and insights in Reformed epistemology, fail to deliver the goods. This wealth of material does not really show how one can get to Christian theism, despite the bold claims to have done this. Once that becomes clearer, this work falls naturally into place as the beginning of the next phase of the discussion.

The primary audience for this work will be philosophers, theologians, graduate students, and the top end of the undergraduate world. It will take some time for some theologians to get on board. They are still suffering from a bad hangover from the hostile reaction to theology by analytical philosophers with which we are all familiar. Most mainline Protestant theologians have either given up divine revelation or are sheltering under the shadow of Karl Barth down now to the third generation. More conservative Protestant

---

4. Ithaca, NY: Cornell University Press.
5. London: Macmillan.

theologians and Roman Catholic theologians will be much more interested, for they never fully abandoned the intuition that revelation is pivotal in the elaboration and justification of Christian belief. The text is serious reading. I would use it immediately in my core seminar in philosophy of religion for incoming doctoral students and in my upper division seminars for seminary students. I regularly teach a course on divine revelation and have been looking for a text like this for some time. I would also use it in my general seminar on the justification of religious belief. I would look to use parts of it in my introductory course in theology.

I cannot recommend this book too highly. It brings back to life a long-neglected topic, divine revelation, which cries out for fresh analysis and attention. It advances a bold, original thesis. The argument throughout is clear, succinct, and rigorous. It advances the current discussion on the justification of theistic belief by calling attention to the shortcomings of the current options and opening a new network of issues. In all, this is a refreshing, substantial contribution to analytical philosophy of religion.

WILLIAM J. ABRAHAM

Acknowledgements

Many wonderful people helped us at various stages leading to the publication of this book. Some assisted years ago as we began to unfold our ideas in journal articles; others helped with drafts of the book itself.

We wish to thank these philosophers and theologians: William J. Abraham, Robert M. Adams, Helen Alford, Frederick Aquino, Gordon P. Barnes, Joseph M. Boyle, Jeffrey E. Brower, Christopher H. Conn, Kevin L. Flannery, J. L. A. (Jorge) Garcia, Laura L. Garcia, Jorge J. E. Gracia, Paul Gavrilyuk, Jerome (Yehuda) Gellman, Frank Gourley, John Greco, William Hasker, Patrick Lee, Anthony J. Lisska, Michael Gorman, Timothy McGrew, Daniel Menssen, Alvin Plantinga, Jeremiah Reedy, Bruce Reichenbach, Patrick Roche, Peter Shea, Quentin Smith, Richard Swinburne, Jerry L. Walls, and Linda Zagzebski; and Kenneth Konyndyk, who never saw a word of this book but inspired it in significant ways.

We are also grateful to the colleagues we interact with daily, who provided commentary, caution, and encouragement. We must single out for special mention John D. Kronen and Russell Pannier, whose ever-ready criticisms and suggestions immeasurably improved our arguments.

We thank our students who worked with earlier versions of the book; their questions and comments strengthened the text, and their enthusiasm for the project reassured us that the book was accessible to nonprofessionals.

Rachel A. Bauder, Ann M. Hale, Nicole W. Mass, Debra Shelito, and Laura Stierman helped with proofreading, indexing, and other matters. Gayatri Patnaik and Sarah Lloyd moved the project forward in its early phases. Jon Pott, Reinder Van Til, and Willem Mineur (Eerdmans) provided indispensable assistance; so did Jennifer Hoffman, to whom we are particularly indebted for her excellent editorial work and guidance. We are grateful to all.

ACKNOWLEDGMENTS

Our deepest gratitude goes to our families, and we dedicate this book to them, the living and our beloved deceased. Sandra Menssen thanks especially her mother, Lee Menssen, and sister, Carla Menssen; their selfless love and their generosity of spirit enrich us all. Thomas Sullivan thanks his Ginny, their children Thomas, Seanne Harris, Julie Brooks, Michael, Patrick, and Kerry LeClair, and their families for their limitless love and understanding.

PART I   Introducing a Preferable
Philosophical Approach to the Question
of Whether a Good God Has Revealed

1 The Need for an Alternative Philosophical Approach to a Perduring Question: Has a Good God Revealed Anything to Us?

1.1. The Search for a Reasoned Case: Starting Points

1.1.1. The Great Question: Inquiry and Meta-Inquiry

In Plato's magnificent portrayal of Socrates' last hour, the condemned philosopher reasons with his disciples about what follows death. At one point during the dialogue Socrates invites Simmias to present objections to the argument for immortality that Socrates has offered. Simmias begins by explaining his general attitude: if it is impossible to attain precise knowledge about immortality in our present life, then one should "adopt the best and most irrefutable of men's theories, and, borne upon this, sail through the dangers of life as upon a raft, *unless someone should make that journey safer and less risky upon a firmer vessel of some divine doctrine*."[1] Wrestling with the mysteries of life and death, Simmias harbors the desire for a revelation from the gods that would provide him a safer vessel, a ship.

Many agnostics today share both Simmias's interest in the possibility of a revelation from on high and his philosophical cast of mind, but their circumstances are otherwise markedly different, in at least two important ways.

First, Simmias could assume that the most noted thinkers in his world believed in a divine order, in the existence of at least one god. Nobody would laugh in his face, least of all the philosophical genius in front of him. Today, however, many of the learned in science and philosophy scorn such belief. In their eyes, all who cherish the idea that a transcendent being exists, including

---

1. Plato, *Phaedo*, 85 c-d; G. M. A. Grube, trans., *Plato: Five Dialogues* (Indianapolis: Hackett Publishing, 1981), p. 124 (italics added).

countless Hindus, Jews, Christians, and Muslims, betray profound ignorance of the evident lessons to be learned from the advance of science. In consequence of widespread doubt among the intelligentsia about the existence of God, a contemporary agnostic willing to take revelatory claims seriously appears to face not just the question of whether a God has revealed anything to us, but a deeper, more basic question: Is there, in fact, a God?

Second, and more positively, today's inquirer can consider revelatory claims that are far more attractive than the stories of Homer and Hesiod. True, many intellectuals see little or nothing to treasure in revelatory religions save those truths that human reason and experience can discover on their own, without reliance on the mythological grotesqueries that have set people against people in battles to the death over the Revealed Word of God. But millions more are drawn to teachings so powerful they have transformed the world, including the world of the rational nay-sayer, who assumes that the God to be denied is the God proclaimed in the great revelatory religions, not the paler divinities of worldviews untouched by these intriguing teachings.

Theistic philosophers today do not, of course, assume that an inquirer interested in the possibility of divine revelation can take the existence of a good God for granted.[2] Accordingly, they set out arguments for God's existence, beginning with the fact of the world's contingency, perhaps, or its apparent fine-tuning for life; they feed in data such as reports of religious experience; they reflect on the import of the world's evils. Abstracting from the content of putative revelations, these arguments are supposed to bring a person to the point of seeing that it is at least as likely as not that there is a good God. After that point has been reached, it is possible to move on to the question of whether there is a true revelation.

But setting things up this way, we will suggest, makes all too likely a negative answer to both the question of whether God exists and the question of whether a revelation has been given. Happily, we argue, another philosophical path is available. It involves moving investigation of the content of revelatory claims — the transformative claims of the great revelatory religions — up toward the beginning of agnostic inquiry. Though the philosophical and theological literature is full of material pertinent to elements of the argument we develop, we know of no other statement of the argument, or anything much like it, let alone

---

2. Although we understand the term "God" to refer to a being who is wholly good, we will sometimes call attention to the attribute of goodness, which has a special significance in our investigation, by speaking pleonastically of a "good God." Notice that we do not say a good God must be *unsurpassedly* good; "wholly good" will do for our purposes. We will be leaving it largely (though not entirely) an open question what attributes other than pure goodness a being must have to count as God.

an extended defense of the argument as a whole. However, while our approach deviates appreciably from that typically taken in works on the philosophy of religion, the process we recommend is far more congenial to actual inquirers' inclinations than the approach seemingly called for by many philosophers. For agnostics who are not philosophically trained often ponder claims that God has spoken in Scripture or other ways. They thus take in two questions simultaneously: whether there is a God and whether there is a true revelation. How can that be acceptable? Is the argument supposed to go: "There must be a good God because it says so in this divinely inspired work"? Hardly. That circular and cynical representation of non-philosophers' reasoning is woefully inadequate. Their insight can be captured in a much better way. In this book we aim to provide a philosophical argument justifying their manner of proceeding.

We write for agnostics — those who do not believe that there is a God.[3]

---

3. Unfortunately, there is no wholly satisfactory term that picks out the set of individuals who do not believe that there is a God.

If we were to place etymology at the fore, we might use the term "atheist" to pick out the set of persons who do not believe that there is a God. Etymological considerations suggest an "atheist" is simply someone who is "without God," which might be taken to mean someone who is not a theist. Generally speaking, etymology clarifies. However, "atheist" is so widely used to designate one who *asserts* the nonexistence of God that it seems improper to insist that its etymological sense is normative.

The word "agnostic" is used in various inconsistent ways. It was coined by Thomas Huxley to describe the view that human reason cannot provide rational grounds to justify either the belief that God exists or the belief that God does not exist (a view Huxley held). Such a conception of agnosticism, now often called "philosophical agnosticism," builds in *allegiance* to the position of neutrality. But many people today regard themselves as agnostics without having made a commitment to the impossibility of human reason settling the question one way or the other. Sometimes "agnostic" is used to mean one who says: "I do not *know* that there is a God, and I do not *know* that there is not a God." But the rather common usage of "agnostic" to designate the individual who disavows knowledge one way or the other conflates the distinction between belief and knowledge and is thus highly tendentious. One may well be justified in believing that there is a God if one has a case for the existence of God stronger than the case against; belief may fall far short of knowledge. Sometimes "agnostic" is used to refer to one who says: "I do not believe that there is a God, *and* I do not believe that there is not a God." But this excludes from the category people (including many scientists) who say: "I believe there is no God — but of course, I could be mistaken about the matter; I do not pretend belief is the same thing as knowledge, and I might be wrong about whether there is a God." Such individuals are sometimes described by philosophers as "atheists," persons who positively assert the nonexistence of God, but the individuals themselves often prefer the label "agnostic." The term "atheism" connotes a definiteness and a militancy that a nonbeliever may want to eschew. And in practice the line between believing there is no God and not believing that there is a God is not always easy to draw, despite the different logical forms of the assertions.

In this book we use the term "agnostic" broadly to include all who do not believe that there

We also write for believers. They can have good reasons to consider, from an agnostic's standpoint, the case for theism and revelation. Not least among these reasons is that one loves best those one knows best, and a believer might come to know God better by studying philosophical grounds for belief, and the variety of philosophical paths to God. Furthermore, there are different kinds of believers: some may possess the "eye of contemplation" and profess certainty that there is a God, but others (we are among them) do not. Those who do not may find it especially useful to reflect on philosophical warrants and approaches. And we write as well for onlookers, meta-philosophers who concern themselves with strategies for arguing for or against the existence of God or the credibility of alleged revelations.

The project of the agnostic inquirer is distinct from our own meta-project. The inquirer wants an answer to the question: Has a good God revealed anything to us? As meta-inquirers who are ourselves drawn to the hopes that inspire the question, we aim to provide a strategy for inquiry with good promise of an affirmative answer. Thus we do not try conclusively to answer the question whether a good God has revealed. An oil company looking for new reserves will call in geologists who can say something about the odds of finding oil in a particular place, and drilling engineers who can explain the best way of digging in identified areas of interest. The geologists and drilling engineers are meta-seekers. As meta-inquirers, we will succeed if we find good reason to believe that a particular strategy is richly promising. Should we find not just good reason but irresistible reason, our success would be resounding. Resounding success is certainly better than mere success; but mere success is, after all, *success*. Should we fail even to reach the threshold of good reason, our failure might be so complete that we will have all but proved that the hypothetical inquirer could not succeed in the way we have proposed. But failure need not be so miserable. Our effort might result in finding that there are no compelling reasons to think it unlikely that a good God has given us a revelation. While that would not quite be success, not even mere success, it would be worth something.

The two projects — that of the inquirer and that of the meta-inquirer — are close to our own hearts. Both of us were at one time philosophically inclined nonbelievers, struggling with the project of natural theology as standardly conceived and experiencing the well-known and nearly universal dissatisfaction with that project when it is taken to be a springboard into religious belief. (Both of us are adult converts to theism and Christianity.) In

---

is a God. We will refer to "atheists" when we wish to speak specifically of those who explicitly deny the existence of God.

some ways, we have written this book for the persons we once were; but our conviction that many people are in similar situations allows us to see the undertaking as something more than self-indulgence.

1.1.2. *An Agnostic's Need for a Reasoned Case*

Given the right kind of revelation, the tools of philosophy could be set aside. Events may overwhelm, making matters too obvious to require deep philosophical reflection. Although Socrates and Simmias philosophized as the hour of Socrates's execution approached, accounts of the last hours of another famous condemned man report a different kind of dialogue. A new disciple responds to events with the words, "Jesus, remember me when you come into your kingdom," and he hears in reply: "Truly I tell you, today you will be with me in Paradise."[4] There is something in the voice, something in the air, something divine, that warrants belief in revelation, in the promise of immortality. Or so it seems to the thief hanging on the cross near Jesus. Paul on the road to Damascus, perhaps, or Moses, or Muhammad, or Teresa of Avila acquired similar convictions, grounded in similar experiences. It is at least conceptually possible that religious experience can impress itself with such force that one no more needs to reason whether light is radiating from God than to reason whether it is radiating from the sun.

Agnostics, however, do not claim such dramatic experiences. Indeed, agnostics typically have not had any experiences they would recognize as definitely religious. And while some agnostic inquirers may be able to accept as veridical the testimony of those who say they perceive God, many agnostics have a skepticism about mystical claims that is too deep for such testimonial evidence to carry great weight, at least at the outset of investigation.[5]

Religious apologists are certainly aware that agnostics lack dramatic religious experiences themselves and regard reports thereof with skepticism. Yet apologists often talk in ways implying that an agnostic can arrive at belief without a reasoned case. How do they imagine conversion occurs?

Some follow the lead of the early John Henry Newman in suggesting that an agnostic may see faith as a *venture* originating with personal experience.

---

4. Luke 23:42, 43 (NRSV).

5. William Alston proposes that belief in God is acceptable on the basis of a kind of perceptual practice that, like any perceptual practice, should be accepted as valid unless undercut by compelling argument; and, he maintains, the testimony of those who claim to perceive God can count as evidence for others. See William P. Alston, *Perceiving God: The Epistemology of Religious Experience* (Ithaca, NY: Cornell University Press, 1991).

Newman, deeply suspicious of what he calls the "paper logic" in much natural theology, announces that "it is as absurd to argue men, as to torture them, into believing."[6] The lame hear the words of Peter and of Paul, Newman says, and believe what they hear, and are healed by their belief: reason and argument do not enter the picture. He reminds us that Jesus reprimands "doubting Thomas" for demanding sensible proof before believing in the resurrection. Nevertheless, an agnostic might observe, Jesus does in fact provide the proof Thomas requested. The reprimand may have come not because Thomas required some evidence, but because he required too much.

Newman does maintain that "antecedent considerations" prepare the mind to accept the gracious gift of faith. That sounds promising. It turns out, though, that the most important antecedent consideration is the judgment *that a revelation is likely*. Given that judgment, a person is supposed to be positioned to see that the Christian gospel is suitable to the human condition — and hence to embrace it. However, vast numbers of inquiring agnostics cannot find evidence that gets them to the point of judging that a revelation is likely. Newman goes on to say that the so-called evidences for Christianity, which will be compelling for the properly prepared mind, often serve "as a test of honesty of mind; their rejection being the condemnation of unbelievers."[7] It is the rare agnostic who will find this appealing. Newman appears to demand that people hand over reason at the gates of faith and march on through. Any member of a cult could tell us the same thing. Newman does say a good deal more that might be marshaled to give a quite different picture of faith and reason; indeed, the later Newman offers arguments left and right — effectively. He made many converts. Still, at certain times and in certain moods he scorns the idea of reasoning one's way to belief.

Again, in the case of a great contemporary philosopher of religion, Alvin Plantinga, we encounter a writer whose extraordinary argumentative skills have immeasurably advanced the field of natural or philosophical theology — even as he lets drop, from time to time, remarks about the role of reason that agnostics may find discouraging. Is Plantinga's discussion of warranted Christian belief, ingenious in so many ways, useful to the inquiring agnostic? Drawing on some ideas in Calvin and Newman, Plantinga gives us a portrait

---

6. John Henry Newman, *Fifteen Sermons Preached Before the University of Oxford* (London: Longmans, Green and Co., 1918), Sermon IV, p. 63. We do not mean to suggest that this quotation represents Newman's best thought on the subject in the Oxford sermons, or that those sermons as a whole convey his best thinking on the subject. In our view, the *Grammar of Assent* and some of his letters are far more helpful. But a number of the ideas in the sermons have been quite influential.

7. Newman, *Fifteen Sermons*, Sermon X, p. 199.

of the believer who finds, deep within epistemic foundations, a basic belief in God, in the same way that we find ourselves perceiving trees, or remembering what we had for breakfast, or realizing that two plus two equals four, or believing in the existence of other people.[8] As Plantinga sees it, these beliefs are *occasioned* by various circumstances, but they are not typically conclusions *inferred* from those circumstances. All of us, he says, have a disposition to form theistic beliefs in certain situations. But our *sensus divinitatis* (sense of divinity) does not always work properly: it may have been inadequately nurtured, or may be diseased. When it does not operate as it was designed to operate, people can fail to have basic belief in God. Plantinga extends his account to cover not merely theistic belief but Christian belief as well. On his extended model, a Christian believer (with the assistance of the Holy Spirit) recovers the use of or access to the *sensus divinitatis* and obtains natural knowledge both of God and of the truths of Christianity. Plantinga says:

> We [Christians] read Scripture, or something presenting scriptural teaching, or hear the gospel preached. . . . What is said simply seems right; it seems compelling; one finds oneself saying, "Yes, that's right, that's the truth of the matter; this is indeed the word of the Lord." I read, "God was in Christ, reconciling the world to himself"; I come to think: "Right; that's true; God really was in Christ, reconciling the world to himself!"[9]

Yet even if Plantinga's explanation of how Christian belief can have warrant for the believer is correct, agnostics are not conscious of having the sorts of basic beliefs Plantinga reports about God or about Christianity. They do not apprehend God in the lilies of the field or the starry skies above. They do not find religious belief lodged safely in their epistemic foundations. Even many religious people will be reluctant to say that they have a "properly basic" belief in God, and agnostics have *no* belief in God. Can an agnostic pull from Plantinga's account directions for acquiring warranted Christian beliefs? Read Scripture; listen to the gospel preached; ask for divine assistance. But many inquiring agnostics have already read some Scripture, and, in the manner of the young Charles Ryder in *Brideshead Revisited*, have mustered the kinds of prayers of which an agnostic is capable ("O God,

---

8. Plantinga calls his account "the Aquinas/Calvin model." See Alvin C. Plantinga, *Warranted Christian Belief* (New York: Oxford University Press, 2000). Plantinga has not always been so friendly to Aquinas; see his essay "The Reformed Objection to Natural Theology," *Christian Scholar's Review* XI, no. 3 (1982), and in the same issue, Joseph M. Boyle, Jr., J. Hubbard, and Thomas D. Sullivan, "The Reformed Objection to Natural Theology: A Catholic Perspective."

9. Plantinga, *Warranted Christian Belief,* p. 250.

if there is a God, show me the truth of this gospel, if it is true"). If you are an agnostic, your reaction upon reading Plantinga's words, reading that "God was in Christ reconciling the world to himself," may well be: "That is a beautiful sentiment; I wish Christians could give me reasons for thinking it is true!" But Plantinga says, "I don't know of an argument for Christian belief that seems very likely to convince one who doesn't already accept its conclusion."[10] Granted, Plantinga's discussion in *Warranted Christian Belief* might be useful to agnostics who have some inclination to believe but who think that one cannot rationally believe in God without good propositional evidence. And it might help agnostics who think that there are good objections to belief that are not de facto objections (i.e., not objections to the *truth* of belief).[11] Still, most agnostic inquirers are likely to find his discussion unsuited to their purposes.

Some say that art offers a path to religious belief. Should an agnostic inquirer interested in religion be going to art museums instead of doing philosophy? Wassily Kandinsky expressed strong views about the power of art to move the soul:

> Generally speaking, colour is a power which directly influences the soul. Colour is the keyboard, the eyes are the hammers, the soul is the piano with many strings. The artist is the hand which plays, touching one key or another, to cause vibrations in the soul.[12]

Kandinsky's art embodies this view. He apparently did not even think people needed to apprehend intellectually the symbolism in his paintings to be awakened spiritually. Moscow will be the third Rome, the world capital dur-

---

10. Plantinga, *Warranted Christian Belief*, p. 201. While Plantinga acknowledges that his model might be stretched to accommodate *inferences* to the existence of the divine, he does not himself favor this move. This is evident, for instance, in his discussion of Jonathan Edwards's understanding of regenerative faith. Plantinga indicates that Edwards *may* have thought a Christian believer, aided by the Holy Spirit, "perceives the divine glory and beauty of the things of the gospel, and then infers from that, in a quick argument, that they are indeed divine, from God, and hence are to be believed" (p. 304). The other possible specification of Edwards's views, and the view Plantinga himself endorses, is that the Christian sees the gospel's divine glory, "and *immediately* forms the beliefs that these things are true and that they are from God" (p. 304).

11. Plantinga distinguishes between *de facto* and *de jure* objections to belief in God. *De facto* objections are objections to the *truth* of belief. *De jure* objections, such as the Freudian claim that belief in God is the result of wish fulfillment, suggest that belief is "not up to snuff from an intellectual point of view," whether or not it is true. See Plantinga, *Warranted Christian Belief*, p. ix.

12. Wassily Kandinsky, *Concerning the Spiritual in Art*, trans. M. T. H. Sadler (New York: Dover, 1977), p. 25.

ing the thousand-year reign of Christ after the Apocalypse, Kandinsky believed, and he represented this view in *Improvisation No. 30 — Warlike Theme*. Most of us, however, can look long and hard at the painting's dark sky, the firing cannons, and the buildings in the upper right that we identify as the churches of the Kremlin because art critics tell us that is what they are, without being moved to accept anything like the proposition "Moscow will be the third Rome." Vincent Van Gogh's ideas about the religious dimensions of his work are more comprehensible than Kandinsky's. Van Gogh used a kind of natural iconography in his paintings, believing that when one sees "indescribable and unutterable desolation . . . the thought of God comes into one's mind."[13] And so it may. Yet, for philosophical agnostic inquirers, the thought of God — the hunger for divine friendship — likely will need to be supplemented by arguments for God (perhaps arguments that refer to the hunger).

Is literature a more fruitful resource for an inquirer? One of the two central theses Martha Nussbaum defends in *Love's Knowledge* is that "certain truths about human life can *only* be fittingly and accurately stated in the language and forms characteristic of the narrative artist."[14] Nussbaum illustrates this thesis by trying to develop a literary argument that human beings cannot intelligibly aspire to have a life after death, an argument based on Homer's Odysseus/Calypso story. Odysseus chooses to leave behind the possibility of everlasting life with the beautiful Calypso on her calm and otherworldly island, deciding — heroically — to risk the perilous journey home to return to his aging wife, Penelope, where he will face her death and his own. It looks as if Nussbaum wants to draw (at least) these two ontological claims out of Homer's story: first, that while humans may aspire to transcend "ordinary" humanity, there is no state to which we can aspire that is preferable to the current human condition; and second, that a person might not be the same individual in another heavenly world.

What in Homer's story supports the first of these claims? Nussbaum observes that Odysseus's island interlude is not all that appealing. But how does that favor the claim at issue? The "heavenly" island requires him to abandon the woman he loves and to whom he has pledged himself. But the picture of heavenly life we get from religious traditions (particularly Christianity) is a picture where there is a *closer* union of husband and wife through the being

13. Vincent Van Gogh, quoted in W. H. Auden, "Calm Even in the Catastrophe," in J. D. McClatchy, ed., *Poets on Painters: Essays on the Art of Painting by Twentieth-Century Poets* (Berkeley and Los Angeles: University of California Press, 1990), p. 133. See Auden's discussion, pp. 133-35.

14. Martha C. Nussbaum, *Love's Knowledge: Essays on Philosophy and Literature* (New York: Oxford University Press, 1990), p. 5 (italics added).

who is their source. An image of this promised union exists in the human family, where husband and wife are drawn together by their children, and where the children are themselves united in the family through the action of the parents. The Calypso story is supposed to suggest that the Christian message of an afterlife wrongly encourages people to be inattentive to the present world. But there is a way in which the Christian account tells us that life in this world is invested with infinite significance. How we treat one another is infinitely important, according to the Christian account. Eternal life hangs in the balance — for ourselves and for others as well. Our world is enlarged by the religious message as we work to transcend our parochialism.

And why think Homer's story shows that translation to a heavenly world would destroy identity? Because, Nussbaum suggests, we cannot imagine our hero as Calypso's constant consort without imagining that he dulls down into a very different person. The human practices that enliven us would lose their meaning in a heavenly world, she says. Athletic contests and politics would be pointless. But this is curiously unimaginative. For creatures go through radical metamorphoses: the pupa becomes a caterpillar that becomes a butterfly. We ourselves have internal experience of the phenomenon of radical change: few adults think they can explain sexual union to a grade-schooler. Furthermore, matter itself can metamorphose. People in equatorial regions have sometimes been unable to believe that water could be solid. Perhaps the glorified "subtle" bodies that certain religious traditions anticipate will facilitate the retention of identity, making possible various analogues of the earthly experiences that Nussbaum believes ground our identity.

There is no denying that some people draw conclusions through art and literature; but the philosophically inclined inquirer will not settle for anything less than a reasoned case. That does not mean the burden of proof is on theism rather than atheism. Perhaps neither side must shoulder the burden of proof. It simply means that the situation of the philosophical agnostic inquirer (indeed, of philosophical believers who lack the "eye of contemplation") calls for an argument.

Our focus on argument is not intended to suggest that tacit or implicit evidence has no role in agnostic inquiry. It certainly plays a part. You, the inquirer, likely will be unable to state in full detail all the evidence of the case that you will judge sufficient in the end: it is possible to have plenty of evidence that is difficult to get up or articulate. Try to think of all the reasons you have for believing one of your friends is trustworthy. Can you recall all the incidents over the course of many years when this person had reason to lie or cheat but did not? Nevertheless, you have evidence for your friend's trustworthiness. Yet, even if, as Newman says, "almost all reasons formally adduced in moral inquiries, are rather specimens and symbols of the real grounds, than those grounds themselves,"[15] these specimens and symbols may for many inquirers be indispensable means to the end. A philosophically inclined inquirer does not need to be able explicitly to state all the supporting evidence in the case, and may in the end need a case suffused by familiarity with a revelatory content, familiarity too intimate for words (which may give a taste of what believers would call "religious experience").

The inquirer needs not merely to have a case but to *recognize* that there is a case. That does not mean it is necessary to have the concepts that would be indispensable to structuring a case in its best form. Euclid understood that theorems should come out of axioms; but he had no expressed underlying logic, no formal deductive system, whether he understood that there was such a thing or not. As a result he made some mistakes. Nonetheless, where he produced theorems from axioms in accordance with some standard logic, he indeed established the case.

How strong an argument, or reasoned case, is needed? An agnostic inquirer who hopes a good God has revealed may mark different stages of success. One hugely important stage would be for an inquirer to come to the judgment that the evidence in view renders the proposition that a good God has revealed more worthy of credence than its contradictory. Any sensible inquirer will recognize that the evidence in view will not be all the possible evidence. And others will work from a different evidential base. But if you are an inquirer, you can only make a judgment on the basis of the case as it presents itself to you, not as it presents itself to someone else, though of course you can reasonably withhold judgment until you personally absorb someone else's case. Though a personalized case, one constructed or apprehended according to the inquirer's lights, grounds the judgment, it does not at all follow that the ground is entirely subjective. The premises of the case stand in a mind-independent relationship to the conclusion. Whether anyone recognizes that the elemental composition of bullets found at a crime scene matches the elemental composition of bullets found in a suspect's possession, the match lends evidence to the conclusion that the suspect is guilty, whereas a mismatch does not. The match or mismatch in no way depends on what anybody thinks. An inquirer needs to bring the personal case into alignment with the mind-independent facts, so far as is feasible, given the inquirer's circumstances and other obligations. And a philosophically minded inquirer will be eager to do just this. Yet, should the inquirer in the end be able to say, "The case before me makes be-

15. Newman, *Fifteen Sermons*, Sermon XII, p. 275.

lief in a revelation more credible than belief in its contradictory," a giant step toward the goal has been taken.

With some trepidation we will say that such a case renders the conclusion more probable than not. The reason for the trepidation is that probability theory is still in an exceedingly unsettled condition, despite all the ingenious work done on mathematical systems many philosophers take to be foundational.[16] Yet, while probability theory today is riddled with perplexities, particularly as the theory applies to reasoning about hypotheses, it is difficult to avoid talking about probable conclusions. With effort, we could avoid such talk. We could always favor longer expressions, such as "the inquirer's evidence renders a conclusion more credible — more worthy of credence — than its contradictory," insist on taking "more worthy of credence" as primitive (in the style of Roderick Chisholm), and refuse to link any such talk with talk about probability, on the grounds that the latter idea is too vexed to be serviceable. Nonetheless, it is convenient to say that the probability of a proposition on the evidence available to the inquirer is greater or less than .5.

As we use the terminology, a *probable* case is the same as a *plausible* or *likely* case for a claim: it is a case with a probability above .5. It may strike some ears as overly precise to attach a numerical value here. A number of experts hold that, strictly speaking, there is no such thing as quantitative confirmation.[17] But rough numerical values may be assigned to probability judgments even if quantitative confirmation is, strictly speaking, impossible. In looking at a range of paint samples, you might be willing to say: "If I had to put that paint chip on a scale of green-ishness from one to five, I would say it is about a four." Such a statement conveys the impression, and that is enough.

Inquirers typically hope for much more than a probable case that God has revealed something. They want a probable case that God has revealed something *significant*. And more than this, they want a case for something significant for their lives. Most inquirers are, with Simmias, looking for a safer vessel

---

16. Part of the reason, as we see it, for this unsettled condition is that probable reasoning is thought to be some kind of inductive reasoning, as opposed to deductive reasoning. But much probable reasoning is deductive; it is merely probable because the proffered premises are not evident. It would be better to start with Aristotle's distinction between demonstrative and non-demonstrative reasoning (both of which can be deductive). At a minimum such a beginning would free theorists from invoking such oddities as "partial entailment" of a conclusion by a premise set.

17. See Wesley Salmon, "Confirmation," in Robert Audi, ed., *The Cambridge Dictionary of Philosophy* (Cambridge, UK: Cambridge University Press, 1999).

for the journey of life, and it would hardly be satisfying to learn that a good case could be made for God's having revealed to some mathematician that a particular Mersenne number with over six million digits is prime. Inquirers are looking for a revelation that gives good guidance for conduct, instruction about how to become intimate with God and others, how to overcome evil, how to repair the damage of personal wrongdoing, and how to reach a condition of eternal bliss. Further still, they may look for a revelation that continues and grows, a revelation that is, so to speak, alive. They may hope for secure and confident belief, certainty that a good God has revealed. Inquirers may look for such things; yet, if an inquirer should merely learn that it is likely there is a good God who has communicated something to us, that by itself is surely success of a highly significant order — even if it is in some sense "mere" success. (In fact, at the end of this book we will be arguing that it is possible for this "mere" success to underwrite the wholehearted, resolute assent required by major revelations. The belief that it is likely a good God has revealed may *rationally* be transmuted into secure and confident faith.) At the outset, then, we urge the inquirer to target a probable case that a good God has revealed.[18]

To reach the judgment that the claim that a good God has revealed is more probable than not, an inquirer must find a case *for* the claim that is better than any and all cases against it. If the case for were simply better than any *particular* case against, the case for might not be very strong at all, since all the particular cases against might themselves be very weak. But if a case for is better than all cases against, taken collectively, then the proposition supported by the case for is more likely than not. Of course, no one can know the particulars of all possible cases against, but we can often surmise that, whatever the possible particulars of the individual cases against, they could not add up to much. Imagine, for instance, that a barely literate student submits to a high-school teacher a paper entitled "The Syzygy and Me." The teacher invites the student to her office.

> T: "I was intrigued by your paper. How did you come to know that unusual fact about the word 'syzygy'?"
> S: "What unusual fact?"
> T: "That it has so many y's in it."
> S: "How many?"
> T: "You tell me."

18. An inquirer who wishes to set the bar lower than a .5 probability that there exists a God who has revealed can construe the argument of our book as recommending a strategy simply for raising the probability that a good God has revealed.

S: "Five?"

T: "No, three: you said in your paper that it is the only word in English with three y's in it. By the way, what is a syzygy?"

S: [Blank look]

T: "Did you get any help with this paper?"

S: "Nope; it's all my own work."

T: "I wonder if you can explain, then, why your paper is nearly identical with a paper on the web?"

S: "Really? What a coincidence!"

A case for plagiarism is building that has every prospect of being stronger than any and all possible defenses, taken collectively.

It is worth noting that it is possible to determine that there is some case for — at least one — better than any and all cases against without knowing *which* case for is better than any and all cases against. Imagine a murder trial. The defense puts up witnesses to furnish an alibi, but the witnesses are inconsistent in some small details. The case as a whole cannot be believed, given the (minor) contradictions; but there may well be a path through it that is believable, that will allow you to set the conflicts aside. For instance, it will not matter whether the defendant was or was not wearing a black jacket at the time in question.

In practice, cases are not fixed: they move and transform. Thus, if an inquirer has *a* case, the inquirer will (in practice) have more than one. The mind processes information much as a visual system does. Our eyes keep moving, saccading from one fixed point to another and viewing things from different angles; we do not have a single vision of the world. Yet we have a vision of the world sufficient to justify many beliefs about it, including the belief that there *is* a world. The mind paints in the world so that we do not notice the discontinuities necessitated by our visual apparatus. So it is with a case: the mind paints in pieces of the case, and the mind goes back, fixing on elements it has just painted in, reflecting on tacit evidence, checking out guesses, and so forth. But the case moves.

While the inquirer need not be able to articulate a case in its best form, our own meta-inquiry requires us to say something about how an inquirer might structure a case. This we do at various points.

1.1.3. Jumping to Conclusions and Freezing in Place

Two problems pointing in opposite directions arise at the outset. The first is *the problem of wishful thinking*: this is the worry that the desire for a positive outcome will prejudice judgment, making it all too easy to accept a revelation without adequate evidence. The second is *the problem of rigidity:* the worry that if one avoids letting desires get out of hand, and takes a "show me" attitude toward putative revelations, it will be all but impossible to accept revelatory claims.

Wishful thinking does, of course, often lead people astray. The gambler is positive the next roll of the dice will pay off; the patient is sure the late-breaking cancer therapy will produce health; the parent is certain the child can make the team if given one more tryout. Hope for a particular conclusion often skews the reading of the data. We will concede that a desire for a particular outcome may affect the way an inquirer reads the evidence, may even prompt a leap to an unwarranted conclusion.

Nevertheless, the cost of eradicating desires for particular conclusions may simply be too high.

Indifference to outcome undermines the pursuit of truth: an apathetic inquirer will have trouble arriving at any result at all. Furthermore, there are some desires concerning outcomes that we can scarcely imagine abandoning — indeed, are morally obliged to hold on to. A parent searching for a kidnapped child cannot be, and should not try to be, neutral about whether the child is still alive. A researcher trying to find a cure for Parkinson's disease should care about outcomes. You cannot reduce your level of care about possible outcomes without changing values — and even beliefs. People who strongly desire to protect the environment likely believe that there is some general obligation to protect it. In order to change their desire, they will need to start telling themselves things like "The quality of water in Minnesota's lakes does not matter in the long run," or "My own efforts to improve things are insignificant." Desire follows upon belief, at least in many cases. The admonition not to care about the truth of a revelatory claim requires investigators to start thinking along the lines of "It makes no difference whether there is a God who loves me."

And even if we could just up and believe what we like about such matters, by eliminating desires about whether God exists we divest ourselves of an important means of testing particular revelations: we try putative revelations in part by whether they address our deepest desires. It has sometimes been remarked that, while the fact that a person is hungry does not prove the cupboard is full of bread, the fact that human beings are capable of hunger may point to the existence of such a thing as food. Whether or not that is true, if you believe you are dying of hunger, surely it is eminently reasonable for you to search the cupboard for food — indeed, it would be incomprehensible if you were not to.

So, to investigate questions concerning theism and revelation, we need not, should not, and probably cannot purge ourselves of all desires about outcomes. What we must do is evaluate the evidence as honestly as we can, being on guard against misleading desires. An inquirer who wants there to be true revelatory claims must be careful about swallowing tales of visions and miracles, and slow to interpret unusual experiences as divine. An inquirer who wants there *not* to be a God must be on guard against raising barriers to belief, careful not to adopt standards concerning proof that are stricter than those we ordinarily employ. And both kinds of inquirers may remind themselves that, though wanting something to be true does not make it true, it does not make it false either.

So caution is in order. And that leads to our second problem. Do not caution and proper regard for sound methodology all but foreclose discussion of the miraculous and wondrous? How does an agnostic inquirer, who must rely on beliefs actually in possession, avoid being so rigid that every amazing claim is dismissed as incredible, every strange ideal deemed unworthy of approach?

It does, indeed, need to be acknowledged that, just as one begins inquiry with the *desires* actually in possession, so also one begins with the *beliefs* already in possession. At the outset of investigation an inquirer has every right to proceed like Aristotle, Thomas Reid, C. S. Peirce, Roderick Chisholm, and many other philosophers who draw on a large pool of deeply ingressed, ordinary, commonsense beliefs. There is a world. There are people in the world. People feel pains and pleasures and have thoughts. People who die tend to stay dead. Things that come into existence tend to have causes. Good is to be done and evil avoided. And so on. What alternative is there but for us to rely on such beliefs? If someone insists that we set aside ordinary, deeply held beliefs, banning them as premises in arguments, there has to be a justification for that prohibition. And while it is conceivable that some particular project (such as Descartes's) might generate a justification, the project of the agnostic inquirer does not appear relevantly specialized. After all, our ordinary, deeply held beliefs did not just mysteriously descend upon us: they have *warrant*. We believe, for example, that birds can fly from tree to tree and not from a tree to the moon, because we have seen the former, and never the latter, and because we are acquainted with enough natural science to think no birds fly to the moon.

As the history of science makes plain, however, ordinary, commonsense beliefs sometimes require revision. Who would have thought, in days gone by, that one identical twin could be twenty-five years older than the other? But revision of our basic holdings must proceed with caution. We do not sever ties with a relative or a good friend without compelling reason, and we similarly should be loath to disown a deeply ingressed belief. The fact that some eminence pronounces against a view is not sufficient. Parmenides says nothing moves. Berkeley says trees in the forest would cease to be if no one were conscious of them. Bohr presents an antirealist interpretation of quantum mechanics that seems to support Berkeley's view. These pronouncements need not — and should not, at least not right away — force us out of our realism. Nor do they make us say: "Well, experts are found on both sides of these questions. Some say things that strike us as bizarre, others do not. Who are we to take a stance?" When quantum physicists tell us that the spin orientation of electrons is indeterminate prior to measurement, it does not require a huge stretch of the imagination to accept the point. However, when a quantum physicist asserts, as a few do, that the moon is not really in the sky unless someone is looking at it, we are going to need an exceedingly strong argument for the conclusion. Challengers to so-far-well-warranted beliefs have the burden of proof.

Challengers also have the burden of establishing that reflection on the challenge is worthwhile. The challenger must say, "I know this sounds wild, but consider briefly the following . . ."; the challenger must put together a little package attractive enough for us to say we want to hear more. Whatever the package contains, it is going to have to be enticing indeed if it is to persuade us to investigate questions such as whether anything moves, or whether trees in the forest disappear when no one is looking. We must avoid the mistake of thinking that, before we can get to the question at hand, we must go back over all starting assumptions because at some point they have been challenged by ancient skeptics, or by the rise of modern science, or by the elusive methods of the deconstructionists. An agnostic inquirer is perpetually in danger of losing sight of the project. It is important to remember that one of the inquirer's ingressed beliefs is that it *matters* whether there is a good God who has given us a revelation. And if it does matter, then the investigation should terminate before the inquirer terminates.

Given the strong presumption in favor of fundamental, ordinary beliefs, can an inquirer avoid being so dug in as to be unbudgeable?

For inquirers are certainly aware that revelatory claims do not have a pedestrian content. Revelations offer a vision of the world — of how things are and ought to be, of how we should behave, and so on — that in some ways is very strange. A god who commands a father to slay his only son and make of him a burnt offering? One god who is actually three different persons? A deity who takes on human form, only to be ignominiously executed as a common criminal, and who expects to be worshiped? Abstaining from pork? Turning the other cheek? Celibacy for the Kingdom? It will be a rare inquirer whose starting beliefs and desires fit these bizarre assertions and demands.

Now everyone is aware that in the theoretical order, openness to the amazing is rewarded. You can get astonishing results starting with very basic beliefs. The mathematician Georg Cantor begins with the simple idea that two sets are the same size if they can be put into one-to-one correspondence; he ends up with endless layer upon layer of increasingly larger infinities. As Cantor was open to the notion that some infinities are larger than others, so should an inquirer be open to the notion that there might be a deity whose character is infinite. Indeed, Cantor himself held that there is an infinitude with respect to God that is altogether distinct from the infinitude with respect to worldly objects collected in a set, and that the "real existence" of the "*Transfinitum*," the concrete existence of transfinite numbers, is a reflection of God's infinite nature.[19]

The theoretical order is one thing, though, and the practical order another. It may be thought that, whereas the history of mathematics and science (and much else) demonstrates the necessity of openness to revision of theoretical beliefs, it is a different matter entirely as far as the practical realm is concerned. Why should we be open to radically changing our behavior or our affections?

In fact, though, openness to radical change in the practical arena is appropriate when we can sense that all is not well with our practices and attachments. And all does not appear to be well when we restrict our view to the secular order.

In the first place, the goods in our lives, incomplete and transient as they are, do not fully satisfy — a point widely recognized by philosophers and others. What is the remedy? One can think in an Aristotelian way about excellence and the virtues, and recognize the limited happiness that comes out of such reflection. Or one may look to other ethical systems, as the Hellenistic philosophers did, systems that overturn the commonsense and Aristotelian picture of values. Return to the foundational conception of ethics, the Stoics said: the only thing good is a good will; you can be harmed by nobody but yourself. Renounce empty desires, the Epicureans said: free yourself from disturbances and fears, including the fear of death; death is nothing to us, since it ends our existence. The Stoics and Epicureans thus repudiate the common morality expressed in Aristotle's ethics. But neither the kind of ethics Aristotle advances, close to the common sense of the matter in so many

---

19. See Joseph Warren Dauben, *Georg Cantor: His Mathematics and Philosophy of the Infinite* (Princeton, NJ: Princeton University Press, 1979).

ways, nor the radical value reversals of Stoics, Epicureans, Machiavellians, or Nietzscheans, lead to deep satisfaction.

Second, the various naturalistic ethical systems are on collision courses with one another, and it appears that no satisfactory resolution of the differences is to be found — that is, not if we eschew appeal to a higher, transcendent order. Henry Sidgwick saw things in this light. Something is wrong with the foundations of ethics, he thought. Utilitarianism made the most sense to him, and he held onto it; still, because he could not see how to reply definitively to the case against it, he worried that some contradictory system might be true (as a person might hold onto Euclidean geometry while simultaneously worrying about an inability to respond to those who deny the parallel postulate). Maybe, Sidgwick suggested, the only way to get a consistent ethic is to postulate a God who rewards virtue in another realm, as Kant had proposed. And this despite Sidgwick's deep skepticism about religion.

Third, no ethical system provides a clear and compelling set of axioms. Where is the system that has us all persuaded? Undergraduates who register for ethics courses not uncommonly expect to be handed such a system. Let us get the axioms and proceed, they think. Instead, what they get is a lot of talk about different systems, much of it unconnected with the bottom-most principles. Self-evident foundational principles of ethics are hard to come by. For that reason, no ethical system presents serious obstacles to an openness to having behavior or desires changed by revelatory teachings. Many ethical systems are at variance with revelations, of course; but the axioms of such systems are not obviously correct.

Fourth, those ethical systems inconsistent with revelatory traditions often are repugnant. Take, for instance, the contemporary philosopher Peter Singer's utilitarian approach to ethics. Newborn infants lack a right to life, Singer says, as do the elderly when their capacities are sufficiently diminished. Some who agree with him accused him of inconsistency when "he did not kill his mother, who had advanced Alzheimer's disease and whose care was consuming money that could . . . more profitably be spent elsewhere."[20] Singer's collaborator, Helga Kuhse, defends him: "Singer has never denied that there is a gap between what pure reason would seemingly demand that people should do and what is practically feasible. . . ." One of the practical circumstances that must be taken into account, Kuhse notes, is the fact that it is against the law to kill people.[21] Or consider Kai Nielsen's conclusions in *Ethics Without*

20. Helga Kuhse, "Introduction," in Peter Singer, *Unsanctifying Human Life: Essays on Ethics* (Oxford: Blackwell, 2002), p. 11.

21. Kuhse, "Introduction," p. 11.

God.[22] While at first insisting that he can work up a purely secular argument for treating people fairly, he ends up conceding that, with respect to torturing and killing the innocent in terrorist acts, "there are circumstances when such violence must be reluctantly assented to or even taken to be something that one, morally speaking, must do."[23] We venture to say that most inquirers will not find Singer's and Nielsen's reversals of values leading to a deeply satisfying ethic. The reversal of values called for by Judaism, Christianity, and so on moves in a very different direction.

Are there limits to openness? Of course. Most evidently, we cannot give up on the principle of non-contradiction, bold but wayward logicians notwithstanding.[24] And we properly resist adopting morals or ideals that strike us as exceedingly pernicious. That is consistent with being open to moving far from our initial assumptions, particularly when we recognize disturbances in the foundations of ethics, or shortcomings in the mode of life we have adopted. In the practical realm our deepest desires must be our guide: implantation of new aspirations and practices may be in order, but they must answer to bedrock desires.

1.2. Objections to Embarking

1.2.1. *Kantian Arguments Purporting to Undercut Natural Theology*

Seeking a philosophical case of the kind we have described — a case for the claim that a good God has revealed that is stronger than any and all cases against the claim — is doing natural theology. There is no universally accepted definition of "natural theology." We adopt the following widely accepted account: natural theology is the enterprise of providing support for theistic religious beliefs, relying on arguments that do not assume that there is a true revelation (i.e., their premises are all accepted on the basis of reason and experience alone, not on the basis of religious authority).[25] Perhaps you

---

22. Kai Nielsen, *Ethics Without God*, 2d ed. (Buffalo, NY: Prometheus, 1990).

23. Nielsen, *Ethics Without God*, p. 132.

24. Still, it can be acknowledged that we might forever be condemned to have inconsistency in conceptual systems due to the inadequacy of human intelligence. See Edwin D. Mares, "Semantic Dialetheism," in Graham Priest, J. C. Beall, and Bradley Armor-Garb, eds., *The Law of Non-Contradiction: New Philosophical Essays* (Oxford: Oxford University Press, 2004). Those who deny the principle of non-contradiction are today called "dialetheists."

25. This is an account very much like the one offered by William Alston, about which we will have something to say later.

think that your project is not at the outset to build a case either for or against religious belief, but rather to discover the *truth* about the matter. You may then engage in natural theology *and* in natural atheology, constructing cases on both sides of the question. As the dialectic progresses and you begin to incline in a certain direction about how the question of revelation should be answered, one of the two projects may be subsumed under the other.

The pretensions of natural theology have long ago been exploded, it is often said. "World-crushing" [*Weltzermalmend*] is what Moses Mendelssohn famously called Kant's criticisms of the traditional arguments for God.[26] And it is indeed Kant whom people typically have in mind when they describe natural theology as impotent, though Hume may be mentioned in the same breath. Iris Murdoch speaks of Kant's "conclusive exposure of the so-called proofs of the existence of God"[27] as though an understanding of the putative exposure is just part of the background knowledge all sophisticated moderns (or postmoderns, or post-postmoderns) have acquired. In a similar vein, Kai Nielsen says:

> [B]oth Hume and Kant provide powerful critiques of the various traditional attempts to prove in any way His [God's] existence. . . . While some of the *details* of their arguments have been rejected . . . there remains a very considerable consensus among contemporary philosophers and theologians that arguments like those developed by Hume and Kant show that no proof (*a priori* or empirical) of God's existence is possible.[28]

Susan Neiman broadens the point: "If one thing might seem to unite philosophers on both sides of the Atlantic, it's the conviction that Kant's work proscribes not just future philosophical references to God but most other sorts of foundation as well."[29] It is not just Kant's criticisms of the "proofs" of God's existence that lead people to speak of the demise of natural theology, but his deeper attack on metaphysics itself.

We both have profound respect for Kant. We heartily embrace "that prerogative of reason which makes it the highest good on earth, the prerogative

26. As Allen Wood reports in "Rational Theology, Moral Faith, and Religion," in Paul Guyer, ed., *The Cambridge Companion to Kant* (Cambridge, UK: Cambridge University Press, 1992), p. 397.

27. Iris Murdoch, *The Sovereignty of Good* (New York: Routledge and Kegan Paul, Ark Paperbacks, 1985), p. 80.

28. Kai Nielsen, *Philosophy and Atheism* (Buffalo, NY: Prometheus Books, 1985), p. 18. Nielsen also writes that Hume's *Dialogues* and Kant's *Critique* "make it quite evident that none of the proofs for the existence of God work, i.e., they are not sound or reliable arguments" (p. 68).

29. Susan Neiman, *Evil in Modern Thought: An Alternative History of Philosophy* (Princeton, NJ: Princeton University Press, 2002), p. 3.

of being the final touchstone of truth" (as our epigraph from Kant has it). But reason underwrites a healthy skepticism of philosophical authority. And an inquirer troubled by persistent rumors of the demise of natural theology would do well to pause briefly to look at some of the allegedly paralyzing difficulties, the problems that are supposed to immobilize the project of natural theology.

Consider the character of the requirement that an investigator take up a particular argument against the possibility of getting anywhere with an inquiry into the question of whether a good God has revealed. The requirement might be understood in at least three ways:

1) One must *first* deal with the allegedly show-stopping argument before undertaking serious inquiry into the question of whether a good God has revealed.
2) One must *simultaneously* work to understand the allegedly show-stopping argument, as well as arguments purporting to show that a good God has revealed.
3) One must, *at least in the end*, take up the alleged show-stopper.

On the second and third readings, the inquiry is not shut down at all. It is really only the first requirement that presents a difficulty. However, it is unreasonable to demand that an inquirer deal with an alleged show-stopper *before* examining arguments purporting to show that a good God has revealed. For suppose you set out a particular argument against the possibility of natural theology. To evaluate this argument, you must compare its premises with the premises of the arguments that purport to point to God's existence, and you must make a judgment about the *relative* plausibility of the premises. And if you engage in this kind of comparison, you are already into the project of examining arguments concerning the case for theism and revelation. The main project not only need not be, but cannot be, postponed indefinitely while you scrutinize arguments against inquiry.

What conditions must be met by an argument that successfully challenges the enterprise of natural theology? Presumably, the conditions are those that govern good argument everywhere. They include the following. First, it should be possible to discern just how the argument is supposed to go: that is, it should be possible to identify with reasonable confidence the fundamental assumptions or premises, as well as the basic conclusion, and understand the terms that figure in the argument. Second, the premises should be relatively secure. In the present case, that means that each premise of the argument purporting to shut down natural theology should be at least as plausible as each premise in the argument(s) of interest within natural theology. Third, the conclusion should be sufficiently strong. Obviously, if someone claims (as Nielsen has) that no proof of God's existence is possible, then the conclusion of the supporting argument cannot simply be something like "Anselm's best-known argument for God's existence fails."

Kant's specific arguments targeting the traditional proofs of God's existence, and also his broader arguments against metaphysics itself, fall far short of what is required if natural theology is to be blocked.

Take the specific arguments first.

We will not stop to argue that they do not meet the first test, the test of lucidity, though we note that Kant's reputation in this regard is not encouraging. Original philosophers such as Kant produce texts that are wonderfully kaleidoscopic, full of brightly colored bits of technical language that shift in sense as their creators seek to articulate utterly new concepts. The problems of determining just what Kant means and just how his argument goes are notorious. Nor will we dwell on whether the attacks pass the second test (security of premises), though we do observe that here, too, there are signs that all is not well. Nielsen acknowledges that "details" of Kant's arguments have been rejected by the philosophical community. Others maintain that there are more substantial difficulties with the Kantian arguments against natural theology. Kant's heavy reliance on mistaken assumptions about space, time, and causality has prompted some who are well informed about physics to dismiss him as having "nothing to say to us who are witnesses of the physics of Einstein and Bohr."[30]

Rather, we focus on the third test. Do Kant's specific arguments against natural theology conclude to a thesis that is sufficiently strong for the purpose of the person who wants to shut down natural theology altogether? Reasons for concern abound.

To begin with, Kant does not say in his critique of "speculative theology" that he shows God's existence cannot be proved; instead, his conclusion is that it cannot be proved on the basis of what he terms "theoretical reason." That leaves wide open the possibility that it can be established in some other way — namely, practically. And in fact, Kant (at times, at least) does seem to think that reason functioning practically might arrive at the theistic conclusion. He says: "[W]e will show about the moral laws that they not only presuppose the existence of a highest being, but also, since in a different respect they are absolutely necessary, they postulate this existence rightfully but, of course, only practi-

---

30. Hans Reichenbach, *The Rise of Scientific Philosophy* (Berkeley: University of California Press, 1951), p. 44.

cally. . . ."[31] Commentators sometimes suggest that Kant's conclusion is that God's existence must be taken as a practical posit for the purposes of motivating right conduct.[32] However, if we put talk of the "theoretical" and "practical" to one side and ask how the passage just cited looks when expressed in terms of premises and conclusion, it appears that Kant is arguing as follows:

1) There is a binding moral law.
2) If there is, then God exists.
3) So, God exists.

This is an argument for the existence of God. It may or may not be sound; but it does illustrate the fact that some arguments in natural theology — maybe even some that Kant endorsed — are immune to his attack on *speculative* theology.

Furthermore, Kant took himself to be exposing the traditional proofs as strict, or pure, proofs — Aristotelian demonstrations. A demonstration or full-fledged proof, according to Aristotle, must satisfy a constraint on form, and another on content. The constraint on *form* is that the argument must be deductively valid. Moreover, the premises must be relevant to the conclusion. (Relevance logicians today concur on this high standard.) The constraint on *content* requires true premises that are also cognitively prior to and better known than the conclusion. Indeed, genuine proof must proceed from premises that are in some sense "evident," Aristotle says. Notice that arguments in modern science meet neither the Aristotelian constraint on form nor the constraint on content. Nevertheless, of course, the "probable" arguments of science are invaluable. So even if the conclusions of natural theology were only probable, much in the way that modern science's conclusions are, one would think they could be of great use. Kant disparages probable arguments for God's existence; but his reasoning on this point is not impressive.[33]

31. Immanuel Kant, *Critique of Pure Reason,* trans. and ed. Paul Guyer and Alan W. Wood (Cambridge, UK: Cambridge University Press, 1998), p. 585 [A634/B662].

32. Some Kant scholars would argue that God is only "practically" postulated in the *Critique of Pure Reason,* and there is no warrant for thinking Kant is arguing that we have either knowledge or opinion of the existence of God as a theoretical sort of cognition. Many commentators have been baffled by Kant's declarations that "practically postulating" does not involve forming an opinion.

33. Here is one example: "It may well be allowed to *assume* the existence of a being of the highest sufficiency as the cause of all possible effects, in order to facilitate reason's search for the unity of its grounds of explanation. Yet to go so far as to say, *Such a being exists necessarily,* is no longer the modest expression of an allowable hypothesis, but rather the impudent presumption

A further problem still concerns the strength of the conclusion of Kant's specific arguments against speculative theology. When Kant argues that none of the traditional proofs of God can succeed, he has in mind proofs that aim to show that there is an *ens realissimum* (a maximally real being). But we will argue in later chapters that, for the purpose of ascertaining whether a revelation from on high has been given to us, it is sufficient to have evidence for the existence of a supranatural[34] being, whatever its character. The claim that no argument can be made out for the existence of a supranatural being of any kind whatsoever is much stronger than the claim that no argument can be made out for an *ens realissimum*. Kant does not even consider the possibility of arguing for a "merely" supranatural being.

Thus Kant's attack on specific arguments within natural theology, his attacks on the traditional "proofs" of God's existence, should not deter an agnostic inquirer.

What of his broader attack on the foundations of metaphysics? On the usual understanding of the matter, Kant suggests that the fact that metaphysics is a battlefield of endless controversies, where no combatant holds ground for long, is rooted in the nearly irresistible temptation to extend concepts and principles that are legitimately applied to the realm of experience (the "phenomenal" realm) to the domain beyond experience (the "noumenal" realm), where they are in fact illicit. "Transcendent" metaphysics, which relies on this overextension, cannot reach its traditional goals, Kant held. The noumenal order is completely closed off from us, closed in such a way as to render judgments about the existence and interconnections of properties and things in that realm entirely inscrutable. So the time-honored claims of metaphysics, in his view, have no solid grounding. If Kant is right, an inquirer would be unable to find even a probable argument for a god of some kind. Kant explains: "*Probability* has a place only regarding the knowledge of things in the world. For anything of which I am to have probable knowledge must be homogeneous with (or a thing of the same kind as) some other thing of which my knowledge is certain. . . . So I cannot say that it is probable that God exists."[35]

---

of an apodictic certainty; for if one proposes to cognize something as absolutely necessary, then that cognition must also carry absolute necessity with it." Kant, *Critique of Pure Reason*, p. 574 [A612/B640]. Kant here appears to conflate metaphysical and epistemic necessity: to say that a being exists necessarily is a metaphysical claim; to say we know with certainty that such a being exists is an epistemic claim.

34. We understand "supernatural" as synonymous with "supranatural," but we adopt the latter term because the former has picked up some unfortunate popular connotations.

35. Imanuel Kant, *Lectures on Philosophical Theology*, trans. Allen W. Wood and Gertrude M. Clark (Ithaca, NY: Cornell University Press, 1978), p. 121. Despite this, Kant himself at

However, there is good reason to doubt that Kant's broader attack comes anywhere close to succeeding. The problem here is not that the conclusion of Kant's attack is too weak: he mounts a bold assault on the possibility of transcendent metaphysics. But his arguments fail to pass either the test of lucidity or the test of having reasonably secure premises.

The obscurity of Kant's case against transcendent metaphysics is legendary. It is hardly possible to read the secondary literature for long without running into statements like Karl Ameriks's in the prestigious *Cambridge Companion to Kant:* "If one looks closely at the *Critique,* it is not easy to show precisely how even on its own terms it has definitely undermined all claims of traditional metaphysics; indeed, from the *Critique* alone it is difficult to find out what all those claims are."[36] And should it be thought that Ameriks is being hard on Kant, consider Norman Kemp Smith's comment that Kant "flatly contradicts himself in almost every chapter" of the *Critique,* in such an obvious way that "every commentator has felt constrained to offer some explanation" of the inconsistencies.[37] Kant's case fails the first test — that of lucidity.

Although it is often unclear just how Kant's arguments run, it is possible to identify some key premises. However, they are anything but secure.

Consider his line of reasoning in support of the claim that cognition cannot be extended beyond appearances — into the noumenal order. Kant presents a *reductio ad absurdum* argument: he asks us to suppose the claim is false, and he generates contradictions from that supposition. His famed "antinomies" are intended to present, side by side, opposed but equally persuasive arguments from traditional metaphysics (where cognition *is* extended beyond appearances), thereby demonstrating the impotence of reason when it attempts to reach beyond experience and appearances. Now there are plenty of criticisms of Kant's discussion of the antinomies: typically, commentators note that the arguments on one or both sides are weak, so the apparent paradox can easily be resolved. We agree that, on close inspection, the antinomies dissolve; but, whether they do or not, Kant's argument tacitly presumes that we can in fact know at least one principle, the principle of non-contradiction. The principle of non-contradiction tells us that no entity

---

times acknowledges that probable reasoning about God's existence is in fact possible. See, for instance, Kant, *Lectures on Philosophical Theology,* pp. 100-101.

36. Karl Ameriks, "The Critique of Metaphysics: Kant and Traditional Ontology," in Paul Guyer, ed., *The Cambridge Companion to Kant* (Cambridge, UK: Cambridge University Press, 1992), p. 258.

37. Norman Kemp Smith, *A Commentary to Kant's "Critique of Pure Reason,"* 2d ed. (Atlantic Highlands, NJ: Humanities Press International, 1992), p. xx.

whatsoever can simultaneously have and lack a particular property. Nothing can be both red and not red, lovely and not lovely, all due qualifications taken into account. But Kant can draw nothing from the antinomies pertinent to his aims unless he assumes that the principle of non-contradiction holds in the noumenal order: without this assumption, the lesson to be learned from the antinomies could just as well be that things in the noumenal order *do* both have and fail to have the very same properties, as the opposed arguments in the antinomies suggest. Kant must thus part ways with philosophers who accept strong versions of dialetheism.

One could respond that Kant sees the principle of non-contradiction as merely "logical" or "semantic," not ontological. The principle would then hold as a rule of language or thought, not a rule of reality. Yet, as Aristotle pointed out, the key question is not about what we can say or think, but rather what can *be* the case. For nothing prevents something from being *called* "F" and "not-F." A word, Aristotle notes, can have opposed meanings. Indeed, there are a few words in English that do have opposed meanings: "contronyms," or Janus words, they are called. "Dust" and "trim" can involve either removing something (dusting the bureau, trimming the hedges) or adding something (dusting the cake with powdered sugar, trimming the Christmas tree). "Inoculate" can mean either "protect against" or "infect with." "Snap" can mean either "break apart" or "join together." The principle of non-contradiction is a statement about entities: not our thought about entities, not our language about entities, but entities themselves. All entities — phenomenal and noumenal.

So it looks as though we can know something about the way things are in the noumenal order after all. Moreover, Kant himself is insistent that we can. While theoretical reason leaves us in the dark about the existence of the self and about the self's power to determine its own course of action, the way to knowledge is not entirely closed. For Kant, what is impossible is to peer into the noumenal on the basis of *theoretical* reasoning, not every form of reasoning. There remains the possibility of inferring the structure of the unseen world from practical principles, as follows:

1) I can know that I ought to do x.
2) "I can know that I ought to do x" entails "I can know that I am free to do x."
3) So, I can know that I am free to do x.

Kant's way of putting the point is more complicated, yet he appears committed to the preceding line of reasoning. For in many places in the *Critique of Practical Reason,* Kant tells us such things as, "freedom is real, for this idea reveals itself through the moral law."[38] And we know freedom exists because it is inferred from a moral law that "is given, as it were, as a fact of pure reason of which we are a priori conscious and which is apodictically certain. . . ."[39] To some extent, then, we can reach cognitively into the unseen world and find there an objective fact, the existence of a mysterious power, the power of free will. No amount of talk about how our knowledge of our freedom is possible only for "practical purposes" or by "practical reason" undoes the fact, if it is a fact, that we have had delivered to us an extremely important component of what we know. The question we need to ask is: Are there premises we *know*, entailing the conclusion that we know we are free? And the answer, according to Kant, is "yes." In fact, he goes further than this, holding that we have something beyond everyday, garden-variety knowledge that the premises of the argument are true: we have apodictic certainty of their truth. The wall of the world beyond experience is thus breached by everyone conscious of duty, which is everyone, period. And given the breach, as well as the possibility of explaining events by appealing to powers whose causality we cannot sensuously intuit, the way lies open to drawing inferences about God.[40]

1.2.2. Wittgensteinian Contentions: Separate Spheres, Separate Magisteria

Some thinkers develop a position not entirely dissimilar to Kant's, though they may care little about the Kantian critiques we have just surveyed. Natural theology is inaccessible territory, these thinkers hold, because religion has an

38. Immanuel Kant, *Critique of Practical Reason,* ed. Mary Gregor (Cambridge, UK: Cambridge University Press, 1997), p. 3 [5:4].

39. Kant, *Critique of Practical Reason,* p. 41 [5:47].

40. Kant holds that we can recognize *a priori* that the moral law makes a claim upon us, and therein also recognize that in the world beyond experience there exists an inscrutable faculty of freedom. Yet he also insists that this grasp of the noumenal fact does not open the way to theoretical employment of the cognized fact. Kant's reasoning on this score is subject to various interpretations, but Andrews Reath seems to express the general consensus when he says that, since "the reality of transcendental freedom is not established though any sensible intuition, it is not an item of empirical or theoretical knowledge that, for example, can enter into the explanation of events" (Andrews Reath, "Introduction," in Kant's *Critique of Practical Reason,* p. xiii). Yet we surely are told that this transcendental freedom is guaranteed by insight into the moral law, and it would appear that, if it can be seen that one is in some circumstances obligated to do something in the world, do something physical, and that if in general ought implies can, then one can freely affect the world. In other words, the mental has causal impact on the physical; the mental — in this case free choice — is not epiphenomenal. And at least part of the explanation of why one's body is stroking through the water is that one freely chose to rescue the drowning child.

internal logic protecting it against outside criticism from philosophy and science, and rendering traditional inquiry into theism and revelation pointless. The so-called "Wittgensteinian fideists" take this position. Evolutionary biologist Stephen J. Gould, a religious believer, famously propounded a similar view, speaking of the "non-overlapping magisteria" of science and religion, with their separate spheres of authority.[41]

Why might it be thought that science and religion, by their very natures, cannot conflict? It certainly looks at first glance as though a religion can teach things that are inconsistent with the weight of scientific evidence. Every standard science text dealing with human origins undercuts a literal reading of the book of Genesis. Furthermore, the possibility of conflict is commonly understood. That is, the ordinary understanding of religious belief — the understanding of the people in synagogues and churches and mosques — is that it includes some empirical hypotheses, and may be falsifiable (though, of course, most people would not put it quite that way).

Like Wittgenstein himself, Wittgensteinian fideists are not fans of explicit argumentation. Still, they say things that at least suggest arguments. One argument of interest, drawn from Norman Malcolm's classic discussion of "the groundlessness of belief," might be stated as follows:[42]

1) General frameworks are beyond question or criticism.
2) Religious beliefs are (or are parts of) general frameworks.
3) Thus religious beliefs are beyond question or criticism.

The argument is puzzling, to put it mildly. For the history of science is full of cases where what at first appeared to be foundational or framework truths were questioned and proved false. As Karl Popper observes, from Pythagoras and Parmenides to Ernst Mach and Max Planck, scientists endorsing different frameworks have criticized one another and fruitfully discussed their differences.[43] Newton and Descartes had fundamentally different frameworks for thinking about cosmology. Newton's basic concepts could not even be expressed in the Cartesian system; but that did not prevent people from arguing

41. See Stephen Jay Gould, *Rocks of Ages: Science and Religion in the Fullness of Life* (New York: Ballantine Publishing Group, 1999).

42. Norman Malcolm, "The Groundlessness of Belief," in R. Douglas Geivett and Brendan Sweetman, eds., *Contemporary Perspectives on Religious Epistemology* (New York: Oxford University Press, 1992). Malcolm does not set out numbered premises, but he does appear to commit himself to the reasoning.

43. Karl R. Popper, *The Myth of the Framework: In Defence of Science and Rationality* (London: Routledge, 1994), p. 34.

about the differences. They argued intensely, eventually siding with Newton. In the area of logic, too, frameworks can be, are, and often should be questioned. It is possible to argue about even the deepest framework proposition, the principle of non-contradiction. The principle is *in some sense* groundless: it is indemonstrable from any absolutely prior principles. But it can be debated and defended by arguing from propositions skeptics must grant if they are to express a meaningful view.[44] And there are plenty of criticizable religious practices. Aztecs thought the sun looked pale in the morning; they reasoned it must want blood, which they provided. It is very hard to see that it was wrong or somehow incoherent for observers of this practice to say that the human sacrifice should stop. Science here provides the wherewithal to stop the killings: the sun does not draw nourishment from blood sacrifices. Banishing science from the realm of religion is the last thing we want to do in this situation.

And anyway, given Malcolm's understanding of a general framework, it looks as though an inquirer can regard the most general framework of religious belief as beyond question and still investigate whether there is a God who has revealed. For Malcolm says that Buddhism is undoubtedly a religion. But Buddhists do not purport to believe in God.

A defender of Wittgensteinian fideism might try a different tack. Some writings of the Wittgensteinian disciples (including Malcolm) suggest the following line:

1) There is no such thing as belief in God apart from the practices of worship.
2) If so, then religious beliefs cannot be evaluated from the outside, apart from the practices of worship.

Is there no such thing as belief apart from worship? On at least one traditional religious understanding of the fallen angels or demons, the demons believe that God exists — they tremble at the thought — but they categorically renounce worship. And even if the deepest, truest belief requires engaging in religious practices, the beginning of belief might not. What is wrong with an agnostic inquirer, a nonbeliever grasping for accessible starting points, investigating whether there is a good God who has revealed? There are certainly churches that have made propositional proclamations about God's revelation, long and loudly, proclamations intended to apply universally, not just to believers: there already exist communities that regard them-

---

44. See Aristotle's *Metaphysics*, bk. IV, ch. 1.

selves as answering the agnostic's questions. The first step toward one of the communities may be philosophical, even if the last step is not.

A popular idea that lends itself to appropriation by Wittgensteinian fideists and those who advocate for "separate magisteria" is that the existence of God is not a hypothesis. And science and religion can conflict only if the existence of God is a hypothesis, it is suggested. In support of the claim that the existence of God is not a hypothesis, it is possible to cite distinguished philosophers who plainly are neither Wittgensteinian fideists nor proponents of the "separate spheres" view. Alvin Plantinga, for example, says:

> Now from this point of view [the view that theistic belief is a hypothesis designed to explain something], most of the beliefs characteristically accepted by, say, Christians are peculiarly ill-founded. How could the existence of a triune God, or the incarnation of the Second Person of the Trinity, or the death and resurrection of the Son of God be sensibly thought of as *hypotheses* designed to explain what we find in B [the universe]? What, in B do these things explain? Could one sensibly claim they are worthy of belief because of their high probability with respect to B, or because they explain some significant portion of B? Obviously not.[45]

And the Catholic priest who was the first to formulate the big bang theory, Lemaitre, seemed to think it wrong — both from the point of view of science and the point of view of religion — to regard the existence of God as a hypothesis.[46]

However, surely if people are running around saying that somebody rose from the dead, it would be possible to explain this phenomenon by reference to the fact (if it is a fact, of course) that somebody actually did rise from the dead. Plantinga's example is misleading because the attributes he refers to (such as God's Trinity) have no connection with attributes of the universe that immediately come to mind when we think of explaining it. Imagine, though, that you are living in Kepler's time and somebody asks, "How could the sun, the thing that warms us, possibly be invoked as the explanation of what moves the earth?" In fact, the sun can be invoked in the explanation. Similarly, the Trinity of God, qua Trinity, is not responsible for the existence

---

45. Alvin Plantinga, "The Probabilistic Argument from Evil," *Philosophical Studies* 35, no. 1 (1979): 51.

46. Lemaitre "was always of the opinion that science and theology were separate fields which, though ultimately leading to the same goals, should not be mixed," according to Helge Kragh in *Cosmology and Controversy: The Historical Development of Two Theories of the Universe* (Princeton, NJ: Princeton University Press, 1996), p. 60.

of the universe, but if the Christian claims are correct, the very same God who is triune is the God responsible for the existence of the universe. Furthermore, in the Christian understanding of things, there are facts that are explained by the Trinity, qua Trinity. By Plantinga's own account, God's becoming incarnate in the Second Person of the Trinity can explain the evils of the world.[47] We will ourselves be arguing at length that various components of revelatory claims have great explanatory power. Now a believer might conceivably attach some sense to the notion of a "hypothesis" according to which God's existence does not count as a hypothesis; but it is not obvious that will be of interest to an agnostic inquirer. One's own existence is not a hypothesis to oneself; but it does not follow that one's existence is in a sphere of inquiry inaccessible to science and philosophy.

Wittgensteinian fideism offers a faith without risk, a faith *nothing* can show to be false. But a faith without risk is a faith without content. If the world ends and there is no afterlife, Christianity has been falsified. If Vatican III is called in accordance with requisite norms and renounces the doctrine of the Trinity or the doctrine of papal infallibility, then Roman Catholicism has been falsified. Religious belief is not merely an empirical hypothesis about the world, of course. Religion has a depth reason cannot fathom. Yet that is consistent with our being able rationally to investigate questions about the truth or falsity of religious claims.

1.2.3. *The Scientific Demystifiers' Promises*

Although Galileo, Descartes, Newton, and other originators of the modern scientific revolution all believed in God, surveys indicate that most top scientists today do not. Physicist and Nobel Laureate Steven Weinberg reports that, on the rare occasion when the topic of religion comes up among the physicists he knows, most express mild surprise and amusement that anyone still takes the subject seriously. Weinberg takes it seriously, but his views provide no encouragement to an inquirer into revelation. On the occasion of accepting the "Emperor Has No Clothes" award from the Freedom From Religion Foundation, he said:

> I personally feel that the teaching of modern science is corrosive of religious belief, and I'm all for that! . . .

47. Alvin Plantinga, "Supralapsarianism, or 'O Felix Culpa,'" in Peter van Inwagen, ed., *Christian Faith and the Problem of Evil* (Grand Rapids: Eerdmans, 2004).

... I can hope that this long sad story will come to an end at some time in the future and that this progression of priests and ministers and rabbis and ulamas and imams and bonzes and bodhisattvas will come to an end, that we'll see no more of them. I hope that this is something to which science can contribute and if it is, then I think it may be the most important contribution that we can make.[48]

We all accept the existence of quarks and electrons on the authority of scientists. Why not also listen to them on broader questions about the nature of the universe, including questions about its ultimate origin and its destiny?

Still, authority is not everything. Argument counts. And it is certainly possible for inquirers who are not scientists to make some judgments about the worth of scientists' arguments, because those arguments do not depend exclusively on technical scientific knowledge. If expertise is required, it often is in philosophy or some other field.

Indeed, in many cases the agnostic assertions by scientists hardly take the form of argument at all. Consider Richard Lewontin:

> We take the side of science *in spite* of the patent absurdity of some of its constructs, *in spite* of its failure to fulfill many of its extravagant promises of health and life, *in spite* of the tolerance of the scientific community for unsubstantiated just-so stories, because we have a prior commitment, a commitment to materialism. . . . Moreover, that materialism is absolute, for we cannot allow a Divine Foot in the door.[49]

Lewontin has plainly let the cat out of the bag. As far as he is concerned — as far as the many who think like him are concerned — the rejection of theism is a manifesto. There is not even a hint of an argument, just naked assertion. It does not take a specialist in genetics or relativity theory to see this. Why cannot we allow a Divine Foot in the door? Newton, the greatest of them all (in top scientists' estimation), certainly thought we could; he held that God "constitutes duration and space."[50]

Nor does it take special scientific expertise to recognize that top scientists who do argue against theism limit their claims, often acknowledging that sci-

48. Steven Weinberg, "Free People from Superstition," *Freethought Today* 17, no. 3 (2000), retrieved Nov. 1, 2005, from <www.ffrf.org/fttoday/2000>.

49. Richard Lewontin, "Billions and Billions of Demons," *The New York Review of Books* 44, no. 1 (Jan. 9, 1997).

50. Isaac Newton, *The Principia: Mathematical Principles of Natural Philosophy,* trans. I. Bernard Cohen and Anne Whitman (Berkeley and Los Angeles: University of California Press, 1999), p. 941.

ence does not prove undeniably that theism is false. Albert Einstein,[51] Richard Feynman,[52] and Steven Weinberg[53] all modestly grant that they cannot prove the negation of the theistic hypothesis.

Nor is the nonspecialist incapable of recognizing that a case depends on scientific claims that are controversial (or worse) among top scientists themselves. A major reason Einstein rejected revealed religion is that he believed necessity rules all, even going so far as to describe the thesis as essential to science. But he was saying this at the very time that science was abandoning determinism. Though most of us are not well placed to judge the scientific evidence for the truth of determinism, we can certainly recognize that Einstein's position on the matter is unpopular among scientists today.

Inquirers without specialized scientific training can, moreover, see that some of the arguments against theism by top scientists obviously have nothing to do with science. The most persuasive argument against a personal God in Einstein's writings we can find (an argument that may have stemmed from Einstein's determinism) poses a quick and speculative version of the problem of evil.[54] Like Einstein and countless others, Weinberg is bothered by the problem of reconciling the world's evils with the possibility of a good creator. Remembrance of the Holocaust, he says, makes him unsympathetic to attempts to justify God's treatment of us.

Furthermore, even when scientists support their agnosticism with arguments that rely on noncontroversial, genuinely scientific premises, commonly the core of their case for agnosticism also rests on at least one premise open to philosophical evaluation without reliance on the latest news from the frontiers of science. In some cases it can rather easily be seen that an argument is, say, formally invalid, or that it covertly assumes what is at issue, or commits some other logical fallacy. For example, consider this from astrophysicist Lee Smolin:

51. Einstein writes: "To be sure, the doctrine of a personal God interfering with natural events could never be *refuted,* in the real sense, by science, for this doctrine can always take refuge in those domains in which scientific knowledge has not yet been able to set foot." Albert Einstein, *Ideas and Opinions* (New York: Bonanza Books, 1954), p. 48.

52. Richard P. Feynman says: "I agree that science cannot disprove the existence of God. I absolutely agree. I also agree that a belief in science and religion is consistent." Feynman, *The Meaning of It All: Thoughts of a Citizen-Scientist* (Reading, MA: Helix Books/Perseus Books, 1998), p. 36.

53. Steven Weinberg says: "The inconsistency between the modern theory of evolution and belief in an interested God does not seem to me one of logic — one can imagine that God established the laws of nature and set the mechanism of evolution in motion with the intention that through natural selection you and I would someday appear — but there is a real inconsistency in temperament." Weinberg, *Dreams of a Final Theory: The Scientist's Search for the Ultimate Laws of Nature* (New York: Random House, 1994), p. 248.

54. Einstein, *Ideas and Opinions,* pp. 46-47.

[The universe] cannot have been made by anything that exists outside it, for by definition the universe is all there is, and there can be nothing outside it. And, by definition, neither can there have been anything before the universe that caused it, for if anything existed it must have been part of the universe. So the first principle of cosmology must be "There is nothing outside the universe."[55]

At the head of a book on the cosmos, this can sound like tough-minded science. Yet it takes only a few seconds to see it for what it is: an all-too-quick philosophical argument based on a tendentious definition of "universe" that insinuates its conclusion without even beginning to give real evidence. Of course, if by universe you *mean* "everything there is," then there is nothing outside it. What we want to know, though, is whether there is anything beyond all this matter and energy, whether there is anything that did *not* begin to be 13.7 (or so) billion years ago.

Do scientists have arguments better than the ones just cited? One would think so. Still, even the best of their arguments often embed premises open to philosophical scrutiny. Let us consider a general argument whose main lines are quite familiar, an argument that crystallizes objections to theism voiced by leading scientists:

1) Without invoking supranatural causes (God or spirits), science adequately explains phenomena once thought to require injection of causality from outside the physical world.
2) If so, then it is highly probable that the "final theory," an expression of the ultimate laws of nature, will explain enough to justify the assured conclusion that the world is a physically closed system.
3) If so, then it is fatuous to look into the case for theism and revelation.
4) So, it is fatuous to look into the case for theism and revelation.

Weinberg is one of the few top scientists to take the trouble to spell out the argument's promissory materialism in any detail.[56] Against the backdrop of the idea of the targeted "final theory," which would answer the deepest questions by appealing to bedrock principles, Weinberg describes "the demystification of the heavens" and the "demystification of life." He says that "our discovery of the connected and convergent pattern of scientific explanations has done the very great service of teaching us that there is no room in

55. Lee Smolin, *Three Roads to Quantum Gravity* (New York: Basic Books, 2001), p. 17.

56. Weinberg, *Dreams of a Final Theory*, especially chs. 2, 3, 11. The formulation of the three-step argument, which we believe represents Weinberg's reasoning, is our own.

nature for astrology or telekinesis or creationism or other superstitions."[57] And our understanding of science, he tells us, is "our greatest aid" in judging which avenues of explanation should be explored.

Is this an argument that only a specialist in one of the physical sciences, only an elite among elites, can evaluate? Not at all. Nonspecialists may reasonably find fault with all three premises. We will focus, for purpose of illustration, on premise 2.

There is plentiful reason to be suspicious about whether scientists will one day explain "enough" for us confidently to conclude that the world is a physically closed system — a system that admits no supranatural causes, and that itself has no impact on anything supranatural.

For instance, science does not purport to explain "historical accidents," as Weinberg notes. And he acknowledges that it is difficult to determine what is a mere accident and what merely looks like one. But his recognition of the problem does nothing to diminish it. Is the existence of the world itself a historical accident? Weinberg is silent on the issue. It is as though science's incapacity to deal with the very existence of the world were on a par with its inability to explain historical accidents long lost in the mist of time, such as the appearance of a small inkblot on one of the letters from Abigail Adams to her husband, John. Philosophers with positivist leanings argue that the question "Why is there anything at all?" poses a pseudo-problem; but it is far from obvious that they are correct.

The goal of explaining the existence of human beings is sometimes also abandoned by the demystifiers. Weinberg states: "Perhaps our best hope for a final explanation is to discover a set of final laws of nature and show that this is the only logically consistent rich theory, rich enough for example to allow for the existence of ourselves."[58] But a theory merely consistent with the emergence of human beings might also be consistent with our failure to make an appearance on the great stage of existence. That is not much of an explanation.

And there is another phenomenon scientists have great difficulty accounting for: consciousness. As Weinberg candidly observes:

> Of all the areas of experience that we try to link to the principles of physics by arrows of explanation, it is consciousness that presents us with the greatest difficulty. . . . I have to confess I find this issue terribly difficult, and I have no special expertise on such matters.[59]

57. Weinberg, *Dreams of a Final Theory,* p. 50.
58. Weinberg, "Can Science Explain Everything? Anything?" *The New York Review of Books* 48, no. 9 (May 31, 2001): 50.
59. Weinberg, *Dreams of a Final Theory,* p. 44.

The best cognitive neuroscientists often admit with Weinberg, "so far *not* so good" if we are talking about consciousness itself and not related phenomena such as the ability to give verbal reports on the content of mental experience. After 532 pages of fascinating detail about cognition and the nervous system, the distinguished authors of the authoritative textbook *Cognitive Neuroscience* lament: "Right from the start we can say that science has little to say about sentience. We are clueless on how the brain creates sentience."[60] And Stephen Palmer tells us, 630 pages into his critically acclaimed *Vision Science,* "[T]o this writer's knowledge, nobody has ever suggested a theory that the scientific community regards as giving even a remotely plausible causal account of how consciousness arises or why it has the particular qualities it does."[61] Then there are the philosophers who agree with scientists that the universe is a physically closed system and yet doubt that science can explain consciousness: David Chalmers, Joseph Levine, Thomas Nagel, Steven Pinker . . . and the list of physicalistic skeptics among the philosophers keeps growing.

If scientists are not explaining consciousness, what are they doing? Typically, investigators do one of three (overlapping) things, all of which are intriguing and important. First, they establish correlations. In ancient societies, physicians attending warriors with open head injuries noticed that sensory and motor impairment regularly occurred on the side opposite the damage to the brain. Now we can probe the brain electronically or scan its structure and activity with a number of marvelous devices, from the familiar functional MRI to the new MEG technology. We learn that vivid memories can be triggered by stimulating areas of the temporal lobe, the sensation of a phantom limb correlates with excessive firing of neurons in the somatosensory cortex, and the anterior cingulate cortex lights up when we do something of our own volition. Second, neurobiologists elaborate the processes involved in those areas of the brain active when consciousness is present. Through neuronal "signaling," chemical and electrical features of cell activity are tracked in marvelous detail. Third, and most interesting, neurobiologists explain why, *given* that conscious experience is somehow grounded in the activity of the nervous system, variations in the environment and within the nervous system itself result in modulation or extinction of awareness.[62]

60. Michael S. Gazzaniga, Richard B. Ivry, George R. Mangun, *Cognitive Neuroscience: The Biology of the Mind,* 2d ed. (New York: W. W. Norton & Company, 2002), pp. 659-60.

61. Stephen E. Palmer, *Vision Science: Photons to Phenomenology* (Cambridge, MA: MIT Press, 1999), p. 630.

62. For a particularly striking illustration, the reader might wish to consult neuroscience textbook explanations in terms of lateral inhibition of neuronal firing leading to the Mach-band

There is, in fact, good reason for thinking that science is *in principle* incapable of explaining consciousness. Consider the following scenario. Your child has a pull toy that features a little man in a box whose head pops in and out of the box as the toy is pulled along. You wonder, why does the head pop in and out? You examine the toy and see that the wheels are affixed to an axle with a rise in the middle; the little man sits on the rise, so his head goes up and down with each revolution of the wheels. Now your friend comes in and asks, "Why does the man's head pop in and out?" So you explain. And your friend says, "I understand all that, but why does the head pop in and out when the toy is pulled along?" The question is bizarre: if your friend has really understood everything you have said, it makes no sense to continue to ask why the head pops in and out. We may generalize from this case to the relevant principle:

> If a putative explanation of a phenomenon is a genuine causal explanation, then if you grasp the explanation in relation to the phenomenon, it cannot reasonably be asked: "But why does the phenomenon occur?"

No matter how much is said about the nervous system, as long as what is said is confined to statements of fundamental physics and chemistry, you will always be able to ask "But why does *that* produce consciousness?"

In any event, given all that Weinberg concedes about the limits of the final theory, it is difficult indeed to see why we should think that the conclusion that the world is a physically closed system is "assured."

A Presupposition of the "Assured" Conclusion That the World Is a Physically Closed System: Circumscribing the "Physical"   To maintain that a purely natural or scientific explanation has been so successful that we can all be confident the world is a physically closed system and inquiry into theism is fatuous, one should have a reasonably clear account of what it is for a thing to be physical, an account consistent with physicalism's axiomatic claim that there is nothing supranatural.

Of course, it cannot simply be said that a physical thing is a thing with physical properties and that physical properties are properties of physical things. That would make no one any wiser. Nor can it be said that physical properties are properties that endow their bearers with extension in space and time: it has been a long while since physicists have embraced a Cartesian view that ties physical things to extension. Pointlike objects without substructure are now acceptable as physical entities. What, then, should be said?

---

phenomenon. Explanations and illustrations are also available on several websites that show up when "lateral inhibition" and "Mach-band" are entered as key terms on a search engine.

We will look first at the two prominent ways of spelling out what physical entities, properties, and processes are,[63] and then turn to a couple of less well-known accounts.

Each of these accounts, we will argue, fails to meet at least one of the following conditions. First, the account of the "physical" should not be too narrow: it should not exclude things one wants to count as physical. Second, it should not be too broad: if the account does not exclude things such as God, or little gods, then it will hardly suffice to support the anti-theistic claims of the physicalist and shut down inquiries into theism. Third, it should not be too vague: the account should not leave it an open question whether it excludes things one wants to count, or includes things one does not want to count. And fourth, it should not be defined in such a way that it turns out to be either obviously false or highly improbable.

The first prominent account of physical things and processes, sometimes called an "object" conception, suggests that a property is physical just in case it is the kind required to give a complete account of paradigmatic physical objects (or it supervenes on such properties). There are many problems with this approach, among them that pounding on the table and saying "By 'physical' I mean the sort of thing I am pounding on" fails to corral an adequate stock of paradigmatic physical objects. It is a good bet that there are some pretty strange physical things we have yet to discover. This account is too narrow: it does not yield a wide enough stock of physical objects.

The second prominent account, sometimes called a "theory-based conception," proposes that physical things and processes are those items that can be characterized in terms of physical properties; and physical properties, in turn, are specified as those properties invoked by standard physical theory (or properties that supervene on or are realizations of such properties).

But which physical theory?

If it is *present* physical theory, there is no guarantee that the present set of postulated physical properties will be adequate for the job of demystification: the account will be too narrow. Andrew Melnyk, who opts for defining physicalism in terms of present physical theory, is untroubled by the narrowness of the account, because he is willing to give up on the standard expectation that one should endorse a theory only if one takes it to be approximately *true*. He declares: "It is perfectly possible to endorse *any* scientific hypothesis, including therefore physicalism, and indeed to endorse it rationally, while ac-

---

63. See Daniel Stoljar's account of the conceptions and their problems in Daniel Stoljar, "Physicalism," *Stanford Encyclopedia of Philosophy* (Spring 2001 ed.), Edward N. Zalta, ed., retrieved Nov. 1, 2005, from <http://plato.stanford.edu/archives/spr2001/entries/physicalism/>.

knowledging that it has only a very low probability of being true."[64] However, no one should halt an inquiry into God's existence or the existence of divine revelation on the grounds that a manifesto has been issued telling us that an endorsable but false physics can explain the world.

If, on the other hand, future physical theory is the point of reference, then we are back to having little idea what we are talking about, and face the very real prospect that the account will be too broad. Consider, for instance, the possibility that physics in the future might return to a view more like that of the early modern period, a view that *includes* the divine. Kepler filled his astronomy with mysticism and appeals to ideas about the holy Trinity. Newton's *Principia,* the most influential scientific work of all time, treated absolute space and time as part of the *sensorium,* or sensory matrix, of God. Whether or not Newton understood God's *sensorium* as a sense organ, as Leibniz charged, Newton's language surely does suggest that he puts God into the fundamental postulates of his physics. "In him [God] all things are contained and moved," Newton contends in the famous "General Scholium" at the end of the *Principia.* "This concludes the discussion of God, and to treat of God from phenomena is certainly a part of 'natural' philosophy."[65] James Clerk Maxwell proposed what was surely thought of at the time as a physical theory. But Robert Mills tells us in an introduction to contemporary physics: "To a present-day physicist, Maxwell's theory of the electromagnetic field seems to give a powerful description of something completely *non*material whose reality has nothing at all to do with matter as we know it. . . ."[66] The philosopher John Searle observes that, if it should turn out that we need to acknowledge a divine force, that would be seen as a part of physics, too.[67] If the focus is on future physical theory, the second prominent account of the physical cannot keep the divine out of the foundations of science.

Two lesser-known accounts of the "physical" worthy of attention are pro-

64. Though Melnyk promises a defense of this startling assertion in chapter 5 of his book, that chapter does little to dispel the sense of unease his position elicits. Andrew Melnyk, *A Physicalist Manifesto: Thoroughly Modern Materialism* (Cambridge, UK: Cambridge University Press, 2003), p. 14.

65. Newton, *The Principia,* pp. 941, 943.

66. Robert Mills, *Space, Time and Quanta: An Introduction to Contemporary Physics* (New York: W. H. Freeman and Company, 1994), p. 2.

67. "If it turned out that God *does* exist and that it's absolutely right, if we became totally convinced of this, given the rest of our worldview that would be a fact of physics like any other. That is to say, instead of four forces we would find five basic forces, the divine force would have to be added or you would see all the other forces as manifestations of the divine force." John Searle, "Rorty v. Searle, at Last: A Debate," *Logos: A Journal of Catholic Thought and Culture* 2, no. 3 (1999): 67.

vided by Wilfred Sellars and Paul Meehl. In the first of their two (nonexclusive) senses of "physical" — they call it physical₁ — an item (entity, constituent, property, or action) is physical if and only if it is in the space-time net. In the second sense — physical₂ — an item is physical if and only if it is definable in the most elementary terms of a theory adequate (without being excessive) to describe completely the states of the universe before the appearance of life.[68]

Will it be helpful to the proponent of non-theistic explanation to spell out a conception of a physically closed system that understands "physical" as "physical₁"? No. For if entities that are physical₁ will be required in the "final" scientific theory, then explaining events in this world may require invoking entities and processes smacking of the divine. It is true that God — if there is a God as traditionally defined — is outside the space-time net. But Aristotelian substantial forms are not, and they qualify as physical₁, as do Aquinas's substantial forms endowed with immortality, which are *in time* to begin with, then *out of time* for a while, and then back *in time* again. Descartes, too, depicted souls in a way that qualified them as physical₁, even though he deemed them to be immortal beings transcending matter. And some modern accounts of immortal selves possessed of freedom of the will do the same.[69] If something alive can transcend matter, then why not God? Indeed, on some nontraditional theistic theories, the deity itself is physical₁, since it is attached to the world in the form of a world-soul. To allow that the theory may need to appeal to physical₁ entities — monads, points of conscious, the property of being conscious, mental direction of a mind toward objects, feelings, or a host of other ethereal entities that have one foot at least in the space-time net — is tantamount to admitting that these kinds of things are inexplicable on the basis of a naturalistic theory that allegedly demystifies the world. The sail snaps, and the argument loses its driving wind.

An understanding of "physical" as "physical₂" faces similar problems. No one knows whether God will need to be part of a theory adequate (without being excessive) to describe completely the states of the universe before living things appeared in it, and we cannot, without begging the question, assume that there will be no need to refer to God. Recall that Searle suggests a divine force could be seen as part of physics, if it turns out we need to acknowledge a divine force. So the second of the Sellars-Meehl accounts of the physical, like the first, is too broad.

---

68. See Paul E. Meehl, "The Concept of Emergence," in *Selected Philosophical and Methodological Papers,* ed. C. Anthony Anderson and Keith Gunderson (Minneapolis: University of Minnesota Press, 1991), p. 182.

69. See William Hasker, *The Emergent Self* (Ithaca, NY: Cornell University Press, 1999).

We conclude, then, that there is no sense of "physical" that is definite enough and strong enough to undercut the project of natural theology. (Nonetheless, in the pages ahead we will keep on talking about physicalistic explanation, in the way people sometimes do in this kind of situation. This is tantamount to saying that the "physical" is the subject of current physics — or current physics, plus refinements. Of course, since we are not committed to physicalism, we are also not committed to the terminology.)

The most interesting aspect of the failures of all these definitions of "the physical," in our view, is that not a single one of them succeeds in cleansing the physical entirely of the divine.[70] If physicalistic explanation is to stand as a barrier on the way to the study of natural theology, then what counts as physical must be clarified in a way that keeps divine beings out of the foundations. Thales declared all is "full of the gods"; future science must purge every one of them. No God. No little gods: no angels, no souls or entelechies, no Leibnizian monads (simple, indestructible, immaterial entities mirroring the universe), and no "points of consciousness" can be permitted in the base laws, axioms, and postulates.

Furthermore, even if one could set forth a definition of "physical" that would prevent references to the divine from entering into physical or scientific explanations, such explanations would not entail that there is no supranatural being: the explanations would be agnostic on that point. It would not be an anti-theistic account of the world that explained so well why balls fall to the ground when dropped, why the temperature falls in the winter, and so on. The scientific or physical explanations of these phenomena are not *anti*-theistic; they are simply *non*-theistic. That point may be obscured by the fact that "physicalism" is standardly taken to name an anti-theistic philosophic position. But again, the scientific explanations of phenomena that are doing so much to demystify the world are not essentially *anti*-theistic; they are simply *non*-theistic. Thus it is possible to combine scientific or physical explanation with theistic explanation; it is possible for theistic explanation to build on physical explanation. Of course, at every moment of the day people give accounts of such facts as "The coffee is too hot" by pointing out such facts as that the burner flame is too high; it would seem preposterous to say that the coffee is too hot because God boiled it. Yet, *if* the truth of the matter is, as suggested in philosophically attuned revelatory traditions, that God, the First Cause, is concurrently active when any secondary causality occurs, then

---

70. It might be thought that the first account does not have this problem (though it is in other ways inadequate). However, the idealist might say, "Pound away on the table as much as you like; but it is all ideas." In that case one is into something spiritual.

the explanation that comes closest to an ideal explanation would involve reference to the First Cause as well as to the fact that the flame is too high.

1.3. The Difficulty of Building a Reasoned Case Solely Through Standard Natural Theology

1.3.1. *The General Problem*

So we may set aside objections to embarking on the project of natural theology, whether from Kantians, proponents of the view that religion and science belong in separate spheres, or scientific demystifiers.

Nevertheless, the task of the agnostic investigator is formidable when the natural theology relied upon is what we will call *standard* natural theology. The standard approach can be introduced through a widely accepted account of natural theology offered by William Alston:

> *Natural theology* is the enterprise of providing support for religious beliefs by starting from premises that neither are nor presuppose any religious beliefs. We begin from the mere existence of the world, or the teleological order of the world, or the concept of God, and we try to show that when we think through the implications of our starting point we are led to recognize the existence of a being that possesses attributes sufficient to identify Him as God. Once we get that foothold we may seek to show that a being could not have the initial attributes without also possessing certain others; in this manner we try to go as far as we can. . . .[71]

"[W]e try to go as far as we can." Can agnostic inquirers go so far with natural theology as to get an affirmative answer to the question of revelation, the question whether a good God has revealed? Many theistic philosophers have said "yes." But that is very optimistic — at least when natural theology is conceived in the way Alston explains it. For natural theology so conceived defers consideration of the content of revelatory claims until one has recognized the existence of God. We will use the phrase "standard natural theology" to refer to projects in natural theology that do not identify the content of revelatory claims as especially important evidence a philosophically inclined agnostic inquirer should seriously consider in an investigation into whether there is a good God.[72]

71. Alston, *Perceiving God*, p. 289.
72. Many who engage in natural theology would freely acknowledge that the kinds of problems they set for themselves might not have occurred to them as problems had it not been for

Practitioners of "standard natural theology" need not — indeed, usually do not — announce that the content of revelatory claims is off limits for an agnostic inquirer. They simply proceed without reliance on that content, and they expect their readers to come with them. One pugilist might boast, "I can floor you with one arm tied behind my back"; another might make no such announcement, but nevertheless not use one of his arms (James J. Braddock had no "left" to speak of before working on the docks). Neither pugilist is working up to capacity. Similarly, neither the practitioner of natural theology who explicitly renounces evidence from the content of revelatory claims nor the practitioner who merely ignores it is working with a full database. Both are handicapped. Or so we will be arguing.

Why be less than sanguine about the prospects of natural theology so conceived? The *general* problem is that this kind of natural theology leaves agnostic inquirers with insufficient resources for assessing particular atheistic arguments (such as the argument from evil) and for generating enough evidence to answer the great question of revelation affirmatively. The general problem with standard natural theology will be well illustrated if we reflect on standard natural theology's restricted capacity to handle the problem of evil.

1.3.2. A Specific Example: Limited Resources for Handling the Problem of Evil

How can the world's evils — its suffering and wrongdoing — coexist with an all-powerful, all-knowing, wholly good creator of the universe? The problem this question poses, the problem of evil, has exercised so many thinkers that a technical term has been introduced to label attempted theistic solutions: they are called theodicies. (As is customary, we speak of "the" problem of evil. In fact, a good number of different problems have been taken up under this rubric. We simply stipulate that we take "the problem of evil" to be the problem posed by the question just articulated.)

The best-known contemporary theodicy — using the term broadly — is

---

the existence of revelatory claims. For instance, the dogma that there is a single God who is providential generates a variety of puzzles for the natural theologian. But this concession does not amount to seeing the fact that revelations make these proposals as itself *evidence* for the truth of the proposals.

Compare: *A priori* justification is justification without appeal to sensory experience as part of the evidence. Still, we might not be able to cognize the relevant propositions unless we first have sense experience of the sentences that enable us to get a grip on the propositions in question.

Plantinga's "free-will defense."[73] His line of argument has earned high respect even from those who have sought to oppose it. Richard Gale, for example, says: "Plantinga's version of the FWD [Free-Will Defense] is a thing of beauty that, it is safe to say, will serve as one of the cornerstones in theism's response to evil not just for many years to come but for many centuries."[74] Plantinga modestly does not aspire in his free-will defense to tell us God's actual reasons for permitting evil. He seeks — in one of his later iterations of the defense — merely to show the consistency of the proposition

g) God exists

with

e) There is as much evil as our world contains.

Of course, many hypotheses that are false or highly improbable are consistent. Plantinga points out that "Henry Kissinger swam the Atlantic Ocean" is a self-consistent statement: it is (or appears to be) logically possible. "My spouse will win the Powerball lottery this week" and "I will win it seven times in the next eleven months" are self-consistent and consistent with each other (compossible).

Given the modest goals of Plantinga's project, it is easy to be skeptical about its utility in persuading an agnostic that an all-good God actually might have a good reason for allowing the world's evils. But matters get worse, because it looks like even Plantinga's relatively modest project of demonstrating consistency will in certain circumstances not succeed without the addition of a persuasive argument that an afterlife is possible.

To understand why, we need a slightly fuller sense of his project. To show that g and e are mutually consistent, Plantinga makes use of a theorem of modal logic that is demonstrable in standard systems:

If there is some proposition that together with g entails e, and if g and that proposition are compossible, then g and e are compossible.

So Plantinga looks for a proposition that satisfies this condition. He ends up with the following conjunctive proposition:

73. Plantinga prefers to call his argument not a "theodicy" but a "defense" of God's goodness. He reserves the term "theodicy" for arguments that purport to present God's actual reason(s) for allowing evil. This is a narrower use of the term "theodicy" than has been traditional.

74. Richard Gale, *On the Nature and Existence of God* (Cambridge, UK: Cambridge University Press, 1991), p. 113.

r) It was not within God's power to create a world containing a better balance of good and evil than our world contains; and God creates a world with as much good and evil as our world contains.[75]

Here, we suggest, the agnostic inquirer encounters a difficulty. There is reason to doubt that g and r are compossible. For it is doubtful that it is permissible for a deity to create if the deity can do no better than produce this world. That is, it may be inconsistent with the hypothesized divine goodness and wisdom to create when the results are so dismal. Necessarily, an inquirer might reason, if there is no afterlife, then a world with the particular balance of good and evil in our world is a world in which many suffer horribly through no fault of their own and without compensation, and hence is off limits for a creator-deity; and, necessarily, there is no afterlife. So it looks as if the compossibility of g and r could easily depend on the possibility of an afterlife. But one might suspect that an afterlife is impossible for various reasons.[76] It might, for instance, be thought that the same person cannot be reconstituted after being destroyed. If it is plausible to think destruction precludes reconstitution (of the very same being), then Plantinga's free-will defense is not yet complete. If Plantinga's modest free-will defense is to work for the agnostic, if it is to show an agnostic merely that evil is *consistent* with God's existence, it may need to be supplemented with an argument that an afterlife is possible.[77]

---

75. See Alvin Plantinga, *God, Freedom, and Evil* (New York: Harper and Row, 1974), p. 59. We have slightly simplified Plantinga's language, granting him the assumption (for the sake of the argument) that all the evil in the world is "broadly moral evil."

76. For a consistency proof to be undermined, one does not have to *know* that there is some necessary truth that torpedoes an argument that two propositions are compossible. It is enough to think it is *plausible* that there may be such a necessary truth. To illustrate, consider a scenario in which there is a dispute about whether two mathematical propositions are consistent. Imagine that in the end it looks like it might have been shown that the two propositions are consistent provided there is no prime number between one hundred trillion and two hundred trillion, say. Imagine too that you suspect there is such a prime number: perhaps you know of frequency tables predicting there will be a prime within the relevant range. In this case the consistency of the two propositions has not been established.

77. Plantinga has more to say about the problem of evil than is said in connection with the free-will defense. In *Warranted Christian Belief* he sets forward — in order to criticize — what he takes to be the strongest anti-theistic objection to God on the basis of evil. "The claim is essentially that one who is properly sensitive and properly aware of the sheer horror of the evil displayed in our somber and unhappy world will simply see that no being of the sort God is alleged to be could possibly permit it" (p. 484). Plantinga rejects this claim by arguing (p. 485) that, "if classical Christianity is true, then the perception of evil is not a defeater for belief in God with respect to *fully rational* noetic structures — any noetic structure with no cognitive

Peter van Inwagen offers a set of defenses against different forms of the argument from evil, defenses more ambitious than Plantinga's insofar as they seek to show not just that it is logically possible that a good God exists, despite the evils of this world, but that it is epistemically possible, possible in the "for all one knows" sense.[78] The various defenses take the form of "just-so" stories, the sort of stories that are told all the time in evolutionary biology with a view to blocking the anti-evolutionary argument that some complicated mechanism could not arise by mere chance. The just-so story is not put forward as true or even highly likely. Still, if it is not so exceedingly implausible that it must be dismissed, it can serve to show that the anti-evolutionist's argument is unsuccessful. Similarly, van Inwagen says, to show that an argument from evil is unsuccessful, it suffices to paint a picture suggesting it could well be the case, if there is a God, that awful evils are permitted for this reason or that. Thus in connection with what he calls "the global problem of evil" — an argument that moves from the existence of many horrendous evils in the world — van Inwagen suggests that God well could have permitted that state of affairs in order to show us what it is like to be cut off from divine love. We are in a hellish world, and "[a]nyone who does not want to live in such a world, a world in which we are the playthings of chance, had better accept God's offer of a way out. . . ." Those who take the way out have eternal light and life in the offing: "this present darkness, the 'age of evil,' will eventually be remembered as a brief flicker at the beginning of human history."[79]

It is noteworthy that on van Inwagen's telling of the stories, manifestly drawn from the Hebrew-Christian revelatory tradition, there is an appeal to the possibility of an afterlife. Moreover, his account runs the risk of driving what van Inwagen calls "neutral agnostics" in the wrong direction, turning them into "weighted agnostics," agnostics leaning toward atheism (van Inwagen suggests, for instance, that there may be horrors that do not lead to

---

dysfunction, one in which all cognitive faculties and processes are functioning properly." *If* classical Christianity is true. Plantinga then goes on (p. 499) to pose the question: "But *is* it [Christianity] true? This is the really important question. And here we pass beyond the competence of philosophy. . . ." We think an inquiring agnostic rightly hopes for more from philosophy.

In the early days, Plantinga contented himself with a "defense," and was suspicious of going beyond. But he has warmed to the idea, sketching a "theodicy," an answer to the question "How should Christians think about evil?" It presupposes the whole Christian economy of salvation, including an afterlife. See Plantinga, "Supralapsarianism, or 'O Felix Culpa,'" in Peter van Inwagen, ed., *Christian Faith and the Problem of Evil* (Grand Rapids: Eerdmans, 2004).

78. Peter van Inwagen, *The Problem of Evil* (Oxford: Oxford University Press, 2006).

79. van Inwagen, *The Problem of Evil*, p. 89.

greater goods; that is a suggestion many *theists,* let alone agnostics, would resist). But van Inwagen sees no risk here. He writes:

> I should be willing to defend the following conclusion, although I shall not explicitly do so: *if* the considerations I shall present indeed show that the argument from evil is incapable of turning neutral agnostics into atheists, these considerations will also show that the argument from evil is incapable of turning neutral agnostics into weighted agnostics.[80]

The conditional is anything but obvious, however, and it would be nice to see an explicit argument for the claim. Various aspects of the just-so stories could easily repel agnostic inquirers, real and "ideal" (in van Inwagen's sense). Nothing van Inwagen *explicitly* argues — or, so far as we can see, *implicitly* argues — makes it clear why a real or ideal agnostic, "weighted" toward atheism by the just-so stories, should not find them altogether too morally or conceptually repugnant to underwrite further investigation into whether a good God exists.

Many theistic philosophers would acknowledge that theodicy must build in the claim that beyond the world we know there exists another that is better. Robert Adams, for instance, says that an eschatological faith is required.[81] And Marilyn McCord Adams notes: "Hick, Swinburne, Stump, and Walls [offer solutions to the logical problem of horrendous evils that] presuppose that postmortem survival is metaphysically possible for humans. . . ."[82] Her own solution to the problem of evil also requires an afterlife.

However, it is extremely difficult to persuade an agnostic (directly) that an afterlife is plausible, and difficult even to show that an afterlife is *possible* if the agnostic is sufficiently skeptical. Joshua Golding calls attention to the general point and the difficulty it creates for Richard Swinburne:

> The problem is that, when Swinburne reaches the end of his argument [in the second edition of *The Existence of God*], it remains the case that in order to establish the probability that there is a God, we also face the challenge of whether there is ample reason to believe in the afterlife. Skepticism about whether there is an afterlife translates into skepticism about whether God exists. Unless there is independent justification for the belief in the afterlife,

---

80. van Inwagen, *The Problem of Evil,* pp. 50-51.

81. Robert Merrihew Adams, "Existence, Self-Interest, and the Problem of Evil," *Nous* 13 (1979): 65.

82. Marilyn McCord Adams, *Horrendous Evils and the Goodness of God* (Ithaca, NY: Cornell University Press, 1999), pp. 178-79.

the probability that there is a God remains seriously in doubt due to the problem of evil.[83]

Even theists who are exceedingly optimistic about how far philosophy can carry us toward theistic and theological conclusions are skeptical about whether philosophy can show that there is, or may be, an afterlife. Aquinas works within a system he takes to provide philosophical grounding for many religious truths, including the truth that there is a God; but he does not deem it easy to get philosophical proofs of the immortality of the human soul. And Cajetan, a prominent disciple of Aquinas, reversed more than once in his judgment about whether immortality could be proved. The switches probably were a function of Cajetan's shifting judgments about whether Aquinas's arguments on the subject were sound. Furthermore, even if the proofs Aquinas offers of human immortality succeeded, much would remain to be shown. For the "separated" condition Aquinas thinks the soul is in after bodily death is, he holds, incapacitating: without a body, there is no sensory supply, and since memory depends on sensory perception, and cognition depends on memory, if there is any cognition at all it is very limited. The sort of immortality that can be proved, if any, turns out to be the immortality of a subject in a kind of persistent vegetative state (without the vegetable). The being in this state might not even know it was alive. To see that a separated soul could be in anything other than a persistent vegetative state, Aquinas depended on revelation, and on his belief that a good God would not leave humans in such a deprived state.

Standard natural theology lands the agnostic inquirer in a quagmire of theodicy-building without adequate resources: absent appeal to the content of revelatory claims, it is difficult to find the notion of an afterlife plausible; yet most theodicies and defenses of divine goodness rely on that notion.

1.4. The Hope for an Alternative Approach to Building a Reasoned Case

1.4.1. A Tacit Presupposition of Standard Natural Theology

Why have theistic philosophers not thought the content of revelatory claims much worth examining at the outset of projects in natural theology? An important ground for deferring its consideration, we suggest, is the following presupposition, often tacit but widely shared:

83. Joshua Golding, review of Richard Swinburne's *The Existence of God*, 2d ed., *Notre Dame Philosophical Reviews* 2005.04.04, retrieved Nov. 2, 2005, from <http://ndpr.nd.edu>.

p) One cannot obtain a convincing philosophical case for a revelatory claim without first obtaining a probable case for a good God (a case that renders the proposition more probable than not).

It is a bit tricky to show that p is common. It is rarely highlighted. But a sampling of accounts of the standard approach to natural theology can, if the gaze is appropriately directed, display the picture to which p belongs.

Contemporary definitions of "natural theology" often build in presupposition p. Recall Alston's definition, which we recently cited. Here it is again:

> *Natural theology* is the enterprise of providing support for religious beliefs by starting from premises that neither are nor presuppose any religious beliefs. We begin from the mere existence of the world, or the teleological order of the world, or the concept of God, and we try to show that when we think through the implications of our starting point we are led to recognize the existence of a being that possesses attributes sufficient to identify Him as God. Once we get that foothold we may seek to show that a being could not have the initial attributes without also possessing certain others; in this manner we try to go as far as we can. . . .[84]

Alston's widely respected account is cited by Norman Kretzmann in his commentary on Aquinas's natural theology in *Summa Contra Gentiles II*. Kretzmann says: "I couldn't do better than to offer William Alston's view of the discipline in the following passage," and then reproduces the text just quoted in its entirety.[85] Scott MacDonald's entry on natural theology in the *Routledge Encyclopedia of Philosophy* also sets forth the key presupposition:

> Natural theology aims at establishing truths or acquiring knowledge about God (or divine matters generally) using only our natural cognitive resources. . . . As traditionally conceived, natural theology begins by establishing the existence of God, and then proceeds by establishing truths about God's nature (for example, that God is eternal, immutable and omniscient) and about God's relation to the world.[86]

---

84. Alston, *Perceiving God*, p. 289.

85. Norman Kretzmann, *The Metaphysics of Creation: Aquinas's Natural Theology in "Summa contra gentiles II"* (New York: Oxford University Press, 1999), p. 3.

86. Scott MacDonald, "Natural Theology," in Edward Craig, ed., *Routledge Encyclopedia of Philosophy* (London: Routledge, 1998), retrieved Nov. 1, 2005, from <www.rep.routledge.com/article/K107>. Given MacDonald's reference to natural theology as "traditionally conceived," one might wonder whether he has some nontraditional conception that rejects presupposition p; however, in the encyclopedia entry, MacDonald does not discuss p at all. Nor does he discuss the

Do natural theologians actually *display* the presupposition when they construct arguments in natural theology?

It is easy to see why a person might think that Aquinas would endorse the order of inquiry p requires. Both his *Summa Theologiae* and *Summa Contra Gentiles* begin by presenting philosophical arguments for the existence of the universal source, God, and move on to establish and explore God's attributes. They then discuss the emergence of created beings from the universal source. Finally, they take up theological questions, and consider how all created beings return to God, the universal goal. But Aquinas had aims in ordering his topics that are not apparent at first glance (as Kretzmann has emphasized). We do not claim that Aquinas presupposed p. However, even if he did not, his work still may lead others to think it is true.

Scholastic philosophers who came after Aquinas recommend a pedagogy — an order of instruction — that all but makes p explicit. Consider Abraham Calov, a seventeenth-century Lutheran scholastic:

> It having been proved, if this should be denied, that God is, and that there must be some method in which God may be worshiped by men, we must teach, that it cannot be but that God has revealed that method, so that He may be worshiped properly; then, that God wishes men to be led to the enjoyment of Himself, and also, that He has revealed unto men the manner in which they are to be thus led; finally, the fact that God has revealed Himself, must be taught from history, which revelation God has seen fit abundantly to accompany with miracles and documents, by which we are rendered absolutely certain that it is truly divine.[87]

For another important case where p is assumed, take Newman's nineteenth-century classic *A Grammar of Assent*. Newman believes that "natural religion" — that is, natural knowledge of God, of God's will, and of our duties toward God — is an essential source of "antecedent considerations" that prepare the mind for Christianity. The beliefs of natural religion set up an inquirer to make the all-important judgments concerning revelation, Newman says.

> I have no scruple in beginning the review I shall take of Christianity by professing to consult for those only whose minds are properly prepared for it;

---

feature of standard natural theology that, we have suggested, p grounds: the lack of identification of the content of revelatory claims as especially important evidence an inquirer should seriously consider in an investigation of theism.

87. Abraham Calov, *Systema Locorum Theologicorum* (Wittenberg, 1653), quoted in Heinrich Schmid, *The Doctrinal Theology of the Evangelical Lutheran Church*, 3d ed., vol. I (Minneapolis: Augsburg Publishing House, 1961), p. 268. We thank John D. Kronen for this reference.

and by being prepared, I mean to denote those who are imbued with the religious opinions and sentiments which I have identified with Natural Religion [including belief in God]. . . . *it is plainly absurd to attempt to prove a second proposition to those who do not admit the first.*[88]

Notice that a person might presuppose p in some significant sense even if the person would not assent to p if it were presented. Imagine a kind of scenario philosophers have sometimes commented on: You walk down a series of steps but reach the bottom step sooner than anticipated, stumble, and say, "I thought there was another step there." The fact is, you did not really *think* there was another step there; that thought did not go through your mind right before the last step. Rather, you presumed that a certain kind of action was in order; you presumed that the steps would continue in the way they had begun. There was a neuromuscular expectation. Would it be correct to say that you were "presupposing" the presence of a step? In one sense, yes, even if you did not consciously entertain the thought that there was another step, and even if you would have been unwilling to assent to the proposition: "Coming up there is another step," were that proposition presented.

Perhaps Kretzmann presupposed p in this sense. Had he been asked whether he would accept it, he might have said "no" — despite his endorsement of Alston's definition of natural theology. Yet his nuanced and illuminating discussion of "the metaphysics of theism" includes a number of comments that can reinforce p in the minds of readers. For instance:

As for . . . the "natural" theology that is at the centre of my interests here . . . it must forgo the unphilosophical headstart apparently provided by putative revelation and accept as its data only those few naturally evident considerations that traditionally constitute data acceptable for philosophy as a whole. So it seems clear that natural theology's agenda for rational investigation will have the existence of God as its first distinctive item — the first item that marks it off as the theological part of philosophy. If God's existence can be plausibly argued for, its second large-scale topic will be what can be inferred about God's nature; its third, the relation of everything else to God. . . .[89]

---

88. John Henry Cardinal Newman, *An Essay in Aid of a Grammar of Assent* (Notre Dame, IN: University of Notre Dame Press, 1979), p. 323 (italics added).

89. Norman Kretzmann, *The Metaphysics of Theism: Aquinas's Natural Theology in "Summa contra gentiles I"* (New York: Oxford University Press, 1997), p. 25. Kretzmann does go on to observe (p. 85): "I think he [Aquinas] overstates his project's need for an existence proof at the outset. Like any feasible natural theology, it really requires no more to begin with than *the working hypothesis* that there is an appropriately, broadly characterized sort of explanatory being,

Swinburne has over the years carefully constructed an extended probabilistic argument, a monumentally important argument, that begins with a case that theism is coherent; and then moves on to argue that it is probable that there is an all-powerful, all-knowing, perfectly good creator; and then that a perfectly good creator would reveal himself to his people; and, finally, that historical evidence gives us reason to think God has made such a revelation in the person of Christ. At each new step, Swinburne makes use of evidence already accumulated: for instance, evidence that there is a good God makes it easier to argue that God has revealed, because we have some expectation that a good God would reveal. Although Swinburne has argued that one can *in fact* get a probable case — a highly probable case — for God's existence before moving to the next stage, he does not hold that one *must* obtain a probable case before moving on. In *The Resurrection of God Incarnate,* he restricts himself to the "moderate initial assumption that the background evidence . . . makes the existence of God as probable as not."[90] Based on that initial assumption, he works to build a case that historical evidence concerning the resurrection makes it very probable that Jesus was God incarnate, and that Jesus rose from the dead.

More recently Swinburne has articulated a distinction between bare and ramified natural theology that is also pertinent. Bare natural theology is "the attempt to demonstrate the existence of God by arguments (deductive or inductive) beginning from premises describing very general and evident public phenomena." Its arguments start "from basic beliefs held very strongly by theist and atheist alike and proceed thence by criteria shared between theist and atheist." Ramified natural theology, he says, is "a natural extension of

---

which needn't be identified as God and, in the absence of a more detailed characterization, really shouldn't be identified as God." Kretzmann's general notion of a working hypothesis is certainly compatible with our own approach. However, he emphasizes that "developing parts of that subject-matter [natural theology] within philosophy of course requires forgoing appeals to any putative revelation or religious experience as evidence for the truth of propositions . . ." (Kretzmann, *The Metaphyics of Creation,* p. 5). This passage marks a decisive difference between Kretzmann and us. We will argue that putative revelations — revelatory claims — should be recognized as part of the database of natural theology. Kretzmann concludes *The Metaphysics of Theism* with the comment (p. 354): "The fullness of God's loving and giving emblazoned in John 3:16 is out of natural theology's reach, though it needn't be out of the natural theologian's mind." We will be arguing that the truth of John 3:16 — if, indeed, it is true — may *not* be out of the reach of natural theology. And the content of John's Gospel can be part of the evidence grounding an agnostic's final verdict concerning the truth of theism and the Christian revelatory claim.

90. Richard Swinburne, *The Resurrection of God Incarnate* (Oxford: Clarendon Press, 2003), p. 31, n. 12.

bare natural theology"; it produces "arguments from generally agreed historical data for the detailed claims of a particular religion."[91] He comments: "In
order to pursue ramified natural theology, Plantinga claims correctly, we
need first bare natural theology to argue for the existence of God. . . ."[92]

Yet none of this entails a commitment to presupposition p. How much
bare natural theology is needed, on Swinburne's view, before an inquirer
turns to detailed claims of a particular religion? It is not entirely clear. However, more may be read into Swinburne's particular way of proceeding than
he intended, especially when his ordering of questions is combined with the
particular conclusions he reaches concerning how probable God's existence
can be made on the basis of bare natural theology. And though Swinburne
does not (we think) actually commit himself to presupposition p, he also
does not identify the content of revelatory claims as especially important evidence an inquirer should seriously consider in an investigation into whether
there is a good God. As we said at the outset of this section, we take the absence of such an identification as the hallmark of what we are calling "standard," or traditional, natural theology. Therefore, though Swinburne does not
endorse p, his approach does fall under the heading of "standard natural theology," as we are using that phrase.

Scientists may also accept p. Physicist Stephen Barr, a religious believer,
writes: "The first article of religion, of course, which must be believed before
any divine revelation can be accepted, is that there is a God."[93] And according
to many atheistic scientists, religion should only be taken seriously if the
world's phenomena cannot be explained adequately via natural means. But
showing the inadequacy of scientific explanation is not far from showing that
there is a cause of the universe (or what it contains) distinct from natural
causes. And that is tantamount to showing that the existence of a
supranatural being is not implausible.

Furthermore, leading textbooks in the philosophy of religion — antholo-
gies and single-author texts by non-theists and theists alike — confirm the
apparent naturalness of p. Such textbooks customarily consider topics in
something like the following order:[94]

91. Richard Swinburne, "Natural Theology, Its 'Dwindling Probabilities' and 'Lack of Rapport,'" *Faith and Philosophy* 21, no. 4 (2004): 533, 535.

92. Swinburne, "Natural Theology, Its 'Dwindling Probabilities' and 'Lack of Rapport,'"
p. 538.

93. Stephen M. Barr, *Modern Physics and Ancient Faith* (Notre Dame, IN: University of Notre Dame Press, 2003), p. 13.

94. See, for instance, Eleonore Stump and Michael J. Murray, eds., *Philosophy of Religion:
The Big Questions* (Malden, MA: Blackwell, 1999); William L. Rowe and William J. Wainwright,

- arguments for the existence of God,
- arguments against the existence of God,
- discussion of the attributes of God,
- miscellaneous issues (including, usually, issues concerning death and immortality, and — occasionally — issues concerning revelation).

Sometimes the texts present discussions of attributes of God before arguments for existence; sometimes there is a beginning unit on the relationship between faith and reason. Invariably, however, the topic of revelation is considered *after* God's existence has been discussed thoroughly (if revelation is considered at all). A reader gets a clear sense that there is a rough natural order for addressing the topics, an order moving from the general to the specific, an order that puts revelation at the end of the line.

Thus far we have pointed to the ubiquity of presupposition p by referencing a) accounts or definitions of natural theology, b) approaches various philosophers — past and contemporary — take as they develop arguments of natural theology, c) assumptions of scientists, and d) organizational schemes for textbooks in natural theology. We have suggested that p is exhibited in all these instances.

Another sort of argument can be given to establish the pervasiveness of presupposition p. It is an inference to the best explanation. The phenomenon to be explained, we suggest, is the paucity of philosophical discussion of whether a good God has revealed anything to us. Many philosophers who are keenly interested in the question of whether there is a good God never philosophically confront the momentous question of revelation.[95] But there certainly are philosophical issues to be addressed, including whether a case can be made on the basis of reason for the contention that a good God has revealed something. Philosophers may avoid the big question concerning revelation in part because, even if the question is not in principle closed to useful

---

eds., *Philosophy of Religion: Selected Readings*, 3d ed. (Fort Worth, TX: Harcourt-Brace, 1998); Louis P. Pojman, ed., *Philosophy of Religion: An Anthology* (Belmont, CA: Wadsworth, 1987), and subsequent editions; Baruch A. Brody, ed., *Readings in the Philosophy of Religion: An Analytic Approach* (Englewood Cliffs, NJ: Prentice Hall, 1974), and the 1992 edition; Michael Peterson, William Hasker, Bruce Reichenbach, and David Basinger, eds., *Philosophy of Religion: Selected Readings* (New York: Oxford University Press, 1996), and the 2001 and 2007 editions.

95. The phenomenon is sufficiently widespread not to require documentation. Pick up any recent major work on God's existence, theistic or atheistic, and chances are that the question of revelation is not mentioned. To take a single example, see the massive (atheistic) work by Jordan Howard Sobel, *Logic and Theism: Arguments for and Against Beliefs in God* (Cambridge, UK: Cambridge University Press, 2004).

philosophical investigation, it seems too heavily historical. What, exactly, did Muhammad teach? Did Jesus rise from the dead? Clearly, the question of whether some particular revelatory claim is true cannot be settled without looking at issues that take us beyond philosophy. Yet philosophers of religion (theistic and atheistic) do not hesitate to discuss the plausibility of claims about miracles, including the resurrection of Jesus: they recognize that, while such questions involve history, they involve philosophy as well. The main reason philosophers are largely silent on the big question of revelation — the question of whether a good God has revealed — may be that they tacitly presuppose that, before asking whether a deity has revealed, one must dispose of a whole list of prior questions about the existence and attributes of the deity. Is there a being of maximal power? A being of transcendent knowledge? One who is immaterial? One who is perfectly good? And so on.

Despite all this, it seems obvious enough that p is not presupposed by the vast majority of inquirers into revelatory claims. Drawn to a particular claim, they meditate on it, and base their decision largely on its content. Noteworthy also is the fact that some writers who are not seen as professional philosophers, people such as C. S. Lewis, propose arguments that could be read as stepping right around the problematic presupposition. Lewis puts the question, "What are we to make of Jesus Christ?"[96] and suggests that none of the alternatives to the proposition that Christ was what he said he was — divine — is acceptable. Such a line of reasoning does not presuppose p — or anything like it (though neither Lewis nor his recent commentators point this out).[97]

But an inquiring agnostic who begins reading the philosophical literature is very likely to judge that the intellectually respectable way of proceeding is by deferring consideration of the content of revelatory claims until God's existence has been established as, at the least, probable.

1.4.2. The Falsity of the Presupposition Underlying Standard Natural Theology

Why is it routinely supposed that the nearly universal presumption about order expressed by presupposition p is correct? Logical considerations about complex questions can appear to support it. In general, it may seem, if you are trying to

---

96. C. S. Lewis, "What Are We to Make of Jesus Christ?" *God in the Dock: Essays on Theology and Ethics* (Grand Rapids: Eerdmans, 1970).

97. See Daniel Howard-Snyder, "Was Jesus Mad, Bad, or God? . . . or Merely Mistaken?" and Stephen T. Davis, "The Mad/Bad/God Trilemma: A Reply to Howard-Snyder," both in *Faith and Philosophy* 21, no. 4 (2004).

answer a complex question, you must first answer any embedded simpler questions. A little more formally, if the truth of complex proposition q is at issue and q embeds $q_1, q_2, \ldots q_n$, then (it seems) each embedded sub-proposition $q_1, q_2, \ldots q_n$ must first be established. The question of whether a good God has vouchsafed a revelation to humankind appears to presuppose a positive answer to the question "Is there a good God?" And it is, indeed, easy to find cases where it is eminently sensible to answer at least some of the subquestions before tackling the complex question. It is, for instance, preposterous for a physician to try to decide whether a certain cancer therapy will benefit a particular patient without first having some sense of whether the patient has cancer.

It turns out, however, that the philosophical rationale supporting presupposition p is defective. That is evident from the existence of counterexamples.

Consider the discovery of Neptune. In 1781, William Hershel discovered Uranus, which he first took to be a comet. Soon astronomers plotted a reasonably accurate orbit for Uranus; but by 1840 they noted a discrepancy of over one arc minute between its predicted and actual orbit. The size of the discrepancy was so great that they conjectured that another object in space might be perturbing Uranus's orbit. J. C. Adams and U. J. Leverrier carried out laborious calculations to pinpoint the part of the sky to be examined. In 1846 astronomers at the Berlin Observatory, responding to Leverrier's request, quickly found Neptune. The statement "There is a heavenly body beyond Uranus that is perturbing its orbit" embeds the sub-statement "There is a heavenly body beyond Uranus," but it was perfectly rational to try to determine the truth of the embedded statement by simultaneously determining the truth of the more complex, embedding statement.

Take another case, one obviously pertinent to inquiry about whether a genuine revelation has been given to us. You might ask whether the author of a letter to you is willing to die for you. If the answer to this question is "yes," that presupposes that *someone* is willing to die for you. Yet it makes no sense at all to investigate whether someone is willing to die for you by listing all the people in the world and investigating each, trying to determine about each in turn, without reference to the letter, whether he or she is willing to make the ultimate sacrifice for your sake. It would be far more fruitful to learn what one can about the author of the letter, and then ask whether the evidence supports the claim that *that person* is willing to die for you.

One might object that there must be something wrong with our counterexamples, that the investigative or argumentative protocols just described *cannot* be proper, not in the way we described them, because they commit "the fallacy of the complex question." In fact, though, there is no relevant fallacy here to worry about. Yes, Aristotle talked about the fallacy of the complex question, and most logic texts that deal with informal fallacies discuss it. However, Aristotle's account is less than luminously clear. His main idea appears to be that we fall victim to the fallacy if we fail to detect that what seems to be one question really involves several questions, and we either proceed to answer with a "yes" or a "no" in a way bound to be misleading, or freeze and fail to answer at all.[98] A familiar example (though not Aristotle's) is presented by the question: "Have you stopped beating your spouse?" Yet no fallacy is committed if one simply distinguishes the questions at issue, and explains one's answer. A truthful answer is available to a spouse who is not abusive: "No, I have not stopped beating my spouse, because to stop something you must have been doing it at some point, and I have never beaten my spouse."

A person might sensibly ask how to distinguish between, on the one hand, complex questions that embed an unanswered question such that the embedded question must be resolved before addressing the complex question, and, on the other hand, complex questions that embed an unanswered question such that it makes very good sense to try to answer both the complex question and the embedded question at once. But it is beyond our purposes to develop an abstract criterion allowing such distinctions to be drawn. The agnostic inquirer can do without the criterion itself. What the inquirer needs to know is whether there might be reason to accept *at once* both the claim that there is a good God and the claim that a good God has revealed.[99]

---

98. See ch. 5 of Aristotle's *On Sophistical Refutations*.

99. If we are right about this, one has a straightforward way of dealing with the "problem of dwindling probabilities." Plantinga has argued that the problem undercuts a historical case for Christianity: at each stage of investigation it looks like probabilities must be multiplied, so the final proposition about the truth of Christianity will have a very low probability on the historical evidence (it seems).

But why think an inquirer must pause at each stage as the argument is developed to ask, "What is the truth of the hypothesis at *this* point?" There is, as we see it, no advantage in doing that, any more than there is an advantage to jurors who constantly ask themselves as a trial proceeds, "What is the probability of the hypothesis that the accused is innocent at this particular point, given just so much evidence?" Of course, nothing *stops* one from asking that question, and it is pretty natural to do so in certain circumstances. Yet the judgments one makes at these intermediate points may have no bearing at all on the judgment one makes when all of the evidence one is going to consider has been put on the table. Darwin had trouble making sense of the age of the earth, as it was estimated in his day: there was not enough time for evolution to have occurred. We do not now say: "Oh, we must factor in the datum that we *used* to think the world was not very old" — the nineteenth-century estimates, and the still earlier estimates, have no bearing on our present judgments.

In the course of defending Richard Swinburne's earlier work, Swinburne and Timothy McGrew appear to make substantially the point about dwindling probabilities that we are making here. McGrew adds some technical criticism of Plantinga's use of probability theory. See

A complex proposition cannot have a probability that is greater than the probability of some claim that is part of, or entailed by, the complex proposition (unless one of the standard axioms of probability theory is rejected — as is sometimes done in the interest of accommodating quantum phenomena). However, the strong claim could still be more *believable* than the weak claim. Some propositions are more credible when they are part of a bigger picture than when they stand alone. It is remarkable that this point is so seldom made, given that the whole function of argument is to render credible a proposition that lacks credibility by itself (i.e., the conclusion) when it is conjoined with other propositions (i.e., the premises). (The distinction between credibility and probability can be invoked to account for the alleged conceptual misconduct of ordinary reasoners in the famous cases examined by Amos Tversky and Daniel Kahneman.)

The standard philosophical approach to investigating theism and revelation points straight up a high mountain, because the approach presumes that, before we get on to the question "Has a good God revealed anything to us?" we must first show that there is a good God. But because the rationale that appears to lie behind the tacit presupposition is mistaken, we can see the glimmer of a hope that an alternative approach is possible.

Swinburne, "Natural Theology, Its 'Dwindling Probabilities' and 'Lack of Rapport,'" and Timothy McGrew, "Has Plantinga Refuted the Historical Argument?" *Philosophia Christi* 6, no. 1 (2004).

2 A Preferable Philosophical Approach to the Great Question

2.1. Overview of the Key Argument

Where, now, do things stand? To inquire into the question whether a good God has revealed, the philosophically inclined agnostic properly seeks a case that is more probable than not. Various objections to embarking on this project of natural theology recede under scrutiny. However, agnostic inquirers are stymied by the standard approach that the long tradition of natural theology has taken to the question of whether a good God has revealed. It is difficult, for instance, to see how a good God could have created this world, with all its evils, unless in an afterlife all wrongs are righted; and unaided natural reason can scarcely find its way to such an afterlife. Theists who accept a revelatory claim that includes a good God's promise of a glorious world to come have resources to confront the problem of evil; but on the standard philosophical approach to the question of revelation, it looks like an agnostic cannot build a case that a revelatory claim is plausible without first building a plausible case for a good God. And this appears nearly impossible under the circumstances. Still, because a basic presupposition of this standard approach is mistaken, an inquirer has reason to hope that a different philosophical approach might be mapped.

In this chapter we begin to map a philosophical path for an agnostic inquirer that veers from standard natural theology by moving to the content of putative revelations soon after reason is satisfied that the existence of some sort of creator is not highly unlikely. Without committing to any particular revelation, an inquirer can look to selected revelations for evidence that there is a good God who has revealed. Among the things that may be discovered are clues to the solution of the problem of evil. The content of revelations can push up the probability that there is a good God, as well as the probability that there is a true revelation. In a nutshell, our overarching Key Argument, the argument we introduce in this chapter and further defend in the chapters to come, runs as follows:[1]

1) If it is not highly unlikely that a world-creator exists, then investigation of the contents of revelatory claims might well show it is probable that a good God exists and has revealed.
2) It is not highly unlikely that a world-creator exists.
3) So, investigation of the content of a revelatory claim might well show it is probable that a good God exists and has revealed.
4) So, a negative conclusion concerning the existence of a good God is not justified unless the content of a reasonable number of leading revelatory claims has been seriously considered.

Most of our attention in this book is devoted to premise 1, the Key Conditional. Some may think that the hard work in defending the argument will come with premise 2. Actually, premise 2 is easier to support than might be imagined, though it is certainly worthy of fuller attention than we are able to provide here. And though premise 1 may strike some people as obvious at first, difficulties arise upon reflection. Does not the Key Conditional naïvely assume that a world-creator would have the attributes of a good God? Does it not overlook the fact that revelatory claims include outrageous assertions and demands? Does it not ignore gargantuan methodological problems? The present chapter includes a basic, prima facie defense of premise 1; the remaining chapters take up objections to 1. The present chapter also includes a prima facie defense of 2. Of course, premise 3 follows from the first two premises. We take 4 to be a corollary of 3, and do not explicitly address it here. It is an exceedingly important corollary, we believe.[2]

---

1. An earlier version of part of our argument can be found in Sandra Menssen and Thomas D. Sullivan, "The Existence of God and the Existence of Homer: Rethinking Theism and Revelatory Claims," *Faith and Philosophy* 19, no. 3 (2002). See also Sandra Menssen and Thomas D. Sullivan, "Religious Belief for the Rest of Us: Reflections on Reformed Epistmology," in Raymond Martin and Christopher Bernard, eds., *God Matters: Readings in the Philosophy of Religion* (New York: Longman Press, 2002).

2. Whether more than one revelatory claim must be considered is a judgment call.

There is, by the way, a weaker thesis than the one at 3 (or its corollary at 4) that the argument of our book supports and that may be of some interest. It is this: the existence of God might be established through a combination of a) arguments in traditional natural theology that leave one with less evidence than would warrant the judgment that God's existence has a probability > .5, and b) evidential credit derivable from considering revelatory content that pushes the probability past .5 without pushing the probability of the revelation itself past .5.

Even a person persuaded by the basic case of the present chapter may find our discussion (in subsequent chapters) of objections to the Key Conditional useful. That discussion continues the project of raising the probability of the general claim that *at least one* revelation has been given to us — and the greater the probability of that general claim, the better the chance of success when examining particular revelatory claims. In other words, our defense of the Key Conditional in this chapter and beyond targets a *midlevel* question, a general question that lies between the even more general question of whether there is a good God, and more specific questions about whether this or that particular revelatory claim is true. This intermediate question is: What is the likelihood that some revelation — one revelation or another — has been given to us, on the assumption that it is not highly unlikely there is a world-creator? We aim to show through our work on the intermediate question that, prior to detailed investigation of any particular revelatory claim, there exists substantial evidence for the existence of a good God who has revealed, evidence that includes warrants provided by reflection on putative revelations in general.

Of course, though we focus on a general claim, we will still need to mention particularities. Consider, by way of illustration, two approaches to refuting an anti-realist about science, someone who holds that we neither know nor have good reason to believe anything that science teaches us about the world. One way would be to produce an argument for a specific scientific fact, and then go on to show that the argument for that fact is more credible than any general argument the skeptic offers against all such knowledge. A second approach would be to find some general account of epistemology that shows how some particular conclusion could be established, and to urge that this general epistemological argument is more credible than the argument produced by the scientific skeptic. The second approach, taken by many who are concerned to refute the scientific skeptic, operates at a general level. But, in arguing along the lines of the second approach, a person might well invoke particularities about the world — for instance, the success science has had in arriving by different methods at Avogadro's number. We will be doing much the same thing, targeting a general, midlevel question, but from time to time dipping into particular revelatory claims.

Mathematicians tell a story about a shepherd who needed to get all his sheep home each night — safely inside the gate. The shepherd did not know how to count. But he devised a strategy: every morning before leading his sheep out to graze he put a pebble in his pocket for each sheep; in the evening he removed the pebbles one by one as he brought each sheep back through the gate. The story shows that the size of sets can be measured using the concept of "as many as" even if one cannot number the items in the sets.

The shepherd has an important immediate goal: keeping his sheep safe. He does not first need to learn to count in order to be sure he brings home all his sheep. While learning to count would be a fine and interesting thing to do, it is not essential to the shepherd's immediate purpose. The intricate arguments of standard natural theology are fascinating and valuable, but, we will argue, it is unnecessary for an inquirer hoping for a positive answer to the "great question" — whether there exists a good God who has revealed — to work step by step through the protocol prescribed or modeled by most natural theologians.

2.2. A Basic Case for the Key Conditional

2.2.1. Homer and God

The statement "There is a heavenly body beyond Uranus that is perturbing its orbit" embeds the sub-statement "There is a heavenly body beyond Uranus"; but, as we have observed, it was quite reasonable for astronomers interested in the simpler statement to focus attention on the more complex, embedding statement. Ascertaining the truth of the complex statement was at the same time ascertaining the truth of the embedded statement. Thus a question presents itself: Might the truth of the claim "God exists" be determined by focusing on the embedding statement "A good God has revealed something to us"?

We will take a step closer to an answer to that question by reflecting on an analogy between investigation of the existence of Homer and investigation of the existence of God. What is it to investigate whether Homer existed? It is (let us stipulate) to consider whether a single individual — call the person "Homer" — was primarily responsible for the great epic poem the *Iliad*.

The ancient Greeks appear to have thought that both the *Iliad* and the *Odyssey* were indeed composed by one man, Homer. However, they seem to have known almost nothing about his life. They were ignorant of when and where he lived. Beginning in the sixth century BCE, stories began to grow up about the heritage and personality of the man believed to have authored the epics. But contemporary scholars find little in those traditions that is plausible except for the claim that Homer was an Ionian associated with Smurne and Khios.[3] Much later, Cicero and Josephus both suggested that the *Iliad* had been

3. G. S. Kirk, *The Iliad: A Commentary* (Cambridge, UK: Cambridge University Press, 1985), p. 1.

composed without the aid of writing; but neither of them seems to have doubted that the composition was the work of a single individual.[4]

The first widespread debate about whether there actually was a single individual who was responsible at least for the *Iliad* surfaced in the eighteenth century. A work by the Abbe d'Aubignac, published in 1715, argued that Homer never lived;[5] and by the end of the century, the powerful and influential work of the German scholar F. A. Wolf had popularized the contention that there never was a Homer and simultaneously inaugurated the field of classical philology. Wolf's work was based partly on the discovery of a tenth-century Homer manuscript with commentary going back to the Alexandrians and partly on the sophisticated methods of biblical scholarship that the German theologians had been developing, which were revealing various substrates within the Hebrew scriptures. In addition, Wolf insinuates in his grand (but unfinished) *Prolegomena to Homer* that a single individual was incapable of composing the *Iliad,* because anyone who had composed so long a poem would have needed to rely on writing, and writing was unknown in the time and place of the *Iliad*'s composition. Cursory examination of either Wolf's *Prolegomena* or the work of his commentators will reveal the frustrations of those who try to pin down Wolf's arguments on this point. His masterful prose is, according to his translators, deliberately designed to avoid articulating theses carefully and definitely. Perhaps the clearest statement of the position that has come to be attributed to him appears not in the *Prolegomena* but in a letter he wrote to a publisher in 1780, where he submitted a plan for an essay arguing that "it was impossible to prepare so great a work as the *Iliad* without writing."[6] Although writing was known to the ancient Mycenaeans who predated Homer, Wolf and other scholars believed that it had disappeared from Ionia by the eighth century BCE, the time of the likely composition of the *Iliad*. The so-called "Dark Ages" filled a stretch of three to four hundred years after the catastrophic collapse of Mycenaean culture. Many scholars, influenced by what they understood as Wolf's argument, began to believe that, despite internal textual evidence suggesting unity of theme and hence unity of authorship, the *Iliad* could not have been composed by a single individual.

However, the field work of Milman Parry during the 1930s provided a basis for resolving the bitter dispute between the "analysts," who took up the

---

4. F. A. Wolf, *Prolegomena to Homer,* originally published in 1795, trans. with introduction and notes by Anthony Grafton, Glenn W. Most, and James E. G. Zetzel (Princeton, NJ: Princeton University Press, 1985), p. 5.

5. See Joachim Lacataz, *Homer: His Art and His World,* trans. James P. Holoka (Ann Arbor: The University of Michigan Press, 1996), pp. 7-8.

6. Wolf, *Prolegomena to Homer,* p. 16.

Wolfian argument, and the "unitarians," who disputed it on grounds of internal textual evidence. Parry showed that there is no doubt that epics the length of the *Iliad* can be composed orally when writing is absent from a culture. In 1934 in southern Serbia he transcribed an epic poem of 12,000 lines from a bard unable to read or write. Since that time, other field workers have documented similar feats of memory (e.g., by Uzbek and Kara-kirgiz bards).[7] Parry described the technique that permits such accomplishments: there is a standardized "secondary language" that includes a stock of formulaic expressions enabling the poet both to remember already established structure and to improvise to fit the occasion.[8] Thus, as the *Oxford Classical Dictionary* tells us: "The early arguments [against the existence of Homer] . . . based on the belief that no man could have composed poems of such a length before writing was known, have now been dispelled by our knowledge of what memory can do when writing is not familiar."[9]

Once it was determined that it is not impossible, not even wildly implausible, for a single poet to have had primary responsibility for the *Iliad,* the question could realistically be posed: Was there in fact one author? And in answering this question the content of the poem could be scrutinized. Its cohesiveness, including the consistency of its characters, could be examined, along with the development, power, and resolution of the main plot. The consistency and richness of the language could be analyzed, and the regular appearance of certain features of vocabulary (including particular abstract nouns, Aeolic forms, and patronymics) recognized. Types and number of similes and types of transitions used between major scenes could be evaluated. Scholars have discussed all of these elements and used them as a basis for making a judgment about whether the *Iliad* (or the *Odyssey*) had a single author — that is, whether Homer actually existed. Furthermore, once Parry had analyzed the formulaic, artificial language of the Serbian bards' oral poetry, Homeric scholars could see that the Homeric epics were composed in the stylized "secondary language" that the contemporary philologists described. The current consensus of opinion among the classicists appears to be that, more likely than not, Homer did actually exist: "Most scholars now accept that the Homeric epics are the result of a developing oral epic tradition on the one hand, the unifying and creative work of an exceptional monumental composer on the other."[10]

---

7. "Heroic Poetry," *Encyclopedia Britannica,* retrieved Oct. 15, 2005, from <http://www.britannica.com/eb/article-9040202>.

8. See, for instance, "Homer," *Encyclopedia Britannica,* retrieved Oct. 15, 2005, from <http://www.britannica.com/eb/article-11597>. See also Lacataz, *Homer,* and Kirk, *The Iliad.*

9. *Oxford Classical Dictionary,* 2d ed. (Oxford: Clarendon Press, 1970), p. 524.

10. Kirk, *The Iliad,* p. xv.

So a curious novice classicist may begin by wondering whether Homer existed. The inquirer may at first think Homer could not possibly have existed, since it seems unimaginable that a single person could have composed the *Iliad* without the aid of writing.[11] But discovering what illiterate peoples are in fact able to retain in memory changes the entire landscape. If it is not, after all, impossible — not even exceedingly unlikely — that a single individual authored the *Iliad,* then the poems themselves can be re-examined and the internal evidence for a single author evaluated. The content of the poem may very well bring the probability of the existence of Homer up over .5.

How does all this bear on the agnostic inquirer's project? It shows that sometimes, when we are in doubt about the existence of some being x, if we come to see that the existence of x is not highly unlikely, then the content of a putative communication from x can show that x exists (and has, indeed, transmitted the communication at issue). And a corollary can be drawn: unless there are special reasons for thinking otherwise, one is unwarranted in dismissing the contention that x exists without giving serious consideration to the content of the putative communications — assuming x's existence is not highly unlikely.

Other examples suggest the same point. Is there extra-terrestrial intelligence? It does not look exceedingly implausible, though perhaps less plausible than the claim "Homer exists" has ever been among classicists. And we may have no way to find out whether there is extra-terrestrial intelligence except by listening to signals from outer space, as is being done in the SETI research program (Search for Extra-Terrestrial Intelligence). The SETI program involves monitoring vast numbers of radio signals from outer space. Many natural objects emit these signals, but the SETI researchers look for signals that almost certainly would have to be sent by intelligent agents. Imagine that radio telescopes detect a candidate signal with transmissions corresponding to the prime numbers from 2 to 101. The statement "Some highly intelligent life form in outer space has sent this signal" embeds "There is (or was) highly intelligent life in outer space." Still, it is eminently reasonable to try to confirm the embedding statement in order to confirm the embedded statement.

Or again, imagine that your next-door neighbor says to you: "There's a man I've never met who has promised to leave me a fortune when he dies. He's a distant admirer and benefactor; he writes me every month." You are

---

11. Some classical scholars argue that there is reason to think Homer did have access to writing after all: they have become convinced that significant aspects of the old Mycenaean aristocratic culture survived the catastrophic event (whatever it was) of about 1200 BCE that was once thought to have extinguished Mycenaean civilization. But whether Homer did or did not read and write does not affect the legitimacy of the reasoning of the novice classicist.

initially skeptical. One day, though, when you and your neighbor are out collecting the mail, she hands you an envelope that has just arrived, saying it is from the admirer, and tells you to open it. You find a check for a large sum of money inside, along with a letter that refers to the sender's recent investment successes, his admiration for the poetry your friend has been publishing in the local literary review, and his own declining health. Now how do you assess the likelihood that some stranger is actually going to leave your neighbor a fortune? Before seeing the letter, you may judge it not extremely unlikely, given what you know about your neighbor's character; still, you may put it below .5. However, seeing the letter from the alleged benefactor would push the likelihood above .5. It surely would have been unreasonable for you to refuse to examine the letter and yet adamantly maintain that no benefactor of the sort she has been describing exists.

2.2.2. *The Concept of a Revelatory Claim*

Our Key Conditional urges investigation of revelatory claims. We understand a revelatory claim to be any claim, written or spoken, that fits — or can be made to fit — the logical form:

g revealed to r that p

where g is a supranatural or entirely nonphysical being, a god, let us say; r, the recipient, is an individual or a group of individuals; and p is a propositional content (possibly a very complex, even infinite, content). A revelatory claim is asserted by a claimant, an individual or a group of individuals (the claimant could be identical to the recipient). A report of such an assertion has the form:

c asserts that g revealed to r that p.

The notion of a revelatory claim, or a report thereof, can be sharpened in various ways. Some indication of the means of the revelation could be built in: perhaps the vehicle was a dream, or a vision, or a voice. The time of the claimant's assertion, or of the god's alleged communication, could be indexed. If the project requires it, the notion can be detailed.[12]

---

12. For more on the concept of divine revelation, see William J. Abraham, *Divine Revelation and the Limits of Historical Criticism* (Oxford: Oxford University Press, 1982); George Mavrodes, *Revelation in Religious Belief* (Philadelphia: Temple University Press, 1988); Richard Swinburne,

Our account sets aside non-theistic religions, despite the fact that some of them may *in some sense* endorse revelations. The Purva Mimamsa school, for instance, held that the Vedas constitute a kind of revelation, providing information about what ought to be done and about what will happen to us after death as a result of what we do in this life. However, they are not supposed to be the revelation of a god or any kind of personal being: the Vedas are self-existent, eternal, and authorless. Since our focus in this work is on the question of whether a good God has revealed, we leave to the side such non-theistic revelations.[13]

We are presupposing that it is possible to make a revelatory claim that includes *propositions*. Some thinkers maintain that revelation does not consist of propositions: "What God reveals is not propositions or information — what God reveals is God."[14] No doubt, if God does reveal God, then Something immeasurably more than propositions is being revealed. Yet the claims *that* God reveals God, *that* God broke into history, and *that* God performed mighty deeds are all propositions, as are the multitude of teachings in the Bible and Qur'an about the nature of God and what God expects from us. And an inquirer has every right to ask whether such teachings or propositions, expressed in the *claimant's* message, are true.

We have been suggesting that the question of God's existence might be settled affirmatively by examining the content of alleged revelations. The content in isolation from context? Not at all. Content always has a context to take into account. Academics reviewing a colleague for tenure will assess the candidate's research by focusing on the content of the candidate's publications. The reviewers take for granted that content cannot be evaluated with-

---

Revelation: From Metaphor to Analogy (Oxford: Oxford University Press, 1992); Nicholas Wolterstorff, *Divine Discourse: Philosophical Reflections on the Claim That God Speaks* (Cambridge, UK: Cambridge University Press, 1995); William Abraham, *Canon and Criterion in Christian Theology: From the Fathers to Feminism* (Oxford: Oxford University Press, 1998); Jorge Gracia, *How Can We Know What God Means? The Interpretation of Revelation* (New York: Palgrave, 2001); and William J. Abraham, *Crossing the Threshold of Divine Revelation* (Grand Rapids: Eerdmans, 2006).

13. Does this mean that we leave aside Buddhism? Not necessarily. The essential properties of Buddha may include many of the attributes associated with God in classical theism — *uncaused, omniscient, immutable,* and, to use Paul Griffiths' words, *"maximally salvifically efficacious."* See Griffiths, "Nontheistic Conceptions of the Divine," in William J. Wainwright, ed., *The Oxford Handbook of the Philosophy of Religion* (Oxford: Oxford University Press, 2005), p. 75.

14. William Hordern, *The Case for a New Reformation Theology* (Philadelphia: Westminster Press, 1959), pp. 61-62. Cited by C. Stephen Evans, "Faith and Revelation," in William J. Wainwright, ed., *The Oxford Handbook of the Philosophy of Religion* (Oxford: Oxford University Press, 2005), p. 325.

out considering context: content is inextricably entwined with context. If the candidate has published derivative, unoriginal work, and has furthermore insufficiently acknowledged sources, the reviewers will judge the content of the research inadequate. The Key Conditional of our Key Argument asserts that the content of revelatory claims may well lift the probability that there is a good world-creator up past .5; however, there is no suggestion that the content can furnish this base without any understanding of the various contexts that are essential to the message.

What counts as the *context* of a revelatory claim?

N. T. Wright observes that core creedal claims must be understood against the backdrop of the religious group's worldview expressed in four ways: "story, answers to questions, symbols and praxis."[15] The stories the Jews tell in the Pentateuch, stories taken up and retold in their own way by both Christians and Muslims, illustrate the first of these background elements. Jewish revelatory claims can scarcely be understood without reference to the Pentateuch's account of creation, of Israel's ancestors, of the exodus from Egypt and wandering in the wilderness, of the entrance into Canaan, of the covenants rooted in God's love. In discussing the second element, "answers to questions," Wright stresses worldview questions: Who are we? Where are we? What is wrong? What is the solution? But there are other kinds of questions and answers, including the all-important question of who speaks for the community. Who has the right to formulate creeds, and under what conditions? What else, apart from the creeds, must be accepted, and according to which authority? By "symbols," the third element, Wright understands both artifacts and cultural events. These would include synagogues, churches, mosques, religious art, liturgies and para-liturgies, distinctive apparel, and such problematic symbols as the Crusades. Finally, "praxis" is a mode of being in the world that distinguishes the believers in various ways. Praxis and symbol overlap: the distinctive dietary practices of Hindus, Jews, Christians, and Muslims not only are ways of being in the world, but marks of their identity.

Revelatory claims must also be read against the backdrop of the wider world of secular events and learning. What conclusions pertinent to our overarching question are to be drawn from the fact that, so far, ancestral narratives in Genesis and biblical traditions in Exodus cannot be connected directly to other ancient sources? Or from the fact that the author of the Gospel of John

---

15. N. T. Wright, *The New Testament and the People of God* (Minneapolis: Fortress Press, 1992), p. 134. While Wright explains his four-component schema with Christianity in mind, the schema clearly fits other revelatory religions. Perhaps Wright's application of the schema would differ some from our own.

writes (in John 5:2) in the present tense of a pool with five porticoes, known as Bethesda, near the Sheep Gate in Jerusalem, and that archaeologists have found such a pool, and established it was destroyed by the Romans in 70 CE?

Inquirers yearn for the unadorned, unspoiled word; they wish to drink from the fresh waters that once gushed up from a new spring, to hear the revelation of God from the lips of Moses, Jesus, or Muhammad. But one need hardly do more than fix on the alleged ideal to recognize that the realization is hopeless. We simply do not, for instance, have a record of the original expressions of Jesus and the apostles: what we have are re-expressions and interpretations. An inquirer does not decide, out of the blue, to get a fix on the revelation to or from Moses, Jesus, or Muhammad without first hearing Judaism, Christianity, or Islam proclaimed in a modern form. *Perhaps* an inquirer will conclude that a judgment about the current claims can be made only after first gaining a clear view of the original revelation, a view that can be obtained through historians, linguists, and other scholars. However, the conclusion that it *must* be recovered should be reached most reluctantly, and only after an inquiry into the credibility of revelations now on offer proves them to be unacceptable. Tempting though it is to focus on the primary recipients of the divine word and seek the unadulterated original revelation, multiple difficulties burden that effort. The easier approach is to focus, at least initially, on contemporary claimants.[16]

2.2.3. Listening to the Voice of the Accused

What must be shown to establish the Key Conditional — the contention that if it is not highly unlikely that a world-creator exists, then investigation of the contents of revelatory claims might well show it is probable that a good God exists and has revealed?

16. A report of a revelatory claim calls attention to the oft-neglected role of the *claimant*. The few contemporary analytic philosophers who have addressed the topic of revelation at any length have attended primarily not to claimants but to questions and problems surrounding divine activity, divine transmission of a message, and human reception of the message. George Mavrodes, for instance, sets out three models of revelation, differentiated by a focus on recipients. See Mavrodes's *Revelation in Religious Belief* (Philadelphia: Temple University Press, 1988), esp. pp. 73-150. Swinburne, too, fixes his gaze on the recipients of revelation (mostly on the recipients of Christian revelation). Identifying and evaluating an original historical revelation is the first step, in his view; once one has deemed a particular historical revelation plausible, one can determine which contemporary interpreter of that revelation is the best interpreter. (We should add, however, that William Abraham's *Crossing the Threshold of Divine Revelation* is a notable exception.)

That depends on an inquirer's grounds for *doubting* that a good God exists and has revealed. Classicists once doubted that a Homer existed because they doubted one person could retain the *Iliad* in memory without recourse to writing. The work of Parry and other field linguists made it possible for classicists to refocus attention on the content of the epic and to look for internal evidence of a single author. In this case, once the doubt about memory was removed, classicists could turn immediately to reflection on the content of the *Iliad;* they did not have other substantial worries interfering with such a move. We need to ask the following: Assuming that it is not highly unlikely that a world-creator exists, what *remaining* grounds might generate doubt about the value of investigating the contents of revelatory claims?

Deep concerns about the problem of evil could constitute grounds. In the face of such concerns, the Key Conditional will be acceptable only if an inquirer is persuaded that revelatory claims could contain crucially relevant information about evil. What is needed — at the outset, anyway — is not a solution to the problem of evil, but rather reason for judging that investigation of the contents of revelatory claims might provide such a solution.

Anyone who has accepted our argument thus far has acknowledged that the content of a putative communication might show that there is a person answering to a certain description. A putative communication from a world-creator might show *something* about the world-creator's character. Now we do not say that an inquirer could reasonably expect to learn about any attribute whatsoever through a putative communication. It strains credulity to suggest that examining a revelatory claim could show that there is a world-creator with a particular fondness for the song "Lavender's Blue, Dilly Dilly." On the other hand, it does not require mental acrobatics to imagine that a revelatory claim could provide evidence of a good world-creator and an acceptable explanation of evil — *if* one does not consider it highly unlikely that there is some sort of world-creator *and* acknowledges that the content of a putative revelation from such a creator might well render it probable that a world-creator exists *and has certain characteristics.*

Acceptable explanations can be incomplete. If a good friend misses an appointment with you and explains that she was prevented from coming by a serious but confidential matter, you will presumably accept her remarks as a satisfactory explanation of the missed meeting — though it is obviously incomplete. Various revelatory traditions purport to give acceptable, though incomplete, accounts of evil. Some obscurity in explanation may be unavoidable: obscurity attends depth.

Explanations in the sciences, after all, almost always butt up against some fact that cannot initially be accounted for — sometimes that can *never* be explained. Galileo's critics pointed out that, if his theory were true, parallaxes (apparent displacements of stellar bodies brought about by a change in an observer's position) should have been observable; but no one had ever observed a parallax. Finally, in 1838, a parallax was measured. Darwin's theory did not at first seem to square with what was known about the age of the earth. Eventually — after the theory was generally accepted — answers to the geological objections were found. There are plenty of situations like this outside the domain of religion. Suppose, for instance, that you are a criminal defense attorney with a strong distaste for defending the guilty (perhaps you are independently wealthy). You screen clients before accepting any case. You are told about a case that is supposed to be hopeless: everyone is sure that the accused is guilty because a couple of very credible eyewitnesses tell a convincing story. However, something about the defendant intrigues you. You talk to the eyewitnesses, and it turns out that their accounts are less decisive than reported. You are sufficiently impressed by the accused that you decide to take the case and gather more evidence. You get DNA tests, which support the defendant's claim. Thus you have key details that make it unnecessary to go back and question eyewitnesses. You have an account of matters that is acceptable despite being incomplete in some ways. Even inconsistency in the explanation can *in one sense* be tolerated. Physicists hold on to some inconsistent theories, though they do so, of course, with a sense of unease. They know something is wrong somewhere, but they often figure that a way can be found to modify the basic content of the theory to eliminate contradictions.

Just how much incompleteness (and inconsistency, of a sort) can be tolerated in an explanation of evil will depend on multiple factors. Crucially important will be the strength of the case one has in abstraction from the world's evils.

It seems only fair to listen to the voice of the accused. Evils are introduced as evidence against the existence of a good God; but, it is assumed by many, no answer provided by putative revelations can be allowed in as a possible explanation because that would not be "doing philosophy." Imagine a legal code that allowed people to be indicted and tried on evidence, and required that the defense be conducted without testimony by the accused — either directly or through representatives. The case against any defendant, then, might look bad. Yet, were the defendant's testimony allowed, a very different picture would emerge. All the relevant testimony must be admitted into the case. What are the explanations of evil? Let us hear them, if not in God's own voice, then through the likes of Moses and the prophets. Which prophets? The false and the genuine, if any be genuine. Socrates claims to speak for Diotima on love. We listen attentively and judge the worth of the message. Paul claims to speak for One infinitely greater than Diotima on the same subject: "And now faith, hope, and love abide, these three; and the greatest of these is love."[17] Why not give the voice of the One the same attention we give Socrates? Mingled with the voices of emissaries, God's voice, it is argued, can be heard in stories, myths, exalted poetry, legal codes, exhortations, spiritual directives, and proclamations about the world and ourselves. It is a strange philosophical method that refuses to attend to any of it.

Not only is it legitimate to introduce the content of revelation into purely philosophical discussions, but there may be no other way to get the results the agnostic inquirer hopes for concerning evil. You cannot trisect an arbitrary angle or square a circle using only a rule and compass, as Euclid requires. But you can do it using other methods, and there is no good reason to refuse to use them, as several centuries of argument have made abundantly clear. These other methods involve assumptions mathematicians have found far less than obvious; they treat the assumptions as postulates and look to see how far they can get with them, what they illuminate and explain.[18] Similarly, an agnostic inquirer may ask what is illuminated and explained by the content of a putative revelation.

All this may be accepted *in the abstract* by an agnostic inquirer. That is, an inquirer may think: Yes, I can see the need to listen to the voice of the Accused, if such a voice can be identified. But the prospects of identifying a divine Word are discouraging. In the first place, we cannot know what a good world-creator would reveal, and thus we cannot know what to listen for. Furthermore, the world's major revelatory claims are full of errors: why turn to them for divine messages? Finally, the major revelatory claims lack well-evidenced miracles, the stamp of the divine. These three concerns might generate doubt about the value of investigating putative revelations even if one were to grant that the existence of a world-creator is not highly unlikely.

Let us, then, examine each of these three sources of doubt.

2.2.4. Knowing What a Good World-Creator Would Reveal

It may look like we are all clueless about what to expect from a god — even one who is all-knowing, all-powerful, and wholly good — for a reason Elliott

---

17. 1 Cor. 13:13 (NRSV).

18. For an intriguing account of the history of the argument, see Henk J. M. Bos, *Redefining Geometrical Exactness: Descartes' Transformation of the Early Modern Concept of Construction* (New York: Springer, 2001).

Sober brings out as well as anyone (in the course of discussing design arguments for God's existence).[19] Design arguments all fail, Sober contends, because they rest on the unwarranted assumption that we know what a divine designer would bring about. And it is no help, he says, to build in the assumption that *God,* a being who is "omniscient, omnipotent, and perfectly benevolent," is the designer in question: "The assumption that God can do anything is part of the problem, not the solution. An engineer who is more limited would be more predictable."[20] The relevance of this to our proposal comes out clearly when Sober invokes the SETI project — which we pointed to in support of our Key Conditional — to prove *his* point. Sober says that the SETI engineers do not look for a signal that satisfies some *a priori* notion of what an intelligent being would communicate. Rather, they look for narrowband radio emissions because, so far as we know, mindless natural processes do not produce them. Although Sober thinks that the strategy may not work, he says:

> [I]t is hard to see how the scientists could do any better. Our judgments about what counts as a sign of intelligent design must be based on empirical information about what designers often do and what they rarely do. As of now, these judgments are based on our knowledge of *human* intelligence. The more our hypotheses about intelligent designers depart from the human case, the more in the dark we are as to what the ground rules are for inferring intelligent design. . . . I suspect that SETI engineers are on much firmer ground than theologians. . . . The problem of extraterrestrial intelligence is . . . an intermediate case, lying somewhere between the watch found on the heath and the God who purportedly shaped the vertebrate eye. . . .[21]

The suggestion, then, is that we are in the dark about what "the God who purportedly shaped the vertebrate eye" would do.

We agree that an agnostic inquirer into revelatory claims needs some idea of what a good world-creator would reveal; still, that inquirer needs much less than Sober imagines.

Think again of Homer and the *Iliad.* It is virtually impossible to produce an estimate of the probability that the *Iliad* would have been written by a single individual on the hypothesis that there was a poet of great skill in ancient Greece; about all one can say is that the probability would be very, very low.

19. Elliott Sober, "The Design Argument," in Neil A. Manson, ed., *God and Design: The Teleological Argument and Modern Science* (New York: Routledge, 2003).

20. Sober, "The Design Argument," p. 41.

21. Sober, "The Design Argument," pp. 40-41.

But the content of the *Iliad* could lead us to believe that there was a Homer if it fit well with our general ideas about the sort of thing a Greek poet of the time might care to compose, and what the poet's method or approach to composition would be. We do, in fact, understand some of the things a Homer might wish to express in song, such as the nature of war as it was then known, and we have learned something about techniques a Homer could use to compose a lengthy epic, such as structural devices that aid memory. We understand enough to say that the content of the *Iliad* is *congruent with* the assumption that there was a single composer, Homer. Should a storyteller greater than Homer arise in our own time, we could confidently predict that the corpus of work would include more than a lone three-sentence story: "I had a dollar. I lost the dollar. I sat down and cried." Likewise, if there is a mind greater than Homer who is going to tell a story, it should be a great story. It should be a story beyond price. If a great storyteller told a one-dollar story, you would say, "I'm disappointed." The storyteller might respond: "What did you expect?" You might say: "I didn't expect any particular story, but I did expect one of a certain quality." And if the question at issue is what a great and good world-creator, a good God, would do (or refrain from doing) — again, certain things can be said. An inquirer can expect sublimity in communications. Words that will heal our deepest wounds; information on how to atone for sin; aids for flourishing — we can anticipate all this. We expect a revelatory content congruent with a good God.

An inquirer will also look at the question of whether the content likely exceeds human capacities of production. If a communication had arrived a thousand years ago with detailed information about the marvelous properties of stem cells, that would certainly indicate forcefully — from our contemporary vantage point — that the revealer was an extra-terrestrial of some sort, perhaps a divine sort. Or again, if somebody claimed that an ancient document contained a revelation from God in the form of an exact prediction of a much later event — not something vague, such as the prophecies of Nostradamus or the prophecies of the coming of the kingdom found in Christian Scripture, but definite descriptions with unmistakable time and place references — that would be weighty evidence of nonhuman intelligence at work, maybe intelligence only a divine being could possess. Or if a communication tomorrow revealed secrets about the origin of the universe, telling us how to get something from nothing through a weird application of some version of the Banach-Tarski theorem, and explaining in the same communication how it could be that humans attain "glorified" bodies in a world beyond the one we know, we might infer that the communication came from above — from a god who is not only powerful but good. Of course, Hinduism, Judaism, Christianity, and Islam contain nothing like the fanciful examples just given. An agnostic inquirer will need to ask on a case-by-case basis whether some aspect of the content of a revelatory claim exceeds human capacities of production.

In sum, where the content of a revelatory claim is congruent with a theistic explanatory hypothesis, and where there is reason to believe that the content exceeds human capacities of production, one may find that the evidence is *illuminated* by the hypothesis that a good God has revealed.

Ours is not a position that requires the bold pronouncements some religious apologists have made concerning what we may expect from a good God.

Newman says of Christianity that it is what a good God would reveal if a good God revealed anything at all.[22] We can get some sense of what Newman is after here; but if the assertion is taken literally, it is a dangerous overstatement, whether made on behalf of Christianity or another religion. It appears to eliminate the possibility of a revelation with surprises, wonderful or dreadful. And does anyone really want to say that a revelation placing the incarnation of God in Palestine during the reign of the Caesars is more probable on the hypothesis that a good God would reveal than a revelation that places it elsewhere? For one can easily imagine a variation on a candidate religion such that the variation appears more likely than the original candidate. Start by removing seemingly approved genocides from the Hebrew scriptures, as well as such conflicting statements from the Christian scriptures as "The Father and I are one" and "[T]he Father is greater than I."[23] If the probability of the putative revelation is higher than .5 on a relevant set of assumptions, it does not follow that the probability of no other putative revelation would be higher.

Swinburne's comments about what we can expect from a good God, though expressed with a confidence that will make some inquirers uneasy, are nonetheless more cautious than Newman's. Swinburne holds that "we have some a priori reason to suppose that God will become incarnate and provide an atonement for us."[24] An inquirer might be willing to join Swinburne here; on the other hand, the inquirer might judge an atoning incarnation very unlikely, *a priori*, but when faced with a set of phenomena, reasonably say: given this evidence, I believe that the incarnation is more probable than its contradictory.

---

22. "He [one to whom the Word of Life is offered] has a keen sense of the intrinsic excellence of the message, of its desirableness, of its likeness to what it seems to him Divine Goodness would vouchsafe did He vouchsafe any, of the need of a Revelation, and its probability." John Henry Newman, *Fifteen Sermons Preached Before the University of Oxford* (London: Longmans, Green and Co., 1918), Sermon XI, p. 203.

23. John 10:30; 14:28 (NRSV).

24. Swinburne, *Revelation*, p. 72.

But what about Sober's argument based on the SETI example — where does it go wrong? Recall that Sober emphasizes that SETI focuses not on the *content* of the communication we might receive from outer space but on the *modality.* SETI engineers look for narrow-band radio emissions. It does not follow, though, that a signal could not be received that would display intelligence. Suppose, as is supposed in the dramatized version of encounter with extra-terrestrials in the film *Contact,* that a signal beeped out the prime number sequence up to some high number. Then what would anybody conclude? Yes, it is certainly true that rational extra-terrestrials might have many ways of reaching out other than beeping out sequences of prime numbers; and yes, among those ways may be many that would elude our grasp. Nevertheless, the point remains: detecting a series of 1,000 prime numbers beeped to us from outer space would be detecting evidence of a content from which we could reasonably infer extra-terrestrial intelligence.

And if, somehow, we received in all the world's languages the message "I Am," etched in crystals of granite or displayed in the stars, the phenomenon would scarcely be dismissible on grounds that we have no reasonable idea what an extra-cosmic being would reveal. We can embrace much of what Sober says about the difficulties of predicting God's revelations, and much of the kindred apophatic theologies of a St. John Chrysostom, St. John of Damascus, or Moses Maimonides, even as we refuse to let ourselves slip into complete skepticism regarding the matter. It is true that a divine mind would have attributes barely intelligible to us. Yet we are not altogether bereft of ideas about what a divine communication would be like or — more pertinently for present purposes — what kind of message would point to a heavenly source. The problem of knowing what a good world-creator would reveal is a specialized version of the problem of knowing what a good world-creator would *do.* We think Sober is right about the inability to know certain things about what a designer would do. We agree that there is no way of knowing whether an omniscient, omnipotent, wholly good designer would have allowed to evolve the allegedly inefficient "panda's thumb," which Stephen Jay Gould takes as evidence against a powerful, intelligent, good Designer. Still, if one were completely at sea with respect to *any* proposition about what a good world-creator would do, the problem of evil would disappear.

However, does not what Sober says in criticizing the design argument apply to our own position as well? He says:

> I have complained that we have no way to evaluate the likelihood of the design hypothesis, since we don't know which auxiliary assumptions about goal/ability pairs we should use. But why not change the subject? Instead of

evaluating the likelihood of Design [the probability of the evidence of design on the hypothesis that God exists], why not evaluate the likelihood of various conjunctions — (Design & GA_1), (Design & GA_2), etc. [where GA_n is a goal-ability pair]?[25]

We are maintaining that there is some combination of goals and abilities that, when assigned to God, would yield a hypothesis that explains the data relatively well. And to say that there is some such hypothesis is to allow just what Sober complains of: various conjunctions involving "goal-ability" pairs. How, though, does this constitute changing the subject? The subject is whether some sort of deity exists. A classicist investigating the unitarian hypothesis concerning the composition of the *Iliad* begins by being interested in whether a single individual (a "Homer") composed the *Iliad*. The classicist will need a fuller description of Homer — whether Homer was or was not literate, and so on — a set of auxiliary hypotheses to pair with the original hypothesis that Homer existed. But the original subject was not just Homer, without any description at all; the original subject encompassed the auxiliary hypotheses.

Sober says that there are two problems with what he calls "changing the subject" in discussions of divine design. The first is this:

> [I]t is a game that two can play. Consider the hypothesis that the vertebrate eye was created by the mindless process of electricity. If I simply get to invent auxiliary hypotheses without having to justify them independently, I can simply stipulate the following assumption — if electricity created the vertebrate eye, the eye must have features $F_1 \ldots F_n$. The electricity hypothesis is now a conjunct in a conjunction that has maximum likelihood, just like the design hypothesis. This is a dead end.[26]

Now the proponent of the design argument puts forward a hypothesis that makes it intelligible, by reason of addition of the right kinds of goal-ability pairs. The hypothesis of design illuminates, explains why we end up with the vertebrate eye (or whatever one is considering). In contrast, the hypothesis Sober adds fails to explain anything. One can, of course, just make up a *modus ponens* argument: If electricity created the vertebrate eye, then the eye must have certain features; and electricity did create the vertebrate eye. But that is unilluminating. Two can play the game — but not necessarily with equal success.

And here is the second problem Sober sees in "changing the subject":

25. Sober, "The Design Argument," p. 41.
26. Sober, "The Design Argument," p. 41.

My second objection is that it is an important part of scientific practice that conjunctions be broken apart (when possible) and their conjuncts scrutinized. . . . If your doctor runs a test to see whether you have tuberculosis, you will not be satisfied if she reports that the conjunction "you have tuberculosis & auxiliary assumption 1" is very likely while the conjunction "you have tuberculosis & auxiliary assumption 2" is very unlikely. You want your doctor to address the first *conjunct,* not just various conjunctions. . . . Demand no less of your theologian.[27]

"When possible," Sober says, conjunctions should be broken apart. Our entire book can be seen as an argument that it may not be possible to break apart the conjunction "A good God exists and a good God has revealed."

2.2.5. Countenancing Errors in the Content of Revelatory Claims

Many people claim to have communicated with extra-terrestrials, but due to aspects of the alleged communications, no sensible person gives their contents a moment's thought. Should the SETI project claim evidence of a communication, we would need to look at it, but not every putative communication is entitled to the same respect. With regard to the case at hand, it could be said that if *certain kinds* of allegedly divine communications had come our way, we might need to examine them carefully, but the better-known divine "revelations," *pace* the apologists, are pretty obviously all too human, full of scientific, historical, philosophical, and moral mistakes.

There are errors in revelatory claims, for there are contradictions. Brand Blanshard enumerates inconsistencies in Judaeo-Christian scriptures: "[T]here is no difficulty in showing that the Biblical books do not constitute . . . a coherent whole," he says.[28] For instance, I Kings reports that the pillars of Solomon's temple are eighteen cubits high; II Chronicles says that they are thirty-five cubits high. Matthew and Luke give different genealogies of Jesus. And so on. Are there inconsistencies on more important matters? Yes, Blanshard alleges. Focusing on Roman Catholicism (a relatively easy tradition to work with, he notes, because the Catholic position "has been defined with care and precision by the doctors of the church"),[29] Blanshard enumerates a series of switches that sixth-century Pope Vigilius made concerning the monophysite controversy.

27. Sober, "The Design Argument," pp. 41-42.
28. Brand Blanshard, *Reason and Belief* (New Haven: Yale University Press, 1974), p. 38.
29. Blanshard, *Reason and Belief,* p. 23.

Only contradictions in core doctrines, or contradictions in a part of a doctrine that the putative oracle of God insists is contradiction-free, have the power to explode a revelatory claim. Although details about the conditions that must be satisfied for a papal declaration to be *ex cathedra* are variously reported in Catholic sources, the substance of the statement makes it quite clear that a good deal of what Blanshard points to concerning Vigilius falls outside the scope of infallibility.[30] Blanshard accuses Vigilius of reversing his approval of the ecumenical Council of Chalcedon in a private letter to Empress Theodora. However, privately expressed papal opinions do not meet the first Vatican Council's standard for infallibility. Blanshard also claims that Vigilius reversed his approval of Chalcedon by signing the formal document *Iudicatum*. We no longer have the text itself of Vigilius's *Iudicatum*, or "verdict," of 548; what we have are fragments of the text quoted in later documents. The *Iudicatum* condemned the "Three Chapters" — writings by three Syrian bishops that *some persons* took to be endorsed by Chalcedon — but the condemnation was apparently offered with an explicit statement that none of the teachings of Chalcedon were being condemned.[31] In our view, Blanshard's criticisms generally miss the mark.

Others, such as Hans Küng, have offered additional arguments that popes have erred in situations where the conditions of infallibility were met. This is no place for a full-scale examination of the charges; we only wish to point out here what must be done to overthrow a dogma such as that of infallibility. In Blanshard we have an analytic philosopher far more alert than are theologians such as Küng to the relevant philosophical distinctions, such as that be-

---

30. The definition of papal infallibility proclaimed by the first Vatican Council, and reaffirmed by Vatican Council II, runs: "We teach and define that it is a dogma Divinely revealed that the Roman pontiff when he speaks ex cathedra, that is when in discharge of the office of pastor and doctor of all Christians, by virtue of his supreme Apostolic authority, he defines a doctrine regarding faith or morals to be held by the universal Church, by the Divine assistance promised to him in Blessed Peter, is possessed of that infallibility with which the Divine Redeemer willed that his Church should be endowed in defining doctrine regarding faith or morals, and that therefore such definitions of the Roman pontiff are of themselves and not from the consent of the Church irreformable." See *The Companion to the Catechism of the Catholic Church: A Compendium of Texts Referred to in the Catechism of the Catholic Church* (San Francisco: Ignatius Press, 1994), p. 891, and the entry on "infallibility" in the *Catholic Encyclopedia* (1917), on-line at <www.newadvent.org>.

31. J. N. D. Kelly says that the verdict held "that the Three Chapters should be condemned, although without prejudice to Chalcedon" (Kelly, *The Oxford Dictionary of Popes* [Oxford: Oxford University Press, 1986], p. 61). Philip Hughes says that the verdict was "so written as to make clear that it in no way involved Chalcedon" (Philip Hughes, *The Church in Crisis: A History of the General Councils, 325-1870* [Garden City, NY: Hanover House, 1961], p. 120).

tween an assertion and a presupposition; but Blanshard nonetheless fails to come to grips with the precise proposition he sets as his target, despite his careful reworking of arguments (which were originally presented in the Gifford Lectures and revised for publication). Establishing that there is a contradiction in a core ecclesial teaching is no easy thing.[32] And the rumor that a doctrine is dead is not the same as an authenticated death certificate.

It is, of course, possible for a community to claim the status of divine messenger without making the additional bold claim to consistency over time. Some members of religious communities might even hold that contradictions in core doctrine are not fatal. We grant that, without absurdity, a community can maintain that the original message from God is *in some sense* inconsistent: "The Lord said: I give you two geometries, one asserting the parallel postulate, one denying it. Ponder them both." And a person might do that — with great profit. Some believers take a view close to that of some later rabbis, who "even in matters of halakhic disagreement sometimes allowed that both opinions were 'words of the Living God,' a God made living precisely by the play of debate."[33] (Presumably, there was a way that the opinions could be "words of the Living God" without imputing to God contradictory beliefs or commands.) An inquirer may find this rabbinic view, while perhaps unrepresentative of Judaism, as intriguing as it is bold. But there are philosophically minded inquirers who are intrigued by an opposing boldness, by declarations about synchronic and diachronic consistency in definitive teachings, declarations that are in principle refutable because it is possible to imagine the occurrence of certain events that would prove the teachings false. Roman Catholicism does declare that its core teachings are consistent over time.

Even if deep reading of troubling and apparently contradictory narratives can yield consistency, there remain elements of the Hebrew and Christian revelations, indeed every major revelation, that resist the most sympathetic modern attempts at understanding. How, for instance, can we believe that a good God approved the utter eradication of peoples and towns that is re-

32. Of course, it also takes work to show that core teachings are *not* inconsistent. It appears inevitable that this work will include identifying a canon within a canon. Sorting through a canon — those materials, persons, and practices that communities officially or semi-officially set apart as means for preserving or attaining a relationship with God — to find an inner canon may, as William Abraham wisely cautions, lead to an overshadowing of any soteriological vision of the heritage. Nevertheless, the work of sorting must be done. See Abraham, *Canon and Criterion in Christian Theology,* esp. p. 471. We have paraphrased and generalized Abraham's definition of "canon"; see p. 1 of his book.

33. Stephen A. Geller, "The Religion of the Bible," in *The Jewish Study Bible,* ed. Adele Berlin and Marc Zvi Brettler (Oxford: Oxford University Press, 2004), p. 2040.

ported in the book of Numbers? That is a gravely disturbing assertion, whether or not it is inconsistent with other assertions in the revelatory tradition. It cannot be denied that there is more than a little to the claim that major revelations contain questionable morality — not to mention scientific and historical mistakes.

It takes no more than such difficulties to threaten the entire case we are making.

But while it takes no more than that to threaten the case, it does take more to defeat it. The apparent errors do not immediately generate the conclusion that the content of putative revelations, understood in context, obviously cannot provide the evidence necessary to raise the probability of God's existence past .5. For the conclusion to follow, it must also be assumed that a divine truth conveyed through humans should bear no mark of the limitations of the messenger, that the rays of the sun should never be obscured in the least by the medium through which the light is transmitted.

The assumption is dubious. As long as we can come to recognize the cultural presuppositions of the human messenger, there remains the possibility of grasping enough of the substance of the divine message — supposing a divine message has actually been sent — to allow the inference to the existence of a good God.[34] In some ways we are like children repeating a message given by an adult: a child may garble elements in such a message, but in many cases one can tell which parts of the message came from the adult. Furthermore, we can often discern the original character of a message transmitted by individuals we know to be self-aggrandizing or jealous, inclined to exaggerate, or to color, or to minimize. And while witnesses in a court case may tell different stories, and a juror may be unable to sort out all the inconsistencies, it may still be possible to judge whether the defendant is guilty or innocent. The philosophers present in the famous incident of "Wittgenstein's poker" have different recollections of what took place, and it is difficult to get a full and accurate picture of what happened. But one can infer a number of things legitimately: Wittgenstein and Popper were both at the event, at some point Wittgenstein picked up a poker, and so forth. The four Christian Gospels give us four different accounts of Jesus of Nazareth, and various elements of the accounts are questionable. Still, few doubt that Jesus was put to death, or that he was a Jew with teachings that were in some sense new, or that he gathered disciples about him, or that he was reputed to have performed wonders.

34. See Swinburne's *Revelation* for an extensive and extraordinarily useful discussion of background presuppositions from a philosophical standpoint.

Billions of people think revelatory claims are worthy of belief. To be sure, many of these devotees are unlearned. But many of them are intellectuals of unquestionable stature. Ignorant and learned alike have been drawn to revelatory religions because the teachings speak in ways that pure philosophy fails to do. Were there some philosophical system that promoted a more attractive worldview, the world's religions of choice would be the choice of few. Standing behind the great theistic religions of the world are great apologetic traditions fully cognizant of the difficulties presented by transmission of a divine message through human beings. In the end, perhaps the apologetics will not adequately rebut sophisticated challenges. But the sheer existence of thousands of subtle arguments should undercut the contention that revelatory claims are *obviously* too defective for the work we would assign them.

Of course, most inquirers have some familiarity with the broad story lines of major revelatory traditions, and most Western readers have more than a little familiarity with the Judaeo-Christian tradition on which we focus. However, reflection on what one thinks one knows can have a high payoff. We all view matters in less than optimal circumstances — in the dark in many ways. To allow for more light, some nocturnal animals have a mirrorlike structure in the back of their eyes, right behind the retina, that returns missed light to the retina, in effect enabling the animal to get a second and better look. A cat, its eyes glowing as the light bounces off the mirrors behind the retina, effortlessly finds what is hidden in the shadows. For us, it takes conscious effort to gather light missed the first time. Even inquirers who have more than a passing acquaintance with the story lines of leading revelatory claims might benefit from careful re-examination, from pondering the messages. Is there enough in the content to satisfy an agnostic inquirer? It seems reasonable to look (again) and see.

A skeptic can offer a challenging response. Let it be stipulated that it is only to be expected that a divine message transmitted by humans will bear the marks of creaturely finitude and that reflective interpretation of the message could yield rationally acceptable doctrine. Still, it might be objected, if the core of the message is acceptable only because reason can purge it of human error, then it is not the original message but rather the human philosophical distillate that is worthy of belief. An inquirer who follows this course is just doing what Socrates or Kant did, it may be suggested, reducing an allegedly but fancifully divine message to credible human teaching. Kant finds much of worth in what religions have passed on, particularly Christianity; but what he finds is only what reason can discern to be so, and thus the title of his most developed statement on the subject: *Religion within the*

Bounds of Reason Alone. So, the skeptic may say, if God is to be found, it will be by reason conducting itself in the tradition of Socrates and every rationalist since his time.

Our inquirer is free to select and interpret revelatory claims in such a way as to sustain the inquiry, and this does indeed often mean doing what Socrates and Kant and others have done, that is, purging a revelatory claim evidently inconsistent with what human reason prescribes. Yet, as we hope to have made clear by the end of this book, from this it does not follow that the process inevitably leaves the inquirer with nothing but philosophy.

Nor does it follow that selection and interpretation with a view to sustaining the inquiry must be an exercise conducted in bad faith. Science is replete with examples of investigators doing their best for a theory despite collisions with facts, and internal contradictions. For example, in "Partial Symmetries of Weak Interaction," the paper that led to his 1979 Nobel Prize, Sheldon Glashow argued that the mass of the charged intermediaries must be greater than zero. But there was a major problem: the photon mass is zero. "Surely," Glashow noted, "this is the principal stumbling block in any pursuit of the analogy between hypothetical vector [bosons] and photons. *It is a stumbling block we must overlook.*"[35] Darwin pressed on with his theory despite its collision with the geological "facts" of the day.

Even in mathematics, the top researchers press forward, despite problems of coherence. The history of calculus provides an instructive example. Newton and Leibniz, taking a cue from Archimedes' "method of exhaustion," developed general, systematic treatments of both integral and differential calculus. Notoriously, though their systems were powerful in application, they had defective foundations. Both thinkers (most regularly Leibniz) spoke of infinitely small quantities, "infinitesimals" or "differentials." The notion had intuitive appeal, but the formal accounts of infinitesimals were internally inconsistent. It was not until the nineteenth century that mathematicians such as Augustin Louis Cauchy and Karl Weierstrass developed the "epsilon-delta" concept of moving toward a limit in a way sufficiently clear and rigorous to ground calculus. Reference to infinitesimals became thoroughly disreputable. But in the 1960s the mathematician Abraham Robinson rehabilitated the concept of an infinitesimal, proposing an approach to calculus that he called "non-standard analysis."[36] He showed that it is possible to set up a rigorous,

---

35. Sheldon Glashow, "Partial Symmetries of Weak Interaction," *Nuclear Physics* 22 (1961): 579-88. Cited by Gerald Holton, *The Advancement of Science and Its Burdens* (Cambridge, MA: Harvard University Press, 1998), p. 171.

36. Abraham Robinson, *Non-standard Analysis,* rev. ed. (Princeton, NJ: Princeton University Press, 1996).

consistent framework of analysis that includes infinitesimals. Drawing on work in mathematical logic, Robinson demonstrated how to extend the real number system to include "hyperreals" (in something like the way rational numbers were extended to include "reals" to allow 2 to have a square root). The hyperreals include infinitesimals. Historians of mathematics now widely acknowledge that Berkeley's charge that the foundation of infinitesimal calculus was laced with contradictions was unanswerable for centuries. Yet the tenacity of mathematicians was vindicated by two entirely different solutions to the conundra. Those inquirers into revelatory claims who show similar tenacity cannot, for this reason alone, fairly be charged with bad faith.

2.2.6. *Doing Without Evident Miracles*

Even religious apologists insist, at least as emphatically as unbelievers, that revelations must be marked by confirming miracles to be credible. William Paley asks: "Now in what way can a revelation be made but by miracles?" He answers: "In none which we are able to conceive."[37] And Richard Swinburne writes in the introduction to his book *Revelation:*

> Part II considers the central issue of the tests by which one can recognize something as revealed truth. . . . how strong we need our historical evidence to be depends on how likely it is a priori that God will give us a revelation. But we do need historical evidence, and that, I shall argue, *must take the form of evidence of a miraculous intervention into the natural order,* reasonably interpreted as God's authentication of a purported revelation.[38]

Swinburne and others have worked out impressive arguments for the possibility of miracles, understood as violations of laws of nature. Our concern at the moment, however, is not whether miracles are possible but whether it should be conceded that, without a confirming miracle, no revelatory claim could be credible.

We resist the conclusion that a miracle is necessary to authenticate a revelatory claim — for three reaons. First, if a miracle in any strict sense of the term is required, then it may be the case, just as Swinburne maintains, that

---

37. William Paley, "Prefatory Considerations," *A View of the Evidences of Christianity* (1794). Paley's remark is cited approvingly by Swinburne in *Revelation,* p. 218.

38. Swinburne, *Revelation,* p. 2 (italics added). Later in the book (p. 112) Swinburne reminds us that he has argued "that a miracle would be needed to authenticate one [a revelation]." Curiously, in ch. 6 of his book, where he presents his argument, it is hard to find a clear statement of the claim that a miracle is necessary to authenticate a revelation.

only Christianity will be believable on the basis of its having been revealed (and that is not a happy consequence). Second, the one revelation Swinburne thinks has a chance of being believable on the grounds that it was revealed promotes the idea that reliance on miracles is not necessary to come to belief; indeed, many have come to believe in that revelation without such reliance. Third, Swinburne's argument for the claim is unpersuasive.

First, then, the untoward consequence of the claim. Swinburne says:

> If the above are the tests for the genuineness of a revelation [the test of content supplemented by the test of an authenticating miracle], I suggest that, *before we ever come to look at the details of its message and method of promulgation,* there is, among the so-called great religions of the world, only one serious candidate for having a body of doctrine which is to be believed on the grounds that it is revealed, and that is the Christian revelation.[39]

With respect to the Muslim belief that the Qur'an contains God's revelation to Muhammad, Swinburne says:

> We have no reason to suspect that illiterate creative genius cannot guess at truths normally accessible only to the literate, or create a new style or a successful movement. So there is no strong reason to suppose that natural law has been violated. We do not know what are the natural possibilities in this area.[40]

And Swinburne takes the same dim view of the claims of Hinduism and Judaism: lacking anything that looks like a plausible confirming miracle, they cannot be believed on the basis of having been revealed. This quick dismissal of all world religions except Christianity is certainly unsettling. It is, however, a consequence of the insistence on a confirming miracle, if, as Swinburne maintains, Christianity is the only live candidate "for having a body of doctrine which is to be believed on the grounds that it is revealed. . . ."

Now it might seem that this consequence is something we two meta-inquirers — both Christian — should find congenial. But we do not. For one thing, it is a Christian teaching that God has revealed at diverse times and places, and it is unsettling to see so many revelatory traditions dismissed as epistemically unworthy of acceptance as revelations. Furthermore, if non-Christian revelatory claims are bypassed, then a source of evidence for Christianity will have been eliminated. For, as we will explain in a later chapter, ex-

---

39. Swinburne, *Revelation,* p. 95 (italics added).
40. Swinburne, *Revelation,* p. 97.

ploration of disjunctive revelatory claims may enhance the probability that some true revelation has been given, thereby decreasing the evidence required on behalf of a particular revelatory claim.

A second reason to resist the claim that miracles are necessary to justify belief in putative revelations is found in the teaching and practices of the one revelation Swinburne thinks has a chance of being believable on the grounds that it was revealed. That teaching is found in the New Testament. Jesus is reported to show some dismay that miracles might be required to convince Philip of Jesus' intimate union with the Father: "Believe me that I am in the Father and the Father is in me; but if you do not, then believe me because of the works themselves."[41] And, in fact, people do come to belief in the way that Jesus asks: by hearing a message and accepting it. John Henry Newman's account of the process is unsurpassed. A word of life is offered. It is believed. Why? The message is thought probable because the believer has a love for it, because the believer has a keen sense of the intrinsic excellence of the message, of its desirability. The revelation

> has with it the gift of staunching and healing the one deep wound of human nature, which avails more for its success than a full encyclopedia of scientific knowledge and a whole library of controversy, and therefore it must last while human nature lasts. It is a living truth which never can grow old.[42]

In effect, Newman is arguing that the message is unsurprising on the assumption that a good God revealed — and not otherwise. And an inquirer may supplement the judgment about the intrinsic excellence of the message with a variety of reinforcing facts, often concerning content in context. The wondrous emergence of a teaching, facts about the lives and, often enough, heroic deaths of messengers who model the teaching, facts about the "chronic vigor" and development of the doctrine over time, may call for explanation. And the hypothesis that the content comes from above may explain all these marvels better than any competing explanation.

A third reason to resist the claim that at least one miracle is required as a mark of authentication is that Swinburne's case for it is unpersuasive.

41. John 14:11 (NRSV).

42. John Henry Cardinal Newman, *An Essay in Aid of a Grammar of Assent* (Notre Dame, IN: University of Notre Dame Press, 1979), p. 376. Newman explicitly criticizes Paley for thinking miracles are required for conversion (though Newman elsewhere treats miracles as striking and conclusive evidence in favor of Jewish and Christian revelation). Newman's case in the *Grammar* draws on the concourse of the history of the Jewish people, on Jewish prophecy understood in light of Christ's life, on the spread of the Christian Church, and on the teaching for which martyrs die.

Swinburne, who is not all that explicit about his reasoning on this particular point, appears to argue as follows:

1) It is possible to infer that a putative divine revelation is genuine only if it is attended by a mark of authentication. ,
2) A miracle, and only a miracle — a violation of the laws of nature — can serve as a mark of authentication.
3) So, if a putative revelation is not attended by a miracle, it cannot be inferred that the revelation is genuine.

This argument is suggested by Swinburne's assertion, recently cited, that the historical evidence for a revelation "must take the form of evidence of a miraculous intervention into the natural order, reasonably interpreted as God's authentication of a purported revelation."[43]

But the argument is problematical. For when "mark of authentication" is understood narrowly, the first premise is false, and when it is understood more broadly, the second is false.

Swinburne's own understanding of a mark of authentication appears to be very narrow:

A mark of authentication such as a seal or signature becomes such in virtue of two considerations. First, no one other than the purported author could, it is generally believed, have made it. . . . Secondly, the local conventions are

---

43. Sometimes it looks as though Swinburne is instead arguing:

1) It is possible to believe a body of doctrine on the grounds that it has been revealed only if it is plausible that the doctrine was initially given to humankind along with a divine mark of authentication.
2) A miracle (a violation of the laws of nature), and only a miracle, can serve as a divine mark of authentication.
3) So, it is possible to believe a body of doctrine on the grounds that it has been revealed only if it is plausible that the doctrine is authenticated by a miracle.

See Swinburne's *Revelation,* pp. 95-97. On this reading of Swinburne, one might reasonably ask: Why is it so important to believe a body of doctrine *on the grounds that it has been revealed?* How is that significantly different from coming to believe, on the basis of the contents of the putative revelation, that a body of doctrine is in fact a revelation? One arrives at the same endpoint either way. But assume that there is something very valuable about believing a doctrine on the grounds that it has been revealed. Nevertheless, perhaps one could, by examining the content of a revelatory claim, come to judge that it is plausible that it is revealed — and *then* accept certain puzzling parts of the revelatory claim that did not figure at all into the judgment that the claim is plausible, that is, accept the puzzling parts *on the grounds that they have been revealed.* At least some of one's beliefs would then have the especially valuable source.

such that a mark of that kind is generally made only in order to authenticate. Signatures and seals are recognized by convention as authenticating devices, whereas fingerprints are not — even though they too are marks very difficult for others than their author to produce.[44]

This is puzzling. Granted, seals and signatures perform their functions due to convention. However, if the question is whether a communication has come from a particular person, evidence that (quite probably) only the person in question could have sent it is clearly relevant. If you get a handwritten letter from a close friend, you do not need a signature to testify to its origin. If a prophet starts making absolutely accurate and precise predictions about events weeks before they occur, that might reasonably be taken as a sign of divine inspiration.[45] Similarly, it does not seem out of the question that the Qur'an might exhibit the stamp of the divine, even if its production did not violate laws of nature. Thus under a narrow understanding of a "mark of authentication," the sort of understanding Swinburne employs, premise 1 is false.

And premise 2 is clearly false under a broad understanding of authenticating mark, for a broad understanding extends beyond violations of laws of nature. Premise 2 *embeds* the claim that a miracle is a violation of the laws of nature.

When "miracle" is understood in this broader way, it is much easier to accept the thesis that revelations must be validated by miracles. Swinburne makes the question of whether something is miraculous an either-or affair. But the etymology of the word "miracle" suggests a different way of looking at the matter. A miraculous event is a wondrous event, a marvelous event, an event for which natural explanations are unsatisfying.

And here we encounter a range of possibilities. At one end are found alleged events such as a person who was certainly dead rising up and walking. Such a shocking event, if witnessed, would elicit the sort of wonder that makes people think they might be hallucinating. Further along the line would be the fulfillment of exact prophecies. Suppose a person prophesies that, because of our sins, God will permit terrorists to detonate a nuclear weapon on May 9, 2025, killing exactly 1,105,111 people the first day, 32,333 the second, and 2,405 the third. Should events come to pass exactly as prophesied, our wonder

---

44. Swinburne, *Revelation,* p. 94.

45. A prophecy fulfilled can help establish a revelation as genuine, Swinburne holds: he says that "the evidence of content would be substantially very much stronger indeed if the content contained elements which subsequently proved true but which at the time could only have been known to God himself" (Swinburne, *Revelation,* p. 89). Nevertheless, Swinburne does not seem to give much credit to such evidence, unless violation of a law of nature is involved.

at the prophecy would be substantial, and it would be madness to dismiss the part of the prophecy that refers to sins on the grounds that the prophet *could* just happen to guess the numbers. Curiously, Swinburne discusses the role prophecies might play in validating a revelation, but still insists on a miracle that is a violation of the laws of nature. (Of course, actual revelatory claims do not contain fulfilled prophecies of the kind just mentioned. Any reasonably precise prophecies in received scriptures have, it is now widely agreed, found their way in after the predicted events.) Further still along the line are events and circumstances that are both highly desirable and highly unlikely. Traditional natural theology draws on some such events, such as the fine-tuning of the universe for the development of human life, the existence of consciousness, and the existence of the world itself. The sense of wonder here may be considerably less, since some of these phenomena are widely acknowledged — though we may suddenly become aware that accounting for some particular phenomenon is not so easy. Arguably, the unexpected emergence of some beautiful teaching, or the apparently providential development of doctrine within a particular community, poses an explanatory question parallel to questions about fine-tuning or consciousness.

While it is not customary to think that all these things would, strictly speaking, be miracles (if they occurred), that may be due in part to the fact that we lack a clear and unproblematic concept of a "law of nature" and of a "violation" of such a law. In any event, a Muslim who infers on the basis of content that the Qur'an comes from God can properly say to Swinburne that no violation of a law of nature is required to draw a probable conclusion, particularly when the content is combined with other facts known to those intimately familiar with Islam. Again, the question to keep our eye on is not whether the content of a putative revelation *must* have come from above, but whether a person could reasonably decide that it did, absent a confirming miracle understood as a violation of a law of nature (and since precise and successful predictions of events that could not be known by a human in advance are not to be had, absent such predictions).

For these three reasons, then, we conclude that a miracle is not required to confirm or authenticate a revelatory claim.

Of course, nothing we have said so far suggests in the least that a confirming miracle would be useless, much less that it would be impossible to find good evidence for one. All we are saying is that there is good reason to think it possible to get by without such a miracle. But now we wish to highlight a point about our suggested procedure that we think throws some light on the evaluation of miracle claims.

Following Hume, critics of Christianity have argued that the evidence for the regular course of nature always overwhelms the evidence put forward on behalf of the miraculous exception. Criticisms of Hume's arguments abound, some of them trenchant.[46] And it does not take a Hume scholar to recognize the shortcomings of his arguments *for an inquirer following the strategy we recommend.* Hume says:

> Though the Being, to whom the miracle is ascribed, be, in this case, Almighty, it does not, upon that account, become a whit more probable; since it is impossible for us to know the attributes or actions of such a Being, otherwise than from the experience which we have of his productions, *in the usual course of nature.*[47]

But if the world may have come to be out of nothing (and we are just about to argue that this is indeed a real possibility), then there is more to go on than the usual course of nature. Moreover, as we have been urging, the *content of revelation* can be taken into account. Hume completely ignores this. Consider how inapt is his analogy between the putative resurrection of Christ and the imagined resurrection of Elizabeth I. Hume asks us to conduct a thought experiment in which Elizabeth I is alleged to have died and three days later to come back to life. Witnesses testify to the miraculous event, we are to imagine. Hume contends, correctly, in our view, that the proper inference in this case, no matter how sincere and reputable the witnesses are, would be that Elizabeth never died in the first place. But this case is hardly parallel to accounts — reverberating through the centuries — of Christ's death and resurrection. There is no context for Elizabeth's "death and resurrection": no teaching, no teleology. We have no reason to think Elizabeth would rise from the dead, no predictions of the event, no rationale for it. We have no marvelous adumbrations on its significance. We have nothing like the unparalleled story of Christ. Indeed, we have no story at all.

---

46. John Earman and David Johnson, for instance, both argue that Hume's attempts to show that belief in miracles could under no circumstances be epistemically justified fall flat. John Earman, *Hume's Abject Failure: The Argument against Miracles* (Oxford: Oxford University Press, 2000); David Johnson, *Hume, Holism, and Miracles* (Ithaca, NY: Cornell University Press, 1999). But see also Robert J. Fogelin, *A Defense of Hume on Miracles* (Princeton, NJ: Princeton University Press, 2003).

47. David Hume, *Enquiries concerning the Human Understanding and concerning the Principles of Morals*, 3d ed., ed. L. A. Selby-Bigge and P. H. Nidditch (Oxford: Clarendon Press, 1975), part II, sec. 38, quoted in Fogelin, *Defense of Hume on Miracles*, p. 82 (italics added).

2.3. Defense of the Key Conditional's Antecedent

2.3.1. A Simple Argument for a Minimalist Conclusion

We turn, now, to the second premise of our Key Argument (i.e., the antecedent of our Key Conditional):

> It is not highly unlikely that a world-creator exists.

The concept of a world-creator, as we understand it, is very thin: it does not even entail intellect. This, together with the fact that we aim merely to show it is "not highly unlikely" that there is a world-creator, means that the second premise of our Key Argument is minimalist, or modest, and so may be relatively easy to support. That will matter to the agnostic inquirer who is determined to avoid Kierkegaard's infinite parenthesis enclosing an endless number of problems that must be solved before taking a religious standpoint.

The tradition of natural theology contains some arguments that are especially well suited to the attempt to establish that the existence of a world-creator is not highly implausible, even if they do not show that a good God is probable. Consider, for instance, John Leslie's argument that the universe's "fine-tuning" makes it probable that either the universe was designed, or that unimaginably many *cosmoi* with radically different properties were generated by chance.[48] Leslie argues that the two hypotheses should be taken equally seriously. If one is searching for a highly plausible argument that there is a good God, this conclusion may be disappointing. But the picture changes if all that is needed is an argument that it is not highly implausible that there is a world-creator. (Often, however, the standard arguments for God's existence are more complicated and more ambitious than is required to secure the antecedent of our Key Conditional.)

Our own argument is designed to establish that the conjunction of the following two apparently independent propositions is not highly implausible:[49]

---

48. See John Leslie, *Universes* (London: Routledge, 1996).

49. We use probabilistic language to express the claim that these two propositions are not highly implausible. Our contention is that if one assigns a probability to the conjunction, it is not going to be anywhere in the neighborhood of zero. Some would insist that propositions of this sort are inscrutable, and that if probabilistic language is to be adopted, the best way to represent a suspension of judgment is by assigning to each hypothesis an interval <0,1>. Such an assignment would amount to conceding our claim: if that interval is assigned, then the probability assigned is *not* in the neighborhood of zero.

1) The physical universe came to be (that is, had a beginning).
2) Whatever comes to be has a cause distinct from itself.

If the conjunction of these two contentions is not highly implausible, then neither is the claim that the universe has a cause distinct from itself, a world-creator. For all the argument tells us, the creator may be crafty, conniving, cruel, or insensate. Or there may be more than one creator: to say that there is *a* being causally responsible for the existence of the universe is not to say there is only one such being. However, if the conjunction of the propositions is not highly implausible, it would be a mistake to claim that it is known or all but known that there is no creator. The argument is thus tantamount to a refutation of one strong form of atheism — a quite common form.

The first proposition refers to the "physical universe." Have we not already argued (in chapter 1) that it is extremely difficult to circumscribe "the physical"? Yes. But if an agnostic is prepared to allow that what is meant by the world's coming-to-be several billion years ago is that there was a transition from nothing to something, then we need not entangle ourselves in an effort to find what is meant by "physical universe." We intend to designate by that phrase what the cosmologists designate when they say that roughly 13.7 billion years ago the universe came to be. This universe is commonly thought to proceed from a singularity, and the singularity thought to be a physical reality such as gravity, mass, or charge, which has an apparent value of infinity. Details regarding alternative understandings of the universe's beginning do not affect our argument, so long as it is understood that we are not claiming that the world came to be in the course of an already existing time.

Taken separately, neither of the two propositions seems, at least at first glance, to be implausible at all.

With respect to the first, "The physical universe came to be," cosmologists keep telling us that the universe began some 13.7 billion years ago, and while the "big bang" may have been preceded by a big crunch, no respectable cosmologist claims that it is highly unlikely that the universe is temporally finite. The theory that the world began from an initial singularity has persuaded even many atheists that it is probably true that the world came to be. Now everyone recognizes that judgments of this kind can be overturned quickly in contemporary physics. There do exist rivals to "big bang cosmology" based on Einstein's general theory of relativity and postulating a beginning of time. The best-known ones include string and ekpyrotic theory. But the existence of these highly speculative and untested rivals has not led to anything like a consensus against the position that the universe began to be. Even on a cautious or skeptical assessment of the evidence, it looks like we have no reason to prefer the hypothesis that the world has always existed over the hypothesis that it has not always existed. It looks like we can assign the claim that "the world came to be" a probability of *at least* .5. We can make this assignment without trying to work through either the arguments of contemporary physicists or the complex philosophical arguments advanced over the past two millennia in support of the claim. (If there were *no* evidence one way or the other, the probability would be inscrutable; we could then judge that the hypothesis that the universe began is not less probable than the denial of the hypothesis.) Moreover, the current consensus of scientific opinion pushes the probability of the claim up a bit.

And what of the second proposition, "Whatever comes to be has a cause distinct from itself"? Few general principles outside of logic and mathematics strike us with the force of what we might call the "universal causal principle" — that whatever comes to be has a cause. The great Scottish philosopher Thomas Reid put it this way: "That neither existence, nor any mode of existence, can begin without an efficient cause, is a principle that appears very early in the mind of man; and it is so universal, and so firmly rooted in human nature, that the most determined skepticism cannot eradicate it."[50] But could it be that, while the universe does require a cause, it brought itself into being? D. H. Mellor expresses the virtually unanimous view of the matter when he says that "no one thinks that anything can cause itself," and again, "No one then will defend self-causation."[51] We will understand the universal causal principle as building in this ubiquitous assumption (though later we will have occasion to critically examine the assumption).

2.3.2. Objection: There Well Could Be Exceptions to the Universal Causal Principle — The World May Just Have Popped into Existence

It has sometimes been taken to be one of the lessons of quantum mechanics that there are exceptions to the universal causal principle. Quentin Smith, for instance, at one point argued that, whether the causal relationship be analyzed in terms of physical necessity or in terms of the regular but non-necessary conjunction of events of a certain kind, "It is sufficient to understand causality in terms of a law enabling single predictions to be deduced, precise predictions of

---

50. Thomas Reid, *Essays on the Active Powers of the Human Mind,* ed. Baruch Brody (Cambridge, MA: MIT Press, 1969), essay IV, ch. 2, p. 267.

51. D. H. Mellor, *The Facts of Causation* (London: Routledge, 1995), p. 17.

individual events or states," to see that, given the Heisenberg uncertainty principle, "there are uncaused events in this sense. . . ."[52]

However, it does not at all follow from the Heisenberg uncertainty principle that there are exceptions to the universal causal principle — given accounts of causality that properly distinguish between causality and determination.[53] As long as it is allowed that non-logical necessary conditions must be in place for things to come to be, that suffices to credit the universal causal principle. And quantum mechanics provides no reason to doubt that there are indeed non-logical necessary conditions for the occurrence of events. The final location of an electron scattered by an atom is not precisely predictable, but that does not mean that the scattering is not a necessary condition (in the circumstances) for the electron's following a particular path.[54] The same holds for the emergence of virtual particles from the physicist's vacuum: there are necessary conditions for their emergence.

But, it may be objected, counterexamples show that causes are *not* necessary conditions. For instance, imagine a student driver riding with an instructor who has an independent brake. If the instructor says, "You must put your foot on the brake or the car will not stop," the instructor is not refusing to come to the rescue should the student freeze and fail to step on the brake. So even though the student in fact hits the brake and causes the car to stop, it does not look like the student's hitting the brake is a necessary condition of the car's stopping.

To see the defect in the counterexample we must distinguish between two understandings of the contention "c is a necessary condition for e." This can mean either

1) c is necessary for e in some circumstance s

or

2) c is necessary for e in any circumstance whatever.[55]

---

52. Quentin Smith, "The Uncaused Beginning of the Universe," *Philosophy of Science* 55, no. 1 (1988): 49.

53. See G. E. M. Anscombe, "Causality and Determination," Inaugural Lecture at Cambridge University, 1971, reprinted in G. E. M. Anscombe, *The Collected Philosophical Papers of G. E. M. Anscombe,* Vol. II: *Metaphysics and the Philosophy of Mind* (Minneapolis: University of Minnesota Press, 1981).

54. For an excellent review of the subject, see Richard W. Miller, *Fact and Method* (Princeton, NJ: Princeton University Press, 1987), esp. pp. 60-64.

55. A couple of points are worth noting. First, we concentrate on *particular* causes in *particular* circumstances. That is to say, we are not talking about properties. But it would be possible

It is possible to think of conditions that might reasonably be claimed to be necessary in all circumstances if anything is to exist or happen. One might claim that unless God acts, nothing at all can happen. But the assertion that something is a necessary condition is rarely to be taken to mean 2, necessary in *any* circumstance whatever. It usually just means 1, that the condition is necessary in *some* circumstance s. And if we hold that causes are necessary conditions in the first sense, then there is no refuting the claim that c is a necessary condition for the emergence of e in circumstance s by producing counterexamples that bring other causal agents into play and thus involve changing s to some other circumstance, say s*. Granted, if the driving instructor says, "You must hit the brake or the car will not stop," the instructor is not refusing to come to the rescue. Yet it remains true that, if the situation is not changed by the instructor's intervention, if you do not do what you must do, the car will not stop. Exactly parallel points could be made about the more sophisticated scientific examples philosophers give when they suggest causes may not be necessary conditions.

Holding that causes are necessary conditions in sense 1 makes it possible to answer another common objection to the claim that causes are necessary conditions. It is often alleged that causes cannot be treated as necessary conditions because many effects are, as the jargon has it, causally overdetermined. Two assassins may simultaneously fire bullets into a victim, who subsequently dies from the wounds; but, had one of the assassins missed, the victim would still have died from the other bullet. So it seems that each agent's action is superfluous; neither appears to be a necessary condition. However, if c_1 and c_2 *each* cause the whole of effect e, then the entire effect derives from each source. And this is no more possible than it is for a river to draw all of its water from two distinct sources. Talk of overdetermination arises when levels of explanation are confused. Suppose you stretch a metal spring by adding two weights to a pan at the end of the spring. The spring stretches in a determinate way, that is, at such and such rate to such and such extent. The actual stretching is not overdetermined; if only one weight were added it would stretch in a different way. Still, we may describe the event abstractly, as just the stretching of the spring. Thus, each weight may be said to cause the spring to stretch, and the stretching, abstractly considered, is overdetermined. But there are not two ef-

---

to translate our claims about particular causes to the more general level of properties if desired. Second, when we speak of a cause operating in a situation s, we do not mean to suggest that there is nothing in s playing a causal role. We claim that *a* cause of the universe is not highly implausible. That does not mean there cannot be additional causes of the universe. See Thomas D. Sullivan, "Coming to Be without a Cause," *Philosophy: The Journal of the Royal Institute of Philosophy* (Cambridge) 65, no. 253 (1990).

fects here — one the spring's stretching, and a second its stretching in *this way*. There are only two levels of description, less and more specific. The actual, concrete event is not overdetermined.

A skeptic might object: "Imagine the world just popping into existence. This *is* conceivable. Conceivability argues possibility. So why not say the universe just popped into existence?"

But while conceivability offers some evidence for possibility, conceivability is, of course, not decisive. It is conceivable that some very large composite number is prime, but if it is in fact not prime but composite, it is necessarily so. In the case of the principle "whatever comes to be has a cause (distinct from itself)," there is reason to think it is true, and necessarily so, despite the conceivability of exceptions. Over time an ocean of evidence swamps islands of doubt. There are no known exceptions. The principle is so deeply grounded in experience that it would be more difficult to give it up than just about any other principle about the world. To appreciate the depth of its ingression, one need only read a little of the history of the cosmological disputes raging in the middle of the last century. Both big bang theorists such as George Gamow, Ralph Alpher, and Robert Herman, who thought the whole world exploded into existence without a cause, and steady state theorists such as Fred Hoyle, Hermann Bondi, Thomas Gold, and William McCrea, who proposed that new matter in the universe was constantly arising from nothing at all, were excoriated by philosophers and scientists alike for talking errant nonsense. You cannot just have energy introduced into the universe without there being any cause of its emergence at all, it was said.[56]

Still, it might be argued, what this ocean of evidence supports is merely a causal law, and the standard view of causal laws is that they are not necessary in the same way that metaphysical or broadly logical propositions are. Thus, for example, in his very thorough examination of causality, D. H. Mellor observes that Don's falling fifteen meters causes Don to die only if the laws involving bone structure, impact, and so forth hold. They may not hold in worlds other than ours. It is thus only necessary that Don dies under these circumstances *in this world*.[57] But if causal laws may not hold in other worlds, then no matter how much intuition and experience speak for the principle

---

56. Helge Kragh, *Cosmology and Controversy* (Princeton, NJ: Princeton University Press, 1996), pp. 202-69. Note the ambiguity of saying that something arises "from nothing." The atheists at the time were saying that nothing at all gave rise to the world or new energy or matter; the theists were saying that some cause was involved, but no matter was required by the creator for the production of new matter or energy.

57. Mellor, *The Facts of Causation*, pp. 17-18.

that whatever comes to be has a cause distinct from itself, it seems possible that the law does not hold for the emergence of the universe itself.

However, what we need to show is not that we infallibly know that the universal causal principle holds always and everywhere and across all worlds, actual and possible. All we need is reason to believe that it is as likely as not that it holds in this one, and that it holds concerning the generation of the universe — not merely events within the universe.

Furthermore, while it is true that philosophers often insist on a distinction between physical and metaphysical necessity, it is hard to see why. Physical laws could be different in a different world only if all the fundamental particles of that world were identical to the fundamental particles in our own world, but behaved differently. However, if two entities are fundamentally disposed to behave differently, then they are different kinds of entities. In short, it seems senseless to maintain that natural laws are necessary, but only softly so, not necessarily necessary.

To develop the point slightly, let us hypothesize a different world, w_2, with physical laws different from the laws here in the actual world, w_1. Either the composition of matter (bones, for instance) in w_2 is somewhat different than the composition of matter in our own world, w_1, or the composition of matter in w_2 is exactly the same as the composition of matter in w_1. In the first instance, where the composition of matter differs, it is misleading to say that different *laws* hold. The bones of bunnies here in w_1 may be somewhat softer than the bones of human beings, but that hardly means different *laws* apply to their bones and ours. So consider the second case, where the composition of matter in w_2 is exactly the same as in w_1. Presumably, the behavioral dispositions of material objects in w_2 are different from those in w_1. But how could the properties of matter in the two worlds be exactly the same, and the behavioral dispositions differ? Of course, we can imagine worlds in which something much like a human being would have bones less brittle than ours. After all, human bones vary in brittleness even in this world. But this cannot be what is meant by the natural laws being different. What must be meant is that there might be other worlds in which a bone, composed exactly the same way that a bone is composed in this world, is less rigid. If it is less rigid, then we can presume that at least some of the ultimate constituents of the bone themselves would have different behavioral dispositions. So, for example, while an electron in this world has a negative charge of $1.60217733(49) \times 10^{-19}$ coulombs, elsewhere the charge would be slightly different. But then what would it mean to say each is an electron, or that they are electrons of the same type? Instead of saying that the laws of physics are different elsewhere, it would seem to make more sense to say that elsewhere things have similar but distinct properties. Thus it is reasonable to understand the necessity involved in the principle "whatever comes to be has a cause" as what is generally characterized in the literature as *metaphysical* necessity.

Further still, it is possible to argue for the universal causal principle in a way that takes us beyond an appeal to Reid-like intuitions and general experience. The argument has two stages.

The first part of the argument depends on an assumption that at least one thing — one object, event, or property — has a cause (distinct from itself) for its emergence. In that case, contrary to what Hume asserts, not everything can come to be from anything or from nothing at all. For, as we have argued, any cause is a necessary condition: without the cause, the effect will not occur (assuming everything else in the situation remains unchanged). And in no situation can a putative cause both be and not be a necessary condition.

Therefore, not everything can come to be from anything or from nothing at all. But that is not the same as showing that nothing can emerge without a cause. Perhaps certain things cannot emerge in this mysterious way, but other things can. And if so, why exclude the possibility that the universe is itself one big exception to the general rule that nothing can come to be without a cause?

This brings us to the second stage of the argument. If one thing, x, needs to be caused, but another thing, y, does not, then it cannot be that this is because the first thing is contingent and the second is not, since by hypothesis both come to be. Therefore, either a) it is just a brute fact that x needs to be caused, while y does not, or b) it is a brute fact that x has some special property or set of properties that makes it dependent, while y lacks those or any other dependent-making properties. Neither alternative is attractive. How could the need for a cause in one case and not the other simply be a brute fact? Just as two garments cannot be *exactly* alike except that one is flammable and the other not, so two electrons cannot be exactly alike except that one would need to be brought into existence by a cause and the other would not. As for the second alternative, if having the property of being contingent does not make a thing causally dependent, how could any other property?

Quentin Smith has proposed two answers to this last question.[58] It may be that the world is so different from anything within it that it does not need a cause, he suggests. First, he argues, the singularity from which the universe sprang is the only thing whose coming to be is not governed by any laws; and

58. Quentin Smith, "Can Everything Come to Be Without a Cause?" *Dialogue* 33, no. 2 (1994): 319. See also Thomas D. Sullivan, "On the Alleged Causeless Beginning of the Universe: A Reply to Quentin Smith," *Dialogue* 33, no. 2 (1994).

since "definitions of causality often make explicit or implicit reference to laws, it is natural to suppose that, if there is only one completely lawless thing, this thing will also be the only thing exempt from causality." Second, "the big bang singularity is the simplest possible thing; it has zero spatial dimensions . . . zero temporal dimensions . . . and is governed by zero laws."

But it is doubtful that either of Smith's reasons for saying the world might have come to be without a cause, taken by itself, is adequate, and taken together they appear incoherent.

Consider the first suggestion: that the singularity does not need a cause because the singularity is lawless. The proposal is replete with difficulties. a) To begin with, while Smith is right about the tie between causality and law being commonly assumed in the literature, some philosophers of science vigorously contest the claim.[59] b) Furthermore, the suggestion that there is a causal nexus only where events are governed by law tacitly assumes that nothing could ever *freely* cause something else to come about. You could not cause your hand to go up by choosing that it go up, since no law can regulate free choices. (Of course, the existence of free will is controverted, but the issues surrounding free acts cannot be stated neutrally given a stipulative definition of "cause" that rules out free causes.) c) And it is not at all clear that the singularity is lawless. As Smith himself notes, Hawking does not think it is. d) Finally, suppose we ask what kind of law is supposed to give expression to a necessary condition for some thing to be an effect. Certainly it cannot be insisted that the kind of law is a physical law, a law whose *relata* are both physical. For to insist on that is blatantly to beg the question against any kind of theism: of course, if the world, or singularity, or anything else can be caused only by something physical, then no non-physical originator could cause the world, or singularity, or anything else to come to be. Smith does not make such a foolish error. He merely says that definitions of causality often make explicit or implicit reference to laws, period. But then it cannot be supposed that the coming to be of the singularity is lawless. Here is a possible law: necessarily, whatever a being with certain divine qualities wills to come into existence, comes into existence. (Smith himself, in one of his later writings, actually invokes this law in arguing that God cannot be a cause of the universe.)

Smith's second reason for thinking that the singularity may begin to be causelessly is that the singularity is uniquely simple. This appears plausible (initially) because ordinarily it takes less to bring simple things into existence than complex things; it takes less to build an airport with one runway than

59. See, for example, Nancy Cartwright, *How the Laws of Physics Lie* (Oxford: Clarendon Press, 1983).

with ten. But simpler things still need proportionate causes. Imagine someone saying: "I believe millipedes have causes, but not centipedes — after all centipedes have fewer legs; they are simpler." Or: "Sure, protons need causes, but they are more complicated than the quarks that compose them. Quarks have no proper parts. So quarks do not need causes." Simple things, even maximally simple things, still have properties. If the big bang singularity is point-like in its simplicity, it is nonetheless infinitely dense. One would think that an infinitely dense object would stand no less in need of a cause to bring it into existence than real and virtual particles, which Smith concedes have causes in the form of necessary conditions.[60]

In any event, Smith's idea that simple things (or maximally simple things) might not need a cause does not comport well with what he says about causality's linkage to law:

> Since no physical laws govern the singularity, it is the case that if it gives rise to something at a later time, it is most likely to give rise to random or arbitrary particle configurations (giving an overall state of maximal disorder) and is not likely to give rise to a highly ordered system such as a flower or ant.[61]

If no physical law connects the singularity with what it "gives rise to," and if, as Smith wants to have it, there is causality only where there is a physical law, then there is no causal connection between the singularity and the ensuing random configuration of particles. It follows that the more complex particle configuration emerging from the singularity is also causeless. And it, unlike the singularity, is not maximally simple.

It is plausible that if the world came to be, it had a cause, as Smith has come to acknowledge.[62] Even so, Smith contends, the argument is not over, because there remains yet one more way to deny that whatever comes to be has a cause distinct from itself.

---

60. Notice how, in the view that complex things need causes, but not simple things, complex things cannot be made up of maximally simple things. The constituents of everything must themselves have constituents: electrons must have proper parts, and so must these parts endlessly. For let x be composed of y and z, and let y and z be maximally simple. Since x is not maximally simple, x needs a cause; since y and z are maximally simple, y and z do not need causes. But if all the parts of x can come into existence without a cause, then it is possible for x to do so also, since no more is required for x to emerge than for all of x's parts to emerge.

61. Smith, "Can Everything Come to Be Without a Cause?" p. 316.

62. In personal communication to Thomas D. Sullivan.

2.3.3. Objection: The World Might Have Caused Itself

We noted that D. H. Mellor articulates the commonsense view that "no one thinks that anything can cause itself."[63] But Mellor wrote those words a little before Smith produced an intriguing argument that the universe might, indeed, have made itself.

Smith begins his argument by providing examples drawn from the history of science, examples that are supposed to suggest that it is possible for a thing to be self-caused. The examples are interesting, but they support a conclusion too weak to damage our thesis. After providing the examples, Smith says: "They [Smith's critics] can no longer say the atheistic theory can be rejected out of hand since it violates the 'self-evident' or 'plausible' principle that uncaused beginnings are impossible."[64] We agree that atheism cannot be rejected out of hand. However, we are not asserting that it can be.

There is more to Smith's case, though, than providing examples that are supposed to suggest that it is possible for a thing to cause itself. It takes some work to see what the case as a whole comes to, since Smith's argument has unfolded over several articles without the connections being made fully explicit (also, along the way, Smith has changed his mind about some key points). His argument, in the end, seems to go like this:

1) The universe came to be. [Smith insists that this is true.]
2) Whatever comes to be has a cause. [Smith comes to concede that this is plausible.]
3) If the universe has a cause, then either it causes itself or something distinct causes it to be. [This appears to be analytic.]
4) Nothing distinct from the universe causes it to be.
5) So, the universe caused itself.

Thus it would follow that it is false that whatever comes to be has a cause distinct from itself.

Smith supports 4 by attempting to show that the concept of cause *cannot* apply to a supranatural creator. And he tries to show this by arguing that there is no theory of causation between events according to which something distinct from the universe can cause it to be. Therefore, much hangs on whether the concept of a cause can be applied to the action of a supranatural

---

63. Mellor, *The Facts of Causation*, p. 17.
64. Quentin Smith, "The Reason the Universe Exists Is That It Caused Itself to Exist," *Philosophy* 74, no. 4 (1999): 586.

creator. In reflecting on this question, Smith considers a variety of causal the-ories.[65] He says that Hume's ideas about temporal priority, spatio-temporal contiguity, and nomological relatedness rule out divine causality; and many theories incorporate one or another of these elements of Hume's analysis. Smith holds that Curt Ducasse's ideas about singular causality do not help the theist, nor does David Lewis's counterfactual analysis, nor John Mackie's INUS definition. Running through all the main theories, he concludes that God could not be the cause of the universe according to any of them, so if the universe has a cause (as Smith now concedes), then it must be self-caused. Smith's argument for 4 thus basically comes down to two propositions:

4a) No standard theory of causality between events is applicable to a being distinct from the universe.

4b) If so, then there cannot be a being distinct from the universe that is caus-ally responsible for it.

Smith could be right about 4a. Consider, for example, Smith's analysis of David Lewis's ideas about causality. Smith summarizes Lewis's account as fol-lows:

> c causes e if and only if (i) c and e are events and both occur and it is the case that either (ii) if c had not occurred, e would not have occurred, or (iii) there is a causal chain linking c and e and each link d in the chain is such that if d had not occurred, then e would not have occurred.[66]

Smith argues that, if we let c be the divine willing of the big bang and we let e be the big bang, then if e had not occurred, c would not have occurred. "But this implies the false proposition that e is the cause of c, since c is counterfactually dependent on e," Smith says. He points out that the solution Lewis offers to a more general problem — the solution that causes are not necessarily effective — will not help here because God's will is necessarily ef-fective. God is omnipotent; thus, necessarily, if God wills the big bang, there is a big bang. Hence God's volition winds up being counterfactually dependent on the big bang. The causality is running in the wrong direction.

This commentary on Lewis strikes us as entirely correct. Can we avoid the problem simply by recalling that our argument in this chapter is about the ex-istence of an agent who may not be omnipotent? It seems unwise to try. Al-

---

65. Quentin Smith, "Causation and the Logical Impossibility of a Divine Cause," *Philosoph-ical Topics* 24, no. 1 (1996).

66. Smith, "Causation and the Logical Impossibility of a Divine Cause," p. 174.

though all we need at this point is an argument for a being distinct from the universe that causally contributes to its existence, a mere creator, it is risky to concede on the way to revelation that the author of a revelation in question cannot be an omnipotent being. It is risky because there are major revelatory claims that make God out to be omnipotent.

Still, all that this argument of Smith's shows (if it succeeds) is that Lewis's theory rules out an omnipotent creator. But even if it were granted that Lewis's theory is the best available, why should we think that 4b would be true? That is, why think the fact, if it is a fact, that no standard theory of causality between events is applicable to a being distinct from the universe entails that there cannot be a being that is distinct from the universe, and causally responsible for it? There are at least three reasons for rejecting the claim that, if no contemporary theory of causality allows for a creator, then there could not be a defensible theory of causality that does allow for a creator.

First, none of the theories of causality Smith considers, including Lewis's, has earned full support from the philosophical community.[67] Imagine an argument that purports to show that mathematics proves nothing because none of the current theories of proof covers what passes for proof in mathematics. The trouble with this argument is that there is no widely accepted theory of proof because all are in some way inadequate to our *concept* (or concepts) of proof. Or again, imagine someone saying that God cannot know anything because no extant theory of knowledge could apply to God. Again, the problem may not be with God's having knowledge, but with theories of knowledge that do not adequately account even for human knowledge.

Second, some of the theories Smith considers might become serviceable for the case of divine causality if they were appropriately modified: that is, conditions that render the theories insufficiently general could be stripped off. A good deal of contemporary theorizing about causality is confined to *physical* causality. The theory of nomological relatedness, for example, can be modified as follows. Typically, according to this theory, causality is defined in terms of laws of nature and a set of non-causal relationships (such as temporal priority and spatio-temporal continuity between two particulars). Smith points out that God's actions are not governed by a law of nature. But the theory can be generalized by dropping the modifying phrase "of nature" from the claim that causality is defined partly in terms of laws of nature. Neces-

---

67. Even the dominant theory of the day, David Lewis's counterfactual theory, is still threatened by seeming counterexamples. In the face of severe criticism, Lewis made substantial revisions to the theory in his Whitehead lectures at Harvard in March 1999, and has since continued to struggle with counterexamples.

sarily, if God exercises a certain power in a certain way, then there will be an effect of a certain kind. It is a law, an ironclad law; we simply do not grasp God's capacity and thus do not know the law. It is not a physical law but a metaphysical law; it is a law that perhaps pertains to a unique entity.

Third, Smith does not consider a wide enough range of theories. Most significantly, he confines his analysis to causal theories where the *relata* are events. He leaves out agent causality. He says: "Considerations of agent causality are not germane to our discussion; our topic is the cause of the universe's beginning to exist, not the cause of God's *act of willing* that the universe begin to exist."[68] He thus rules out the possibility of accounting for the emergence of the universe as an immediate effect of a world-creator itself. Given his rules, the world can only arise from an event. But this stage setting is unfortunate. In some traditional views of God, the world emanates directly from God. Divine volitions are not distinct from the one who acts. God is not an event, and there are no events in God. Of course, this theory is full of obscurities, as is the theory of mere human agency, which attempts to defend the not implausible idea that we are responsible for at least some of our basic acts. But the agent theory of action, with roots in medieval thought (including the thought of Aquinas) and in the Scottish philosophers Thomas Reid and Douglas Stewart, and defended by Arthur Danto, Richard Taylor, and Roderick Chisholm in our time, remains a live option. So long as it does, no argument that ignores it succeeds in demonstrating that a creator cannot give rise to a world in which there dwell agents like us.[69]

Surely, one who becomes intrigued by theism will want to know more about the causality of the one referred to in the classic text expressing a common belief of Jews, Christians, and Muslims: In the beginning "God created the heavens and the earth. . . ."[70] For the present purpose, though, a full theory of divine causality is not necessary.

---

68. Smith, "Causation and the Logical Impossibility of a Divine Cause," p. 170.

69. The fact that Smith sets up his discussion in such a way as to rule out agent causation is noted and discussed by Richard T. McClelland and Robert J. Deltete in "Divine Causation," *Faith and Philosophy* 17, no. 1 (2000): 4. McClelland and Deltete impose a Humean view on Smith, a view according to which there are no substances underlying events, and criticize Smith for the view. However, we do not think Smith is committed to such a view. He can respond to McClelland and Deltete: "I am not denying that there are substances underlying the events involved in causation; rather, I am saying that the *relata* involved in causation must be events." We think Smith's exclusion of agent causation ought to be resisted, but on grounds different from the grounds that McClelland and Deltete take. The exclusion should be resisted because one of the *relata* involved when one thing causes another may not be an event. The causation may go directly from the agent to the thing caused.

70. Gen. 1:1 (NRSV).

Each of our two apparently independent propositions, then, is at least equiprobable with its contradictory:

The physical universe came to be (that is, had a beginning).
Whatever comes to be has a cause distinct from itself.

Indeed, the second premise appears to enjoy a very high probability. Thus it looks like the conjunction of the two propositions has a probability considerably higher than .25. In other words, it looks like it is, at the very least, not exceedingly improbable that there is a world-creator.

2.3.4. Objection: An Immaterial Mind Cannot Interact with the Physical Order

How could a spiritual entity interact with the physical order? How could a god, an immaterial mind, affect or move matter? If mind cannot interact with matter, then a supranatural entity cannot create a natural or physical world.

Admittedly, we have no idea how mind can move matter. But how big a problem is this? It could be monumental if it were not for one thing: in the end, we have no idea how *matter* moves matter. Despite what is sometimes said, we do not actually experience physical causality in any deep way. We see *that* matter moves matter in some sense, but we do not see *why* or *how* it happens. We see someone throw a pencil across the room: we can see the hand grasp the pencil, we can see the arm move back, and we can see the pencil leave the hand and fly across the room. We do not, however, see the causation. Hume was right on this point: all we have are laws *associating* causes with effects.[71] (It does not follow that there is no necessary connection between cause and effect. The belief that there is a necessary connection might be warranted even if we are clueless as to how the connection operates.) There was a time when physical or mechanical causation, matter moving matter, was seen as more perplexing than mind moving matter. As Philip Frank long ago observed, the ability of matter to move matter was, in the days after Newton, held to be understandable by analogy to *mental* causation. "We express this analogy by saying that the wind exerts a 'force' on the sail, where the word 'force' reminds us of our will, of force in the mental sense. In this way, the mental concept of 'force' entered technical mechanics."[72] The wind exerts a

---

71. Actually, Arab thinkers noted the point prior to Hume.

72. Philip Frank, *Philosophy of Science: The Link Between Science and Philosophy* (Englewood Cliffs, N.J.: Prentice-Hall, 1957), p. 98.

"force" upon the sail. The pencil "flies" across the room. We have no conception of how mind can move matter, but neither do we understand how matter can move matter. We do not in either case actually observe the causal nexus. Indeed, given contemporary physicists' uncertainty about what matter is, it is easy to imagine that the day might return when the more fundamental kind of causation is thought to be mental.

Still, do not physicalists put forward arguments on behalf of the claim that mind cannot move matter? Sometimes. Here is one:

1) The world is physically causally closed.
2) If the world is physically causally closed, mind can have no causal impact.
3) So, a divine mind can have no causal impact on the world.

Of course, the causal completeness of physics (asserted in the first premise) cannot simply be laid down as an axiom. True, in a great many philosophical works the belief that the world is a physically closed system is just announced at the beginning, as if it were part of a creed. But the whole question is whether mind can move matter.

Beyond that, however, we may ask: how is the causal completeness of physics to be understood? For if we take what seems to be a sensible statement of it provided by philosopher of science (and physicalist) Elliott Sober, a difficulty is evident. Sober puts forward the following principle as expressing the causal completeness of physics:

$$Pr(b|p) = Pr(b|(p\&m))$$

The principle says that the probability at some time t that a bit of behavior b will occur at a later time is fixed by the physical properties p the system has at t: the system's mental properties at time t do not affect the prediction. As Sober puts it, "the physical properties instantiated at time t 'screen off' the mental properties instantiated at that time from behaviors that occur afterwards."[73] If something is predictable on the basis of the physical, then the mental cannot have a causal impact, according to the causal completeness of physics.

Given this understanding of causal completeness, there appears to be a problem with premise 2. It can be seen through simple thought experiments. Imagine a situation in which a person with a certain illness displays a signa-

---

73. Elliott Sober, "Physicalism from a Probabilistic Point of View," *Philosophical Studies* 95, no. 1-2 (1999): 135-74, retrieved Nov. 2, 2005, from <http://philosophy.wisc.edu/sober/papers.htm>, p. 4.

ture symptom of that illness, one that provides a basis for predicting future developments in the course of the illness. The symptom does not itself *cause* the future developments. Or imagine that it is possible (someday it may be possible) to predict what an individual is going to do by looking at the electromagnetic field above the person's skull. Still, our electromagnetic fields do not *cause* our behavior. In both these scenarios, Sober's principle makes it impossible to recognize causal connections that even the physicalists routinely accept. Now imagine a situation in which God is a sustaining cause of all that goes on. That is, if God were not to sustain the world, not to be present with respect to each action and event that takes place within the world, then the actions and events would not take place. The traditional religious view is, indeed, that there is a divine intimacy involved in all causality. In the imagined case, God's action would be a necessary condition for worldly actions and events and hence would be part of the cause of those actions and events. But everything could still be predictable from the physical goings-on. There seems to be no more reason to exclude God's action as relevant than to exclude the mental as relevant in the example involving an electromagnetic field above a person's skull.

This problem for the expression of the causal completeness of physics echoes the problem (mentioned in chapter 1) of how the physical is to be defined. In both cases, the physicalist maintains that we must accept some form of physicalism. But it became apparent in chapter 1 that it is hard to define "physical" without admitting "little gods" as physical. And in the present case concerning the causal completeness of physics, a principle is put forward that is meant to capture the idea of causal completeness but that has as a consequence the eradication of the distinction between cause and symptom.

Let us turn in another direction to try to find an argument forcing the position that mind does not move matter. It is sometimes suggested that the claim that mind *does* move matter conflicts with physics:

1) Any theory that breaches the law of the conservation of energy is highly improbable.
2) All theories that allow that conscious states and acts are other than physical and yet have impact on the world violate the law of the conservation of energy.

What should be made of these premises?

Premise 1 may look plausible enough. Formulated over a century and a half ago, the conservation law has remained intact. It is worth nothing, however, that the law has often been called into question by scientists, not all of them friendly to theism or dualism. In the middle of the twentieth century, for example, a theory diametrically opposed to the big bang theory was proposed. At first called "the new cosmology," then "the steady state theory," it postulated the continual creation of matter throughout the universe out of absolutely nothing. The trio of leading steady-state theorists, Fred Hoyle, Hermann Bondi, and Thomas Gold, all shared the views promoted outspokenly by Hoyle, the group's senior member. The big bang theory was "quite characteristic of the outlook of primitive peoples" who explain nature by invoking gods, they judged.[74] These theorists just shrugged off the worry of fellow cosmologists that their theory was a flagrant violation of the conservation law. As noted earlier, the position of the steady-state theorists was decidedly a minority position, scorned by many. Still, other physicists and philosophers of science who did not embrace the steady-state theory nonetheless felt just as free as Hoyle, Bondi, and Gold to jettison the law of conservation of energy. Philosopher of science and atheist Adolph Grunbaum did. George Gamow, a founder of the big bang theory, refused to attack the steady-state theory on the grounds that it violated the law of the conservation of energy. "Matter is not conserved — so what?" he asked.[75] Gamow knew something Hoyle, Bondi, and Gold apparently did not know: Bohr had earlier rejected the conservation law for very different reasons. So had many others, including the brilliant Leningrad physicist Lev Landau, who labeled Bohr's deviation a "beautiful idea." In the 1930s, Dirac, Jordan, and Schrödinger joined Bohr and Landau in developing quantum theory in ways that departed from the fundamental law.[76]

So, one might just say, with distinguished contributors on physics such as Schrödinger and Wigner, that "in order to deal with the phenomenon of life, the laws of physics will have to be changed, not only reinterpreted."[77] But of course, it would be better for an anti-physicalist theory of mind if it did not run afoul of the law of the conservation of energy. Which brings us to premise 2. Does every form of dualism require a violation of the law of conservation? That depends in part on what the law is supposed to be. It is understood in different ways.

In both philosophy and physics, the law is often stated quite simply: "Energy cannot be created or destroyed." But if this is what is meant, the modal assertion seems completely unwarranted by the evidence. How could anyone

74. Hoyle is quoted by Kragh in *Cosmology and Controversy,* p. 253.

75. Gamow is quoted by Kragh in *Cosmology and Controversy,* p. 249.

76. See Kragh, *Cosmology and Controversy,* pp. 227-28.

77. Wigner is quoted in John C. Eccles and Karl Raimund Popper, *The Self and Its Brain* (London: Routledge, 1993), p. 544.

know on the basis of the limited experiments done relatively close to home, that it would be impossible for an additional unit of energy to be produced somewhere inside or outside this universe, even by God? It certainly would be weird if precisely the mass-energy in the universe, not a bit more, not a bit less, had to exist. To accept as axiomatic that energy cannot be created (i.e., in this context, cannot come into existence out of nothing) is to accept as axiomatic either that the physical world did not come into existence out of nothing, or that its coming into existence out of nothing somehow involved no increase in energy. There is thus no reason for a dualist to worry about the conservation law on this construction of it.

A more sensible reading of the conservation law goes like this: "[I]n any isolated or closed system, the sum of all forms of energy remains constant."[78] This expression of the law, however, is still open to interpretation. Is the constancy absolute or statistical? The experimental evidence for the law indicates that *"within the limits of small experimental uncertainty* no change in total amount of energy has been observed in any situation in which it has been possible to ensure that energy has not entered or left the system in the form of work or heat."[79] While the evidence is commonly taken to sustain an absolute interpretation, a statistical interpretation seems to fit at least as well. This is one reason physicists have felt free to see "exceptions" to the law. If the law is only statistical, then it is possible that the causal impact of consciousness is immeasurable, a line taken by John Eccles, Karl Popper, and others. But suppose that either the conservation law is best understood absolutely or that, even if it is taken statistically, the difficulties of making much of this opening for mental causation are too great to help any form of dualism.[80] Where would that leave the dualist? Not necessarily out in the cold. Following Schrödinger, Popper has made another and quite neglected suggestion: in a closed system the energy transfers due to consciousness involve offsetting losses and gains.[81] One way this could happen is by the system requiring energy to produce the conscious state and the conscious state infusing energy back into the system.

There is more. Among the points that the dualist can make is that the first law presupposes that the system is closed. Closed to what? Conscious input? On some versions of quantum mechanics, physical systems require con-

78. Duane E. Roller and Leo Nadelsky, "Conservation of Energy," in Sybil P. Parker, ed., *McGraw-Hill Concise Encyclopedia of the Sciences* (New York: McGraw Hill, 1994), p. 463.

79. Roller and Nadelsky, "Conservation of Energy," p. 463.

80. See David Chalmers, *The Conscious Mind* (New York: Oxford University Press, 1996), pp. 333-57.

81. Eccles and Popper, *The Self and Its Brain,* pp. 541, 176-80, 562-66.

sciousness to collapse the wave function. Consciousness, on this interpretation, is part of the physical theory itself — and interwoven with it in such a way as to preserve the conservation of energy. It is true that for someone like Weinberg the ideal physics of the future will contain no reference to consciousness. But that is just a bet on how the physics of the future will evolve, not an argument about what is or is not consistent with current physical theory as we know it.

Along very different lines, there is yet another way to reconcile the movement of matter by mind without registering a violation of the conservation law: appeal to modes of causality that do not require injection of energy into the system. Aristotle, in effect, made this move when he postulated goals as causes. An image of his view shows up in modern philosophical talk about the distinction between reasons and causes. Both are required for certain kinds of actions, but they are very different kinds of causes. Consciousness might cause by supplying reasons.

With all these possibilities in mind, Popper holds that the idea that Michelangelo's works are simply the result of molecular movements and nothing else is "very much more absurd than the assumption of some slight and probably unmeasurable violation of the first law of thermodynamics."[82] One may disagree with Popper's judgment that the first law is not even a serious problem for non-physicalism, but given the trouble both physicalists and non-physicalists have in explaining consciousness, problems with the first law of thermodynamics may be seen as constituting something less than an overwhelming objection to non-physicalism.

Are there other arguments for the conclusion that mind cannot move matter? Commonly, physicalist Jaegwon Kim opines, arguments put forward in support of the claim are mere expressions of "vague, inchoate dissatisfaction" and inadequate to the task.[83] Kim seeks to remedy this situation, advancing a line of reasoning for the thesis that "the very idea of immaterial, nonspatial entities precludes them from entering into causal relations. . . ."[84] It goes as follows (this is our reconstruction):

82. Eccles and Popper, *The Self and Its Brain*, p. 544.

83. Jaegwon Kim, *Physicalism, or Something Near Enough* (Princeton, NJ: Princeton University Press, 2005), p. 74. We earlier dwelt on the difficulty of pinning down a distinction between the physical and non-physical adequate to support confidential declarations that the world is a physically closed system. While this difficulty of pinning down an appropriate sense of "physical" and "non-physical" might affect Kim's argument, we do not press the point here, but settle for his depiction of the immaterial as non-spatial.

84. Kim, *Physicalism, or Something Near Enough*, p. 92 (in the chapter entitled "The Rejection of Immaterial Minds").

1) An immaterial entity could affect a physical entity only if the former had a "pairing relationship" (r) to the latter. [A pairing relationship pairs a cause and an effect; for example, the spatial relationship of distance and orientation may pair the firing of a gun with the death of a person. The pairing relationship is required to ensure that the agent's causal action terminates in one object rather than another.]

2) Either the pairing relationship r would be grounded in (or constituted by) a spatial causal relationship, or a psychological causal relationship.

3) The pairing relationship r cannot be grounded in a spatial causal relationship, because immaterial entities do not have any position in space.

4) If r is grounded in a psychological causal relationship, then r is grounded in an intentional relationship that picks out some particular entity.

5) If r is grounded in an intentional relationship that picks out some particular entity, then the agent with the intention must perceive the particular entity.

6) If an agent perceives a particular entity, then the particular entity causes the agent's perception (as a tree causes an agent's perception of the tree when the agent looks at the tree).

7) If a particular entity causes an agent's perception, then there must be a spatial causal relationship between cause and effect.

8) So, an immaterial entity cannot affect a physical entity (for a spatial causal relationship was ruled out in premise 3).

Sometimes Kim is drawn to weaker versions of these premises. For instance, he says at one point that "it is plausible that spatial relations provide us with the principal means" for "distinguishing intrinsically indiscernible objects in causal situations. . . ."[85] That is much weaker than the claim (at 7) that there *must* be a spatial relationship between cause and effect. The weaker claim will not, however, suffice to support his concluding assertion, cited above, that "the very idea of immaterial, nonspatial entities precludes them from entering into causal relations." We have used strong premises to support the strong conclusion.

The argument is certainly in trouble by premise 5, if not before. Kim says that, if we are going to pick out a particular entity, "we must perceive it somehow"; and he says that the only credible account of what this perception involves "is the familiar causal account. . . ."[86] However, "the familiar causal account," the kind of account one would give in the example Kim uses, where a

---

85. Kim, *Physicalism, or Something Near Enough*, p. 85.
86. Kim, *Physicalism, or Something Near Enough*, p. 81.

tree causes a person's perception of the tree, is not the only kind of causal account. The familiar causal account is appropriate if perception is understood as *discernment or cognition via a sense organ*. But perception might be taken more generally to be *discernment or cognition*. One may discern that Kim's argument is deductively valid without discerning through a sense organ. So, even for humans, "the familiar causal account" may be inadequate. And there may be a special kind of causal account available for the kind of agent God is supposed to be: God might perceive a tree by causing the tree to exist. The causal account here would run from agent to object, from God to the tree, rather than from object to agent. It was a standard medieval view that such "agent-out" causal relationships exist.

The ambiguity of the term "perceive" in premise 5 — the fact that it can be read as referring either to bare discernment or discernment via a sense organ — affects the remaining premises of the argument. If we adopt the thinner, more general reading of "perception" as "bare discernment," then the rest of the argument falls apart. Go to premise 6 and ask: Why must the particular entity at issue cause the agent's perception? It is possible to discern that an argument is valid without causally interacting with the object. There is nothing about the object of the act that moves the agent to awareness, not in the way that a tree moves an agent to awareness (through the movement of photons, and so on). Or, if you want to say that in *some* sense there is causal interaction between the cognizer and the deductively valid argument, then let 6 pass, but go to 7: it is false that there is a *spatial* causal relationship between a deductively valid argument (which is not in space-time) and your cognition of the argument's validity.

Actually, Kim's argument can be recognized as problematic without identifying any particular premise as problematic. And this recognition can be transferred to other arguments that might be devised for the conclusion that an immaterial entity cannot affect a physical entity. For if this conclusion is correct, then something very interesting follows: we can know the falsity of the conjunction "The world came to be, and whatever comes to be has a cause distinct from itself." One of these conjuncts must be false if an immaterial entity cannot affect a physical entity, given that the world is the totality of physical entities. Imagine the reception the *Journal of Astrophysics* would give to a paper whose accompanying abstract begins: "I prove that either the world is a permanent entity (did not begin to be approximately 13.7 billion years ago) or events come to be without causes. My proof is a simple deduction from the conclusion established by philosophers such as Jaegwon Kim, that nothing immaterial can bring about an effect in the physical world." No editor of a journal of astrophysics would give that sort of argument half a moment's thought. Try turning the argument around: assume the evidence shows that the world did come to be. In that case one has an amazingly quick disproof of a widely accepted version of the principle of sufficient reason — that whatever comes to be has a cause distinct from itself. The disproof is much too quick. If you have to bet on whether it is more likely that Kim's analysis is wrong, or that it is false that the world came to be and whatever comes to be has a cause distinct from itself, the choice seems obvious.

2.3.5. The Quiet Concessions of Atheists

We have given an argument for the claim that it is not highly unlikely that a world-creator exists, and buttressed it by way of responses to some possible objections. Now, briefly, we offer confirmation by calling attention to some quiet concessions made by atheists with respect to the claim that a world-creator exists.

Though the point may have been obscured by our compression above of Quentin Smith's argument, his writings on the origin of the universe present concessions of substantial interest. Smith initially argued that, although the great weight of evidence was in favor of the world coming to be, it could come to be without a cause, because quantum mechanics has given up on the causal principle. Abandoning that position — because quantum mechanics gives up only on necessitating conditions, not necessary conditions — he moved to the view that, however plausible the proposition "Whatever comes to be has a cause" may be when applied to events within the universe, the universe itself may be an exception to the rule. Then, retreating once more, recognizing the plausibility of the position that causes are everywhere necessary for the emergence of events, Smith proposed that the world generated itself. This position is a bare possibility at best, unless it can be shown that there is no alternative. The assertion of a bare logical possibility is obviously a very long way from the confident original assertion that the world came to be without the action of any god. Smith at one point suggested that a person could reasonably judge "the argument against God's existence based on the occurrence of gratuitous evil to be more convincing than the causal principle [nothing comes to be without a cause]."[87] And he has argued (in conjunction with an attack on design arguments for the existence of God) that if the universe was created by a supranatural being, the being was malevolent.[88] Perhaps Smith's ingenious

---

87. Quentin Smith, in William Lane Craig and Quentin Smith, *Theism, Atheism, and Big Bang Cosmology* (Oxford: Oxford University Press, 1993), p. 183.

but desperate proposal that the world caused itself to exist would drop by the wayside if he judged that a theistic resolution of the problem of evil were available.

This sort of thing — thumping denial of God's existence coupled with a barely audible concession that we really do not know that there is no agent cause of the universe — is anything but rare.

Consider Richard Dawkins. In his capacity as holder of the Simonyi Professorship of Public Understanding of Science at Oxford, Dawkins has for some time been informing the world that religious belief is a disease, a virus transmitted like other viruses from one individual to another, usually from parents to children. Yet when pressed, he has conceded that he really does not know that there is no creator. Indeed, he acknowledges that deep reasons have been offered for thinking there is.

> There are possible good reasons for believing in some sort of grand supernatural intelligence. They are never anything to do with the biblical God, which is just an ancient bronze age belief having no semblance of reality. But there are modern physicists who believe that the universe — if you actually look at the laws of the universe, they are to some physicists too good to be true. This suggests a very interesting case for a possible very, very deep reason why we might believe in some sort of grand fundamental intelligence underlying the universe.[89]

Diffident about passing judgment on these arguments, Dawkins more confidently goes on to say:

> But I must really stress that has nothing whatever to do with the kind of God that people go into a church and worship, pray to, fear, ask forgiveness of sins from, the sort of God who cares about whether your sex life is sinful or anything like that. That has nothing whatever to do with what I am talking about now, which is a highly sophisticated physicists' theory.

But how can one be so sure that there is no connection? How would a person know that the god the physicists' theories (perhaps) point to is not the same god billions worship? What would we expect of a god — a "grand supernatural intelligence," to use Dawkins's words — who had gone to the trouble of creating a universe in which there emerged beings capable of good and

---

88. Quentin Smith, "The Anthropic Coincidences, Evil, and the Disconfirmation of Theism," *Religious Studies* 28, no. 3 (1992).

89. Richard Dawkins, BBC talk given March 16, 2003, retrieved Aug. 28, 2004, from <www .bbc.co.uk/northernireland/religion/sundaysequence/archive-interviews.shtml>.

evil? Why would the god have no interest in what went on, no interest in creatures' behavior? Is that plausible *a priori*? Of course, it does not *follow* from the cosmological considerations that a creator would have the attributes assigned by one or another religion, but should it not remain an open question what the further attributes are? More precisely, is it not just what we need to find out by investigating the content of revelatory claims? Dawkins proclaims that the god the physicists' theories point to has nothing to do with the kind of God that cares about your sex life. His rhetoric would not be nearly so effective if he had written that the god of the physicists has nothing to do with the kind of God people worship when they contemplate the Grand Canyon or the starry skies above — or even the moral law within. The god of the physicists *may* be the same God who made the canyons and the stars and who set within us a moral law — perhaps even a moral law that has implications for sexual behavior. One should not rule out the possibility before carefully examining the evidence.

And then there is the case of Anthony Flew, famously a longtime champion of atheism, who has moved to a position he describes as "deistic," commenting that "the most impressive arguments for God's existence are those that are supported by recent scientific discoveries."[90] Big bang cosmology, fine-tuning, and "intelligent design" arguments are among the trends in theistic argumentation that impress him. Flew emphatically states that he does not believe in "the God of any revelatory system," and asked to comment on his "openness" to the notion of theistic revelation, he responds:

> I am open to it, but not enthusiastic about potential revelation from God. On the positive side, for example, I am very much impressed with physicist Gerald Schroeder's comments on Genesis 1. That this biblical account might be scientifically accurate raises the possibility that it is revelation.[91]

It is interesting that, on the basis of the content of a revelatory claim, Flew moves from his judgment that there is some sort of world-creator to the possibility that the revelatory claim might be true. He also imagines that there might be "a knock-down falsification of Islam" on the basis of the content of the Qur'an, commenting that a parallel falsification "is most certainly not possible in the case of Christianity." However, when asked whether there is any chance he might in the end move from theism to Christianity, he re-

---

90. Anthony Flew, "Atheist Becomes Theist" (interview with Gary Habermas), *Philosophia Christi* 6, no. 2 (2005), retrieved Aug. 27, 2005, from <www.biola.edu/antonyflew>, p. 4 of PDF file.

91. Flew, "Atheist Becomes Theist," p. 3.

sponds: "I think it's very unlikely, due to the problem of evil."[92] Flew, then, agrees that the existence of a world-creator is not highly implausible, but he finds the problem of evil a formidable barrier to accepting what might be in his judgment the most appealing of the major revelatory traditions: the tradition of Christianity.

We have already briefly argued that the problem of evil should not stand in the way of careful reflection on the content of revelatory claims. But a fuller case can be made, and to that task we now turn.

92. Flew, "Atheist Becomes Theist," p. 15.

3 Objection: Inquiry into Revelatory Claims
Is Pointless Due to Problems about Evil

3.1. The Objection

Our proposal — our Key Argument — may strike some as obviously wrong-headed. Even if it should be granted that the existence of a world-creator is not highly unlikely, it scarcely seems to follow that it would be worth looking at revelations. For our Key Conditional makes a big jump from antecedent to consequent:

> If it is not highly unlikely that a world-creator exists, then investigation of the contents of revelatory claims might well show it is probable that a good God exists and has revealed.

Each chapter from here on addresses a specific version of the protest that the jump is too big. In the first place, the antecedent of the conditional makes no mention of the creator's *moral character*, but the consequent does. How can that leap be justified? Second, it looks like investigation of the contents of revelatory claims will have the promised payoff for the ordinary philosophically inclined agnostic only if there is a reliable *method* for assessing the multitude of revelatory claims that does not require extensive familiarity with the intricacies of probability theory. What could that method be? Third, a method will be fruitless unless the contents of revelatory claims have substantial *explanatory power*. Why think revelatory claims have such power? And finally, the requirement of *faith*, common to leading revelatory claims, can seem irrational — perhaps even vicious. Can we not see prior to an investigation of revelatory claims that no revelatory religion requiring faith will be able to show what the Key Conditional promises?

In the present chapter we focus on the first of these objections (each subsequent chapter takes up a subsequent objection).

The problem of evil has blocked more inquiries into theism than all other problems combined. Scientists, from giants of the past such as Darwin to more recent standard-bearers such as Einstein and Weinberg, have seen evil as a barrier to religious belief. Innumerable philosophers have rejected theism because of the world's evils. And it is not merely nonbelievers who are troubled by the problem. Augustine's great attraction to Manichaeism, with its hypothesis of a supreme Evil constantly warring with a supreme Good, can be ascribed to the force of the problem of evil. Leibniz, codiscoverer of calculus, published but one book in his lifetime: *Theodicy*. Many agnostic inquirers confronting the problem of evil simply fold their tents and go away.

In chapter 2 we argued that, before pronouncing a world-creator guilty of wrongdoing, account must be taken of the explanations of evil that revelatory claims provide. The explanations are neither comprehensive nor perfectly clear; however, defendants in court cases can rightly be acquitted despite defenses that leave unanswered questions, that are at points confused and even inconsistent. The accused must be given a hearing. But given the enormity of the problem of evil, it will not be surprising if inquirers want more than the few quick words we offered in chapter 2. We face this objection: given the magnitude of the problem of evil, the Key Conditional is credible only if, abstracting from the content of revelatory claims, the hypothesis that a creator of our world would be good is not highly implausible; and this hypothesis *is* highly implausible.

Now the demand here to abstract from revelations is of questionable legitimacy. For the core of the problem of evil is that a good God would have no reason to allow the world's evils, and it is in revelatory claims that clues about possible reasons are found. It would hardly make sense to discuss endlessly the abstract possibility that a defendant in some particular criminal trial might have an alibi without looking at the alibi actually provided.

Nevertheless, we will go on in this chapter to speak fairly abstractly about options concerning the character of a world-creator (though here and there we will refer to particular revelatory claims). One reason for doing so is that engaging the problem of evil at a general level can aid discovery of whether in fact a revelation has been given, because it helps establish tests for the credibility of particular revelatory claims. To give a quick example: if some group purports to have a message from on high that evil is illusory, but general reflection makes it clear that evil is not illusory, then the group's claim to be an oracle of a good God can be discounted (assuming that the claim about evil is a core contention that cannot be read in a more intelligible way). Furthermore, engaging the problem of evil at a general and philosophical level can set up examination of concrete revelatory claims by raising or lowering the likelihood that there is a good God. And further still, we want to introduce a couple of lines of thought that are not only useful in discussing the problem of evil but also helpful in seeing the explanatory power of revelatory claims. One line of thought concerns the tie between the moral law and certain kinds of goods (we discuss this in connection with "pie-in-the-sky theodicy"). The other line concerns God as the extrinsic end, or *telos,* of the universe (we take this up in connection with "substandard worlds"). Both lines of thought reappear in chapter 5 in our exploration of what we call "divine ordination theory."

The possibilities concerning a world-creator's moral character may be divided into three main options. A world-creator might be amoral, altogether outside the realm of moral evaluation; or a world-creator might be in some measure wicked; or a world-creator might be wholly good.

We argue, to begin with, that the first option is unattractive. It is not credible that a creator of this world would be either non-conscious, or crazy, or possessed of some mode of consciousness so different from our own as to place it beyond the reach of our judgments concerning good and bad, right and wrong.

Furthermore, the second option is unappealing: it is implausible that a creator of this world would be wicked. We argue, centrally, that the project of the "demonist" seeking to establish the credibility of an omnipotent, omniscient, wicked world-creator is more difficult than the project of the theodicist. It is harder to construct the *converse* of a theodicy than it is to construct a theodicy itself. An asymmetry between evil and good advantages the theodicist.

If the first and second options are eliminated as possible choices for an inquirer, all that is left is the option of a wholly good world-creator (assuming, of course, a world-creator exists). Yet our talk of amoral and wicked gods will leave some skeptics unmoved. For one thing, it may strike some as altogether too frivolous. Think, for instance, of the likely reaction of a John Stuart Mill, who introduces his discussion of the moral attributes of a deity by commenting:

> We have not to attempt the impossible problem of reconciling infinite benevolence and justice with infinite power in the Creator of such a world as this. The attempt to do so not only involves absolute contradiction in an intellectual point of view but exhibits to excess the revolting spectacle of a jesuitical defense of moral enormities.[1]

1. John Stuart Mill, "Theism" (from *Three Essays on Religion*), retrieved Nov. 3, 2005, from <www.philosophyofreligion.info/theism8.html>.

Our speculation about amoral and wicked gods may appear to be "jesuitical sophistry," philosophical sleight of hand. Furthermore, our reasoning is probabilistic: we do not claim it compels an inquirer to reject the first two options, only that it considerably lessens their attractiveness. Thus we conclude with an examination of the third option concerning a world-creator's character, the possibility that it is wholly good. Of course, we cannot fully engage the vast literature on this topic. Our focus is on likely concerns of an inquirer who is insistent on rejecting the third option *prior* to examining the content of revelatory claims.

3.2. Exploring the First Option: The World-Creator Is Amoral

3.2.1. The Difficulty of Arguing That a World-Creator Would Be Amoral

An argument that a world-creator would be amoral — that is, non-moral, outside the moral realm — must identify some property in virtue of which the amorality obtains. What could that property — call it F — be?

Perhaps it will be hazarded that the property is that of *lacking consciousness*. However, there is a serious problem with this proposal. A world-creator would have to be immaterial, for a world-creator is by definition a cause of all that is material; and as we have already argued, it is wildly implausible that the world caused itself. Now, everything we have reason to describe as immaterial appears to be causally inert — minds and mental acts excepted. This is one reason philosophers since Aristotle have been suspicious of abstract entities. Aristotle criticized the Platonic Forms as useless because they cannot *explain* anything, and it is because they are causally impotent that they cannot. Paul Benaceraff has notably argued that numbers could not be abstract objects because we would be unable to come to know them if they were abstract objects, since whatever we know, we know through cause-and-effect transactions with objects of knowledge — and of course, abstract objects have no causal efficacy. Whether the conclusions Aristotle, Benaceraff, and others reach are acceptable, the nearly universally shared premise that abstract objects cause nothing has tremendous appeal. If the premise is correct, and if abstract objects are our only examples of immaterial entities apart from conscious minds, it appears that if a world-creator is both immaterial and causally efficacious, it must be conscious.

And there is further reason for thinking that an originator of *this* world would be conscious. Given the assumption that there is a world-creator, an immaterial cause of the world, is it more likely that the world's order is in some manner a reflection of Mind, or that it arose without any conscious mental activity at all? The assumption that there is a world-creator increases the likelihood that some kind of intelligence is responsible for the world's order. Imagine modern discoverers of the Chauvet cave art reflecting on the question of what produced the pictures on the cave walls. Given that early human beings were in existence at the time the images were produced — were, indeed, cave dwellers — it is a pretty good bet the images of bison and horses were drawn by those agents, though it is possible the likenesses could have come about by chance, and in some cases, where the images are obscure, we might hesitate to infer to a designing hand if we did not already believe cave dwellers existed at the time the images were produced.

If the world's making were necessitated by the maker's nature, that might constitute some evidence that the maker lacks consciousness (though there certainly are those who hold that human consciousness is consistent with determinism). But why would an originator of the world be compelled ontologically to make any world at all (let alone this particular world)?[2] If a being is obliged to make a world, the being would need to have some property G, such that anything that is G produces a world. What might that property be? A long tradition of argument relies on the neo-Platonic or pseudo-Dionysian principle that goodness is essentially or necessarily *self-diffusive*. Does a self-diffusive being diffuse its very own goodness? Does it merely endow with goodness? Does it diffuse goodness to a maximal degree? Does it exercise final rather than efficient causality in diffusing goodness?

These and related questions are not easily answered. And even if the diffusiveness principle could be expressed precisely, a major problem would remain: What would *ground* self-diffusiveness? In the tradition, the grounding property is goodness. But that property is off limits if the project is to establish that a world-creator would be amoral.

---

2. For a discussion of these issues, see Sandra Menssen and Thomas D. Sullivan, "Must God Create?" *Faith and Philosophy* 12, no. 3 (1995). William L. Rowe criticizes part of the argument of "Must God Create?" in his book *Can God Be Free?* (Oxford: Clarendon Press, 2004), pp. 127-31. He maintains (p. 120) that "If an omniscient being creates a world when there is a better world that it could have created, then it is possible that there exists a being morally better than it." If this is true, and if a number of other propositions are true, this would lead to the conclusion that there is no being of unsurpassable goodness. While we must leave for another time the project of engaging Rowe, we wish quickly to note two points. First, our project in this book is concerned with whether a *wholly good* God might have revealed something, not whether there is a being of *unsurpassable goodness*. At most, Rowe's argument would show only the latter. Second, Rowe's arguments depend on the possibility of grading worlds independently of divine intentions or standards. We will have something to say about that possibility later in this chapter.

Can we get further with the property *being impersonal?* If an impersonal god is simply one who is indifferent to other persons though it knows they exist, then an impersonal god is certainly not necessarily non-moral. Disregard for other persons is callous and immoral.

What if we let F be *self-sufficiency?* A self-sufficient god might be a god focused solely on itself. Aristotle is sometimes alleged to have thought of the First Mover in this way: the best being thinks exclusively about the best object. But thinking about the best object could require thinking nonexclusively after all. For thinking about the best object involves thinking about the best object's properties, and those properties can be relational, extending to things beyond the bearer of the property. For example, the properties might extend to the effect of the best being's causal efficacy, the world. A creator's reflection on its own properties would then include reflection on the created world, and that would bring a creator into the sphere of morality (assuming it has some power to affect a world once created). Alternatively, a self-sufficient being might be understood as a being whose *existence* is independent of other beings. But why should independence place someone outside the sphere of morality? Or, a self-sufficient being might be one whose *properties* do not depend on anything outside it. Then one could say that a creator with moral obligations would not be self-sufficient; it would be bound by some outside (moral) law. In this case, assuming self-sufficiency begs the question.

Could the elusive property F, the property in virtue of which a creator would stand above morality, be that the creator is the *cause of all beings?* Brian Davies argues that, because God is the cause of all beings, God is not a moral agent. Other theists take similar stances. Marilyn Adams holds that God has no moral obligations. Yet she also thinks that "God must be not only the source and sustainer of being and goodness, but also the defeater of horrors."[3] So no one would satisfy the concept of "God" who did not defeat horrors. In the sense of "amoral" that is relevant to us, this means that God is not amoral. In any event, Adams *uses* revelation to make her case that God is a defeater of horrors. Her fine work in this regard certainly does not send the message that it is a waste of time to inquire into revelatory claims.

Judaeo-Christian revelation itself surely represents God as a moral agent. In the dramatic encounter between Abraham and God over the fate of Sodom and Gomorrah, God informs Abraham of his intent to destroy the cities, all but inviting the series of brave questions posed by one through whom all nations are to be blessed.

---

3. Marilyn McCord Adams, *Horrendous Evils and the Goodness of God* (Ithaca, NY: Cornell University Press, 1999), p. 80.

Then Abraham came near and said, "Will you indeed sweep away the righteous with the wicked? Suppose there are fifty righteous within the city; will you then sweep away the place and not forgive it for the fifty righteous who are in it? Far be it from you to do such a thing, to slay the righteous with the wicked, so that the righteous fare as the wicked! Far be that from you! Shall not the Judge of all the earth do what is just?"[4]

God does not reject the broad rule, but rather lets Abraham bargain, lowering the number of righteous needed to save the city. We believe that Abraham's assumption is correct: the Judge of all the earth does what is just, what is right.[5]

3.2.2. *Good Reason for Thinking Moral Categories Apply to a World-Creator*

So it is difficult to see how to argue that a world-creator would be amoral. Furthermore, we now suggest, there is independent reason for thinking moral categories would indeed apply to a creator of our world. We will defend the following argument:

1) If the world has a maker, it is likely the maker knows it brings about a state of affairs that could well issue in emergence of agents to whom moral categories apply (e.g., human beings).
2) If an agent knows it brings about a state of affairs that could well issue in emergence of agents to whom moral categories apply, then it is plausible that moral categories apply to the maker-agent.
3) So, if the world has a maker, then it is plausible that moral categories apply to the maker.

Begin with premise 1. We have already argued that a world-creator would be conscious. It is hard to imagine that a conscious maker of this world would fail to know that human beings would be part of the world. For if the world has a maker, by far the most likely candidate for causal action producing conscious humans would be the direct action of the maker, and it is hard to believe a conscious maker would be unaware of its own direct action. It is un-

---

4. Gen. 18:23-25 (NRSV).

5. The NRSV translates the question at the end of Gen. 18:25 as "Shall not the Judge of all the earth do what is just?"; the older RSV translates it as "Shall not the Judge of all the earth do right?"

necessary to go that far, though: all that is required for the argument we are defending is that a world-creator know that the world includes humans.[6] Complete knowledge of what is involved in world creation is *not* required. A human being never intends an action exactly, in all its particularity. You may intentionally raise your arm; you do not, however, intend the particular velocity with which you raise your arm, and you do not intend the precise pattern of precise angles your elbow takes as your arm rises. In order for an action to be subject to moral evaluation, it is sufficient that the agent intends to bring about an effect that satisfies certain concepts (and that the agent be sane). Raising your arm with the intention of thereby knocking your colleague down the stairs to keep him out of a softball game is an action that can be morally evaluated, despite the fact that you do not intend it in all its particularity, and thus lack complete knowledge of what you are doing.

Premise 2 is more controversial.

Consider a thought experiment. If you are a laboratory scientist curious whether it is possible to breed hairless dog-faced monkeys — and you undertake the experiment and succeed — you have some special responsibility for the monkeys. You cannot, for instance, just toss the monkeys into a fire once you have satisfied your curiosity. Creation of sentient beings carries with it responsibilities. And creation of rational beings carries additional responsibilities. It is one thing for a laboratory scientist to breed hairless dog-faced monkeys; it is quite another to breed hairless dog-faced humans.

And now reflect on parental obligations. Parents have obligations to offspring that are far more serious and specific than the general obligations humans have to one another, and parents who pretend otherwise are universally despised. And the particular ways in which parents raise their children contribute to particular desires, inclinations, and aspirations in the children. Special obligations may result. A wealthy parent who implants and nurtures in a child the desire to attend Harvard may have some duty to help foot the bill. Similarly, a maker who builds human beings to desire happiness may have some obligation to provide for the possibility of that desire's being fulfilled.[7] Human parents' obligations to their children are in some ways specific, unique to the human species. Human parents must, for instance, be especially careful and especially courageous in protecting their children. An

6. An argument similar to the one we set out, but based on a world-creator's *belief* that the world includes humans, could be defended. But most people who will grant that a world-creator would have the appropriate belief will also grant that the world-creator has the knowledge.

7. Jerry L. Walls concurs: "A God who made us in such a way that we naturally felt approval for whatever promoted human happiness, but did not Himself desire human happiness would be evil." Jerry L. Walls, "Hume on Divine Amorality," *Religious Studies* 26 (1990): 262.

omniscient and invulnerable being could be neither careful nor courageous. But the fact that we humans have laws pegged to our own condition does not entail that nonhuman agents who create humans can do with them as they please. The bringing-into-existence of agents capable of rational deliberation and moral agency is a grave matter, and it automatically triggers a general responsibility. Dr. Frankenstein had responsibility both for his children and for his monster.

The curious scientist we were imagining *intended* to bring sentient beings into existence, and most parents intentionally have children. However, this sort of intention is not essential to responsibility. Knowledge of the consequences of action will suffice. If an agent intends to bring about p, and believes that bringing about p will also bring about q, then the agent is morally responsible for the conjunctive state of affairs p and q. Being morally responsible for a state of affairs does not automatically entail being blameworthy, but it does entail that one can be called to account. A judge may know that imprisoning a particular individual will likely make that person a worse human being. The judge does not aim at the convict's moral deterioration, but — to the extent that discretion is involved in sentencing — can nevertheless be called to account, asked to answer for the fact that the prisoner is hardened in wickedness. The answer may be that the sentence is justified; or it may be that the price here is too high, the imprisonment unjustified. Either way, we are applying moral categories, undertaking moral evaluation.

The only support we have offered for premise 2 has appealed to examples about human agents. Can such examples suffice to establish the premise's more general claim concerning *all* agents, including world-creators?

If the examples cannot suffice, there must be a reason why. What difference between human and divine agents could confine humans to the moral realm but loose a divinity from the moral realm? Is it that humans are under ten feet tall? That we do things in time? That we need help? Imagine a small, weak person picking up a baseball bat and, unprovoked, killing his enemy with a series of blows; and then imagine a large, strong person striking his enemy once with his fist, killing him. The fact that the second agent is stronger than the first is irrelevant to our moral assessment of the acts. Why should the fact that a creator is bigger or stronger than we are pull the creator outside the realm of morality? Samuel Johnson dramatizes the point in his scathing reflections on Soame Jenyns's speculation that all is right with the world because superior beings are enjoying their sport with us:

[Jenyns] might have shown that these hunters whose game is man have many sports analogous to our own. As we drown whelps and kittens, they amuse themselves now and then with sinking a ship. . . . To swell a man with a tympany is as good sport as to blow a frog. Many a merry bout have these frolic beings at the vicissitudes of an ague, and good sport it is to see a man tumble with an epilepsy, and revive and tumble again, and all this he knows not why. As they are wiser and more powerful than we, they have more exquisite diversions. . . .[8]

Could the relevant difference be that divine intelligence is qualitatively different from human intelligence? Now, two things that are not in every respect similar can certainly be compared; in fact, any comparison necessarily involves dissimilarity. How much sameness does comparison require? Why should it be insufficient that both things being compared are intelligences? And a creator of our world would have relevant features in common with humans *in addition to* intelligence. The god we are imagining is a designer and creator; but then, so too are humans: we are designers and builders and procreators.

Are the Gods Crazy?   Human beings are, as a class, moral agents. Yet there can be exceptions within the class. A human being who is insane is an inappropriate subject for moral blame. (Interestingly, we often act as though praise can befit such a person, suggesting that some tie to morality remains — but we will set that aside.) The concept of "insanity" is, of course, problematic. Still, we understand enough about the concept to ask: Might a creator of this world be insane?

Many experts maintain that insanity is caused by some breakdown or failure or deficit in the brain. But a maker of the material world — a maker of everything material — will not itself have a brain or a body. We may set aside the question whether, for instance, a divine maker might at some point have used LSD or have been deprived of oxygen.

How can insanity be characterized in a way that avoids reference to bodily deficits? Insane people get things wildly wrong: "I'm a poached egg." Or "I'm Napoleon." Or "I'm the maker of the world; I can make things out of nothing." The insane person is marked by *cognitive incoherence,* detachment from reality. This general characterization can be tested against a listing of psychiatric disorders based on the DSM-IV.[9] There are anxiety disorders, which involve an inability to apprehend or process manifest facts (you are convinced that snakes live under your bed or that your hands need washing eleven times an hour). There are dissociative disorders, which typically involve feelings of

8. John Wain, *Samuel Johnson: A Biography* (New York: The Viking Press, 1974), p. 199.

9. See *The Merck Manual of Diagnosis and Therapy,* 17th edition, ed. Mark H. Beers and Robert Berkow (Whitehouse Station, NJ: Merck Research Laboratories, 1999), pp. 1503-98.

unreality (you feel like you are dreaming; you feel like your body is disconnected from you). Then there are mood disorders, which involve features such as reduced interest, inability to make decisions, unwarranted lack of self-confidence, and feelings of worthlessness. All of these signal that facts are not being processed, that there is a detachment from reality. Schizophrenia and related disorders probably provide the paradigmatic examples of insanity: they are characterized by such symptoms as delusions, hallucinations, and disorganized thinking and speech. In other words, they are paradigmatic cases of cognitive incoherence and detachment from reality. Lacking cognitive contact with reality, mentally ill people cease to be autonomous agents. They lack sufficient freedom, self-control, and self-directedness to *act*. The cognitive incoherence of insanity eviscerates the autonomous self. It is absurd to suppose that a creator of this world would suffer such a deficit.

3.3. Exploring the Second Option: The World-Creator Is in Some Measure Wicked

3.3.1. *The Difficulty of Arguing That a World-Creator Would Be Wicked*

What reason is there for thinking a world-creator is in some measure wicked?

Because we want to set up the options explored in this chapter dichotomously, we will use a very expansive conception of "wicked." When we speak of the possibility that a world-creator would be "in some measure" wicked, we mean to include even the slightest degrees of wickedness, the edges of wrongdoing. If you canoe in Minnesota's Boundary Waters and neglect to pack out a Snickers Marathon wrapper, you will count as wicked in some measure — as we are using the term here.

Given this broad understanding of wickedness, either a world-creator will be amoral or not; and if not, either a world-creator will be wicked or not (and if not, it will be wholly good). It follows from these definitions that an argument *against* the claim that a world-creator is wholly good will be an argument *for* the claim that a world-creator is in some measure wicked (assuming amorality is ruled out). Most of our substantive discussion of the difficulty of arguing that a world-creator would be wicked will be deferred to section 3.4, which takes up the "third option" concerning a world-creator's character, the option of goodness.

A few preliminary comments, however, are in order.

In Hume's *Dialogues*, Philo pronounces upon a set of options similar to those we have articulated:

There may *four* hypotheses be framed concerning the first causes of the universe: *that* they are endowed with perfect goodness; *that* they have perfect malice; *that* they are opposite and have both goodness and malice; *that* they have neither goodness nor malice. Mixed phenomena can never prove the two former unmixed principles; and the uniformity and steadiness of general laws seem to oppose the third. The fourth, therefore, seems by far the most probable.[10]

We agree with Hume's Philo that the uniformity and steadiness of the world's laws, its integration and stability, tell against the hypothesis that a committee or family of gods exhibiting a whole range of moral characters created the world. It tells also against the conjecture that a lone world-creator (if there exists only one) has a mixed moral character. No divided committees; no divided selves.

Another line of reasoning moves against the plausibility of mixtures, at least in the long run. There is a tremendous drive in religion in the direction of thinking that if there are supranatural agents creating or organizing or ruling the world, at least one of them is good. Some gods eat children. Others do worse. Yet, while wicked gods populate the old myths and turn up here and there in contemporary religions, the picture is never utterly horrific. No polytheism[11] altogether eliminates good deities. Or so we are told by standard surveys of religion. And even if it should turn out that someone, somewhere, at some time, held a narrow theism that did not countenance good deities, the significant fact remains that there is a drive toward thinking that if there is a god, there is at least one good god. Arguably, one good god — or one good part of a god with a mixed character — is enough for the eventual triumph of good. Many dualistic religions do predict the ultimate eradication of evil. (If our arguments concerning "cacodaemony" in the next section are correct, there is an asymmetry between good and evil that supports these predictions.)

In any event, the hypothesis that there are gods with mixed moral characters, or that there is a collective of gods, some good and some bad, is hardly a live option for most agnostic inquirers.

Now we have recently argued at some length — greater length than Hume

---

10. David Hume, *Dialogues Concerning Natural Religion,* ed. Richard H. Popkin (Indianapolis: Hackett Publishing Company, 1980), p. 75 [part XI].

11. Dualists posit an evil uncreated spirit, the ultimate source of all evil. But Zoroastrians and Manicheans (at least) would adamantly deny that the evil spirit is a god. As we are using the term "god," though, a god is not necessarily worthy of worship, and an evil spirit could count as a god.

goes to, anyway — that the position Philo gravitates toward is uninhabitable. It is implausible that a creator[12] of the universe is non-moral, neither good nor wicked.

Philo rejects the two remaining options: that the first causes have perfect malice and that they have perfect goodness. His argument for setting them aside is exceedingly compressed: he says merely that "mixed phenomena" can never prove "unmixed principles." When we go on to our "third option" concerning a world-creator's character, we will move more slowly. Perhaps certain *kinds* of phenomena would suffice to prove — or make it very likely — that a world-creator is not wholly good (and hence is wicked). We will entertain that possibility, thus taking the atheistic objections more seriously than Hume does.

Still, for a good number of inquirers, Hume's quick dismissal of the legitimacy of inferring from "mixed phenomena" to the wickedness or goodness of a creator will be instructive. Many who share Hume's skeptical bent will be inclined to agree that the sorts of "mixed phenomena" he has in mind are inconclusive. It appears difficult to infer from these phenomena that a world-creator is good; it appears difficult to infer the opposite.

Note, though, that the kinds of "mixed phenomena" Hume focuses on in the *Dialogues* — the travails of the flesh and torments of soul, on the one hand, and the captivating pleasures of body and mind, on the other — are not the only kinds of phenomena the world presents for our inspection. Hume leaves out of the calculation the lessons to be learned through study of the content of revelatory claims. One might easily think that if the sorts of facts on which Hume is focused do not obviously support any of the available hypotheses about a world-creator's character, then it is eminently reasonable to go ahead and look at putative communications from a world-creator, thus expanding the evidential base. That should be an especially attractive option for an inquirer who has accepted our argument thus far, and has come to believe both that it is not highly unlikely that there is a world-creator and that it is plausible that moral categories apply to a world-creator.

The sense that it is indeed reasonable for an agnostic inquirer to examine putative communications from a world-creator can be reinforced when we consider a line of argument that focuses on a striking fact: it is exceedingly difficult to construct a cacodaemony, and more difficult to construct a cacodaemony than a theodicy.

---

12. For ease of discussion, we have been speaking of "a" creator of the universe, though our argument in the last chapter concerning a world-creator's existence did not rule out the possibility of multiple causes, multiple creators, which possibility Hume entertains. However, the argument could be re-expressed to apply to the possibility of multiple creators.

3.3.2. Good Reason for Thinking a World-Creator
Likely Would Not Be Wicked

Philosophers do not labor to produce "cacodaemonies" that explain how the *good* in the world might coexist with a maximally evil Demon.[13] William James said that there is no problem of good, and in one sense he is right: there is no gnashing of teeth over the world's sweetness and grandeur, its people's loving and noble deeds. Nevertheless, the exercise of cacodaemony-construction is illuminating. We will argue that whatever the obstacles to building theodicies, they are less formidable than those blocking the construction of cacodaemonies.

Think, first, of an idea at the core of theodicies prominent in the Middle Ages: evil is a privation of good. It is highly counterintuitive to suppose that good is a privation of evil. Why? On a definitional level, the goodness of a thing may be understood without reference to any privation (though it cannot be understood without reference to its contradictory opposite), while the evil of a thing cannot be understood without reference to the desirable. A desirable condition can be depicted without the idea that it might be lost. Furthermore, the idea that evil is a privation is played out in moral theories as well as theodicies; but no moral theorist (atheist or theist) supposes good is a privation of evil. And further still, the idea that evil is a privation is rooted in metaphysical speculations that antedate monotheism and that are developed by a variety of non-theistic philosophers, but atheistic metaphysicians do not argue that good is a privation of evil. For all these reasons, then, the supposition that good is a privation of evil is a nonstarter for cacodaemony-construction.

Another kind of long-standing theodicy explains the evil of suffering as punishment for sin. (This broad type of theodicy may overlap with theodicies emphasizing that evil is a privation of good.) Might physical or natural goods be explained as a "reward" for sin, an inducement to wrongdoing? Not easily, because correlations we would expect to see in the natural order — wrongdoing generally producing deep joy — are nowhere to be found. Real pleasures supervene on good actions. Long before the advent of neuroscience, Aristotle observed that pleasure completes an action properly performed. Biologists today explain how pleasure facilitates a being's proper operation.

---

13. Steven Cahn used the term "cacodaemony" to refer to a converse of a theodicy. See Steven Cahn, "Cacodaemony," *Analysis* 37, no. 2 (1977). Cahn briefly sketches a soul-breaking cacodaemony that he holds to be "just as strong as Hick's [soul-making] theodicy," though he thinks that "neither . . . is successful" (p. 73).

Aesthetic theodicies also have an extended genealogy. The suggestion that our world as a whole might be ugly, horrid, or revolting, might offend our aesthetic sensibilities, will strike most people as bizarre. For the bigger our picture of the universe and its workings, the more order we discern, and the more beautiful the whole appears. Nor is it clear that a world that as a whole has some degree of complexity could be ugly, for where there is complexity, it is difficult (if not impossible) to elude order, and where there is order, a key component of beauty exists. People may allow that our world contains much that is bad and yet be hard-pressed to view it as ugly. Plato's Socrates says in the *Republic:* "[G]ood things are fewer than bad things in our life."[14] Nevertheless, Plato judges the world to be a *cosmos,* a thing that is beautiful.[15]

So it is difficult even to know where to begin in constructing a cacodaemony on the cornerstone that good is the privation of evil, or that the world's goods are rewards for sin, or that good is an essential part of a universe that is on the whole ugly. And the problems encountered do not parallel the problems of theodicy-construction; they are worse. The "problem of good" for demonists is less manageable than the problem of evil.

The project of constructing cacodaemonies isomorphic to standard theodicies could be much more broadly and deeply engaged. We will limit ourselves here to one further comparison, a more detailed comparison than we have thus far provided. Though initially it may look as though it is possible to construct converses of free-will theodicies, upon closer examination it appears that the converses lack foundations as strong as theodicies' foundations. We will not argue that free-will theodicies or defenses of divine goodness succeed. Rather, we will argue that free-will cacodaemonies are less successful than their counterpart theodicies.

Let us take as a paradigmatic example of a free-will theodicy (using "theodicy" broadly) Alvin Plantinga's free-will defense of God's goodness. As earlier noted, this defense is intended to show that God's existence is consistent with the existence of evil: evils are justified by referring them to the good of free will. Can we invert Plantinga's line of reasoning and thus obtain a cacodaemony? The inverted account would assert that it is possible that this world contains more moral evil than moral good, and that any other world a Demon could have created containing free creatures would have had a ratio of evil to good less desirable from a demonistic standpoint, and that all of the world's goods are moral goods (goods attributable to the

---

14. Plato, *Republic* 379c; G. M. A. Grube, trans., *Plato's Republic* (Indianapolis: Hackett Publishing, 1974), p. 49.

15. The etymology of "cosmos" is reflected in the word "cosmetic."

free actions of spirits). On this analysis, we would explain goods by seeing them as unavoidable consequences of a world with agents freely choosing to perform evil actions.[16]

However, there are at least two points at which the symmetry between free-will cacodaemony and free-will theodicy breaks down.

In the first place, free will itself has positive value. (Kant argues that freedom gives the world "inner worth.") True, the free-will theodicist typically emphasizes all the wonderful things that can come when free will is rightly used. In and of itself, though, apart from any of its consequences, the possession of free will is a great good. Free will confers dignity and value. This fact helps the theodicist and hurts the cacodaemonist.

The second asymmetry between a free-will defense and a free-will cacodaemony can be uncovered when we consider two situations:

1) A person performs an evil action, and then comes to repent of it, and uses the repentance to better love individuals wronged by the evil action.
2) A person performs a good action, then turns to wickedness, and "repents" of the good, using the recollection of performing good to better appreciate and extend the depths of depravity.

Scenario 2 ill fits the psychology of wickedness. Mary Midgley masterfully depicts human wickedness as a perversion and corruption of positive capacities.[17] In most cases, she points out, evildoers carefully avoid thinking about what they are doing. For the sake of the argument, however, let us assume that both situations 1 and 2 might obtain.

Now we are ourselves inclined to say that in scenario 1, the evil action is redeemed or transformed, used to build something highly valuable, whereas in 2, the original good is *not* co-opted, or transformed, or used to build something evil. Freely chosen good actions have a value that cannot be diminished, regardless of what else happens. Freely chosen evil actions have a disvalue that can be transformed, redeemed by repentance and atonement. Our point is not that good actions cannot have evil consequences, or that it is impossible for a thoroughly wicked person to acknowledge authorship of past good actions. Rather, the point is that a freely performed act of compassion or self-

16. There are various questions a critic of this cacodaemony might raise; perhaps (as Cahn suggests) some of them point to difficulties with the theistic free-will defense. But see John King-Farlow's response to Cahn in "Cacodaemony and Devilish Isomorphism," *Analysis* 38, no. 1 (1978).

17. Mary Midgley, *Wickedness: A Philosophical Essay* (London: Routledge & Kegan Paul, 1984).

sacrifice or bravery cannot be tarnished regardless of subsequent occurrences, while a freely performed act of cruelty or greed or cowardice actually can be redeemed. Good can be drawn out of evil; evil cannot be drawn out of good. Or so we are inclined to say. Good and evil are radically asymmetrical.

Can our view of the matter accommodate the following scenario?[18] Suppose there is a maximally evil creator who knows that free will is a necessary condition for moral good and evil. Suppose also that the evil creator knows what is just, and that justice is more or less what we take it to be. Presumably this maximally evil creator would aim to be as unjust as possible. Suppose it knows that to fulfill this aim it must repay moral good with evil. So the Demon creates beings who are capable of moral good and moral evil. If some are morally evil, its goal of having moral evil is realized. If some are morally good, and ultimately repent of early evil acts, then the Demon can realize moral evil in the form of injustice by giving them hellfire in proportion to their moral goodness. So, even though moral agents can transform their own evil acts by later redeeming good action, even though good can in this manner be drawn out of evil, and even if evil cannot be in the same way drawn out of good, it looks like evil triumphs in the end: the Demon unjustly punishes redemptive human acts of good, and any human act of good provides the Demon with another opportunity for injustice.

However, two elements of that scenario undercut its utility for the cacodaemonist.

First, this cacodaemony appeals essentially to the moral evil involved in the Demon's wicked infliction of pain on good human beings: good acts are "punished" with suffering. Without counting the Demon's wickedness in assessing the balance of good and evil in the world, there is no hope of getting evil to come out on top. Traditionally, though, free-will theodicies or defenses of God's goodness exclude God's good action (in and of itself) as part of the total when weighing up the good and evil in the world. Perhaps because the Demon's evilness has the mark of the inexplicable, the mark of the absurd, there is a tendency to sweep it together with the evils of the material world.

Second, in a free-will theodicy or defense of God's goodness, moral evils are actually *integrated* into a larger picture. In a cacodaemony, the "punishment" inflicted by the Demon — the wicked infliction of pain — plays no integrative role at all. The pain the Demon administers is not deserved by the

---

18. This scenario was described by Charles Kielkopf in his commentary on Sandra Menssen's 1997 ACPA presentation on the possibility of cacodaemony (Sandra Menssen, "Maximal Wickedness vs. Maximal Goodness," *Proceedings of the American Catholic Philosophical Association* LXXI [1997]).

humans; it is not proportional to the choices they have made. Thus there is no whole that integrates the good into a larger evil state of affairs. Evil cannot integrate good into a larger whole because of objective facts about what good and evil are: evil is destructive.[19]

We may underscore this second point by recognizing a couple of different ways in which evils might be said to be necessary for goods. First, *your losing an apple* (it is stolen, you drop it, and so on) is necessary$_1$ for *your apple being replaced*. Second, *a thief's stealing your apple* is necessary$_2$ for *the thief's returning your apple repentantly, and your forgiving the thief.* In the second scenario we have an initial evil that is integrated into a larger whole. This is not the case in the first scenario. Even though the first scenario can, like the second, be specified in a way that makes the particular evil (you lose an apple) logically necessary for a particular good (your lost apple is replaced), the *sort* of evil in the first scenario is not logically necessary for the *sort* of good. The fact that the replacement of your lost apple is a good depends on the fact that the apple serves some valuable purpose (most basically, it provides nutrition). Your losing an item of food is not necessary for your being provided with nutritive goods. When we move to the second scenario, things change: the general moral goods of repentance and forgiveness presuppose moral evils. So, in traditional theodicy, evils integrated into a larger counterbalancing whole are in a special way logically necessary for the greater good. The same cannot be said of the good acts that give rise to the Demon's wicked infliction of pain in our cacodaemony. In the cacodaemony the good acts of humans trigger the Demon's infliction of pain. Moral good is not, however, a kind of thing that is necessary$_2$ for wicked infliction of pain.

A critic may respond that this just plays into the hands of the cacodaemonist. We have said that an evil Demon who "punishes" good acts does not produce a unified, integrated whole. But a cacodaemonist might not want to argue that a Demon would create a world with integrity, a unified whole. It might suit a cacodaemonist perfectly well to imagine a Demon making a disunified, chaotic whole.

If the cacodaemonist takes this tack, however, a new difficulty arises. Due to the difference just described between the two kinds of logically necessary connections, the theodicist can *explain* the whole in a way the cacodaemonist cannot. Superficially, the cacodaemonist can "explain" what goes on in the

---

19. When Aquinas indicates that God is so powerful that he can draw good even out of evil, he phrases the point, not by saying that God can always produce a good great enough to counterbalance evil, but rather by indicating that the evil is in a way developed or integrated into a whole that is good. Aquinas, *Summa Theologiae* I, q. 2, a. 3, ad 1.

world by referring to the evil character of the creator. Yet that evil character cannot be explained as well as a good character could be explained. Explanations go beyond correlations: the best explanations provide intelligibility, rooted in the structure of the thing being explained. (The Socratic view that virtue is knowledge, and that evil involves ignorance, is linked to the inexplicability of evil. Choosing not to do what you know is right to do is absurd.) As an insane world-creator would be marked by *cognitive incoherence,* one sort of detachment from reality, a wicked world-creator would be marked by *appetitive incoherence,* a different sort of detachment. Now an inability to explain the evilness of a creator does not mean that it is impossible for an evil creator to exist. But it counts for something, maybe for quite a bit, in assessing the relative likelihoods that a world-creator would be good, and that a world-creator would be evil.

Therefore, reflection on free-will theodicy and cacodaemony reinforces the conclusion we tentatively reached when briefly considering other kinds of theodicy and cacodaemony. We cannot conjure up evil-twin cacodaemonies for standard theodicies. It looks as though it is a better bet that there is a successful theodicy than that there is a successful cacodaemony.

3.4. Exploring the Third Option: The World-Creator Is Wholly Good

3.4.1. Two Pertinent Problems: "Pie-in-the-Sky" Theodicy and Substandard Worlds

The upshot of our exploration thus far concerning the moral character of a world-creator is this: there is good reason to think a world-creator would not be amoral, and good reason to think it is more difficult to establish that a world-creator would be wholly wicked than that it would be wholly good (and little reason to be drawn to the hypothesis of a partially wicked world-creator). This does not *compel* adoption of the position that a world-creator would be wholly good. Even so, these considerations should undercut resistance to considering seriously the content of revelatory claims — if it is granted that a world-creator's existence is not highly unlikely.

However, a skeptical agnostic inquirer may think that something must have gone wrong somewhere in our argument, even if it is difficult to say exactly where. An inquirer may think that the world's evils make it pretty obvious that some rule of world-making has been violated by any supranatural agent who created our world, *if* the agent is all-powerful and all-knowing. (Here we assume a world-creator who is omnipotent and omniscient because without that assumption the problem of evil is all too easily handled. In this context the assumption handicaps the theist.)

If an inquiring agnostic has a strong inclination to think that putative revelations will be unable to show that evil might exist in a world made by a good God, a leaning that persists through reflection on the possibility of an amoral or wicked creator, it likely will be lodged in something pretty close to a conviction that *a rule of world-making has been violated,* if a world-maker exists. Will a good God necessarily set things up so as to achieve the very best that can be achieved for each of us? Will a good God necessarily give each creature a life that is on the whole worth living? Will a good God necessarily bring it about that each instance of suffering results in a justifying good for the sufferer (unless the sufferer refuses to cooperate)? An extensive philosophical literature has explored such questions, along with the rules for world-making that their answers have generated.

The world-making rules that have any plausibility will have to take into account the fact that major revelatory traditions foretell a world to come in which God's goodness to creatures is made manifest. Surely it would be premature to decide that one of these rules definitely has not been followed without pondering the goods promised by putative revelations. How can a person judge that a creator has failed to do the very best for some individual, or has failed to give an individual a life on the whole worth living, or has failed to set things up so that each instance of suffering produces a justifying good for the sufferer, without getting some sense of the dimensions of the entirety of the individual's life, which, revelations tell us, includes existence in a promised world to come? Now "rules" concerning goodness to creatures can be set forth such that it can be seen right away that they have been breached by a creator of this world, if there is a creator. For instance: "Never make a creature that is susceptible to pain." That is, by the way, a rule that precludes the making of human beings, and hence precludes your existence. ("I exist; therefore there is no God.") But the rules that have a modicum of plausibility will need to countenance the promises of revelations.

So, generally speaking, determining that a rule concerning a creator's goodness to individuals has not been met, or could not be met, or probably has not been met, will require carefully examining the nature of promised *compensations.* And that means pondering the content of revelatory claims. This, of course, is what we urge agnostic inquirers to do.

"Wait," the skeptic may protest. "This entire scheme dreamed up in major revelatory traditions, in which a master deity builds evils into this world and then compensates the afflicted by providing benefactions in a world to come, is preposterous. And that can be seen without looking closely at revelatory claims to ponder the wonderful nature of the promised compensations. Compensatory schemes of the kind described in revelations are themselves foul affairs. And this for at least two reasons. First, as Socrates, Plato, and Aristotle contend, there are certain things a virtuous person will never do. (Some religions, including Christianity, forbid humans from doing evil to achieve good.) But the point applies to the gods as well. A world-creator must not do evil, no matter what: the end does not justify the means. So a world-creator must not intend evil, regardless of the loss of potential great goods, and despite compensations promised the unfortunates who get used for some allegedly glorious end. And second, as Kant has shown, an omnipotent and omniscient creator who promises compensations in an afterlife thereby undercuts the moral order, and so cannot be good. For these two reasons, there is no point in looking into the specifics of the promises made by revelatory claims: the rough contours of these consequentialist religious fantasies suffice to show that they cannot evidence a purely good God."[20]

In the following section we take up this protest.

Another protest may follow (and in the section after the following section we address it). The new protest, which focuses on the quality of the world *as a whole,* has, in one form or another, engaged natural theologians for a long time. Some critics of theism lament that we humans obviously dwell in a world far from the best. Others, uncertain that there is such a thing as a best possible world, maintain merely that the world is *not good enough* to have been made by a wholly good creator who is omnipotent and omniscient. These are philosophers' objections, abstract and general. But after all, our inquirer is philosophical, and so the questions may easily arise. *These concerns — unlike those based directly on the prevalence and magnitude of suffering — are not obviously addressed by revelatory claims.* For that reason, an inquirer may think that it is pointless to go on to thorough exploration of the content of these claims. How could revelations possibly handle philosophical objections about the goodness of the world as a whole?

---

20. Another reason for being reluctant to attribute the intention of evil to a creator if the creator is to be identified with anything like God (though not a reason pointing to the immorality of divine compensatory schemes) is that the attribution seems to limit God's omnipotence, since it seems to imply that God would have no way to bring about a good except by doing evil. See John Haldane, *An Intelligent Person's Guide to Religion* (London: Duckworth, 2003), p. 91.

3.4.2. Handling Objections Concerning "Pie-in-the-Sky" Theodicy

3.4.2.1. Intending Evil

Many have said that Judaeo-Christian Scripture itself pictures a consequentialist god who intends wrongdoing. The Lord says to Moses: "I will harden Pharaoh's heart, and I will multiply my signs and wonders in the land of Egypt. When Pharaoh does not listen to you, I will lay my hand upon Egypt and bring my people the Israelites, company by company, out of the land of Egypt by great acts of judgment."[21] Here it appears as though God *intends* Pharaoh's wickedness, planning to use Pharaoh's hardened heart as a means to some (putatively) good end. However, highly reputable readings of Judaeo-Christian Scripture understand God's "hardening hearts" as metaphorical: the initially troubling language is by itself no proof that the God of Scripture is immoral.

Still, the objection goes, regardless of how Judaeo-Christian Scripture is interpreted, it can be shown that an omnipotent, omniscient creator of this world does intend evil.

What is it to intend something? *Intendere* is formed on *tendere* (to stretch out toward or tend toward): to intend a thing is to seek that thing. In particular circumstances, it is quite possible to aim at or seek things that one would in some abstract sense prefer to avoid. To take Aristotle's example, if you throw cargo over the side of a ship to keep the ship from sinking, you are intending to throw the cargo over, though you regret its loss.

Now a world-creator's intending suffering would not automatically preclude its being wholly good. For to intend suffering is not necessarily to fix the will on evildoing. Indeed, it would be very difficult to defend the proposition that an omnipotent, omniscient creator of this world wills no suffering, for nociceptors, containing unmyelinated C fibers and lightly myelinated Aδ fibers, appear designed to produce pain. A world like ours could, for all we know, be built without excesses of suffering but not without creatures who feel pain. Scarcely any pleasure is *not* associated with some sort of pain.[22] No thirst, no slaking of thirst; no hunger for food or sex, no satisfaction. To request to exist in a world without pain may be to request to be a Cartesian mind attached to . . . well, not to a human body — perhaps to a plant. In any

---

21. Exod. 7:3-4 (NRSV).

22. Plato argues in the *Gorgias* that intellectual pleasures are, among all pleasures, least bound up with pain. Aristotle ties this thought to the essence of happiness, describing contemplation as the purest, least mixed, pleasure. In so doing, he points in the direction of a heavenly state in which pleasures are in no way bound to pain.

event, as we say, willing suffering is not necessarily a matter of fixing the will on the *doing* of evil. If a creator wills suffering, the question of how the suffering might be compensated is surely raised. And here, we have suggested, the content of revelatory claims must be brought into the picture.

To intend wrongdoing is to fix the will on evildoing, and that is itself evil: the assertion that a particular omnipotent and omniscient creator is good is automatically invalidated if the creator intends wrongdoing.

Why think that an omnipotent and omniscient creator of our world, if such exists, must intend wrongdoing?

In the first place, it might be suggested, wrongdoing exists. And if an all-powerful, all-knowing deity intended that there be no wrongdoing, then there would be none. So, *if* there is such a deity, then the deity intends that there be wrongdoing.

However, as Aquinas noted, although "There is wrongdoing" and "It is not the case there is wrongdoing" are contradictories, the contradictory of "God intends that there is no wrongdoing" is not "God intends that there is wrongdoing" but rather "It is not the case that God intends that there is no wrongdoing."[23] An intermediate state exists between the two extremes of "God intends that there is wrongdoing" and "God intends that there is no wrongdoing." The intermediate state is the state in which God *permits* but does *not intend* wrongdoing. As an illustration of this point, consider the following.[24] A young boy has been taking money from his mother's purse. The mother knows what has been happening. She asks her son if he has been taking the money; he denies it. Soon afterward, she walks into the kitchen and sees him reaching toward the purse on the counter. She stops and remains silent. The boy takes five dollars from the purse. Only then does his mother force the confrontation that makes possible a serious discussion of lying and stealing, of trust and forgiveness. She does not stand silent in order for her son to steal. If he had stopped his hand halfway to her purse and withdrawn it, she would have been thrilled. She permits, but does not intend, the wrongdoing. Similarly, an omnipotent, omniscient world-creator might merely permit wrongdoing. The book of Job gives us a picture of Yahweh as doing just that: Satan goes to God for permission to afflict Job.

Another reason for thinking an omnipotent, omniscient creator of our world could not but intend wrongdoing is that such a world-creator would *foresee* wrongdoing attached to intended states of affairs; and, it might be maintained, that entails that the world-creator would intend the accompany-

---

23. See Aquinas, *Summa Theologiae* I, q. 19, a. 9, ad 3.
24. We thank Peter Shea for this illustration.

ing wrongdoing. For, it might be said, whenever a person intends to bring about a particular state of affairs, the person intends any states of affairs that are foreseen to attach to the targeted state of affairs.

We would grant that Roderick Chisholm's principle of "the diffusiveness of intentions" entails the skeptic's claim.[25] But that diffusiveness principle can be defeated. Imagine a man with an injured knee who cannot avoid limping to some degree. If he is in the path of an oncoming car and he intends to save himself, then he will try not to limp, insofar as it is within his power, because the limping slows his effort; and trying entails intending, so he intends not to limp, though he believes he will limp — and he does.

One final reason for thinking that an all-powerful, all-knowing creator of our world would necessarily intend wrongdoing is worth considering. It may look as though a creator (at least a creator who acts anything like the God portrayed in major revelations) uses wrongdoing as a *means* to its ends. If a creator does indeed use wrongdoing as a means to its ends, then we agree that it intends wrongdoing. However, we deny the following contention, which will need to figure in the objection:

> If some human act of wrongdoing or sin, s, is necessary for some good end, e, then necessarily: if a world-creator wills not to assist the human being in refraining from s (not to give "grace"), and the world-creator intends or wills e, and wills for the sake of e not to provide assistance, then the world-creator wills s.

Why think this contention is correct? The reasoning may go something like this: If an agent intends an end, then the agent must will whatever means are necessary for the end; and if s (my delight in your pain, let us say) is necessary for e (your feeling pity for my depraved condition), then if an agent wills e, the agent wills s. But this argument is invalid. Instead of the claim that

s is necessary for e,

one needs the claim that

s is a necessary *means* to e.

But s is not a necessary means to e in the particular example given.

What could be wished to underwrite the claim that an agent uses s as a

25. See Roderick M. Chisholm, "The Structure of Intention," *The Journal of Philosophy* LXVII (1970): 636. See also Joseph M. Boyle Jr. and Thomas D. Sullivan, "The Diffusiveness of Intention Principle: A Counter-Example," *Philosophical Studies* (Holland) 31, no. 5 (1977).

means to e other than that s is a necessary condition of e? We grant that there is a loose and improper sense of "means" where it is taken as something that is necessary if something else is to obtain. A stricter sense of "means" is, however, often operative in our talk. Imagine that Robin Hood wants to hit a bull's-eye with an arrow. All kinds of things are necessary conditions for him to do so: he must exist, certain laws of physics must obtain, and so on. But neither Robin Hood's existence nor a certain set of physical laws is properly called a means to his end of hitting the target. Even if Friar Tuck explains the laws of physics to Robin, that scarcely makes them means. To identify means, we must ask: What must the agent *do* to achieve the end? Robin Hood might himself bring about certain states of affairs that figure in his shooting but that do not count as means. He might, for instance, put an apple core on the stump of a tree and walk off; later, as he passes by, he shoots his arrow through the apple core. His placing the apple on a stump is not a means to his end because he did not do it as part of a plan. A stage for action is needed, but the action is what the agent *undertakes to bring about* on this stage. A man who limps out of the way of an oncoming car, moving as quickly as possible, is not using his limp as a means of escape, though it is a necessary condition for escape, given, let us say, a knee with two torn ligaments. Presented with an end that is sought and a question concerning whether something that necessarily accompanies that end is intended, we need to ask: Is the "something" constitutive of the end (as humming the first bar of a song is constitutive of humming the whole song)? Is the "something" actually productive of the end (i.e., does the agent, in a certain context, structure a situation so as to gear it for an end)? If the answer to both these questions is "No," then the concomitant is not necessarily intended.

3.4.2.2. *Undercutting the Moral Order by Promising Other-Worldly Compensations*

Let us then assume that an all-powerful, all-knowing world-maker might permit but would not intend wrongdoing. Still, an objector may continue, if the creator is anything like the one portrayed by leading revelatory traditions, the creator promises compensations for the evils it permits . . . and thereby undercuts the moral order itself.

This difficulty appears prominently in Susan Neiman's thought-provoking reflections on evil in modern thought. Following Kant, she suggests that, if we knew the connection between right action and rewards, then right action would become impossible. Kant is at his most stunning, she says, when he denies that it would be good for us to know the connections between right action and virtue. He sees such knowledge as "not only metaphysically impossible but morally disastrous."[26] Neiman illustrates the point. She asks that we imagine our relationships with people in power: it is virtually impossible to completely eliminate hope for the goods they can bestow. Only a saint could manage that; only a saint could treat the very powerful in the right ways, for the right reasons.

So a skeptic may urge our agnostic inquirer to resist the notion that a creator who builds evils into the world can get off the hook by promising and then providing pie-in-the-sky, individually tailored compensation packages that will make up for each person's suffering. A purely good creator would set things up differently, the skeptic charges. On the religious picture of things, we all are living in occupied territory: it is occupied by a deity. Everything we think and do is known to the deity, who enumerates not only every hair on our heads but every wayward impulse we fail immediately to check. And because *we* know that an omnipresent God knows everything, pure and true moral action is impossible.

A simple response can be made here. People (most of us, anyway) do not know the connection between right action and rewards; at least, we are not vividly and habitually — or constantly — aware of any such connection. Even believers feel the need to remind each other of what it is all about. "Do you think you can get away with that? You're a Christian!" The regular (weekly, daily) exhortations to good behavior that believers offer one another show the tenuousness of our grasp of the implications of a final reckoning.

Furthermore, though the particular case Neiman mentions involving our relationship with the rich and powerful provides some support for her point — it is indeed hard to tell whether you are being nice to such people for the right reason — if we consider matters more fully, it looks as though many normal human relationships cannot be honorable within the view she is presenting, which is some evidence against that view. After all, many people are attracted to each other — form intimate unions with one another — for the purpose of having children. Are all these relationships degraded? Neiman observes that it is difficult to smile at the powerful for the correct reason. But imagine being asked why you are smiling at your fiancée. You would not say: "Ethical, gracious people are smiley people. That's just what one does . . . I'm certainly not smiling at my beloved because I *like* my beloved, or find my beloved attractive." Now there may be some kinds of activities (almsgiving, say) where, if you think of any good at all, it should be the good of others. But in

26. Susan Neiman, *Evil in Modern Thought: An Alternative History of Philosophy* (Princeton, NJ: Princeton University Press, 2002), p. 67.

many other kinds of relationships — with neighbors, friends, soldiers at arms, comrades, spouses — it is impossible to keep the nature of the relationship out of mind. You think, what a loss it would be to *me* if this person were to die! That is the fact of the matter. We are inclined to tie goods to ends.

Not only does Kant concede this fact, but in the very work to which Neiman gives serious attention, Kant infers from the impossibility of acting without attending to the good a remarkable consequence concerning the connection between morality and religion:

> But now, if the strictest observance of the moral laws is to be thought of as the cause of the ushering in of the highest good (as end), then, since human capacity does not suffice to effect happiness in the world proportionate to the worthiness to be happy, an omnipotent moral being must be assumed as ruler of the world, under whose care this would come about, i.e., morality leads inevitably to religion.[27]

So, how can it be a mark against a revelation (on the Kantian view) that the revelation assures us that what Kant postulates is in fact the case?

Still, the objector or skeptic may persist: "While Kant concedes that it is impossible to *motivate* conduct in accordance with the law without appealing to goods, on his view those goods have nothing to do with what makes a law a law. You might ask a mathematician: 'Could you unfold the laws of mathematics for me?' The mathematician responds: 'Why should I? Give me some motivation.' You will not get mathematics unfolded without reference to motivation, but it does not follow that whatever motivation is provided is part of the mathematical system. Similarly, morality stands above motivation, though it is possible to ask 'Why should I be moral?' In fact, you have looked right past Kant's famous claim that morality cannot be based on ends. He has a deeply challenging argument that moves against your position. The passage you have just quoted from Kant is either inconsistent with his deepest thinking, or, if consistent, is expressive not of his conception of the moral law itself but of a theory of human motivation."

What, then, is the argument in Kant that grounds this famous position that morality cannot be based on ends? It is hard to say. One thinks, of course, of the *Groundwork of the Metaphysics of Morals* as making things plain, plain enough to be unfolded before generation after generation of undergraduates. But consider Paul Guyer's comment:

27. Immanuel Kant, *Religion within the Boundaries of Mere Reason,* trans. and ed. Allen Wood and George di Giovanni; intro. by Robert Merrihew Adams (Cambridge, UK: Cambridge University Press, 1998), p. 36 [6:8].

In spite of two centuries of study and many fine commentaries, Kant's *Groundwork for the Metaphysics of Morals* remains a deeply perplexing book. . . . [There are many questions about his three formulations of the categorical imperative, CI] — about which ones they are, about the relationships that Kant intended to establish among them, about the basis from which he thought he could derive them and the manner in which he intended them to be derived from this basis, and about the relationship between the argument for and about the three formulations of CI in *Groundwork* II and the argument of the remainder of the book. . . .[28]

That is enough to put one on notice that a problem with Kant's work we mentioned in chapter 1 reappears in a new connection: his argument that morality cannot be based on ends flunks the test for clarity.

We could quit with this observation; yet it is worth pushing on a bit.

Consider Kant's striking argument from *Religion within the Boundaries of Mere Reason,* which can look like a concise refutation of the idea that morality rests on any ends. As Kant puts his point, since the laws of morality "bind through the mere form of universal lawfulness . . . morality needs absolutely no material determining ground . . . that is no end. . . ."[29] And if it binds through the *mere* form of universal lawfulness, then it cannot have a material determining ground. His argument seems to go as follows:

1) Either in all cases the ground of duty is merely formal, or not.
2) If not, there are three possibilities: first, the ground is found in self-love directed to one's own comfort; second, the ground is directed to one's perfection; and third, the ground is directed to the happiness of others.
3) The first possibility mentioned in 2 can be eliminated: rank egoism is unacceptable; everyone concedes that self-love directed to one's own comfort is not the ground of the moral law.
4) The second possibility mentioned in 2 can be eliminated: one's perfection can be understood in only two ways, neither of which works — either a) it is understood as *natural* perfection, enhancement of skills in the arts and sciences, physical agility, and so forth, in which case the perfections can be misused, and so cannot ground duty; or b) it is understood as *moral* perfection, in which case one would be "defining in a circle."
5) The third possibility mentioned in 2 can be eliminated by applying the

---

28. Paul Guyer, *Kant on Freedom, Law, and Happiness* (Cambridge, UK: Cambridge University Press, 2000), pp. 172-73.

29. Kant, *Religion within the Boundaries of Mere Reason,* p. 33 [6:3-4].

reasoning in 3 and 4 to cases in which the focus is on the comfort and happiness of others (rather than oneself).
6) So, in all cases the ground of duty is merely formal.

What can be said in reply? Quite a lot. We limit ourselves here to two brief comments on premise 4; in chapter 5 we continue the discussion.

In the first place, we should note that Kant's division in 4 between natural and moral perfections is not exhaustive. *Supranatural* perfections are left out of the picture. If the only kind of ethics that works is ultimately supranatural, then natural and moral perfections are subordinate to a supranatural and encompassing end. Aquinas, commenting on Aristotle, noted that the fullest perfection requires an attendant affection for the highest objects, and that if knowledge and affection are considered as natural capacities or perfections, they both must bear on the right objects to fully perfect the bearer of the perfections. When *that* is the understanding of "natural perfection," it cannot be misused. It must be left as an open question whether there is a supranatural end in prospect.

Second, consider the claim that natural perfections can be misused. It is true enough that intellectual and artistic perfections, for instance, can be applied to perverted ends. But not every natural perfection can be misused. And to block the conclusion of the argument, all it takes is a single natural perfection that cannot be misused. Here is one: the disposition for social relationships, and especially for friendship. Parents who want to endow their children with natural perfections would surely aim to foster this disposition. Now if you are going to have real friendships, you must actually be worthy of trust: being such that people *believe* you are trustworthy cannot ground true friendship. Being trustworthy cannot be misused, not in the way that intellectual or physical talents can be. (*Others* may take advantage of a person's trustworthiness, but the well-socialized individual who is trustworthy cannot misuse the trustworthiness.)

It might be objected: "You have smuggled in under talk of 'socialization' a moral virtue, a fixed disposition to behave well. So you are not arguing from the goal of instilling natural perfection, but rather from the goal of instilling moral perfection." However, it is quite possible for natural perfections to presuppose virtues or fixed moral habits. Reasoning superbly, for instance, presupposes studiousness. But that does not mean natural perfections are themselves virtues. Thus we are not "defining in a circle."

We have aspired here to put our finger on some deficiencies in Kant's purportedly "knock-down" argument against the idea that moral laws are grounded in ends. Admittedly, a great deal more remains to be said on both sides of the question. Yet we are entitled to hold on to ordinary beliefs unless driven from them by philosophical arguments based on premises at least as secure as our pretheoretical assumptions. It is a natural assumption of any mature person that laws make sense only if they are attached to goods in prospect. The mere existence of a philosophical position that denies the connection should not neutralize the initial assumption. A compelling argument is needed. And the above argument scarcely looks compelling. Moreover, when we look at Kant's more positive account of his own theory, what do we find? A theory so obscure in its essentials that, as Guyer notes, two hundred years of study have produced little illumination.

When Guyer himself lights a lamp, we see beneath the three or four or five distinct formulations of Kant's categorical imperative the idea that what gives binding force to the moral law is its connection to what constitutes human dignity. In Kant's judgment, what elevates human beings above the brutes is the human capacity to achieve independence from the demands of nature, which is achieved through freedom and self-legislation. And the notion that freedom is an end is reconciled with Kant's bedrock principle that the moral law has to be necessary and universal. Respect for humanity, grounded in our capacity for freedom, is not a contingent, but a necessary end. The categorical imperative thus becomes a means that is subordinated to the end of freedom, including the preservation and enhancement of freedom. And the distinction between "teleological" and "deontological" ethics is undercut.[30] Now this understanding of Kant may be defective. Still, Guyer's is an understanding seemingly as justified by the text as that of any other commentator in the long struggle to bring Kant's theory to light. (In our opinion, Guyer's suggestions, and the texts from Kant, far from undercutting the idea that ends can be grounds for morality, give strong support to a thesis we later introduce concerning divine ordination as the foundation of morality.)

On this reading, then, the cornerstone of the Kantian system is the achievement of a certain kind of end. It is not Aristotle's end, contemplation of a deity, nor Aquinas's end, contemplation of a deity attended by appropriate affection, and certainly not the end of a utilitarian celebrating the maxi-

---

30. Guyer observes that his reading might be seen as implying that Kant's theory turns out to be teleological rather than deontological. That is not problematic in Guyer's view, for on his reading, Kant's stated reason for insisting on a deontological theory should be rejected. Guyer adds: "In the end, however, it is probably better to say Kant's theory undercuts the traditional distinction: his final view is surely that the freedom that is intrinsically valuable is freedom that governs itself by law, or autonomy, and this conception incorporates ideas of both value and duty in itself." Guyer, *Kant on Freedom, Law, and Happiness*, p. 133.

mization of pleasure. Nonetheless, it is an end. It is the end of transcending nature, becoming — insofar as possible — godlike. It is our glory to be able to act freely, in a way responsible to freedom itself.

What in Kant epistemically justifies this postulate that the end is the achievement of freedom? Nothing. It is simply a practical postulate. And that leaves open the possibility that there is another end that is necessary: a tie to the glorious One. Various revelatory claims teach that the moral law is linked to goods, *but goods of a special sort.* We are bidden to aim at a great overarching good, a shareable common good. Some goods are unshareable. A piece of pie is a particular good, and it is unshareable (you can cut it in two, but two people cannot both have the whole piece of pie). "The greatest good for the greatest number" is unshareable; it involves a heap of particular goods. But community life is shareable. And the great common good revelation identifies is *not* pie in the sky, but God, the extrinsic good of the universe, and our attachment to and enjoyment of God and the children of God in communal life. The attachment contributes to the profound satisfaction of the deepest human desires and capacities. Revelations that point in the direction of God give us a ground for the moral law, for what is right and wrong, by setting conditions for attachment to God. They tie right and wrong to the great common good, unencumbered by the Kantian concept that disconnects the two. Morality does not hang free of all good. Nothing is wrong with linking morality to the production of good.

3.4.3. Handling Objections Concerning Substandard Worlds

3.4.3.1. The Difficulty of Finding a Non-Theistic Standard for World-Grading

Imagine an objector unable to accept our Key Conditional because the world as a whole does not look good enough to have been made by a good God, and it is judged unlikely that revelatory claims will have anything useful to say about this fairly abstract philosophical concern.

If the world as a whole is less good than it should be, then there is a standard for grading worlds: there are properties in virtue of which it is less than good, aspects or features of the world as a whole that count against its goodness. (In this context, terms such as "property" and "aspect" and "feature" are used broadly and interchangeably.) Picture someone saying, "That is a good argument" or "That is a bad argument," but insisting that there is nothing that *makes* the argument at issue good or bad. A good argument has subvenient properties that ground the supervenient property of being a good argument: a valid form, true premises, and so on.[31] And if our world as a whole is so evidently substandard that there is no point in examining revelatory claims even if it is not highly implausible that there is a world-creator, then it should be obvious both that a) there is a non-theistic standard of goodness for worlds, and b) our world fails to meet this standard.

But, we will argue, it is not obvious that these two claims are true.[32] In the present section (3.4.3.1) we engage the position of an objector who contends, "I know there is a standard of goodness for worlds; I know what it is and I know our world flunks." In the next section (3.4.3.2) we take up a fallback position: "I may not know what the standard for world-grading is, but whatever it is, I know our world flunks."

Now, given all the philosophical discussion there has been of whether God must create the best possible world, it might be expected that there would be quite a lot of direct discussion of what it is that *makes* a world good, of the standard according to which worlds count as good or bad. In fact, however, these days precious little is said about standards for world-grading. So we will largely be on our own.

We will assume that a standard of goodness for worlds must correspond to general intuitions about which worlds count as good and bad, and about which worlds an omnipotent, omniscient, wholly good creator might make. Intuitions and standards need not perfectly match. Our intuitions help us discover standards, and standards refine intuitions. Yet there must be some rough correspondence between intuitions, on the one hand, and standards, on the other. Without such a tie, a critic of theism will be unable to mine intuitions to win assent to the claim that our world is bad, or less than the best possible, or in some other way not up to snuff.

It would be helpful to have a satisfactory account of what the world, or a world, *is* before reflecting on standards for grading worlds. It is, unfortunately, extremely difficult to give an account of either *the* or *a* world. G. E. M. Anscombe offers a suggestive characterization of what she calls the universe, and we could call the world: "I take the universe to be the totality of bodies and physical processes, together with whatever is contained in any manner within the compass of that whole."[33] Note that, on this account, there cannot

31. Note, however, that to assert that there is a standard for grading worlds is *not* to assert that all worlds are commensurable. Two worlds might both be good, but incomparably good, or bad, but incomparably bad.

32. An earlier version of this line of argument appeared in Sandra Menssen, "Grading Worlds," *Proceedings of the American Catholic Philosophical Association* LXX (1996).

33. G. E. M. Anscombe, "Times, Beginnings and Causes," in *The Collected Philosophical Pa-*

be more than one world, though there may be sub-worlds that do not causally interact with one another. All sorts of questions arise. To begin with, what counts as a body or a physical process? We have already seen how difficult it is to circumscribe the physical. What sorts of things might be contained within the compass of the totality of bodies and physical processes? Anscombe's characterization counts souls *in* on an Aristotelian-Thomistic understanding of souls, but it counts God *out*. And God needs to be counted out if we want to say that God created the world: God does not create God. Does "the world" include an afterlife, an "afterworld," if there is such a thing? It is hard to see how "the world" *could* include an afterworld, if God is left out of the picture, since an essential part of an afterworld, on major revelations, is union with God. However, if an afterworld is not included, and there is in fact an afterworld of the kind Christianity promises, then there will be bodies left out of the picture, because in the afterworld, we are told, humans will have resurrected bodies. Either way, something gets left out. We do not know of a satisfactory account of "the world" that accords with ordinary, non-philosophical usage, not to mention scientific usage. We will simply stipulate that, when we speak of "the world" and "our world," we refer to the world *without* any afterlife or afterworld, and without (i.e., abstracting from) God. We leave it as an exercise for the interested reader to replot our argument if "the world" is understood as including an afterlife, should such exist. This alternative understanding should make it no more difficult (and would probably make it easier) to establish that, if there exists a standard for world-grading, it is theistic.

Any discussion of questions about world-grading requires envisioning alternative worlds. In what follows, however, we can abstract from the sense in which other "possible worlds" exist. For our purposes, it will almost always suffice to attach a minimal sense to the expression. Thus, when we use the term "possible world" (or speak elliptically of "a world") — unless otherwise stipulated — we will mean just *a hypothetically posited world*. We are committed to no more than the idea that one could suppose that there are worlds different from our own.[34]

---

pers of G. E. M. Anscombe, Vol. II: *Metaphysics and the Philosophy of Mind* (Minneapolis: University of Minnesota Press, 1981), p. 156.

34. The philosophical literature that discusses the meaning of the phrase "possible world" is vast — and highly technical. Here is a hint of the problems: although it is very commonly said that a "possible world" is "a way the world might be," logic textbooks may introduce *reductio ad absurdum* proofs in modal logic, allowing one to posit a "possible world" and then, upon generating a contradiction within an indexed world, back up and drop one of the assumptions. All the while the language of "possible world" is used, even when the aim is to show that no such world is possible. Furthermore, theists and agnostics will have different views of what the possi-

What putative standards of goodness for worlds might an objector call on in an effort to argue that our world is deficient? To explore that question, we will find it useful to divide possible standards into nonfunctional and functional.

Nonfunctional Standards for Grading Worlds   *Eudaimonistic* standards for world-grading — often called utilitarian — lay it down that happiness or pleasure or some such state is to be maximized. This sort of standard may initially be attractive to a person putting forward some version of the problem of evil, since those who are inclined to press the problem of evil often comment on the pervasiveness of the world's pain and suffering, on the large quantity of pain and suffering relative to pleasure and happiness.

Various more or less routine objections to eudaimonism will surface. If worlds are good insofar as they maximize happiness or pleasure or utility, then it must be possible in principle to sum the utility in the world as a whole. But that this is possible is even less plausible than the oft-criticized claim that the total amount of human happiness or pleasure can be summed. And there is the further problem that the happiness of the majority is purchased by the suffering of the few. (The intuition that there are some things individuals should not be asked to sacrifice for the greater good underlies Ivan Karamazov's objection that nothing can justify some kinds of suffering.) And anyway, a usable standard of goodness requires more than an "in principle possibility" that happiness or pleasure or utility can be summed.

Even if these common objections to eudaimonism are set aside, a serious difficulty remains. A eudaimonistic standard rests on an intuition that it is important to make sentient and rational creatures happy or to satisfy their preferences. But then surely the desires or preferences of beings *outside* the world, should there be any, will also be important: there is no good reason to

---

ble worlds are. A theist who takes God to be a necessary being will say that God exists in every possible world. And if God is wholly good, then any world that is really possible must be a world a good God can create (or actualize). But agnostics are unaccustomed to thinking along these lines. It will seem natural to a (philosophical) agnostic to ask questions about whether a good God can create or actualize possible worlds of one sort or another.

Given our minimal understanding of "possible world," we are certainly not committed to anything like David Lewis's idea that every possible world is an actual world, or even to Alvin Plantinga's idea that possible worlds are abstract entities, "maximal possible states-of-affairs." Thus there is no need for us to worry here about the ontological commitments that exercise Charles Chihara in *The Worlds of Possibility: Modal Realism and the Semantics of Modal Logic* (Oxford: Clarendon Press, 2001) or in his review of Plantinga's *Essays in Metaphysics* (Oxford: Oxford University Press, 2003), published on-line in the *Notre Dame Philosophical Reviews* 2003.06.03 (retrieved Jan. 23, 2006, from <http://ndpr.nd.edu>).

exclude such preferences. A powerful and highly knowledgeable maker's wishes and wants would have to be very heavily weighted: the eudaimonist reasonably counts human happiness as at least sometimes outweighing the happiness of nonhuman creatures, and likewise, the eudaimonist will have to count divine happiness or satisfaction of preferences as outweighing human happiness. So the hunter-gods Samuel Johnson imagined, "whose game is man," with "sports analogous to our own," could with abandon sink ships and suffocate those who look to the seas for life — and engage in whatever other amusements they fancy. If it is only happiness or the satisfaction of preferences that matters, then there could be no complaint if the world is constructed so as to satisfy the desires of an infinite creator.

Is there an acceptable *aesthetic* standard of goodness for worlds? Perhaps one world will be better than a second if the first has a higher degree of harmony or organic unity. That will be a function of the number of things or kinds of things it unifies, as well as the complementarity of the parts. It is, however, unclear that there can exist disharmonious possible worlds, worlds with a negative score on the scale of organic unity. If not, if all possible worlds have some degree of harmony, how do we determine where the mark of "sufficiently beautiful for a good God to create" gets placed? For any mark picked, the question can be raised: Why is a world below this mark a world that a good God could not or would not create? Imagine a very simple world, with few constituents (no sentient beings, let us say) and little diversity. Why maintain that a good God would not create such a world? If, as orthodox theism teaches, there was no necessity attached to God's creating — that is, if God could have chosen not to create at all — then it is hard to see what would stand in the way of God's making this simple sort of world. Furthermore, there may be worlds that *do* have a high degree of harmony or organic unity that we would think a good God should *not* create. Many atheists probably think that the actual world is of exactly this kind. We do not want God to be an aesthete who can look on a child murdered in her bed and think: "How beautiful the red blood is on the snow-white pillow!" or who can pronounce the atrocities in Darfur a nice touch in the symphony of the ages. Aesthetic standards, like eudaimonistic ones, fail to correspond in any obvious way to our general intuitions about which worlds count as good and bad.

Could our objector appeal to some kind of *moral* standard for world-grading? Recall that Kant holds that freedom gives the world "inner worth." (He may mean that the power of freedom alone suffices, or that it does so when exercised in accordance with the moral law.) Kant seems to suggest at times that, were the world destitute of free beings, it would have nothing good in it or about it. If this is his view, then he tacitly rejects the medieval view that everything that is, is good. However, even if it is true that the existence of freedom — either freedom in and of itself, or freedom exercised well — confers inner value on the universe, that truth does not provide a standard that matches our broad expectations. There could be all too much sorrow and pain in a world with freedom for us to count the world as a whole as good. No matter how sublime freedom is, we cannot automatically move from the goodness of the part to the goodness of the whole.

Might a *combination* standard, mixing some of the preceding standards, serve? Many questions would arise. What standards should be combined? How are they to be joined? Disjunctively? Conjunctively? How are the standards that are being combined weighted? And even if there is some sort of standard that has these multiple dimensions, there is hardly a *criterion,* a rule you could actually use to make assessments about whether a particular possible world does or does not count as good, or whether one possible world is better than another.

We come up empty-handed in our search for a nonfunctional, non-theistic standard for grading worlds.

Functional (and Non-Theistic) Standards for Grading Worlds   Can sense be made of a functional standard that does not presuppose or entail that there is a supranatural maker of some sort (that is, can sense be made of a non-theistic functional standard)? Not easily.

The trouble at bottom for all such standards is that, absent a creative intent, worlds do not seem to have natural functions. If there is no designer with a goal in mind, the world is not *for* anything at all. A world qua world does not do anything essentially. No modern cosmology book written by a physicalist contains a chapter entitled "On the Function of the Universe." The texts discuss questions about whether the universe will keep on expanding or will collapse into a pointlike structure. Whether one or another eventuality would be in keeping with the universe's function is not a question that is even thought about in cosmology.

We might try saying that the function of the universe or of the world is to provide a good environment for the flourishing of the species within it. Both what constitutes the flourishing of the species and what promotes it can be established without any reference whatever to God, it might be said. Libraries are full of environmental literature on both points. But libraries decidedly are not full of accounts of how any of this would show the existence of a function for the universe. It does not follow from the fact that all the organisms in a world flourish biologically that the world as a whole is good (in any sense matching our limited intuitions), even if the organisms have functions. Do we really want to describe as "good" a hellish universe full of "flourishing" demonic beings?[35] Furthermore, the assumption that organisms have functions, which is necessary for the claim that the environment supports the functions, is dubious unless the functions are referred to a creator. Biology books no more talk about the functions of species than cosmology books talk about the function of the universe. Indeed, it is hard enough to find writers who take functional language about the organs of animals and plants as anything more than a convenient way of talking.[36] A biologist will say that the heart's function is to pump blood. But that only means, it will be explained, that if the heart does not pump blood the organism will die, while the organism is not similarly dependent on the heart's making a thumping sound (for instance). It does not follow, however, that pumping blood is the function of the heart, as if it had a design. It is rather that there is a series of conditionals: no pumping, no circulation; no circulation, no life. Period. Modern physicalist philosophers turn Aristotle on his head. Aristotle argues in Book I of the *Ethics* that humans qua humans have functions, because the whole must have a function if its parts do — and the parts do. Modern physicalists argue that humans have functions qua humans only if the parts do — and the parts do not. Functionless parts, thus functionless whole, thus functionless universe: the world has no purpose or meaning — or value, as a unity.

Could a world's function be identified by its capacity to sustain itself, to promote its own benefit, to flourish as some sort of organism? Plato's *Timaeus* portrays the world in such a way. But here again we do not find a close match between our intuitions about good and bad worlds, and the kind of sorting this standard would provide. Presumably, the standard at issue would direct us to count as "bad" those worlds that are short-lived, or perhaps worlds that lack mechanisms for regeneration or replication. Perhaps worlds that include whole categories of creatures whose entire lives are excruciatingly painful would count as good, because the species properly balance one another in self-sustaining ecosystems. We do not get the requisite match between intuitions and standard.

---

35. Medieval thinkers held that the fallen angels have a measure of goodness about them since they fulfill their natures. Everything that exists with a nature in some way is good, Boethius and others argued. But so far as we know, nobody drew the conclusion that hell was a fine abode. See Scott MacDonald, "The Relation Between Being and Goodness," in Scott MacDonald, ed., *Being and Goodness: The Concept of the Good in Metaphysics and Philosophical Theology* (Ithaca, NY: Cornell University Press, 1991).

36. Fred Dretske takes it as more than that. See Fred Dretske, *Explaining Behavior: Reasons in a World of Causes* (Cambridge, MA: MIT Press, 1991), and *Naturalizing the Mind* (Cambridge, MA: MIT Press, 1995). Dretske acknowledges that he is in the minority.

Might there be a functional standard for grading worlds that is tied to the *intentions* of the world's designer or maker? A good world, on this line, would be a world that does what its maker intends it to do. (Such a standard would not be theistic if there is no requirement that the designer be a good god.) Once again, there is no guaranteed match with our intuitions about what a good world would be like. And in any event, very few of us would think we could tell whether a world succeeded in satisfying its designer's intentions. So the standard would not be usable for present purposes.

3.4.3.2. *The Difficulty of Doing Without a Standard for World-Grading*

Even if nobody can *articulate* a standard of goodness for worlds, it may be protested, it is evident enough that there is some such standard, and that our world flunks. Have we committed what Peter Geach has called the "Socratic fallacy"? Socrates tells Euthyphro that he is wrong to prosecute his father for murder unless he knows his father has done something impious, and that Euthyphro cannot know that unless he can define piety (which he cannot). More generally, Socrates apparently held that one cannot judge a proposition to be true unless one can define all its terms. But paradigm cases show the folly of the Socratic dictum about definition. You tell your neighbor that when he cut down the tree in your yard he wronged you. You may be unable to define "wrong," and you may be unable to define "tree"; it is nonetheless wrong for your neighbor to cut down your tree. So it might seem that even if it is impossible for an objector (or anyone else) to identify a standard for grading worlds, a *particular* possible world might be recognized as too sorry an affair for it to be created by a good God.

The protest, however, is problematic. Even if, despite our lack of a standard, some possible worlds might be identified as less than good, and others as good, the world that is actual is too complicated an affair to be so identified. If the world were nothing but pain, from one end to the other, or if every creature died by spontaneously combusting and then burning in agony for (apparently) all eternity, in plain view of the living so that they see what is in store for them, we would not need a standard for world-grading to say the world is far from good. And if we all had a constant, blissful, beatific vision of God, in a world without pain or wrongdoing, we would not need a standard to say the world is very good indeed. The actual world, though, falls between these extremes.

In rejoinder, a critic might say:[37] "We can evaluate states of affairs, even if

---

37. This is the way we would phrase an objection coming out of some concerns Russell Pannier expressed to us.

we do not have a clearly articulated standard for doing so. You claim that the state of affairs in which agnostic inquirers attend to the content of revelatory claims of major religions is better than the state of affairs in which they do not. More dramatically: a state of affairs in which no child is tortured is better than a state of affairs in which some children are tortured (other things being equal). But a possible world simply *is* a state of affairs.[38] A possible world in which no child is tortured is better than a possible world in which some children are tortured (other things being equal). Such judgments about preferability can be made without tacit reliance on theism, and without any articulated standard of goodness for worlds. So we can reasonably say that a good, all-powerful, and all-knowing world-creator should make a world better than ours."

We would reply in three ways.

First, it is less easy to evaluate states of affairs than the objection makes it out to be. There may be some states of affairs that are unqualifiedly good. There may be no states of affairs unqualifiedly bad. Yet some states of affairs may be good only with qualification. Is getting the best brain surgeon in town to remove your brain tumor good or bad? Given that you need surgery, it is good to get the best surgeon; but it is bad that you need surgery. Is John's suffering pain magnificently a good state of affairs? Given that John is suffering, it is good that he is doing it magnificently. Is the state of affairs in which God becomes incarnate and atones for the sins of humans good? Given that humans have sinned, it is good. But how does a possible world in which humans never sin compare with one in which they do sin, but God becomes incarnate and atones for the sin? That comparison is extremely difficult to make.[39] In the end, God may thank you for your suffering, as Julian of Norwich imagines. But will God also thank you for your sin?

Second, it is not obvious that we can reach in and change one aspect of an ontologically possible world — our own world, or another — holding every-

38. Plantinga says: "How shall we think of the value or goodness of a possible world? Well, what sorts of things are good or valuable or excellent, on the one hand, or bad or unhappy or deplorable on the other? The answer is easy; states of affairs (perhaps among other things) are good or bad. John's being in pain is a bad state of affairs, and John's suffering pain magnificently, a good one. . . . Since possible worlds are states of affairs, they are precisely the sorts of things that are good or bad, valuable or disvaluable." Alvin Plantinga, "Supralapsarianism, or 'O Felix Culpa,'" in Peter van Inwagen, ed., *Christian Faith and the Problem of Evil* (Grand Rapids: Eerdmans, 2004), p. 5.

39. Plantinga's theodicy turns on the claim that, among the possible worlds of great value, there are some that include incarnation and atonement (and these entail evil: no sin, no atonement). See Plantinga, "Supralapsarianism, or 'O Felix Culpa.'"

thing else fixed, and get a new world that is *really* possible, ontologically possible. Imagine that a surgeon recommends surgery on your arm, telling you that the ulnar nerve either will be severed, or not. You surely will not say to yourself: Okay, let me assume it will be severed, and hold everything else fixed, and then see whether I like that possible world. For everything else cannot be held fixed. If the nerve is severed, you will lose your ability to move your fingers, and so lose your ability to write, and so have a diminished capacity to develop your thoughts. Things will definitely be different. Even in the simplest cases, we cannot make little changes and hold all else fixed. Take a checkerboard: try to change one of the red squares to black, keeping everything else, including your perceptions, exactly the same. It may be impossible, because our perceptions of colors depend on the contrasts of surrounding colors.

Third, and finally, even if we assume that it is possible to change one aspect of our world, substituting a more valuable for a less valuable part while holding everything else fixed, and get a new world that is genuinely possible, it does not follow that the new world will be better than the old. The value of a part does not automatically transfer to an aggregation of parts or to a whole. The *relations* in the world may block the transfer. It may be that degradation of a part enhances a whole, as changing the color of a small patch of a painting may make the small patch uglier but may amplify the beauty of the whole. This point holds whether or not the possible world is a genuine *unity* of states of affairs — an organic whole, as some might speak of it.

Must a theist maintain that there is a standard for grading worlds? It is easy to think that, at the very least, a theist is obliged to affirm that the world is good. In the course of discussing (and rejecting) the claim that God must create the best possible world, William Mann observes: "Genesis 1:31 says that the world God created was very good, not that it is the best."[40] And Robert Adams says that the Judaeo-Christian theist "must hold that the actual world is a good world."[41] Their view is unsurprising. God's awe-inspiring "Let there be" in the magnificent account in Genesis of origins results in a creation God calls "good" six times and once — when the creation has been completed — "very good."

However, the picture is complicated. Genesis and the whole of Scripture, from the Pentateuch through the New Testament, lament human frailty, infidelity, and vice: the testaments paint a picture of a world that at times appears

40. William E. Mann, "The Best of All Possible Worlds," in Scott MacDonald, ed., *Being and Goodness*, p. 276.

41. Robert Adams, "Must God Create the Best?" reprinted in *The Virtue of Faith and Other Essays in Philosophical Theology* (Oxford: Oxford University Press, 1987), p. 51.

far more bad than good. The same scriptures that assert that the world was originally good portray an angry, "repentant" God bringing a flood on the entire earth. Later, brimstone and fire rain down on Sodom and Gomorrah because there are not ten who are righteous in the entire city. Apocalyptic pictures fill the closing chapters of the New Testament, reminding us that "many are called, but few are chosen."[42] The world may once have been good, but have turned all too rotten to be counted as good at present. As a consequence of our "living to ourselves," our world may be, as Christian philosopher Peter van Inwagen suggests, "a hideous world."[43] Nothing in the Hebrew or Christian scriptures bids us see the world as good *as a whole,* from start to finish. For this world is no permanent dwelling place. Pray "thy kingdom come," we are instructed: this world is "passing away."[44]

The theist who says *either* that the world is good or bad is committed to the existence of a standard for world-grading. A theist can appeal to a standard that does not have the defects of the non-theistic standards earlier discussed. A theist can appeal to the idea that God is the extrinsic *telos* of the world: the world is ordered to a good God. The general idea may be illustrated by analogy. If you are a physician, what do you work to improve? You are not concerned with the well-being of the bits of food found in patients' bodies, nor with carcinogens that may be stuck inside, nor with parasites; you want to sustain human bodies. And how are the bodies identified? How are requisite distinctions drawn? Reference to patients' minds (or souls) may be required. A human body is ordered to an end, and that end is provided by the organizing mind or soul. The soul informs the body, as Aristotle saw it. As a human body is ordered to the human mind or soul, so may the world be ordered to God (which does not mean that the world is God's body). This is not a kind of standard for world-grading that easily yields a criterion we can actually apply to the world to see whether it is good or not. But that is not problematic for the theist. It is only the atheist arguing from the alleged defectiveness of the world who needs a criterion. Of course, since the standard entails that there is a good God, a person who accepts it may have limited interest in attempting to apply it to the world.

While we believe that there *may* be a defensible theistic standard for world-grading,[45] we wish tentatively to suggest that at least some worlds may

42. Matt. 22:14 (NRSV).

43. Peter van Inwagen, "The Magnitude, Duration, and Distribution of Evil," in Peter van Inwagen, ed., *God, Knowledge and Mystery: Essays in Philosophical Theology* (Ithaca, NY: Cornell University Press, 1995), p. 110.

44. "For the present form of this world is passing away" (1 Cor. 7:31 [NRSV]).

45. For two extended treatments of Thomistic standards for world-grading, quite diverse in

not be fit subjects for bearing either the predicate "good" or "bad." The number 3 does not see, nor is it blind. It is not the kind of thing of which we can predicate sight — or lack thereof. Nor is an infant who cannot focus its eyes "blind." It does not suffer deprivation of sight; it simply is not supposed to be seeing yet. It may be that at least some possible worlds are neither good nor deprived of goodness. No subject can elude contradictories, but some subjects can elude contraries and privatives, as Aristotle pointed out. Now it will never be fitting to predicate sight of the number 3. But it is a different case with a newborn child: the child grows into its capacities. And the world is a-borning. At the end, when the trumpet sounds, it may be possible to pronounce on whether the world as a whole is good or bad. Or maybe even then the world will elude such judgment: if God exists, we should perhaps be asking not about the goodness of the world, but about the goodness of what exists *in complement with God.*

3.4.4. Glimpses of Revelatory Accounts of Evil

Why think that this is a world that a good God could create? Not because it looks like the best possible world. That is not a common judgment. And probably not because it appears to be a good world, even a good world ruled according to strict justice. A world ruled according to strict justice would be terrifying indeed. Instead, one might think this is a world a good God could have made because it is a world full of promise, containing beings of great dignity who can cooperate with divine love. God makes covenants with Noah, Abraham, Moses, David, and others, and through Israel all nations are blessed in "the covenants of promise."[46] The promise to the world, through the promises of the Hebrew and Christian scriptures, is that all are fit subjects, willing and unwilling, to the transforming love of God. Understandings of the promises of the testaments vary considerably, and vary even more widely across the entire domain of revelatory texts. Still, many agree that the promise built into human beings, the beings of wondrous worth, the promise that can be brought to fruition by the ever-reliable promises of a good God, makes this world, with all its grief, a world worth creating, even though the world as we know it is passing away. In short, this is a world a good God could create if it is a world perfused

---

style and substance, see Oliva Blanchette, *The Perfection of the Universe According to Aquinas: A Teleological Cosmology* (University Park, PA: Pennsylvania State University Press, 1992), and Norman Kretzmann's two essays, "A General Problem of Creation" and "A Specific Problem of Creation," both in MacDonald, *Being and Goodness.*

46. Eph. 2:12 (NRSV).

by God's transforming love — and is followed by an afterworld of the right kind. The world may be such that a good God can create it, even if it is not a good world. (Thus it is a mistake for an objector to think that, if it is shown that this is not a good world, then a good God could not have created it.)

But one wonders. Could it really be the case that the world in which some suffer the sorrows of Job is governed not only by justice, but love and mercy?

The question carries us back to Genesis and the beginning of all things. Out of chaos — or from nothing at all — God brings forth heaven and earth. God recognizes created things, if not the world itself, as good — very good. The goodness of every created thing is a real property of the thing itself, conferred on things that did not exist prior to the creative act. Up to a point, philosophy can offer support for this view, for, as we have seen, there is at least an appreciable likelihood that the world came to be through the action of a cause external to it, a creator. If the world was created, then love and mercy were there from the outset, and there more fundamentally than justice — which presupposes love and mercy.[47] Anything due a creature is due on account of something already existing in the creature. But when a creature does not even exist, there is nothing in it to which something is due. Hence, any being owes its existence and ultimately all that it has and does to a primordial act of loving-kindness and mercy on the creator's part. If, then, there is a creator, love and mercy perfuse the world. The argument can be extended to the creation of minds, souls, and selves, especially if the emergence of any of these things transcends the productive power of nature. The mercies of the moments of the creation of each overlie the primordial mercy of creation.

Revelatory traditions (or strains thereof) also teach that love and mercy are constantly operative, moving already established beings in the direction of right action, good acts and great acts proceeding from the gracious impulse of a loving Creator. Experience of gracious influence on their acts, real or illusory, steadies many believers and prompts agnostics to embrace religions that teach that loving, merciful aid comes from above. Wonder at heroic love displayed by others can all but impose the conviction — even on those who recognize little or no gracious influence in their own lives — that Love perfuses love.

Can philosophy offer any resistance to or support for this claim? Of course, arguments against the existence of God are automatically arguments against divine assistance. But what if it is not assumed that no God exists, if instead it is assumed that there is an appreciable chance that there is a world-

---

47. An argument for this claim is to be found in Aquinas, *Summa Theologiae* I, q. 21, a. 4, corpus.

creator? How, then, should we assess the probability that divine grace is at work in good acts? Though the question of whether divine grace is operative is now rarely raised in moral philosophy, Socrates, Plato, Aristotle, Kant, and a host of other philosophers have dealt with it.

Kant was conflicted. On the one hand, he could see no way an agent who had fallen from goodness, abandoning the right maxims to satisfy inclination, could climb out of the moral pit. Against the proposal that it is achievable through divine assistance, Kant argues that it is impossible to make theoretical sense of the gracious influence, since we cannot extend the use of the concepts of cause and effect beyond the objects of experience, that is, beyond nature. And it is impossible to make practical use of the notion, Kant holds, because good acts presuppose a rule concerning what we ourselves must do, while to look to an effect of grace means that the moral good is not of our doing but *the doing of another*.[48] Kant's argument is a variant of arguments debated at length in medieval philosophy, coming to a head in the great debates between Dominican and Jesuit thinkers.[49]

In response, we would only draw attention to a point made by a pagan. Aristotle argues that moral acts presuppose deliberation. But deliberating is itself something we do, and while we deliberate about deliberating, we cannot do it ad infinitum and still act. So there must be a first cause of deliberation itself, either chance (the agent just happens to start deliberating) or some other cause. Aristotle opts for the latter. The First Cause moves the soul along with all other things, he holds in the penultimate chapter of the *Eudemian Ethics*. It does seem that at some point the thought "Shall I perform this action?" just arises without its being due to a deliberative act on the agent's part. Thus we are left with the alternatives that the source of a particular act is mindful (that is, due to a Mind beyond mind), or not. In either case, what proceeds from deliberation is not wholly ours, and thus it is a mistake to insist with Kant on complete ownership of our moral acts if they are to be ours at all. The acts will in all cases begin with a suggestion that comes our way through the prompting of nature or something higher than nature. Although this reflection does not remove the mysteries surrounding divine influence

48. Kant, *Religion within the Boundaries of Mere Reason*, p. 73 [6:53]. Of course, one who listens to Kant on the supreme categorical imperative, say, has been influenced; the action of the listener is then not *owned*, on Kant's view. Why cannot God do what Kant does — whisper "Don't!"?

49. For a superb account of the debate and the underlying metaphysical issues from both a medieval and contemporary standpoint, see Alfred J. Freddoso's introduction to Luis de Molina, *On Divine Foreknowledge: Part IV of the Concordia*, trans., intro., and notes by Alfred J. Freddoso (Ithaca, NY: Cornell University Press, 1988), pp. 1-81.

on human actions, it provides grounds for taking the view that Kant, somewhat ambivalently, adopts in the end. Kant allows that, if we make efforts to improve our moral condition, we can hope that what does not lie within our power can be made good by cooperation from above.[50] If we do our part, God will do God's. Or perhaps more accurately — if God acts, so may we.

Though philosophy can point to a religious remedy for evil, no remedy philosophy has to offer can compete with the religious remedy. The Stoics had a solution for the problem of suffering. You harden yourself to loss; you cease to love others, so their misfortune cannot become your misfortune. A person with a good will is invulnerable, the Stoic says. But hardening oneself to loss is not a solution. Theistic religious solutions offer an amendment, saying that there is no *permanent* damage to a person of good will. The amendment is a radical one: it moves in the opposite direction from the Stoics. The Stoics aimed to extinguish affection. But the solution lies in its expansion, an extending of the self toward God. Compensation for suffering comes from love and charity given and received, from opening oneself up through love and becoming vulnerable, from the satisfaction of desires associated with love and charity. In what does that final satisfaction of desires consist? How can we understand it? What God has prepared for those who love him "no eye has seen, nor ear heard, nor the human heart conceived."[51]

This world, then, is such that a good God could make it because love and mercy are integral to the creative act manifested in the emergence of the world, in the entities that transcend nature, and in moral acts — some sublime — that give the world, in Kant's phrase, "inner worth."

Yet some voluntary acts are horrendous and their effects appalling. They compound the evils of a world subject to violent eruptions, corrosion, disease, and every manner of affliction. The question remains insistent: Is this *really* a world a good God could create?

If what we have said offers any help, it certainly is not enough. Nor are the revelatory traditions completely satisfying. And it looks as though no entirely satisfactory explanation should be expected this side of the world's last night. Yet perhaps revelatory traditions, backed by whatever philosophy can muster, can provide enough of an explanation of the problems of evil and good for an inquirer to conclude that the world began with love, will end with love, and is moved by love all the while — appearances notwithstanding.

Key to one account is the salvific value of suffering. In the Christian tradition, the afflictions of Jesus are thought to have the power to merit the for-

---

50. Kant, *Religion Within the Boundaries of Mere Reason*, pp. 71-72 [6:52].
51. 1 Cor. 2:9 (NRSV).

giveness of God. The sacrifice of the Son shows the divine mercy as nothing else does.[52] The concept of salvific suffering is not absent from the Jewish tradition, though debated within it, as also in the Christian tradition. The Christian tradition takes the reality for granted ("For God so loved the world that he gave his Son") and debates how salvation is effected. The Jewish tradition is more tentative about the fact, though generally united in denial of the salvific value of Jesus' death. The Christian citation of Isaiah 53 as prophetic of Christ has been staunchly protested. Yet, whether the passage refers to Christ, or Israel, or Moses, or Jeremiah (as variously suggested), it appears to support the notion of the power of vicarious suffering:

3   He was despised and rejected by men;
     a man of sorrows, and acquainted with grief;
     and as one from whom men hide their faces
     he was despised, and we esteemed him not.
4   Surely he has borne our griefs
     and carried our sorrows;
     yet we esteemed him stricken,
     smitten by God, and afflicted.
5   But he was wounded for our transgressions,
     he was bruised for our iniquities;
     upon him was the chastisement that made us whole,
     and with his stripes we are healed.[53]

Somehow suffering has meaning, a meaning God has assigned to it through a providential determination that binds us together and binds us to God in a friendship far greater in intimacy and joy than we can imagine. *Our own* suffering can be efficacious: "I am now rejoicing in my sufferings for your sake," the author of Colossians tells us, "and in my flesh I am completing what is lacking in Christ's afflictions for the sake of his body, that is, the church."[54] What can be lacking in the suffering of Christ? Our suffering is a necessary condition for Christ's atonement, some say: suffering is a natural consequence of sin, and without sin there cannot be an atonement. True enough, but Christians have sought a fuller way of understanding the enigmatic assertion, and have found one. God wills that we share in Christ's works, that we be, through our suffering, channels for the application of the wholly adequate suffering of

52. In the Catholic tradition the case is made in John Paul II's Apostolic Letter "Salvifici Doloris" (11 Feb. 1984).
53. Isa. 53:3-5 (RSV).
54. Col. 1:24 (NRSV).

Christ to each individual. Our sufferings are caught up with Christ's, so that it is literally the case that our sufferings are salvific. The sufferings adequate for the redemption of the world include our own, which Christ has willed to make his own, as he offers himself and his mystical body, the church.

We have bypassed the thesis that the world is good, arguing rather that the world is *such that* a good God could have created it. The analogy between divine procreation and human procreation provides some support for our argument. Prospective parents do not ask whether this is a good world when they think about bringing children into it. In the image of God we are created, Genesis tells us; and acting in imitation of our creator's gift of life, we have "scatter'd [our] Maker's image through the land."[55] We choose to have children, even when it is easy to avoid conception, and even when children are not required to supplement a family income. And we do this even though we can predict that they will undergo substantial mental anguish and serious physical suffering. Parents know with certainty that their children will commit moral evil. Prospective parents sometimes do decide to remain childless when genetic testing indicates a high risk of extraordinary physical suffering. Interestingly, couples do not typically refrain from having children when the chance that the children will commit moral atrocities appears especially high.[56] Those areas of the world where the risk of physical suffering is lowest may be areas where the risk of moral evils is especially high: wealth and prosperity are heavy burdens. Who in a relatively highly developed country, though, says, "I will not have children because I fear they would not give sufficient help to those in need"? The whole world adheres to the practice of procreation. We love and nurture our young, guiding them toward a maturity in which they will safeguard new life. Indeed, we vigorously work to sustain not merely our children but *ourselves*. We consciously, deliberately seek long life; suicide is very rare, and when it occurs, very sad.

In prescientific cultures, people labored to assist the rising of the sun, the changing of the seasons; not seeing the causal connections in nature, they provided them through ritualistic sacrifices to the gods. Was it only to warm themselves that they assisted the rising of the sun? Only to feed themselves that they propitiated the gods and helped the seasons turn? Or were they also celebrating and consenting to and loving the world itself? Today we protect endangered species, and not because we want them for food or clothing or zoos: our actions bespeak affirmation, and broaden the consent to the world we give by procreating, and sustaining our children and ourselves.

---

55. In the words of John Dryden, in "Absalom and Achitophel."
56. We thank Peter Shea for this observation.

We receive and cooperate with divine love as we upbuild an order extending beyond the familial and the parochial.[57] God's abiding love helps us love one another, and love the world itself — helps us achieve a glorious liberty, and, together with the whole creation, groaning in travail, find redemption.[58] This world, it is reported, is loved by the One Being who understands everything.[59] Is there something about the world that the One Being sees that we do not see, something that makes it good as a whole, and worthy of the love of the One? Perhaps. Yet whether or not the world is good as a whole, it may be such that a good creator could make it. And whether or not it is good as a whole, its most valuable aspects, the freedom and love that give it "inner worth," may owe their existence and power to another kind of freedom and love — a love that binds the world to Love itself.

57. "God is love, and those who abide in love abide in God, and God abides in them" (I John 4:16 [NRSV]).

58. See Rom. 8:19-23.

59. See John 3:16.

4 Objection: No Acceptable Method Exists for Assessing the Content of Revelatory Claims

4.1. The Objection

There is no method an inquirer can use to sort through and assess the multitude of revelatory claims, no method that will steady judgment and guard against unreliable results, no method that will permit the reliable construction of a case rendering the conclusion that a good God has revealed more probable than not. So goes the objection.

Were there to be no good answer to this objection, it would not necessarily tell against the strategy we are proposing. Arguably, science advances without a commitment to any kind of overarching method.[1] The possibility of progress in assessing revelatory claims without using explicitly articulated methods is evidenced by our confidence in *condemning* certain revelatory claims as improbable. An inquirer completely at sea as to how to assess the content of a revelatory claim would be in no position to condemn any revelatory claim, no matter how absurd; but we all rightly reject revelatory claims made by religious fanatics advocating mass suicide or the sexual abuse of children. Furthermore, progress can be made in philosophy itself, even though philosophers disagree profoundly about method. And while some charge that there really is no progress in philosophy, our inquirer will be suspicious of that charge. For our inquirer (along with all philosophical inquirers, we would say) is committed to an approach that includes identifying bad and good moves in philosophy.

Despite this, we will — for the sake of the argument — assume that, if our

---

1. Though presenting an extreme view about the limits of method, Paul Feyerabend's *Against Method,* 3d ed. (London: Verso, 1993) makes this point effectively.

Key Conditional is defensible, some non-demonstrative procedure or method, at least one, must be identified for evaluating the content of revelatory claims. The assumption is not that an inquiry into revelation is properly conducted only if some particular method is consciously adopted, but rather that the inquiry must conform to at least one appropriate method of non-demonstrative reasoning, even if no conscious effort is made to employ the method. (Compare: one reasons validly if and only if one's reasoning *exemplifies* a formal pattern of reasoning, e.g., *modus ponens,* even if one is completely innocent of formal logic, has never studied it, has never even heard of it.)

In our discussion of "choosing a method" we will argue that at least one such method is available, a method quite familiar to most inquirers. It is not the method many philosophers now assume must be used to investigate religious hypotheses — Bayesian reasoning. We begin by explaining why we think an inquirer should resist the suggestion that responsible philosophical investigation of revelatory claims requires mastering Bayesian models of probability. Rather, the method we recommend for consideration is *inference to the best explanation,* a method familiar to most inquirers, though not by name. It has its problems, but the problems are manageable. And facing those problems will require not only taking some care to formulate the pattern in a way that avoids standard objections, but also dealing more directly with certain issues concerning *ideal* explanation than is customary in the literature.

Having formulated a particular pattern for inference to the best explanation, our method of choice, we move on to discuss one aspect of implementing the method: "choosing a hypothesis." Are there just too many hypotheses — competing revelatory claims — for an inquirer to handle? How should an initial hypothesis be chosen? How particular or specific must a revelatory claim be for investigation to be worthwhile?

Finally, under the heading of "choosing the data," we introduce the neglected concept of a CUE-fact and urge a few other points that put the method of inference to the best explanation under an uncommon light and help set up the illustrations (in the following chapter) of the explanatory power of revelatory claims.

It is true that probability is sometimes a tricky business. But it is also true that we can make plenty of confident judgments about probability prior to arriving at a conclusive judgment concerning competing theories of probability. We can confidently say, for example, that it is entirely improbable that an old man lives in a grass hut on the face of the sun. And it is quite probable that no living human being is more than three hundred years old. The judgment that a particular revelatory claim is probably true will be more difficult.

But it is not impossibly difficult, even for an inquirer who lacks formal training in probabilistic reasoning and in theories of explanation. Or so we say.

Have we any right to say it?

4.2. Choosing a Method — Inference to the Best Explanation (IBE)

4.2.1. Hesitancy about Bayesian Reasoning

At the beginning of his book *On the Nature and Existence of God,* Richard Gale says:

> I completely ignore inductive arguments. . . . A proper discussion of these arguments is the topic for a separate book of considerable length, since it would have to deal with the applicability of Bayesian models of probability to the aggregation of the premises of all the different inductive arguments for and against God's existence. . . . [T]he issues are exceedingly complex and need to be treated by those who are steeped in probability and confirmation theory, which eliminates me.[2]

This is troubling. A gifted, highly analytical philosopher completely eschews inductive arguments when dealing with questions about God because such arguments are just too difficult for him to assess. How, then, can an ordinary philosophically inclined inquirer expect to succeed in investigating an even broader, more complex question? Gale leaves aside revelation; our inquirer takes up the complex question "Has a good God revealed anything of significance to us?" Must an inquirer into revelatory claims master Bayesian models of probability and apply them to a vast aggregation of premises?

The theorem attributed to Thomas Bayes follows from the axioms of the probability calculus. In modern notation, one version of the theorem runs:[3]

$$\overset{\underset{\displaystyle 1}{\downarrow}}{\overline{\Pr(h|(e\&k))}} = \overset{\underset{\displaystyle 2}{\downarrow}}{[\underset{\underset{2a}{\uparrow}}{\underline{\Pr(e|(h\&k))}} / \underset{\underset{2b}{\uparrow}}{\underline{\Pr(e|k)}}]} \times \overset{\underset{\displaystyle 3}{\downarrow}}{\overline{\Pr(h|k)}}$$

---

2. Richard M. Gale, *On the Nature and Existence of God* (Cambridge, UK: Cambridge University Press, 1991), p. 1.

3. "Pr" stands for "the probability of"; "h" for "the hypothesis under consideration"; "e" for "the new evidence," that is, the evidence under consideration; "k" for "background knowledge"; "|" for "given"; and "/" for "divided by."

The theorem tells us that the value labeled 1 — the probability of h, the hypothesis under consideration, on the new evidence e and the background knowledge k — is equal to the value labeled 2 — sometimes called the explanatory power of the hypothesis[4] — multiplied by the value labeled 3 — the prior probability of the hypothesis. What is sometimes called the explanatory power of the hypothesis, 2, is the predictive power of the hypothesis, 2a, divided by the probability of the new evidence, 2b.

Should an inquirer resist the suggestion that Bayesian reasoning must be used to investigate the content of revelatory claims?

Yes.

To begin with, substantial testimony from experts supports such resistance. Experts suggest that there are serious and widespread problems about the applicability of the Bayesian theorem — not merely problems connected with difficulties in mastering received probability theory, but deeper problems. Bayesianism seems to work quite well in certain circumstances, such as settings that involve making predictions about the colors of balls drawn out of urns (given the relevant information about the color composition of the whole set of balls, etc.) and settings that involve assessing some kinds of evidence in legal cases.[5] But John Earman, philosopher of science and one of the most articulate defenders of Bayesianism, expresses a hesitation about applicability that taps into widespread concern. Earman tells us in *Bayes or Bust?* that he is a Bayesian only on Mondays, Wednesdays, and Fridays:

> On Tuesdays, Thursdays, and Saturdays, however, I have my doubts not only about the imperialistic ambitions of Bayesianism but also about its viability as a basis for analyzing scientific inference. . . . I hasten to add that my own schizophrenia on the topic, deplorable as it may be, is symptomatic of a deep schism in the philosophical community.[6]

And many others concur.[7] If experts often find it problematic to apply

4. Although $\Pr(e|(h\&k))$ / $\Pr(e|k)$ is sometimes labeled "the explanatory power of the hypothesis," the number that results from dividing the first of the two probabilities by the second is, in our view, *not* an acceptable measure of how good an explanation the hypothesis provides.

5. See the discussion of Regina v. Denis John Adams in A. P. Dawid, "Bayes's Theorem and Weighing the Evidence by Juries," in Richard Swinburne, ed., *Bayes's Theorem* (Oxford: Oxford University Press, 2002).

6. John Earman, *Bayes or Bust? A Critical Examination of Bayesian Confirmation Theory* (Cambridge, MA: MIT Press, 1992), p. 2.

7. See recent encyclopedias of philosophy, such as the *Stanford Encyclopedia of Philosophy* at <plato.stanford.edu>, and Edward Craig, ed., *Routledge Encyclopedia of Philosophy* (London: Routledge, 1998). Consult entries such as "Bayes's Theorem," and "Probability, Interpretations of," and "Probability Theory and Epistemology."

Bayesian reasoning in the area of science, which should admit of quantitative methods if any area does, an inquirer may reasonably hesitate to apply it in the area of religion.

Why do some experts have problems with application? The answers are many, varied, interconnected, and sometimes quite technical. Some of the experts have problems with the interpretation of the axioms of probability. Some complain that accurate knowledge of probabilities is generally unavailable because "there is almost always a certain arbitrariness about which reference class is chosen as a base for the probabilities. . . ."[8] Others believe that probability theory in general is, as standardly formulated, woefully inadequate for the purpose of handling causality, which lies at the heart of science.[9] And many note that the values in Bayes's theorem are highly resistant to being figured, both in science and — even more obviously — in the areas of theism and revelation: there are problems at points 2a, 2b, and 3 of the theorem. We will illustrate problems of applicability by focusing on this last difficulty, the difficulty of fixing the values at points 2a, 2b, and 3.

Whatever the subject under investigation, there may be a problem about scrutability at 2a. When the subject is theism and revelation, though, the problems are huge. Some probability theorists say as much with respect to at least a significant part of the case for theism. Elliott Sober, for instance, as we have seen, contends that there is a serious problem about the inferability of the data on the hypothesis that a creator exists. He says it is absurd to think one can fix the probability of what a being infinitely more intelligent and powerful than humans would do. We have given reason to doubt Sober's contention. We have said that inquirers are not altogether bereft of ideas about what kind of communication would constitute evidence of a heavenly source. Yet it would not follow from this cautious conclusion that, given merely that a good God has revealed, one could assign a probability to a sentence expressive of the evidence at hand. Swinburne assigns a value of 1/3 at 2a (where h is the hypothesis of theism). Then he adds: "*More loosely and accurately,* my point is simply that our universe is of a kind such that, given God's character, he might well choose to create."[10] But if the nonquantitative assessment is more accurate, why think that Bayesian reasoning is necessary?

8. John R. Josephson and Susan G. Josephson, eds., *Abductive Inference: Computation, Philosophy, Technology* (Cambridge, UK: Cambridge University Press, 1996), p. 27.

9. See, for example, Judea Pearl, *Causality: Models, Reasoning, and Inference* (Cambridge, UK: Cambridge University Press, 2000).

10. Swinburne, *The Existence of God,* 2d ed. (Oxford: Clarendon Press, 2004), p. 339 (italics added).

Turn briefly to 2b. Let "e" be "a universe of the sort we have." What are the chances we would have gotten *this,* the sort of universe we inhabit? A difficulty here is brought out by Timothy McGrew, Lydia McGrew, and Eric Vestrup. There are infinitely many possible universes. If you want to say that the chance of getting a universe like our own is one in n, then you need to assign each of the possibilities a fixed probability. But, however small you make the probabilities, the sum will be infinite — and that violates the laws of probability theory as standardly set out and construed.[11]

And it may be no easier to calculate values at point 3. Probability theorists like Elliott Sober insist that it is nonsense, for instance, to assign a prior probability to the truth of the law of gravity. Whether or not it is always nonsense, it is generally difficult. Consider, for example, the difficulty of assigning values at 3 when certain religious hypotheses are under consideration. Prior to reflection on the evidence under scrutiny, what is the probability of the hypothesis that there is a good God who has revealed? Objective prior probabilities can be extremely difficult to fix upon. When Swinburne sets up his Bayesian argument for theism, he takes the prior probability of h to be the intrinsic probability of h, and he vigorously defends the thesis that the intrinsic probability of a hypothesis is a function of its simplicity, which he takes to be an *a priori* matter. He presents his argument powerfully. Yet, on close examination, the history of science might reveal that the simplest hypotheses have not proved in the main to be true. In any event, we are less sanguine than Swinburne about the role simplicity can play in Bayesian reasoning — as have been many of his critics.

We might summarize these various problems concerning calculating values for Bayes's theorem by taking note of Swinburne's approach in the last couple of pages of his book *The Resurrection of God Incarnate,* where he reviews the values he has assigned to calculate the probability that Jesus was God Incarnate, who rose from the dead. Swinburne challenges readers to say at what point he has gone wrong in constructing his argument, at what point he has made a mistake in his calculations, and to propose an alternative value assignment. But he leaves out one important option in the choices he offers: it is the option of not knowing what value to assign at some point in the argument. At various stages in Swinburne's extended argument, when he reaches a conclusion such as "It is probable that such-and-such" or "It is very unlikely that so-and-so," an inquirer may think: "I simply don't know whether this is proba-

11. Timothy McGrew, Lydia McGrew, and Eric Vestrup, "Probabilities and the Fine-Tuning Argument: A Skeptical View," in Neil A. Manson, ed., *God and Design: The Teleological Argument and Modern Science* (London: Routledge, 2003), pp. 203ff.

ble or not." That is, an inquirer may think that the values are inscrutable. How does one "scrute" the inscrutable? The judgment that a value is inscrutable is different from the judgment that the probability is fifty-fifty (that is, .5).

The artificiality of trying to calculate the values required to apply the Bayesian approach in some areas can be illustrated by reflecting on the following question: Were the five books of the Pentateuch written by a single author, Moses? The hard work in answering that question involved learning ancient languages and developing techniques of literary criticism that allowed different traditions to be identified in the stories woven together in the first five books of the Hebrew Bible. Though one might conceivably use Bayes's theorem to figure the probability of the hypothesis that the Pentateuch was composed by multiple authors, it would be very artificial to make the calculation. Indeed, there is a good chance one would be at sea when trying to assign the values in Bayes's theorem, so that the calculated probability of the hypothesis on the new evidence would not match the judgment arrived at independently of Bayes's theorem. The theorem simply does not provide an algorithm for handling tradeoffs between explanatory virtues such as scope and simplicity. The focus on the mathematics can easily obscure this point.

And if classicists *did,* through Bayesian reasoning, arrive at a judgment concerning the authorship of the Pentateuch or the *Iliad* that conflicted with the judgments made independently of the use of Bayes's theorem, they might well alter the value assignments in Bayes's theorem, not their independent assessments. That is what scientists do in troublesome cases. Einstein's general theory of relativity predicts the "anomalous" advance of the perihelion of Mercury, and we all reasonably take this fact to help confirm the theory. But some standard accounts of Bayesian reasoning theory give the prediction zero weight, because when Einstein proposed his theory, the peculiarities of Mercury's perihelion were already known.[12] Ways have been suggested of trying to repair Bayesianism, but there is no consensus about how the "problem of old evidence" is to be handled. Nobody seriously proposes dumping Einstein's theory on the grounds that it runs afoul here and there of some version of Bayesian reasoning. Rather, what we do is the reverse: we use our conviction that the resolution of the perihelion problem helps confirm general relativity theory to evaluate the adequacy of Bayesian principles (or their application). Similarly, we use our intuitions about particular cases to justify the axioms of probability that generate Bayes's theorem.

Furthermore, even where it *is* possible to figure the values in Bayes's theo-

---

12. For discussion, see Colin Howson and Peter Urbach, *Scientific Reasoning: The Bayesian Approach* (LaSalle, IL: Open Court Press, 1989), p. 257.

rem, Bayesian reasoning may add relatively little to the picture. Bayes's theorem may simply come in too late — after the hard work has been done. Consider an analogy with what we find in mathematics and logic. A mathematician who proves a theorem does the real creative work. A logician can come in and formalize the mathematical proof, and the formalization can add a bit to our security about the mathematical result. Still, the issue has essentially been settled prior to the formalization. Storrs McCall has provided what appears to be the first axiomatization of quantum theory.[13] It consists of a formal language of quantum theory, based on vectors and operators in Hilbert space, a minimal adequate set of axioms for the derivation of the theorems, formal derivations using first-order logic, and — to top it all off — a sketch of the formal semantics for the system. This is a fine contribution to understanding quantum mechanics. But McCall nowhere claims that he is one of the creators of the theory of quantum mechanics.

We must remember that an agnostic inquirer does not need a complete answer to every question encountered to arrive at a reasonable final judgment. Did a single individual compose the *Iliad?* The question admits of a variety of kinds of answers. Yes, there was one person who composed the *Iliad*, in exactly the form we have now (nobody holds this). No, there was a succession of dozens of bards, each of whom had an equal share in composing the epic (nobody holds this either). There are various positions in the middle. However, if any of a range of positions in the middle is correct, then there was a Homer. Perhaps, in order to opt for refined positions in the middle, the classicist will need sophisticated methods that involve math and statistics. But classicists have already made the case for the unitary thesis concerning the authorship of the *Iliad* almost entirely on qualitative grounds.

So there is reason to hesitate before judging Bayesian reasoning adequate to the task of the agnostic inquirer, and even more reason to hesitate before judging such reasoning obligatory.

Despite the deep reservations we have expressed about the prospects for Bayesian reasoning in the area of religious belief, though, we are open to the possibility that it will turn out, in the end, that the best and most exact way to articulate reasoning in the area of theism and revelatory claims is to invoke some species of Bayesian reasoning. Yet even if that should be the case, our contention stands: evidence from revelatory claims must be taken into account when one tries to ascertain whether the existence of a good God is more probable than not. An inquirer can reason in the way we began describ-

---

13. Storrs McCall, "Axiomatic Quantum Theory," *Journal of Philosophical Logic* 30, no. 5 (2001).

ing in chapter 2, from the data we will be discussing in the remainder of this book, to (perhaps) the existence of a God who has revealed.

4.2.2. Specifying a Pattern for IBE

It is legitimate to rely on deeply ingressed, ordinary, commonsense beliefs unless forced by conclusive arguments to discard them, as we have observed in chapter 1. When one thinks about such beliefs, what first comes to mind are beliefs about the world: there *is* a world; people feel pain; people who die tend to stay dead; and so on. Yet some beliefs about method also count as deeply ingressed and commonsensical. Almost nobody believes that the most probable explanatory hypothesis can always be identified with the first explanation that pops into one's mind. Almost nobody thinks, before the evidence is examined, that every explanatory hypothesis is objectively equiprobable. What is it that people do believe? At least implicitly, they believe that, if one hypothesis explains the facts better than another, the first hypothesis is thereby advantaged epistemically. And sometimes, at least — again, perhaps implicitly — people think that they are warranted in inferring that the best explanation of some event is probably true.

Ubiquitous (though largely implicit) pretheoretical judgments continually generate verdicts about probable truth. By far the best explanation for muddy footprints on the floor may be that someone walked all over the floor with muddy shoes. In that case, you judge that someone probably did walk all over the floor with muddy shoes. In fact, you may think that while you can imagine other explanations, imagining them is all you can do: you cannot really give them any credence. The explanation that someone walked on the floor with muddy shoes sufficiently approximates an ideal explanation so as to allow the conclusion about probable truth to be drawn with confidence. The hypothesis that a single individual composed the *Iliad* may better explain the poem's thematic cohesiveness, imagery, vocabulary patterns, sentence structures, and so forth, than does the hypothesis of multiple authorship. In that case, a classicist may conclude that the *Iliad* probably had a single author. And so on.

Philosophers have dubbed patterns of reasoning drawing on these pretheoretical beliefs "inference to the best explanation" (IBE). Though there is a good deal of discussion of IBE in the literature, it turns out to be surprisingly difficult to get a grip on the form of reasoning.

One big question that arises at the outset is whether the pattern includes a move to the claim that a particular hypothesis is probably true. Some philosophers do *not* include it, regarding IBE simply as "the procedure of choosing the hypothesis or theory that best explains the available data."[14] But that stops short of the main question an inquirer typically has: Is the chosen explanatory hypothesis *true?* So most of those who endorse IBE take it to include the move to the probable truth of the hypothesis under consideration. That is what we will do. This longer pattern of reasoning might be termed "Inference to *and from* the Best Explanation": one first chooses the hypothesis that best explains the data — in other words, infers *to* the best explanation — and then infers *from* that point that the hypothesis is probably true. And indeed, there is no reason the acronym IBE cannot be taken to stand for "Inference to and from the Best Explanation." (One could even choose to understand IBE to stand for "Inference from the best explanation, to the probable truth of the Best Explanation," though this leaves out of the picture entirely the procedure of choosing the hypothesis that best explains the data, and thus is unappealing for our purposes.)

Once we move past this big question, there are additional challenges. In light of these difficulties, we will be proposing our own scheme, which, though it does not avoid the vagueness that attends every formulation of IBE, does avoid one significant problem that shows up in leading accounts.

The problem we want to circumvent appears in the account of IBE offered by Peter Lipton, author of the best-known work on the subject. Lipton explains that one of the two "signal distinctions" in his account of IBE "is the distinction between the explanation best supported by the evidence, and the explanation that would provide the most understanding: in short, between the likeliest and the loveliest explanation."[15] And he suggests that we get at the explanation that would provide the most understanding, the loveliest explanation, by asking how good the explanation would be *if* it were true. He describes the "two-filter process" of his favored version of IBE:

> We begin by considering plausible candidate explanations, and then try to find data that discriminate between them. . . . Inference to the Best Explanation also suggests that we assess candidate inferences by asking a subjunctive question: we ask how good the explanation *would* be, if it were true.[16]

14. Jonathan Vogel, "Inference to the Best Explanation," in Edward Craig, ed., *Routledge Encyclopedia of Philosophy* (London: Routledge, 1998), retrieved June 17, 2005, from <http://www.rep.routledge.com/article/P025>.

15. Peter Lipton, *Inference to the Best Explanation,* 2d ed. (London: Routledge, 2005), p. 57.

16. Lipton, *Inference to the Best Explanation,* pp. 64-65. It looks like the two filters can be applied in either order. Elsewhere (p. 56) Lipton describes IBE: "Given our data and our background beliefs, we infer what would, if true, provide the best of the competing explanations we

One question helps us identify likely explanations; the other, lovely explanations.

Yet, despite the initial appeal of Lipton's distinction between "likeliness" and "loveliness," when we look closely at the latter notion, we run into trouble (let us call the latter notion "loveliness-L," as a reminder that this is loveliness as Lipton understands it). The problem, we emphasize, comes from "loveliness-L," not from the general, uninterpreted notion of a lovely or illuminating explanation. The problem comes from the fact that Lipton cashes out "loveliness" in terms of "how good the explanation *would* be if it were true." Lipton's subjunctive condition helps capture the notion of the loveliness or illuminating power of an explanation only if it is possible to abstract from the question of whether the explanation is in fact true, and focus solely on whether it would aid understanding *if* it were true. But this question about truth cannot be set aside.

Why not? The following example illustrates the problem. Imagine a prosecutor giving the following explanation of how the defendant could have committed the crime: "He flew like Superman, faster than a speeding bullet." Would anyone really think that such is an explanation with the power to illuminate, to provide understanding? Probably not. The world would have to be very different indeed if the defendant were able to fly like Superman. It would have to have different laws, or different constituents. We cannot make sense of the subjunctive situation — the fantasy world — in which the hypothesis is true.

Is the Bohr theory of the atom, in its amplitude, a lovely or illuminating explanation? If we cash that question out in the terms Lipton suggests, if we take the question to be about loveliness-L, we will be asking whether the theory would be able to explain *if it were true*. It is generally thought that the theory does illuminate some phenomena. But it cannot be true as a whole. Now, either the theory (as a whole) does or does not have a certain degree of loveliness-L. If it does, that is supposed to increase its probability. But nothing can increase its probability, because an inconsistent theory has a probability of zero. If it does not have any degree of loveliness-L, why is that? Presumably because it is inconsistent. But the only reason consistent hypotheses are considered prettier than inconsistent hypotheses is that, of course, inconsistent hypotheses cannot be true. An intrinsically inconsistent hypothesis does not illuminate (neither does one that is intrinsically consistent, but inconsistent when conjoined with what we know, such as the fact that it is impossible

---

can generate of those data (so long as the best is good enough for us to make any inference at all)."

for an ordinary human being to fly like Superman). The fact that loveliness as Lipton glosses it, loveliness-L, does not always increase probability indicates a problem with his general setup.

Indeed, by far the most important mark of the power to illuminate is consistency. It is much more significant than, for instance, simplicity (though simplicity is also supposed to play a role). Of course, you can ask plenty of questions about a hypothesis if you put aside the question of its truth. You can ask about certain aspects of simplicity: you can ask, for instance, how compressible the hypothesis is, how many words it takes to express it in its most compact form. But you cannot make a judgment about the power of a hypothesis to illuminate without bringing its plausibility or likeliness into the picture.

And just as one cannot abstract from the truth of a proffered explanation to evaluate its loveliness or power to illuminate, so also one cannot abstract from its power to illuminate to evaluate its likelihood. The "evidence" that underwrites the explanation "best supported by the evidence" (to return to Lipton's description of the "likeliest" explanation) must include evidence about the power to illuminate. The line Lipton tries to draw between likely and lovely explanations appears to be badly smeared.

We think, then, that any formulation of IBE that rests on the concept of what would explain *if true* will be unsatisfactory.

Unfortunately, formulations of IBE do commonly rely on the problematic concept of "what would, if true, explain." As one more example, consider John R. Josephson's framework for IBE:

> *D* is a collection of data (facts, observations, givens).
> *H* explains *D* (would, if true, explain *D*).
> No other hypothesis can explain *D* as well as *H* does.
> Therefore, *H* is probably true.[17]

Josephson cautiously introduces the pattern by indicating that abductions, or inferences to the best explanation, "pretty nearly" follow the specified form. (A good reason for the qualification is that the plausibility of the hypothesis under consideration needs to be built into the form; but, given the form's use of the concept "what would, if true, explain," it is unclear how and where plausibility enters the picture in this particular specification of IBE.)

Still, even though it is difficult to articulate a precise and definitive form

---

17. Josephson and Josephson, *Abductive Inference*, p. 5. The chapter of *Abductive Inference* that includes the pattern of inference was authored by John R. Josephson. He indicates (p. 29) that the formulation "is largely due to William Lycan."

for IBE, there is something to our pretheoretical beliefs concerning explanation. If one hypothesis explains the facts better than another does, the first hypothesis is advantaged in terms of probability. And you can hardly think that one explanation is better than another without thinking that there is some sort of ideal, and that the less good explanation, at least, declines from the ideal.

We will put forward an argument frame that takes us somewhat beyond pretheoretical beliefs, while avoiding cashing out the power to illuminate in terms of what "would, if true, explain."

The frame we propose has a further attraction: it operates at a *general* level, subsuming both explanations that refer to agent causes, and those that do not. It might be thought that this is ruinous to our proceeding. Millennia ago, Aristotle taught us not to expect the same kind of argument in all disciplines. Furthermore, he speaks in the *Analytics* about scientific explanation, but treats of practical reasoning elsewhere, and includes personal explanation as a subtopic under practical reasoning. However, while Aristotle says that we should not look for the same measure of exactitude in practical matters that we do in mathematics, that simply underscores the point that the account of practical explanation is best seen against a backdrop of theoretical explanation, which is taken as an ideal.[18] The argument frame we set out pertains to practical reasoning (including personal reasoning), so long as one is prepared to allow that good and bad, right and wrong, intentions and desires, count as properties, where a property is an attribute or characteristic in the broad sense, a characteristic of things, actions, persons, states of affairs, and so on. Now, that good and evil and right and wrong are such properties is presupposed by the whole project here. We have spent significant time talking about the problem of evil, and were there no such property as "wrong," there would be no substantive problem to deal with. And that there are *actions* subject to evaluation, as opposed to things that just happen to people — that also is presupposed as a reality.[19]

18. For a careful analysis of Aristotle and Aquinas on this subject, see Kevin L. Flannery, *Acts Amid Precepts: The Aristotelian Structure of Aquinas's Moral Theory* (Washington, DC: Catholic University of America Press, 2001).

19. It is worth observing that what is *not* presupposed by our argument or by our analysis of personal explanation is any form of dualism — substance dualism or property dualism (though we admit to having great sympathy with some forms of dualism). Thus our argument here is accessible to an inquirer who takes a position like Berent Enç: "[B]y assuming nothing more than a world of material things, we can understand the nature of decisions, of intentions, of voluntary action, and the difference between actions and things that we do when we are merely passive recipients of courses of events. . . ." Berent Enç, *How We Act: Causes, Reasons, and Intentions* (Oxford: Clarendon Press, 2003), p. 2. What we say concerning explanation should make sense even

Here, then, is the argument frame for IBE we propose:

1) If a hypothesis sufficiently approximates an ideal explanation of an adequate range of data, then the hypothesis is probably or approximately true.[20]
2) h_1 sufficiently approximates an ideal explanation of d, an adequate range of data.
3) So, h_1 is probably or approximately true.

This frame is in certain respects vague (as is every formulation of IBE); we will try to make matters clearer shortly.

4.2.3. Ideal Explanation and Pretheoretical Beliefs

Because inference to the best explanation is so widely used — both by people who never employ the label and by scientists and philosophers who do, but who never bother to set out the inferential form — we might excuse ourselves from the task of detailing the form. But we will take the middle ground (between ignoring the task altogether and devoting extensive time to it) and offer some brief comments.

---

to a materialist, provided the materialist holds on to the relevant concepts (such as intention), as Enç does. Some theists invoke an explanatory apparatus that depends centrally on "personal explanation," which is contrasted with scientific explanation. They argue for the existence of personal explanation by seeking to establish that human beings have something immaterial about them, which allows explanation in terms of intentions. But establishing that theism is probable does not require *first* establishing that humans have an immaterial element. We seek to bring divine intentions into the picture without assuming that intentions cannot be physical actions.

20. It may seem that we need to insert "better than any rival" in propositions 1 and 2. However, sufficient approximation to the ideal carries with it the idea of being superior to any rival hypthesis.

To say that a proposition is "probably true" is to say it has a probability > .5; to say a proposition is "approximately true" means that the statement is not as it stands completely accurate, so taken literally it might have a probability of 0, but that it is not far from an accurate statement that is probably true. Some argue that verisimilitude or approximation to truth is notoriously difficult to explicate satisfactorily, and therefore you cannot maintain that one hypothesis is preferable to another inasmuch as it is a better approximation to the truth. (See, for instance, Andrew Melnyk, *A Physicalist Manifesto: Thoroughly Modern Materialism* [Cambridge, UK: Cambridge University Press, 2003], p. 225.) But the inference is too quick. It seems to rest on the Socratic fallacy that a term cannot be used unless it can be defined. There are plenty of counterexamples. For example, we can recognize some instances of sound argument despite the difficulties of pinning down the concept of soundness (difficulties, for instance, concerning the relevance of premises to conclusion).

For the purpose of specifying the concept of "ideal explanation," we suggest that it is useful to think back to Aristotle and his ingenious explication of an ideal that stays close to pretheoretical concepts.[21] Our intention here will not be to track Aristotle very closely in scholarly exegesis. The *Posterior Analytics,* the work that bears most directly on the topic of ideal explanation, is in some places quite opaque. Rather, we will try to extract from Aristotle some useful ideas that have dropped out of many discussions and are only implicit in others, and we will develop the Aristotelian points in our own way.

Why turn to Aristotle?

In the first place, when philosophers consider Nagelian explanation, Hempelian explanation, revised Hempelian schemes such as Swinburne's, and other kinds of explanation, they inevitably do so in light of pretheoretical beliefs about explanation, and perhaps nobody has thought harder about the pretheoretical beliefs than Aristotle.

Moreover, unlike many of our contemporaries, Aristotle analyzed not just explanation but *ideal* explanation. The two concepts are distinguishable, as are the concepts of a ship and an ideal ship, or the concept of civil law and that of ideal civil law. One reason Aristotle's theory of explanation (i.e., of proof-explanation or demonstration) is mistakenly considered passé is that readers looking for a definition of explanation that actually fits scientific practice find instead a model of an ideal that any actual explanation must in some measure fail to satisfy. But whether the project of working up an ideal is in vogue or not, it clearly can be useful. Consider, for example, how helpful it is to think about the ideal of a *decisive experiment.* It certainly makes sense to ask what a decisive experiment might be, even if you think there is no such thing. The idea can be spelled out in this way. Suppose there are two competing hypotheses, h_1 and h_2, where h_1 entails some observation o, but h_2 does not. The hypotheses are tested in the lab, and what is found is ~o. That shows decisively that h_1 cannot be correct. Or so it had been said in the past, when the idea of a "crucial experiment" was popular. However, as Quine and many

---

21. Among the few distinguished philosophers of science and mathematics who share this conviction that it is important to reconsider Aristotle is Evert W. Beth. Beth begins *The Foundations of Mathematics: A Study in the Philosophy of Science* (New York: Harper and Row, Harper Torchbooks, 1966) with an extensive discussion of Aristotle in relationship to other philosophers of science and mathematics. Beth writes (p. 55): "Aristotle gives, in his *Analytica posteriora,* a quite remarkable methodology of the deductive sciences . . . which — apart from the evidence postulate and the connections with the theory of the νοῦς — is in many respects strikingly up-to-date." Beth, who treats Aristotle rather freely (as do we), curiously leaves out of consideration the key concepts of cause and explanation in his synoptic account of the essentials of Aristotle's theory of science (pp. 31-32).

others have argued, there is never a straightforward entailment between a hypothesis all by itself and an observation. Hypothesis h_1 entails o only in conjunction with auxiliary hypotheses. Faced with contravening evidence, then, it is always possible to give up one of the auxiliary hypotheses rather than the main hypothesis. Now whether Quine is right or his opponents are, there can be no discussion of the issue without some concept of an *ideal* crucial or decisive experiment. The same is true of ideal explanation.

There is yet another reason to turn to Aristotle, albeit a reason more difficult to grasp than the preceding two, particularly in the current environment. The reason turns on the concept of what we will call a *CUE-fact,* little if ever noticed in current discussions of explanation, but worked out in detail by Aristotle, who joins what others today separate: *proof* and *explanation.* Later in this chapter we will explicate the notion of a CUE-fact and indicate its importance for our purposes.

What, then, is an ideal explanation? We suggest that the following are necessary conditions.[22]

(1) The form of the explanation is valid. Ideally, the form of an explanation is deductively valid. The preservation of deductive validity is what was alluring in the Hempelian scheme of explanation. And it prompted philosophers to go along with Nagel when he proposed bridge laws connecting psychological and physical states. As a simple example of a deductively valid explanation, take the following: This ring is made of gold, and no artifacts made of gold corrode, so this ring does not corrode (the fact to be explained is the conclusion of the argument: this ring does not corrode).[23]

---

22. Aristotle intends to set out these conditions, or something much like them, as necessary. It appears that he does not intend them to be jointly sufficient. He continues to add conditions throughout the *Posterior Analytics.* But we think that the conditions we list are the main ones. In Aristotle's *Topics,* see bk. V, ch. 3, 131 b25-37. The whole of the *Posterior Analytics* is to the point. See especially *Posterior Analytics,* bk. I, ch. 2, 71 b20-24.

It may be noted that we do not include *simplicity* among our conditions. Simplicity is an ideal only if nature is, in fact, simple.

23. That the form is valid does not mean it must be syllogistic — unless one understands "syllogism" broadly enough to include argument patterns not usually identified as Aristotelian (or categorical) syllogisms. Aristotle himself, in giving a *definition* of "syllogism," does take it broadly, though his *examples* all fall under a narrower conception. The substance of Aristotle's definition is that a syllogism is an argument from which a conclusion distinct from the premises necessarily follows; see Aristotle, *Prior Analytics,* bk. I, ch. 1, 24 b18-23. While we detach from the sorts of examples Aristotle gives of syllogisms, we want to keep Aristotle's condition of *relevance,* located in the definition's requirement that the conclusion follows of necessity from the premises, which Aristotle takes to mean that the premises "cause" the conclusion. Just what he means by saying that the premises cause the conclusion to be true is open to interpretation. But he is clearly insisting that the premises at least be relevant, which is by no means insisted on

(2) *The premises are true.* Because the premises must be true, the explanation is anchored in the real world. Thus the plausibility or likeliness or probability of the explanation is secured.

(3) *The explanation cites a causal property or properties precisely in virtue of which the effect ensues.*

This condition takes a little more unpacking than do the others.

Aristotle argues that all explanation is causal. The appeal of his position is enhanced by his proposing a broad sense of "cause." He famously identifies four types: efficient or agent causes, material causes, formal causes, and final or teleological causes. Within each type, "cause" has focal and extended senses. An ideal explanation need not always invoke all these kinds of causes. Aristotle himself did not require this. He argued that mathematical and logical explanations, for instance, do not involve agent causes, and even more surely, do not involve final causes. However, he contended (rightly, we think) that there is causality even in mathematics and logic: formal causality. We cannot pause to argue over this; we will simply stipulate that by explanation we mean causal explanation — in this broad sense.

We take the commonsense view that there are, in fact, causes for explanations to disclose. One might agree that, in some abstract sense, explanations must disclose causes, but maintain that, since there are in fact no true causes, there are in fact no true explanations. On this Humean view, all we can get is concomitance, one kind of thing after another, with relentless regularity, and explanation becomes articulation of co-variance. Again, this is not the commonsense view.[24] It might be protested that the commonsense view rests on a naïve idea that there is a secret connection between objects and events. But it certainly is hard to shake off the idea that the explosion of a nuclear weapon above a city, followed by the city's devastation, is not *simply* a matter of one thing followed by another. The bomb has power — everybody believes this (including Hume, it appears).[25]

Further, we maintain the commonsense position that causes are explicable in terms of the interconnections of properties. This seems as obvious as it

---

these days. We think that it is as sensible as can be to say that premises of an argument actually ought to have something to do with its conclusion.

24. See Barbara Koslowski's excoriation of the social scientists' habit of faulting the reasoning of ordinary folk because it is all too tied to causal intuitions, and insufficiently beholden to the mandates of Humean reasoning. Barbara Koslowski, *Theory and Evidence: The Development of Scientific Reasoning* (Cambridge, MA: MIT Press, 1996).

25. See Thomas D. Sullivan, "Coming to Be Without a Cause," *Philosophy* 65, no. 253 (1990), and Galen Strawson, *The Secret Connexion: Causation, Realism, and David Hume* (Oxford: Oxford University Press, 1992).

could get. The wood burns because there is a fire *and the fire is hot*. It is not that you cannot find denials of this obvious point in the philosophical literature; you can find denials of just about anything. Along with some nominalists, one could deny, in a radically skeptical way, that there are properties in any sense whatsoever. And one could deny, somewhat less radically, that properties have any role to play in the account of causality and thus, derivatively, in explanation.[26] But these positions are extremely counterintuitive.

With all this in mind, then, what does it mean to say that a causal nexus must be cited *in virtue of which* the effect ensues? In Fred Dretske's famous example, the soprano's aria breaks the goblet in virtue of the sound waves produced, not in virtue of the meaning attached to the words she sings. Using older language, we might say that the sound waves are the per se cause of the breaking of the glass, or that the singing broke the glass qua consisting of sound waves, not qua consisting of Italian words. Incidental factors, "confounding variables" (as they are sometimes called in statistics), are excluded from consideration.

The requirement that an explanation cite a cause *in virtue of which* the effect ensues makes it impossible to reduce explanation to prediction. That certainly accords with commonsense intuitions. Suppose that every time you think about eating pea soup a certain neural pattern forms under your skull. At the same time, because of the neural activity, the electromagnetic field above your skull is disturbed in a certain characteristic way. You may ask: How did I come to think about eating pea soup? The neural activity in your head is part of the explanation (perhaps all of the explanation, on physicalistic assumptions). However, the formation of a signature disturbance above your skull is not at all part of the explanation, even though the probability of the thought on the neural event is the same as the probability of the thought on the special disturbance of the electromagnetic field. Indeed, it might be easier to make predictions off the events above your head than the events within your head, because it is more difficult to get at what is in your head. Nevertheless, no one would say that the disturbance in the electromagnetic field above your head caused you to think about eating pea soup.

If an explanation cites a causal property or properties in virtue of which the effect ensues, then all forms of causality that are active must be cited. In particular, *if* the state of affairs being explained includes something that has a functional cause, the cause must be cited. We emphasize the word "if." It may

---

26. Donald Davidson appears to take this position. For discussion, see Josep E. Corbi and Josep L. Prades, *Minds, Causes and Mechanisms: A Case Against Physicalism* (Oxford: Blackwell, 1999), pp. 13ff.

be that some thing being explained does not have a function; but *if* it does, you have not given a complete explanation of the thing unless you have invoked the function and explained its causal role. For example, suppose archeologists find some ancient object made of gold. It does not look like an ornament, but they cannot figure out how it could have been used for anything. The attempt to explain the state of affairs in which the ancient society had this object is not successful unless the function of the object has been cited. (It is worth noting that, while physicalism seems to go hand-in-hand with the elimination of teleology, some physicalists in fact found their whole view on the assumption that natural things have functions.)[27]

Degrees of precision are possible in the characterization of causes and effects. In explaining why gold resists rust and corrosion we might correctly cite the following cause in virtue of which the effect ensues: the atomic structure of gold is such that it has a relatively large number of protons, seventy-nine, in its nucleus. It is that property — not, say, the property of being yellow — that is responsible for the fact that gold resists corrosion. But the explanation becomes more precise if we say: because gold has seventy-nine protons in the nucleus, the nucleus exerts a large gravitational effect on its electrons, which causes them to move almost as fast as the speed of light, resulting in an increase in the mass of electrons, which in turn moves the electrons closer to the nucleus, which means the outermost electron cannot easily bond with anything else. We should not deceive ourselves into thinking an explanation has been laid bare when we have only looked at the beginnings (as if it is time to enjoy the shade of an oak tree when all we have done is planted the acorn).

(4) The explanation bottoms on fundamental substances and properties (including powers), and on the exercise of such. By a "substance" we mean, roughly, an ontological host rather than an ontological parasite. A substance is not a mode of anything; it is a thing that has modes of existence. A horse *has* a shape; the horse is the host, and the shape is the parasite.[28] Ideally, the

27. For example, Melnyk's "realization physicalism" maintains "that *everything* of a kind that is not mentioned as such in fundamental physics is nevertheless purely physical in the same sense in which the can opener is purely physical: its existence just consists in the existence of something that meets a certain job description." Melnyk, *A Physicalist Manifesto*, p. 7.

28. Exactly what is a substance? What makes a property essential? To answer these questions would take us deep into ontology. We offer just two quick observations.

First, regarding substance: There is an argument in the literature about whether Aristotle held that substances could be composed of substances. Many medieval philosophers were insistent that they could not be. The alleged substance made up of substances would be an aggregate of substances, not itself a unified substance. Commonly these days, however, writers both in science and philosophy talk of substances being made up of substances. For example, the hydrogen atom may be referred to as a substance made up of one proton and one electron,

substances and properties that figure in an explanation eventually bottom in ungrounded grounders, ultimate substances and properties.

Because an ideal explanation bottoms on fundamental substances and properties, there are explanations of explanations. That does not mean that there is some one explanation of everything: we will not necessarily arrive at the bottom of everything — a brute fact, if you wish to call it that. (If you think there is no end to the series of grounding properties, then while there is no such thing as an essence in the sense of an ultimate structure of the nature of a thing, there are more and less basic attributes, and some definitions are more expressive than others. If essence is a matter of degree, so is definition.)

(5) *Each of the above conditions is perspicuously satisfied.* For instance, the premises must not only be true; they must be known to be true.[29] And the explanation must not only bottom on fundamental substances and properties; the fact that it has bottomed must be perspicuous. That is a difficult thing to make out. Aristotle asks: How do you know when you have a thing's definition? Could you prove that you had it? The second book of the *Posterior Analytics* attempts to answer these questions. Having noted that the work is opaque, we now add that the second book is the most difficult part of the whole, and it is hard to see that Aristotle gives us much of an answer to the questions. But we know of no contemporary philosopher who does better in providing a convincing account of how we can know that we have reached bottom in an explanation. Consider the statement that, necessarily, anything that is F is G. Suppose — which is supposing a lot — that we can have an intuition into the necessity of the connection between F and G. It still leaves the question of whether something is F in virtue of being something else, say E. And even if that is self-evident, the question can be pushed back. Why is any-

---

each of which is in turn called a substance. And the proton is in turn made up of further substances. And so on.

Second, regarding essential predication: For Aristotle (unlike some contemporary philosophers), saying that F is essentially predicable of x is not the same as saying that F is such that x could not exist without it. Aristotle's conception of what is essential is tied to the idea of defining things: F is essentially related to x just in case it properly enters into the definition of x. Incidentally, this allows Christians to follow Aristotle, at the same time maintaining that Jesus was truly a human being, and that being human was his nature or his essence, but that there was no necessity in the Logos's taking on a human nature.

29. Evert Beth's view is that the requirement that the premises be *known* to be true is what most deeply divides Aristotle from the modern scientist. But as an ideal it is unobjectionable — and Beth agrees (see Beth, *Foundations of Mathematics*, pp. 38ff.). Beth notes that Aristotle takes as ideal a divine kind of knowledge — knowledge with certainty — that humans cannot possibly have. The very fact that Beth thinks of such knowledge as godlike shows that it is an ideal (see pp. 34-35).

thing an E at all? To bring the sequence to a halt, it is insufficient to maintain that one sees necessary connections between the givens, E, F, and G, and whatever else one wishes to add. It is also necessary to be able to intuit that whatever property undergirds the sequence is such that no explanatory property could be prior to it. And how would one know that?

Declination from the Ideal   Aristotelian ideal explanation, in its original form and in our adapted version, is, we must emphasize, unrealizable. So is ideal friendship; nevertheless, friendships may approximate the ideal to greater or lesser degrees. And so is ideal health — after all, humans are mortal; nevertheless, humans may approximate to greater or lesser degrees a state of ideal health. So long as one does not make the mistake of thinking that one must have the ideal or nothing at all, an ideal is helpful. To illustrate conditions for ideal explanation, Aristotle chose mathematical examples in the main, and for good reason. It is much more difficult to make out a case for our having ideal explanations in the *physical* order that bottom on substances and properties perceived to be ultimate. In modern science, we peer into a deep ocean, and what looks like bottom may be merely a shadow falling far above the floor, if indeed there is any floor. Yet the question, again, is not whether the ideal can be reached but what the ideal is.

While perfectly ideal explanations do not exist, there is, obviously, such a thing as an *acceptable* explanation. You can explain the mud on the floor by talking about someone tramping across it with muddy feet. Though you say nothing about why or how mud is transferred from foot to floor, that does not preclude you from drawing the conclusion that it is probable — highly probable — that someone walked across the floor with muddy feet.

Explanations that decline from the ideal can do so by failing to satisfy any of the conditions just mentioned. Of course, an argument that parachutes down from a high-flying ideal might not land safely; not just any kind of falling off from the ideal is acceptable. Accordingly, it might be asked: "So what criteria do you have for saying when an explanation has fallen beneath the threshold; where do we draw the line?" We do not draw a line, any more than we draw a line with respect to the question "When does a person cease to be a friend?" Perhaps there are no lines to be drawn in either case; in any event, we do not know how to draw a line, either with respect to friendship or acceptable explanation. And so far as we can see, neither does anybody else. However, as we consider the explanatory power of revelatory claims (in the next chapter), we will point out that, in the areas of both science and religion, explanations can fall pretty far below the ideal and still be valuable.

4.2.4. Putting Problems with IBE in Perspective

We have said that problems applying Bayes's theorem are serious enough to prompt a cautious inquirer to seek another method. Yet there are also problems associated with IBE; and even if they are (as we believe) more tractable than those associated with Bayesian reasoning, they deserve some attention.

Bas van Fraassen articulates a problem for IBE of some significance:

> [T]here are many theories, perhaps never yet formulated but in accordance with all evidence so far, which explain at least as well as the best we have now. . . . most of them by far must be false. I know nothing about our best explanation, relevant to its truth-value, except that it belongs to this class . . . most of which is false. Hence it must seem very improbable to me that it is true.[30]

It is possible to concede a good deal to van Fraassen's way of thinking about IBE without despairing of the general method. What may be conceded without courting disaster is that IBE — or, for that matter, any method in science — yields only approximate truth. For approximate truth will do well enough. It may be said that our bodies are made of cells and that cells in turn are composed of molecules and that molecules themselves are composed of more elementary bits of matter . . . and so on. As the analysis proceeds, the theory gets more and more tenuous. Perhaps, as a result, we had better say that our bodies are made of cells and that they are made of molecules — *whatever exactly molecules turn out to be.* For most purposes that will be good enough, even for most purposes in biology. Thus, because our pattern refers to what is "approximately true," it blunts the objection van Fraassen makes against the use of IBE. (Other replies to van Fraassen's objection can be given as well.)[31]

Another problem for IBE, a practical problem, is this: the argument forms or patterns expressing the mode of reasoning leave a great deal to be deter-

---

30. Bas C. van Fraassen, *Laws and Symmetry* (Oxford: Oxford University Press, 1989), p. 146.

31. As Samir Okasha asks: "What licenses van Fraassen in thinking that underdetermination of this sort is ubiquitous?" Samir Okasha, "Van Fraassen's Critique of Inference to the Best Explanation," *Studies in the History and Philosophy of Science* 31 (2000): 698. And any defense of van Fraassen's position would have to confront recent empirical work demonstrating the effectiveness of abductive computational models. See, for example, Josephson and Josephson, eds., *Abductive Inference.* In their fine (but neglected) study, the Josephsons and their associates demonstrate through the development of six generations of effective abductive computational models of knowledge-based systems that the problem of competing hypotheses can be controlled when it comes to the identification of red cell antigens, human gait analysis, word recognition, legal evidence, and speech recognition. IBE works.

mined by the inquirer. Our pattern is not an algorithm; in fact, it is nothing like an algorithm, let alone a magical formula. It may look pretty skimpy. But regarding our own pattern, and other patterns for IBE as well, a couple of things should be borne in mind.

First, IBE is not significantly worse off than demonstrative patterns in what it leaves to an inquirer. This fact is obscured by the unfortunate language currently dominating discussions in logic texts about arguments. Those discussions draw a distinction between valid and sound arguments, and they convey the impression that one cannot do better than have a valid argument with true premises — that is, a sound argument. But a sound argument can be utterly worthless. "Fermat's last theorem is true, therefore it is true" is sound, since it is true and it follows from itself. Who would offer this as a substitute for Andrew Wiles's proof? Now philosophers from Aristotle to G. E. Moore and beyond have, in one way or another, brought up the question of what else besides soundness is needed to yield a genuine proof, a *demonstration*. Some say that the premises must be self-evident; and some boldly go on to say what they mean by "self-evident." The topic of self-evidence is highly controversial, though, and it is always possible to ask, with respect to a putative demonstration, "How do you know that you have produced a *demonstration?* What are your criteria for evident propositions, and how do you know that these true propositions meet the criteria?" Both the pattern for IBE *and* patterns of deductively valid argument forms require filling of the right kind.

Second, though articulated patterns for IBE, our own and others, may move only slightly beyond pretheoretical beliefs — indeed, perhaps *because* they stay close to intuitions — they avoid a problem afflicting Bayesian reasoning. Our pattern for IBE, like other patterns such as Lipton's, hooks on to the essential notion of *illumination*. It is of the essence of explanation to illumine. And because a hypothesis may illumine even when its initial probability is inscrutable, the problems with inscrutability that affect application of Bayesian reasoning recede under IBE. Take, for instance, a case in which you think that the probability the world began to be is inscrutable, even on the assumption of a good God, because you think, as Jews and Christians have thought for centuries, that God was free to either create or not create. Unless you take the position that God *must* create, there is little reason to suppose that it would be probable that there is a world — or a world finely tuned for life, for that matter. However, given the existence of a world finely tuned for life, the best explanation of it, if there is any explanation at all, may appear to be that there is a good God who wants to bring into existence intelligent life. Thus we have the possibility of an explanation of a given fact that leaves the probability of the fact explained inscrutable. It renders it *intelligible;* but intelligibility is not solely determined by probability.[32] Imagine that neon-like signs start flashing in the sky every night, signs that say, "I am the Lord thy God; thou shalt not have strange gods before me" in every known language, and scientists have ruled out the naturalistic explanations that come to mind. What are the odds that the universe would be built that way? The odds are inscrutable. But perhaps one can nevertheless *explain* the phenomenon by appealing to a theistic hypothesis.[33]

Various arguments purport to show that IBE has some other intrinsic flaw, but they need not detain an inquirer bent on getting an answer to the question of revelation. After all, various arguments purport to show that there is something intrinsically wrong with *every* respectable form of argument. Mill argues that the Aristotelian syllogism begs the question; intuitionist mathematicians and relevance logicians discard basic logical laws.

But might there be some special problem in applying IBE to the subject matter at hand — to the content of revelatory claims? The main worry critics

32. While it may be true that the occurrence of a cause ups the probability of its effect, in actual cases it will be an open question just how much the probability goes up. Of course, if the hypothesis is that there is a good God who wanted to bring intelligent life into existence and had the capacity to do it, the probability of intelligent life is 1 (we assume here — with reason — that God would not suffer from weakness of will). But if the hypothesis is just that there is a good God, you might well think the probability of the world's coming to be, or coming to be in this form, is inscrutable. The fittingness arguments in Aquinas here come to mind (*Summa Theologiae* III, q. 1). Aquinas argues that the incarnation and passion of Christ are fitting. But that does not mean that they are probable. We differ here from Swinburne, who sees the incarnation and passion as probable.

33. Thus there is a way of saving the fine-tuning argument even if, as some very able philosophers have contended, the argument cannot be worked out on the basis of probability calculations. See Timothy McGrew, Lydia McGrew, and Eric Vestrup, "Probabilities and the Fine-Tuning Argument." The McGrews and Vestrup rule out fine-tuning arguments (cosmic design arguments) on formal grounds. They may be right about the impossibility of normalizing what has to be normalized. Their argument seems to presuppose that infinitesimals cannot be invoked in the application of the probability calculus. (For an account of the use of infinitesimals in this connection, see Richard Swinburne, *Epistemic Justification* [Oxford: Oxford University Press, 2001], pp. 243-44.) In any event, it does not directly follow that the fine-tuning argument fails. Why cannot an "inference to the best explanation" be made without invoking the probability axioms? The hypothesis of fine-tuning provides an explanation, where otherwise we would have no explanation. The argument from fine-tuning apparently persuaded philosopher Anthony Flew to give up his lifelong atheism. Many people are immensely impressed by it. Can there really be nothing to it? There may be something to it *even if* the probability of the evidence on the theistic hypothesis cannot be determined. There may be something to it if a theistic explanation of the phenomena at issue is better than non-theistic explanations.

are likely to have is this: it may seem very difficult to say what we should expect by way of revelation from a good world-creator.

That is a question that can partially be addressed in the abstract (as we have already done). However, the question is best considered in the context of application.

Indeed, as long as the consideration of any method floats in the nearly empty regions of hyperspace, little or nothing gets settled definitively: whether we are right or wrong about the utility of IBE in answering the question of revelation should be determined in part, at least, by attending to the method as it is in fact applied. The importance of assessing and revising methods in the context of *application* comes out in all sorts of examples. Take Hume's claim that accounts of the resurrection of Christ could not possibly render the event plausible, since the evidence makes the judgment that dead people stay dead about as certain as any empirical claim can get. On Hume's principles, it turns out that the resurrection (assuming it occurred) would be improbable for you even if you witnessed it. In such cases the inferential principles themselves become suspect.[34] Or imagine that the words "Made by God" are found all over the world, etched in micro-patterns of crystals of granite (let us say in *koine* Greek).[35] Some accounts of probability seem to require that we say that the rock-writing does not add even a tiny bit to the probability that theism is true. That is because, so far as we know, the rock-writing occurs only in our world, and we need a run of worlds to make the judgments about probability. But if a critic claimed to have a theory of probability showing that we should not think such rock-writing is any evidence in favor of theism, people would respond by saying: "So much the worse for the theory." Or consider G. E. Moore's hand-waving demonstration of the existence of the external world. Moore had listed three criteria, necessary and sufficient for a proof, and contended that his announcement ("Here's one hand, here's another" as he gestured) satisfied the requirements. The skeptic would see this as blatantly begging the question. Moore, however, was in our view correct to this extent: his "proof" did satisfy *his* criteria for proof. "So much the worse for the adequacy of the set of criteria," people would say, and correctly so.[36]

And in reflecting on IBE in the context of application (as we will do in chapter 5), it may be useful to keep the following point in mind: A revelatory

---

34. See John Earman, "Bayes, Hume, Price, and Miracles," in Richard Swinburne, ed., *Bayes's Theorem* (Oxford: Oxford University Press, 2002): Proceedings of the British Academy — 113.

35. John Leslie imagines this possibility in *Universes* (London: Routledge, 1989), p. 16.

36. Actually, and quite surprisingly — and mistakenly, in our view — some analytic philosophers take Moore to have been joking.

claim is in great shape if it is acknowledged that it offers the best explanation of the phenomena but complained that the argument-form of "inference to the best explanation" is suspect in general. Consider the following: "Yes, the tomb of Jesus was found to be empty, many claimed to have seen Jesus after he was crucified, and the early Christian community came to believe he had risen from the dead; and yes, the best explanation of all this and other facts is that he did in fact rise from the dead. But that is just an inference to the best explanation, and we all know how suspect inferences to the best explanation are."

4.2.5. What No Method Can Do: The Ineliminable Subject

It is time to face an inevitable objection. All this talk about method appears to be aimed at assuring objectivity. But the investigation cannot really be objective, can it? In truth, it cannot be. Not entirely. The person — the subject — cannot be eliminated. And so the investigation must in some measure be subjective.

However, mere admission of that fact scarcely dispels the worry.

The reason for the worry is illustrated by this portion of Pascal's argument for Christianity (quoted and endorsed without qualification by Newman):

> Consider the character of its Founder; His associates and disciples . . . the state at this day of the Jewish people who rejected Him and His religion; . . . after considering these things, let any man judge if it be possible to doubt about its being the only true one.[37]

Against the backdrop of the horrors of the twentieth century, and indeed the entire history of the hellish oppression of the Jews — and the complicity of many Christians in that oppression — Pascal's reference to the state of the Jewish people who rejected Jesus properly provokes negative reactions, from embarrassment to rage. Do not such arguments as Pascal offers and Newman sanctions serve to remind us of the reason so many have turned from religion to science as the chief informant about reality? The confidence of some that they have located the one true path to God has led to religious persecution and wars, with fanatics cheering as those who resist the True Way are put to the sword or burned alive. An onlooker might think that, neither with respect to the evaluation of the content of a professed revelation nor the interpreta-

---

37. Pascal, *Thoughts*, cited by John Henry Cardinal Newman in *An Essay in Aid of a Grammar of Assent* (Notre Dame, IN: University of Notre Dame Press, 1979), p. 244.

tion of supporting events, is there anything to go on except vague feelings, imagined illuminations, and the subjective certainty of assured possession of an "illative sense."

So why not admit what many think, that is, that no method can transform a subjective response into an objective case? Many do indeed accept the contention that, if any articulated case for revelation will contain indispensable premises whose evaluation will vary according to the subjective psychological condition of the inquirer, then no good case can be made out for a revelatory claim. John Earman exemplifies a common attitude when he says:

> I personally do not give much credibility to religious miracles and religious doctrines. And while I acknowledge that those who do can be just as rational as I am, I suspect that degrees of belief in religious doctrines cannot have an objective status if a necessary condition for such a status is the existence of a reliable procedure for learning, from all possible empirical evidence, the truth values of these doctrines.[38]

We would begin to respond by noting that, when writers talk like this, they often say things in tension with what they say elsewhere. Earman, for example, dismisses Hume's arguments against miracles as a "shambles," full of "posturing and pompous solemnities," and declares that among the absurdities not unreasonably attributable to Hume is: "Eyewitness testimony is incapable of establishing the credibility of a miracle deemed to have religious significance." If this thesis attributed to Hume can be judged absurd, why must the differences between a religious believer and Earman be "matters of taste in that there is no objective basis to prefer one over the other"?[39]

It is not as though there is no objective basis in the sense that there are no facts of the matter to get straight, or that it is impossible to get a grip on some of them. Indeed, many elements of a revelatory claim can be easily set in place. The claim that the Jewish people, at some time in their history, became monotheists is not so freighted with feelings that we have no hope of getting it straight. Nor is the proposition in the Christian creed that Jesus suffered under Pontius Pilate. Nor the proposition that the final recession of the Qur'an was made after Muhammad's death. That there are ascertainable facts of the matter follows from what the critics of revelatory claims themselves maintain. For if there is ground for doubting that God dictated every word of the Torah or the Christian Gospels or the Qur'an because those scriptures abound with contradictions, errors of fact, and dubious ethical

---

38. Earman, "Bayes, Hume, Price and Miracles," p. 108.
39. Earman, "Bayes, Hume, Price and Miracles," pp. 108, 94, 105.

judgments, then there are objectively ascertainable facts about the content of these works.

It could be said in response that, while it is possible to get a grip on some facts pertinent to judgments about religious matters, the issue will always be underdetermined. But if that response means that certainty can never be achieved, then the observation is irrelevant (see our discussion of "the problem of resolute belief" in chapter 6). And if the response means a religious hypothesis can never be shown to be *less* probable than .5, then it is obviously false. The Roman Catholic Church's claim of infallibility would be decisively defeated were a future Vatican III to reverse a defined doctrine of Vatican II. And if the response means that a religious hypothesis can never be shown to be *more* probable than .5, then it needs to be argued. Earman begs off providing the argument.[40] It cannot simply be said that it is impossible to show a religious hypothesis to be more probable than .5 because the judgments involved are too subjective; that is the very point at issue.

Furthermore, those claiming that religious teachings are "strongly underdetermined" must explain why the standard they have in mind is not too high. Earman anticipates this objection, arguing that scientific theories are not underdetermined — except in rare cases. But by his own admission, Earman here stakes out a position held by few philosophers of science. And even if it should be conceded to Earman that interesting scientific theories are rarely underdetermined, the same certainly cannot be said about philosophy, Earman's own field. As philosophy underdetermined by the empirical facts is nonetheless criticizable, so too are revelatory claims. Exact religious predictions and prophecies can be tested with the passage of time. Religious claims about things that have happened in the past can be evaluated by historians. Evidence concerning consistency of religious claims or concerning the coherence of theory or doctrine can be examined. Religious claims about the superiority of a certain way of living can be tried by entering into the life. (We will not go into further detail here about testability; the entire set of illustrations in the upcoming chapter constitutes a discussion of the testability of hypotheses about a divine origin of revelatory claims.)

There simply is no escaping the fact that subjective judgments come into play in every field of inquiry. As philosopher of science Ronald Giere points out, there often is no exactitude about handling scientific data: the scientist "*visually compares* the theoretical curves with the data points and judges whether the fit is 'extraordinarily good,' 'very good,' 'good,' 'reasonably good,' 'lacking in agreement,' 'seriously lacking in agreement,' and so

---

40. Earman, "Bayes, Hume, Price and Miracles," p. 107.

on."[41] And when it comes to judging whether the *Iliad* is a great work or whether it was composed by a single author, subjective judgments abound. Yet those judgments are not all on a par; we may compare and evaluate the reasonableness of the subjective judgments. There is no reason to think that investigations into religious matters must be all that different from investigations into other domains.

Indeed, subjective experience plays such a large role in constructing cases that virtually no two people will ever have the same case. The case varies by virtue of the mode of presentation. Two people look at the same case for theism: one accepts it, one does not. But maybe one of them understands the case better. Or suppose their understanding is exactly the same; suppose (what is, in fact, incredible) that they even have the same associations when they think about particular aspects of the case. Yet perhaps one of them has conceived of the case while the other has merely absorbed it. Your case is *your* case; your view from the window is *your* view. Two people will have, not two copies of the same picture, but rather, at best, two pictures from different angles. You might think that your picture or your case can always be shared. But if a case is shareable, it is by reason of a gift. One person is the recipient, the other the donor. That in itself can affect how the case is viewed.

Religious communities have long insisted that "the evidence can be accurately assessed only by men and women who possess the proper moral and spiritual qualifications."[42] (However, we would emphasize that Scripture does portray prophets and apostles as especially concerned to address sinners.) Still, whether or not one accepts the traditional thesis about the significance of moral dispositions, it surely is the case that some personal experiences can better position us to make judgments about a revelatory claim. It is often argued, for instance, that the experience of poverty or oppression confers a hermeneutical privilege. Newman contrasts Montaigne, softly settled into his comforts, a man who could afford "to play with life, and the abysses into which it leads us," with the poor, dying factory girl who says, "[I]f all I have been born for is just to work my heart and life away . . . if this life is the end, and . . . there is no God to wipe away all tears from all eyes, I could go mad!"[43]

---

41. Ronald N. Giere, *Explaining Science: A Cognitive Approach* (Chicago: The University of Chicago Press, 1988), p. 190.

42. William J. Wainwright, *Reason and the Heart: A Prolegomenon to a Critique of Passional Reason* (Ithaca, NY: Cornell University Press, 1995), p. 3. Wainwright's penetrating study follows this theme through the works of Jonathan Edwards, John Henry Newman, William James, and others.

43. Newman, *An Essay in Aid of a Grammar of Assent*, p. 247.

Either there is a God, or nothing makes sense; and the factory girl may have as good reason as the scientist for thinking the world has to make sense.

There is no denying the fact that method can take us only so far. The subject, the entire person, is ineliminable. The world must be viewed from a certain angle, the data refracted through the prism of a mind that is not free from impurities. Assessment of the data will vary a little or a great deal from person to person in light of personal disposition and experience. Much can be done to steady the judgment, but not everything. There are limits to what a disembodied method can produce. Would we want it to be any other way?

4.3. Choosing a Hypothesis

4.3.1. Practical and Theoretical Problems

In a *general* sense, then, we have a method of investigating hypotheses, and no good reason has surfaced to think it cannot be applied to hypotheses about revelation. However, there are some significant practical questions, questions of implementation, to be addressed.

We begin with some questions about choosing a hypothesis from the vast number of revelatory claims in existence. It may be very difficult to see how to sort through the plethora and zero in on the most likely candidates.

We emphasize that this is a *practical* problem. A *theoretical* problem concerning the multitude of revelatory claims might also be posed: How could there be such a welter of revelatory claims today if there really is a good God who communicated something important? Is not the multitude of claims evidence *against* the existence of such a communication?

With respect to the theoretical problem, we need to ask ourselves what should be expected if a true revelation had been given in the somewhat distant past. Suppose a revelation had been given ages ago that was simple and clear, as well as easily remembered and transmitted: suppose, for example, that the Pythagorean theorem had been revealed to Pythagoras. (It is said that on the occasion of its discovery, Pythagoras sacrificed a bull in honor of the gods, the mathematical illumination being conceived, we might suppose, as something like a revelation from on high.) How would the revelation of that theorem look now? The human mind refracts data through a complex structure of associations and in time poses new questions about the given, whatever it is, and poses new answers to match those questions. What is the theorem true *of*? Space? Abstract entities? Nothing? Is the theorem system-relative? Can it consistently be denied, like the fifth Euclidean postulate? Are the lines of a triangle made up of points? Can the theorem properly be expressed in terms of numbers, or would that be alien to the revelation? And so on and so on. We could expect a variety of answers to such questions, not all consistent. Contemporary mathematics and logic offer a bewildering range of options. Even if the ancients had thought that bits of geometry had been revealed, the devotees of the god of mathematics would have found, as later thinkers have found, plenty to argue about.

And there is little reason to suppose that things would be otherwise if there had been a revelation bearing more directly on the big questions of life. What should one expect if an original revelation had been given, much in the way Maimonides conceived, God conveying the extant Torah to Moses? As events transpired and the recipients of the Mosaic revelation reflected on their experience and the meaning of the divine gift, there would inevitably arise a variety of questions and an even greater variety of answers. Not least among the questions would be the issue of what is essential. Someone, someday, surely would deny the essentiality of the sacrifices. Maimonides himself, after all, construed them as divinely ordained only because of ancient custom: he suggested that God adjusted the pagan practices for his own purposes so the Hebrews would not sacrifice to foreign gods. Others would go further. The philosophically minded believers could come to see in the original revelation nothing more essential than ethical theism, purging the message of sacrifice, Shabbat, and Hebrew prayers, utterly rejecting the authority of the rabbis. Reactions would set in. And if, as seems natural, this is what would be expected if the original revelation were to have occurred in the way Maimonides thought it did, how should things look now if it were to have been made instead to an ancient people dwelling in the Kalahari desert or New Guinea? And how would things look if, instead of there being one revelation, there had been more than one, God speaking "to our ancestors in many and various ways"?[44] Things would not look all that much different, it would seem.

Thus our focus in the next two sections will be on the *practical* problem for an inquirer presented with the plethora of revelatory claims. Does the multitude of claims constitute an insurmountable obstacle for the agnostic inquirer? Perhaps — if the pool of serious revelatory claims is as large and as full of contradictions as is often imagined, and if it is necessary to find the one true revelation. Happily, however, as we now go on to argue, *there is little reason to think either of these antecedents is true.*

---

44. Heb. 1:1 (NRSV).

4.3.2. The Pool of Serious and Independent Revelatory Claims

The first step toward cutting down the pool of claims that must be considered is to set to one side religious claims that are not revelatory. Central forms of Buddhism and Confucianism are notable examples of religions that do not appeal to a revelation. Of course, these religions have their attractions. Still, an inquirer interested in revelatory claims properly sets them aside. Such an inquirer also excludes all purely philosophical claims, even if some people cling to them with a religious fervor, some philosophers include them in the *denotata* of their concept of religion, and some legal systems count them as religions. The same goes for claims concerning the worth of spiritual exercises, meditation techniques, diet, and various asceticisms, when the claims do not purport to be sanctioned by divine authority.

Furthermore, not every revelatory claim deserves consideration. The inquirer is looking for a revelation that speaks effectively to the problem of evil. Pythagoras sacrificed a bull in thanksgiving for the revelation of his famous theorem; Cantor believed some ideas of set theory had been revealed to him from above; Ramanujan ascribed his theorems to the consort of the lion-god. Mathematical theories, however, tell us nothing about the problem of evil. And an inquirer need not be concerned with private claims that do not purport to have public implications, even if the claims speak to the problem of evil in a particular person's life, for the inquirer is looking for a general solution to the problem of evil. Nor is an inquirer bound to study every general revelatory claim that speaks to the problem of evil, since some are outlandish.

Even so, the pool of relevant revelatory claims is considerable. Are there just too many competitors?

In answering this question it is imperative to give due weight to the obvious point that religious *differences* do not necessarily amount to *contradictions*.

One reason putative contradictions are often only apparent — or at any rate open to interpretation — is that two apparently inconsistent revelatory claims will each have an associated array of possible interpretations. Only if each possible interpretation of the first claim is inconsistent with each possible interpretation of the second claim will there be genuine inconsistency. It is, of course, difficult to be sure that a listing of possible interpretations of some particular revelatory claim is complete. And even if study were restricted to *plausible* interpretations on the list, options would be vast.

A case in point is the historic dispute between Lutherans and Catholics over the concept of justification, central to the Reformation. The 1999 Joint Declaration of the Lutheran World Federation and the Roman Catholic

Church indicates that there are no differences on justification that should be church-dividing: while Trent condemned certain of the key statements Luther had affirmed, we now realize that Luther and Trent used the word "faith" in different ways. Similarly, it is not always clear what the doctrinal differences are between Christianity and Islam. People assume that Islam rejects the divinity of Christ; surprisingly, that is not so clear.[45] And Christians can accept many propositions Islam offers concerning the unity of God. It is not part of Christian doctrine that Muhammad was not a prophet, though it is implicitly part of Christian doctrine that any teaching of Muhammad contrary to Christian teaching is not revealed. And while most people who count themselves Jews today do reject Christ as Messiah, no one appears to claim that it has been *revealed* that Christ is not the Messiah. Indeed it has been argued by one specialist in Jewish theology, Michael Kogan, that nothing prevents Jews today from believing that it is at least possible that God became incarnate in Jesus, and that Jesus was vicariously sacrificed for the sins of the world and rose from the dead.[46]

Furthermore, when packages of claims made by two religious groups *do* include irreconcilable propositions, the irreconcilable claims may turn out to be inessential to one or both packages. Christians and Muslims reject the ninth principle in the famed statement of Maimonides that the entire Torah we now have is the one given to Moses and there will never be another given by God. But is this ninth principle essential to Judaism? Other parts of Maimonides' creed have been abandoned by believing Jews who take a much narrower view of what is essential. Why not this principle as well? Christian groups have often talked in ways strongly suggesting that public revelation has come to an end; no more is to be expected before the Second Coming of Christ and the end of time. Is this really essential to Christianity? And exactly what proposition is it that is essential? Furthermore, whether a statement is essential to a package of revelatory claims depends, at least in large part, on the status of the one speaking for the community that supposedly received the revelation, and it is often unclear who is entitled to speak for the community and under what conditions.

We should not for a moment dream of repeating the fatuity that all religions are really saying basically the same thing in diverse languages. Homer's

45. See R. C. Zaehner, *At Sundry Times: An Essay in the Comparison of Religions* (London: Faber and Faber, 1958), pp. 195-217.

46. See, for instance, Michael S. Kogan, "Toward a Jewish Theology of Christianity," *The Journal of Ecumenical Studies* 32, no. 1 (1995), retrieved Sept. 24, 2004, from the Institute for Christian and Jewish Studies, <www.icjs.org/scholars/kogan/html>. See also Michael S. Kogan, *Jewish Theology of Christianity* (Oxford: Oxford University Press, 2004).

Iliad, purportedly revealed by the muses (deities), portrays a divine realm surely inconsistent at some level with Jewish, Christian, and Muslim scriptures. Jews, Christians, and Muslims take opposed stances on a large number of issues, across and within the basic groups. Yet, for the reasons just given, many allegedly irreconcilable differences appear, upon scrutiny, to be reconcilable after all — or at least not clearly irreconcilable.[47]

4.3.3. Investigating Disjunctive Claims

The inquirer's task would indeed be exceedingly difficult if it were necessary to find, among all the conflicting claims, *the one and only true* revelation. But if there is at least one true revelation, it is doubtful there is only one. That is to say, it is doubtful that God has revealed divine doctrine to only one people. Major religions, in fact, teach that God has spoken at diverse times and places. And while it would be wonderful to have the full truth, something far less may suffice for important purposes: it may be possible to settle for a sufficiently rich, true disjunction. The sought-for conclusion concerning God's existence would follow from any one of several revelatory claims. An inquirer uncertain about the truth of central contentions distinguishing Hinduism, Judaism, Christianity, and Islam, but confident that one or more revelations contain important truth, can reason in accordance with a constructive dilemma: Either h or j or c or i. If h then g. If j then g. If c then g. If i then g. So g.

With regard to investigating disjunctive claims, an agnostic inquirer is not in a radically different position from one who is inquiring into scientific claims. A physicist may decide that relativity theory is a substantially true account of the world without committing to a particular version of the theory. Relativity prohibits *something* from traveling faster than light. But what? On one interpretation, it is matter or energy, on another it is signals, on another causal processes, on yet another it is other information.[48] The typical researcher in biology also need only believe in a disjunction of evolutionary theories. It may be unnecessary for a biologist investigating the circadian behavior of mice to determine which of the many versions of evolution is true; it may be enough if any one is.

In fact, in some ways the problem is actually worse in science than it is with

---

47. Of particular note is the examination of orthodox Christianity taken pair-wise with world religions East and West. See Zaehner, *At Sundry Times.*

48. For discussion, see Tim Maudlin, *Quantum Non-Locality and Relativity: Metaphysical Intimations of Modern Physics,* 2d ed. (Oxford: Blackwell, 1994), ch. 1.

respect to revelatory claims. One major problem with evaluating scientific hypotheses is anticipating what will be proposed in the future. The agnostic inquirer, however, is not focused on anticipating what will happen in the future; rather, the inquirer is concerned with whether a revelation *has been* given — and again, there are only so many revelatory claims out there. Also, it is necessary in exploring revelatory claims to determine whether a given hypothesis is true, but not to *construct* hypotheses (at least not initially). The agnostic inquirer steps right over one of the most difficult tasks for scientists.

Someone might protest that, once the project of examining the content of revelatory claims is underway, it is, in fact, complicated by hypothesis-construction. For at some point the thoughtful inquirer is bound to confront statements that challenge understanding. "Human beings are made in the image of God." What can this mean, given that God has no body? "Before you is the Eucharist, the body, blood, soul and divinity of Christ." Can this claim about what appears to be bread be construed without absurdity? These and dozens of other issues may force an inquirer to think of explanatory hypotheses — unless the theologians have adequately mapped out the possibilities in a manner accessible to the inquirer.

Yet, to the extent that an agnostic inquirer shares the problem of hypothesis-construction with scientific investigators, the inquirer can benefit from the kind of methodological solutions offered by scientists. Furthermore, to accept or reject the original revelatory claim, the additional hypotheses that an agnostic inquirer needs to consider may not have to be accepted or rejected. All one may need to accept is a disjunction of explanatory hypotheses — and the last disjunct might read: "or something like this." Even the Roman Catholic church, far more inclined to "define" than most believing communities, says that the faithful are free to take or leave certain accounts theologians give of the nature of the Eucharist (just as one is free to take or leave mathematicians' interpretations of the nature of numbers even as one works with numbers and believes in their existence). Finally, and perhaps most significantly, the invention of new hypotheses may *strengthen* an inquirer's case for the truth of some particular revelatory claim. The abductive movement, the inventive movement, opens new possibilities that may end up strengthening the case in the long run. For example, while the development of hermeneutical principles over the last century and a half created many problems for believers, it also eased some difficulties. In Scripture, Jesus appears to predict the Second Coming within a generation, twenty years or so. The hypothesis now widely received, however, is that he never said any such thing.

If an inquirer is targeting a disjunction of revelatory claims, less evidence may be required than suspected. Imagine that soldiers under siege report hearing a loud noise. One says there was a big explosion; another reports a great clap of thunder; another says a bridge collapsed; a few say they heard no loud noise. You might have trouble assessing the probability of any one soldier's contention, but nevertheless think it pretty likely that one claim or another that there was a loud noise is true, and hence that the disjunction of those reports is true. (And it will be even more likely that there was a loud noise.) Or, to switch examples, you may observe a hundred people walking by; you might not bet that any particular one of them carries over $200 in cash, but you might think it a very good bet that some one of them has more than $200.

So, less is necessary if a disjunction is targeted. And in the end there is a way in which all the live options among revelatory claims may be disjunctive. For while there can be a verbal disclaimer — you might say "I'm a Roman Catholic of the strict observance, and reject any claim that another doctrine is the sole true religion" — the doctrine strictly adhered to keeps unfolding. The Council of Trent defined transubstantiation in response to Luther's teachings. Prior to that, two Catholics of the strict observance might have disagreed about the manner in which Christ was present in the eucharistic bread. After Trent, which rejected the Lutheran formula that Christ was "in, with, and under" the eucharistic bread, it became evident that the earlier disjunction of possibilities for a Catholic had been pruned back.[49]

Because an inquirer is always looking for a disjunction, many difficult questions can be put to one side. Whether Moses was the human author of the Pentateuch, whether capital punishment is always wrong, whether purgatory exists — these questions can be set aside, at least at the outset. Revelatory claims unfold over time. Proponents of particular revelatory claims are well aware that some difficult questions are best pushed off at the beginning. (It might surprise an inquirer to learn that Aquinas thought that some mandates concerning sexual ethics were less obviously correct than the precepts of the Decalogue.)

On the other hand, you may not want to set the hard questions aside. Focusing initially on a problematic or troublesome claim may have a high payoff. Consider *King Lear*. The play has various apparent defects. But what at first appears as a kind of overcrowding, an indistinctness, may in time be seen as contributing to a sense of vastness. What at first seems an unimaginative doubling of plot and subplot may, on reflection, be seen to drive home the thesis that something has gone wrong with the world: fathers are divided against loyal offspring. By attending to putative shortcomings, we can see the

---

49. See Denzinger-Schönmetzer, Section 1652 (a passage from Trent).

play's greatness become manifest.[50] Hobbes was struck by a proposition in Euclid that seemed to him to be impossible; he worked his way back to the axioms and amazed himself by deciding that the proposition was true.

This point may be made as well in connection with revelatory claims. Galileo's treatment by the Roman Catholic Church has long been a source of embarrassment for Catholics. But it is noteworthy that, despite the great interest the ecclesial community had in silencing Galileo, through the whole sorry sequence of events no official definitively pronounced both that the Catholic Church has the authority to teach infallibly about Galileo's scientific claim, and that Galileo was wrong. What is the best explanation of this fact? Could the Catholic Church be correct in asserting that the core of its revelatory claim has been developed with perfect (one might say, superhuman) consistency over the centuries? Taking up such questions may result in a relatively easy disproof of Catholicism; but if it is not disproved, then the case supporting it may be considerably strengthened. The point also holds with respect to broad disjunctive claims. The assertion common to Christian denominations that one man made a sacrifice atoning for the sins of many might be scrutinized. The claim common to many Judaic, Christian, and Islamic religions that there are certain actions that are absolutely prohibited, regardless of the consequences, might be investigated (see chapter 5).

Where does an inquirer begin, given all the possible starting points — all of the different levels of generality, and all of the claims found at the different levels?

It can be eminently reasonable to focus initially on a single explanatory hypothesis.[51] Now, in a way, when you pick one hypothesis, you are picking two: the hypothesis and its negation, h and ~h. Ordinarily, however, ~h will not properly be seen as an explanatory hypothesis, since to deny that something is an explanation is not itself to give an explanation. In special cases, however, the negation of the hypothesis may be tantamount to an alternative proposal. For instance, if h is the hypothesis that a single individual com-

---

50. See A. C. Bradley, *Shakespearean Tragedy: Lectures on Hamlet, Othello, King Lear and Macbeth* (New York: St. Martin's Press, 1992).

51. In light of what we have been arguing, one might wonder whether there *are* single hypotheses. But there certainly are hypotheses that are expressed non-disjunctively. And this is what we mean here. Given what we have said earlier, the reality may be that all prima facie simple or single hypotheses unfold into many.

John and Susan Josephson, who report on six generations of increasingly sophisticated "abduction machines" for medical diagnosis and other similar inferential tasks, argue that it is often desirable to postpone consideration of other hypotheses, which can be reserved for a later cycle of "confidence up-dating." Josephson and Josephson, *Abductive Inference*, p. 268.

posed the *Iliad*, ~h may be taken as tantamount to the thesis that the *Iliad* was composed by ~more than one individual, since it is the only live alternative. But often the negation of a hypothesis of interest will have no explanatory power: that is the case, for instance, when h is the hypothesis that your son walked across the floor with muddy shoes.

The most natural way to proceed in selecting a hypothesis or hypotheses may simply be to start with what is most attractive or most intriguing. The attractive claims may be overarching claims, "denominational" revelatory claims such as the claim of Orthodox Jews or of Southern Baptists or of Roman Catholics, or still broader claims, such as the Abrahamic claims common to Judaism, Christianity, and Islam. Or, instead of an umbrella claim, a very specific contention might be identified, such as the claim that it has been revealed that the prophet Jeremiah was an oracle of God, or the claim that it has been revealed that it is always wrong intentionally to kill the innocent. As an alternative to simply picking what is attractive or intriguing, a hierarchical ordering method could be devised to help with the process of selection. Despite obvious dangers, *a priori* judgments could be attempted about the most likely kind of revelation for a good God to give, and the next most likely kind, and so on; an inquirer could go down the line, searching for an actual revelatory claim that meets the named conditions. Or a hierarchy of claims could be constructed based on the strength of the assertions contained in those claims identified as live options: the stronger and the more specific, the more audacious the claim, the easier it will be to invalidate if false, and quite possibly, the easier to validate if true. In practice, the method of starting with what is attractive will often yield results similar to the method of devising a hierarchical ordering: judgments made about the attractiveness of certain aspects of revelatory claims will likely be embodied in the principles chosen for constructing a hierarchical ordering.

4.4. Choosing the Data

4.4.1. CUE-Facts and Other Putative Facts

Questions concerning how an agnostic inquirer can implement the method of IBE arise not only about choice of hypotheses but also about choice of data.

There is a category of facts that is all too easily neglected in investigation of revelatory claims: *putative* facts, "quasi-facts," facts that fall short of being "observations" or "givens."

This sounds strange, no doubt, since on any standard formulation of IBE, the explanation is crafted to explain *data*. We have put it this way ourselves: "If a hypothesis sufficiently approximates an ideal explanation of an adequate range of data, then the hypothesis is probably or approximately true." Is not data what is given, known, or at least accepted as true? Putative facts, of course, are not given, known, or accepted — not by anyone who calls them putative. Must not a philosophical inquiry into the truth of a revelatory claim eschew data that is not evident, data that is not accepted by theist and atheist alike? It is common for philosophers to think that arguments in natural theology begin either from "very general and evident public phenomena" (the starting points, Swinburne suggests, for "bare natural theology"), or from "generally agreed historical data for the detailed claims of a particular religion" (starting points for "ramified natural theology").[52] As Kretzmann comments:

> [N]atural theology, a branch of philosophy . . . provides the traditional and still central means of integrating philosophy with (some of) theology.
>
> Integrating them by means of natural theology amounts to developing within philosophy some of the subject-matter specifically associated with theology. Developing it within philosophy amounts to forgoing appeals to any putative revelation or religious experience as evidence for the truth of propositions, and accepting as data only those few naturally evident considerations that traditionally constitute data acceptable for philosophy generally.[53]

However, putative facts often figure in explanations and can play an essential role in agnostic inquiry into revelation. To see how they can play a legitimate role, consider a practical matter. Somebody tells you that you would be better off reserving a room at hotel x rather than y because the accommodations at x are superior and x is less expensive. If you are satisfied with that

---

52. Richard Swinburne, "Natural Theology, Its 'Dwindling Probabilities' and 'Lack of Rapport,'" *Faith and Philosophy* 21, no. 4 (2004): 533.

53. Norman Kretzmann, *The Metaphysics of Theism: Aquinas's Natural Theology in "Summa contra gentiles I"* (Oxford: Oxford University Press, 1996), p. 2. Kretzmann goes on to note that Aquinas needs Scripture to carry off his project of natural theology, to provide "both a chart to guide his choice of propositions to argue for, and a list of specifications that can be consulted to see that reason's results in Book I of *Summa contra gentiles* are in fact building up a picture of 'God considered in himself'" (p. 7). However, Aquinas is still doing philosophy "from the top down," undertaking a project in metaphysics that begins with consideration of God; and it counts as philosophical "because the starting-points and ultimate justifications of its arguments are all accessible to 'natural reason,' and because it never uses revealed propositions as more than occasional guides to its agenda" (p. 50).

explanation, it would make no sense for you to say, "Very well, I see why I'd be better off, but can you justify the claim that x is a better selection?" The explanation *is* the justification. You do not start with the fact that the selection at x is preferable and then explain it. You explain the superiority of the selection, which becomes a fact upon your recognition of the truth of the explanation.

The point holds not only at the practical level; it holds as well with regard to theoretical questions. You have a hard time believing that continents once formed a single gigantic land mass until it is explained to your satisfaction how it could have happened. Cosmologists doubt that the entire universe was once packed into a single pointlike entity of infinite density — until it is explained to them how that could happen. Some evidence suggests that sexual activity improves health. You regard it as wishful thinking, until you learn that frequent sex ups the production of immunoglobulin A, which promotes immunity to everything from common colds to HIV. You doubt whether one illiterate person composed the *Iliad,* until experts explain how oral poetic traditions developed techniques for holding that much, and more, in human memory.

It is easy to be blind to the role putative facts play in solid explanations, since they often present themselves as established facts. In some situations it can take genius to see clearly what is going on — the genius of a Darwin, for instance. A less astute naturalist might be sorely tempted to conclude from the data collected in a number of fields that the *fact* that species evolve is well established, even though no explanation of how it could take place is available. Darwin resisted that temptation, as he explains in the introduction to the first edition of *Origin of Species by Means of Natural Selection:*

> In considering the Origin of Species, it is quite conceivable that a naturalist, reflecting on the mutual affinities of organic beings, on their embryological relations, their geographical distribution, geological succession, and other such facts, might come to the conclusion that each species had not been independently created, but had descended, like varieties, from other species. *Nevertheless, such a conclusion, even if well founded, would be unsatisfactory, until it could be shown how the innumerable species inhabiting this world have been modified,* so as to acquire that perfection of structure and coadaptation that most justly excites our admiration.[54]

Darwin is saying that a satisfactory *case* for the facts would not exist without an explanation of the putative facts.

54. Cited by Niles Eldredge in *Darwin: Discovering the Tree of Life* (New York: W. W. Norton & Company, 2005), pp. 93-94 (italics added).

A subclass of putative facts deserves special attention. These are facts one does not accept as true but *would* accept, provided they are appropriately linked to a plausible explanation. Such facts, which are *conditional upon explanation,* we dub "CUE-facts." In the paradigm case, a CUE-fact is one you are inclined to accept, are pulled toward, and would accept *if only* it were explainable. Given the tug toward the fact, all that remains — all that is required for acceptability — is a respectable explanation. Declining from the paradigm case, one finds facts that would be accepted *if and only if* they could be explained, and others that would be accepted *only if* they could be explained. The strength of the initial inclination or pull toward the fact helps determine not only which of the conditions just mentioned apply ("if only" it is explainable, "if and only if," or "only if") but also the kind of explanation required for respectability. You may be willing to accept the CUE-fact that your intentions affect your actions if you find any halfway decent explanation of the possibility, so confident were you of the "fact" before encountering the physicalistic line of reasoning that appears to force you to abandon the initial, commonsense position. On the other hand, you may be willing to embrace a moral precept such as "Never secure the death of the innocent" only if an explanation approximating the force of an Aristotelian demonstration — a proof-explanation — crushes opposing arguments.

Mention of Aristotle returns us to a cryptic comment we made a couple of sections back, where we said, without explaining the concept of a CUE-fact, that Aristotle discoursed on it. What we had in mind should now be clearer. Aristotle introduces CUE-facts, though not by that name, when he says in the *Posterior Analytics* that for perfect scientific understanding, we need to reason in a way that establishes *that* it is the case by explaining *why it has to be* the case. The *Posterior Analytics* is devoted to explaining more fully what this reasoning process looks like.

CUE-facts, highlighted by Aristotle but only implicitly acknowledged today, abound. Their implicit acknowledgment comes out in the discourse of the philosophically literate, who often must accord at least some weight to skeptical arguments against common assumptions in everyday life and science. One function of philosophy is to subject the putatively given to the acids of reasoned dissent. It casts into doubt things that were once taken for granted. Just how strong an explanation is required to remove the doubt depends on how much of a battering the "given" has taken. Situations in which explanations make putative facts acceptable are so common that philosophers such as Roderick Chisholm think that a good deal of philosophical activity is directed toward showing how one can hold on to ordinary beliefs seemingly undercut through skeptical arguments. Virtually all of us, for example, are strongly inclined to believe that certain things get larger over time. Chisholm suggests that it is puzzling how such increase occurs.[55] His "problem of increase" derives from Aristotle, who poses a yet deeper problem, one concerning not artifacts and other mere aggregates (Chisholm's focus), but more unified entities, such as organic beings. You may really feel the pinch when Aristotle is done, and say: "I am convinced I grow, but cannot understand how. I would accept the fact that I grow, if only I could find an explanation." Aristotle has an explanation, one invoking deep and difficult metaphysical concepts.

Skeptical arguments can be given too much weight. If used with abandon, the acids of dissent may corrode deeply ingressed commonsense beliefs that anchor not only our ordinary lives but the philosophical enterprise itself. Refusal to accept the fact that you grow unless you can find an explanation of how you grow is within shouting distance of the line of abandon. An inquirer with a skeptical philosophical bent needs to resist overidentifying facts as merely "putative," needs to resist *denying* facts that there is no good reason to deny.

For example, it would be a serious mistake — one depriving an agnostic inquirer of valuable data — to join the more radical physicalists in denying the very existence of consciousness. John Searle (himself a physicalist) reports that, when he began to read the philosophy of mind seriously in order to back up his work on the philosophy of language, he was "appalled to discover that with few exceptions these authors routinely denied [implicitly or explicitly] what I thought were simple and obvious truths about the mind," truths concerning the existence of beliefs, desires, intentions, and perceptions.[56] Searle proceeds to elaborate, contending that both older and currently fashionable views such as logical behaviorism, type-identity theory, token-identity theory, black-box functionalism, strong AI (Turing machine functionalism), eliminative materialism (rejection of folk psychology), and the naturalizing of epistemology — all really leave out the mind.[57] Searle may go too far, but he certainly is right about the widespread tendency among physicalists to explain away the existence of consciousness.

---

55. Chisholm says that a thing increases in size if and only if it exists at some time with one size, and at a later time with a greater size. But is this possible? You may build an addition onto a house. Has the house increased in size? The house either does or does not include the addition; and either way, it looks like it cannot have increased. For it is a necessary condition of the increase of anything that it be smaller at one time and larger at another, and this condition will fail to hold (seemingly) no matter which reference one intends by "my house." See Roderick M. Chisholm, *Person and Object: A Metaphysical Study* (Peru, IL: Open Court, 1976), pp. 157ff.

56. John Searle, *The Rediscovery of the Mind* (Cambridge, MA: MIT Press, 1994), p. xi.

57. Searle, *The Rediscovery of the Mind;* see especially pp. 1-53.

Eliminativists do have some defense of this move. It is worth taking a look at their basic justification: it is an occasion for thinking about what counts as neutral description of the data. The "final theory," eliminativists say, will have to get rid of consciousness because it is part of "folk psychology," and as mistaken as "folk physics" of an earlier time. They suggest that it begs the question to start with the assumption that people have pains, see red, and so forth; for, they claim, the language of qualia is theory-laden, *folk-theory-laden.*

We certainly grant that it is possible to describe phenomena in such a way that a putative explanation begs the question. To label someone's frenzied state "diabolic possession" or "possession by a supernatural devil," and to ask for an explanation under one of these descriptions, is to beg the question. A scientist or physicalist might reasonably say: Stick with the observables: to describe the frenzy as diabolic possession begs the question; it is probably an epileptic fit. To ask for an explanation of "St. Teresa's levitation by God" or of "the divine wounds in the body of St. Francis, the stigmata," is to beg the question. We need to stick to the data, to the fact (if it really is a fact) that Teresa is in the air or that there is blood coming out of St. Francis's hands.

Of course, it is also possible for a *scientific* description of a phenomenon to beg the question, by characterizing some phenomenon in terms of causes. A person might ask for an explanation of "the tug of gravity on bodies falling toward the earth." In response, it could be said: Stick to the data. What one observes is a body moving toward the earth in accordance with the formula "$1/2 \, gt^2$." Whether gravity or something else is responsible should be (at the outset) an open question. (These days some scientists do *not* want to say gravity is responsible.) A person might go to a doctor and ask, "How do I treat this terrible sunburn?" And the proper response might be: "It is not sunburn — you have had an allergic reaction to sulfa drugs."

But what are the core data, the data the scientist is trying to account for in attempting to explain, say, aches and pains? The data at the core seem to be: aches and pains. The pains need not be described as "God-given" or "nonphysical." And they need not be described as "physical" either. It certainly does not seem that an account of the raw sensations begs the question one way or the other. The referents at the core do not appear to be theory-laden, not obviously so, not in a way that begs the question.

Think, for a moment, about the analogy between "folk-physics" and folk-psychology offered in support of eliminativism. The idea is supposed to be that our folk-physics — our pretheoretical views about physics — can be wrong, and similarly that our folk-psychology could be wrong. Maybe we do not really have pains and aches. What are the core beliefs in folk-physics? Stephen Stich gives us an example of what the eliminativists have in mind.[58] He reports that when people are shown a diagram of a metal ball swinging back and forth at the end of a string, and they are asked to draw the path the ball will follow if the string is cut when the ball is in a particular position, their drawings suggest that the ball would continue along the original arc of the pendulum for a short time. In fact, however, the ball would not do this. Thus, Stich concludes, our folk-physics is wrong. But Stich's analogy is improperly drawn. If we want to describe a folk-physics that parallels folk-psychology, we should be talking about a folk-physics according to which people believe such very basic propositions as "Things move."[59]

It is worth noting that Stich's eliminativism has "unraveled" (to use his terminology). He describes the process as one in which he gradually became aware that he was not defending — indeed, was not even conscious of — the full set of premises supporting his eliminativist conclusion:

> It is a bit odd that, despite its fundamental importance in eliminativists' arguments, the step linking the Premises to the conclusions has not been the focus of much attention in the literature. In my own writing, at least until recently, it was a step I took quite unself-consciously. . . . But gradually over the last several years I have come to realize that this crucial step in eliminativists' arguments is anything but obvious.[60]

How is this kind of thing possible? In one respect, it is all too understandable. The questions Stich has been working on are difficult, and the big picture can disappear. Stich's acknowledgment is a useful reminder of the importance of articulating the immediate premises of arguments.

The existence of consciousness, then, should be treated as a fact, and it has been properly so treated by theists who argue that it cannot be explained on physicalistic principles. While it is open to the agnostic to argue that consciousness actually can be explained on physicalistic principles, now or sometime in the future, it is not really open to the agnostic to deny the datum. And it is a mistake to think that the denial is "scientific." Herbert Feigl once asked Einstein: "Wouldn't the qualities of immediate experience be left out in a perfect physical representation of the universe?" Einstein replied: "Why without

58. Stephen P. Stich, *Deconstructing the Mind* (New York: Oxford University Press, 1996), pp. 11-14.

59. Stich does not comment on the fact that the subjects of the experiment he mentions were beginning students at schools like Harvard. This surely is not the cohort one wants in exploring "folk physics"; Harvard students already know too much about physics. Their tendency is to reach beyond the patterns they are actually witnessing toward some hypthesis.

60. Stich, *Deconstructing the Mind*, p. 5.

them, the world would be nothing but a pile of [dirt]!"[61] So one datum that needs to be acknowledged is the existence of consciousness. It is a datum that theists have argued is exceedingly difficult to explain on physicalistic principles. But another datum regarding consciousness that is equally significant in the debate about God is that consciousness has a causal role. This is perhaps not treatable as a fact, even though it is often said to be so by physicalists and non-physicalists alike. It is a point we will have occasion to return to later.

In sum, while some explanations take for granted hard facts, like that of the existence of consciousness, and should not be demoted to the status of putative facts because of wildly skeptical arguments, many explanations legitimately concern softer "facts" that really are only putative facts or CUE-facts.

4.4.2. Organizing Frameworks

A database can be too small to warrant a particular inference. An adequate range of data will be large enough to allow an inquirer to avoid the possibility of a situation in which hypotheses come in second best or third best (or worse) in explaining a certain set of data, but win out over the long run after one has examined a larger database. For example, the best explanation for someone's laughing hard at one point may, when taken in isolation from other facts, be that something very funny was said; the same might hold for that individual's laughing hard at another time. But the best explanation of a person's laughing hard almost continuously may have nothing to do with funny things being said; rather, the explanation may be that the person is suffering from a nervous disorder or is just a very silly person. To take an example involving revelation: it is easy to fall into the trap of thinking that, because a natural explanation is the best explanation of the monotheism of the Jewish people, abstracting from their extraordinary history, and a natural explanation is the best explanation of their extraordinary history as a people, abstracting from their monotheism, a natural explanation is the best explanation of both.[62] The best explanation of both may be supranatural.

---

61. As reported in Herbert Feigl, "The 'Mental' and the 'Physical': The Essay and a Postscript," quoted by John Perry in *Knowledge, Possibility, and Consciousness* (Cambridge, MA: MIT Press, 2001), p. 25 (with the bowdlerization).

62. W. Gunther Plaut holds that it is reasonable to think that the Jews received a revelation just on the basis of their monotheism; Newman is not so explicit but thinks it is reasonable, given all the rest. See W. Gunther Plaut, ed., *The Torah: A Modern Commentary* (New York: Union of American Hebrew Congregations, 1981), xxxvi; Newman, *An Essay in Aid of a Grammar of Assent*, pp. 335-46.

However, though an inquirer needs a database that is sufficiently ample, there is such a thing as having an active database that is too large. A hypothesis can be declared best only if it explains all the data, it is commonly said. But investigators who have attempted concretely to work out explanations in a variety of fields have a different view. Restricting the database is essential to making progress. The task of "finding the best explanation for all of the data" is generally "computationally intractable."[63] Examples abound of respected explanations that eliminate even *relevant* facts. Chomskyan linguistics restricts itself to core grammatical phenomena, that is, the data that can be handled by highly general accounts. The idiosyncratic and the peripheral are largely ignored.[64] Whether this is the best way to do linguistics is open to question. Yet the existence of such an influential school of linguistics conducting its work in this way signals that it is naïve to insist that a winning explanation take into account "all the facts." To make the same point with a homier example, consider the case where a friend of an innocent defendant is called to the stand to provide an alibi for the defendant. Cross-examination of the friend may produce such an abundance of inconsistencies that the testimony hurts more than it helps. Still, the jury may reasonably declare the accused "not guilty." This judgment provides no explanation at all of the friend's confusion, and it may be in tension with the friend's testimony. Yet it may rightly be felt that, while there is some explanation of the confused testimony, no explanation need be sought, since the exonerating evidence is compelling. Similarly, it may be unnecessary to explain every puzzling aspect of a revelatory claim.

Indeed, one could (in principle) substantiate a revelatory claim by pointing to a lone fact about the world that the content of a revelatory claim explains very, very well — and that nothing else explains. Suppose, for instance, that some fantastic event described in the book of Revelation occurred, a phenomenon that appeared wholly inexplicable on naturalistic grounds. Would it not be reasonable to take that event as strong evidence in favor of the revelatory claim? We will not be arguing that there *is* such a fact that an agnostic inquirer can latch on to. But its theoretical possibility should not be forgotten. And we need not look to "fantastic" examples to make the point that the verification of a single precise claim can tell volumes. From one sentence written on a piece of paper, the author may be recognized as highly educated — or practically illiterate. Darcy helps the Bennets in *Pride and Prejudice;* and from that single magnificently generous action, he can be judged

---

63. Josephson and Josephson, *Abductive Inference,* p. 203.
64. John R. Taylor, *Cognitive Grammar* (Oxford: Oxford University Press, 2002), pp. 7-8.

good, despite the fact that there is a lot of evidence against him, and it may be hard to say just where that evidence goes wrong. The Lascaux cave paintings, a bit of paint on a wall, tell us an enormous amount about a people.

However, it will usually not be appropriate to restrict the database to a single fact. Inquirers will generally need a database that is fairly large. How can a relatively large database be handled without becoming unwieldy? How can it be expanded without becoming totally unmanageable?

Organizing frameworks or storylines will play a central role. Not uncommonly, finding a framework or storyline allows an inquirer to see old data as new; that is, the framework organizes, and hence sheds new light on, old data. Consider a story Charles Chihara tells (in the course of a discussion of problems with Bayesian confirmation theory).[65] The King locks up a prince. The prince has one week to solve a problem fashioned by the King's logician; if he succeeds, he wins the princess, and if he fails, he is executed. On each morning of that week he is given a crimson ball that contains a number; on the last morning, he is required to guess the number in the last ball. Day six comes, and the prince still cannot discern any pattern in the numbers inside the six crimson balls that he has received so far. They have all been odd, two-digit natural numbers; but there are eighty-four equiprobable numbers left, and the prince sees no reason why one rather than another of them should be in the crimson ball he gets the seventh day. Then, on the afternoon of the sixth day, he gets a sudden illumination: he sees that the six numbers he already has are the Gödel numbers of the first six letters of the word "crimson" (using the system of Gödel numbering that the King's logician favors). He guesses, correctly, that the Gödel number of the letter "n" will be in the seventh ball. The prince has brought to bear on the issue at hand something he already knew; he has used a framework to reorganize what he already knows, and he has come to a saving insight.

Dimitri Mendeleyev, a chemist at the Technological Institute of St. Petersburg in Russia, set out in 1869 to get some control over the developments that were rapidly occurring in chemistry. He made a list of the properties of the sixty-three known chemical elements, arranged the list in order of increasing atomic weight, and noted what was salient in the behavior of each of the elements. Then came the insight: similar chemical properties made their appearance at regular intervals. This gave rise to the famous "periodic table," which permitted Mendeleyev to predict the discovery of other chemi-

---

65. Charles Chihara, "Some Problems for Bayesian Confirmation Theory," *British Journal for the Philosophy of Science* 38 (1987): 551-60. Cited in Samir Okasha's "Van Fraassen's Critique of Inference to the Best Explanation," p. 708.

cals that would slot into the table. How did he make his great discovery? Just by organizing what was already known. There was no special probing, no special experiment.

Really, all of armchair philosophy (which is most of philosophy) provides examples of ways in which one can reorganize, rework, and draw implications from what one already knows — and likewise with all of mathematics and all of logic. Socrates helps people to remember and bring forward what they already know. They end up drawing conclusions contrary to what they have explicitly held. Aristotle says in the *Topics* that, when dealing with somebody who is particularly contentious, one will find it useful to scramble the order of the premises rather than present them naturally, so that the balky individual does not see until the end where the argument is going.

As all these examples illustrate, an agnostic inquirer could be in the position of *already believing* relevant propositions — but failing to see how they are relevant. Reorganization may make a difference, may provide the *gestalt*.

Stories not only help us reorganize data so that facts we already know stand out; they also provide a framework into which we can fit new data. Oswald Steward's account of a scientific discovery he made in 1979 illustrates the point. He discovered clusters of polyribosomes in and around dendritic spine synapses. He saw the polyribosomes on his micrographs at the same time the idea occurred to him that "the ability to synthesize certain proteins at individual synaptic sites would provide a mechanism that would allow neurons to modify the molecular composition of *individual synapses* on a moment-by-moment basis." He saw a reason for the presence of the polyribosomes at a certain place, and hence noticed something no researcher had yet seen. When Alan Peters, a pioneer in the area, looked at Steward's micrographs and confirmed the identification of the polyribosomes, he observed: "In electron microscopy, you may not notice something unless you're looking specifically for it." Steward speculates that a comment by John Eccles, winner of a Nobel Prize for his studies of synaptic transmission, may have helped him discover the polyribosomes. "The trick is to develop a *story*," Eccles had said to Steward about a year before the discovery.[66]

What kind of framework or storyline can the agnostic inquirer use? The content of revelatory claims itself provides multiple frameworks and storylines; it provides aids to its own interpretation. Revelations provide the equivalent of the key concerning Gödel numbers (in Chihara's story) and the key concerning a possible reason for the existence of polyribosomes in and

---

66. Mark F. Bear, Barry W. Connors, Michael A. Paradiso, *Neuroscience: Exploring the Brain*, 2d ed. (Baltimore: Lippincott, Williams, & Wilkins, 2001), pp. 44-45.

around dendritic spine synapses (in Steward's story). What do these keys, these frameworks and storylines, look like? They are of various kinds. We here briefly mention three kinds found (interwoven) in the Judaeo-Christian tradition.

The first kind involves *historical narratives,* which identify significant events and, by means of their teleological nature, point to new data. The Deuteronomic account of the Hebrews' exodus from Egypt and entry into the Promised Land provides essential structure for one who would understand Jewish (or Christian) revelatory claims. Likewise, the historical narrative of the Jews provides context for understanding the significance of the "I am" statements of Jesus, and the calling of the twelve apostles. And insight into historical narrative sets up an understanding of the Christian eschatological vision.

A second kind of storyline emerges when we examine the Judaeo-Christian historical narrative. Often presented via parable, it focuses our attention on *personal data,* subjective data that may not be shared easily, that may not, in fact, even be acquired easily. "Know thyself," Socrates said; but it is difficult. Think of the power of Sartre's famous vignette of self-deception, in which a woman allows herself to be touched in a compromising way, while she persuades herself that nothing is going on. To attend to what is going on would be to give consent; to pull back would be to break the charm of the moment; so she simply "does not notice" what is going on. One can read Sartre's vignette and think, "Yes, I too am a self-deceiver." In a way, one has known this all along, but the story spotlights evidence already in possession, and it takes on new significance. Similarly, inquirers may see in the content of a revelatory claim a fitting account of shortcomings and personal weakness. Consider an incident reported in the book of Samuel in the Hebrew Bible.[67] King David saw Bathsheba, wife of Uriah, bathing, and he desired her; David ordered that Uriah be sent to the battlefront, where he was killed; David married Bathsheba. The prophet Nathan came to David, telling him a tale of two men, one who was rich and had many sheep, and one who was poor and had but a single ewe lamb. A traveler came to visit the rich man; the latter, not wishing to slaughter one of his own sheep for the evening meal, took the lamb of the poor man. On hearing Nathan's story, David became incensed; he declared that the rich man deserved to die. Nathan responded: "You are the man!"

A third kind of framework or story is especially important for a philosophically inclined agnostic inquirer: these stories or frameworks provide *accounts*

---

67. 2 Sam. 11–12.

of a doctrine or theory in terms of first principles. One of Euclid's accomplishments was to organize and systematize geometry in a way that revealed its axioms — though not all of them. The task of supplying the missing axioms was left to later mathematicians such as David Hilbert. At one point, Hilbert consulted a physicist about some of the new ideas being introduced in physics. The physicist said that when he would finish providing the requested explanation, Hilbert would repeat it — but with the material rearranged, organized systematically in a way that emphasized what was foundational. Euclid hits a "Euclid button" with geometry; Hilbert hits a "Hilbert button" with physics. The data fall into a pattern. And such patterns can be used to bring new data into the picture.

Aquinas pushed what might be called an "Aquinas button" with regard to the content of Christian revelatory claims. While his great *Summa Theologiae* is not part of the content of the Christian (or Catholic) revelatory claim, it can be a vehicle for understanding such content. The *Summa* arranges doctrine in a way that displays the doctrine's philosophical foundations. Peering into the *Summa* is like walking into a cathedral for the first time, or reading Euclid for the first time ("Euclid alone has looked on beauty bare"). It is impossible to miss the surface structure of the *Summa:* three parts, arranged into subparts (the subparts themselves have parts, and so on, and so on). But it takes considerable work to see *why* the parts have the arrangement they do. Understanding the individual questions requires tracing the lines of reasoning all the way back to the beginning of this compendious work. For Aquinas, following Aristotle, tries to provide *propter quid* demonstrations wherever possible — that is, arguments that at once prove and explain a proposition. Such arguments present causal structures that require a knowledge of the essence of any item whose properties are under discussion. Given Aquinas's project of producing *propter quid* demonstrations where possible, he finds it particularly fitting to proceed by gradually building up propositions, demonstrating first the weaker and then the stronger (proposition x is stronger than y if and only if x entails y and y does not entail x). God's existence is more basic than God's simplicity, in Aquinas's view: "God is simple" entails "God exists." Thus the proposition "God exists" comes first. When Aquinas wants to show that God is omnipotent, he shows first that God has power, and then, using that claim as a premise, he argues that God's power is infinite. And so on.[68]

The three kinds of storylines converge. Though Aquinas's focus is on first

---

68. No philosopher has, so far as we know, plotted exactly and in detail how the lines of dependence in the *Summa* run.

principles, references to Scripture (including historical narrative and parables) adorn the rigorous account of foundations, and his whole multivolume work is set up to display a Judaeo-Christian (and ultimately Christian) narrative: the *Summa* begins with a discussion of God, moves to the *exit* of all creation from God, and considers how creatures *return* to God through willing the good, exercising natural virtue, and relying on the mediation of Christ.

Of course, integration of a revelatory claim, particularly integration that includes a display of foundational truths, is difficult — and can be expected to evolve over time. Integration in any field, after all, even the most exact, presents serious challenges, as we have learned from the history of mathematics. In an effort to supply for the deficiencies of Euclid's geometry and the Leibnizian-Newtonian calculus, mathematicians sought to rest the whole on a most secure foundation of evident axioms leading by unquestionable steps to all the theorems they thought could be proved. This effort met with severe challenges in the form of a variety of paradoxes that sprang directly out of the mathematicians' initial assumptions. Paradoxes are deemed genuine by most logicians on the grounds that they contain no obvious logical flaws. Nonetheless, "logical" paradoxes are more important than "semantic" paradoxes, because the former use concepts only from the theory of sets, while the latter use additional concepts such as "denotes" and "true." It is for this reason, as Mendelson notes, that "the logical paradoxes are a much greater threat to a mathematician's peace of mind than the semantic paradoxes."[69] Various means for avoiding the paradoxes have been produced, such as Russell's theory of types, and radical reinterpretations of the paradoxes by the Intuitionist school of Brouwer.

Just as some mathematical paradoxes are more troubling than others, so also in religious matters. Far less problematic are those religious paradoxes that involve reconciliation of the imaginative language of Scripture and tradition with a sane philosophical view. It is easy enough to fit the statement "God hardened Pharaoh's heart" with the view that a good God does not will evil. The biblical statement can be read as an expression by an unphilosophical people of what we would regard as a more acceptable concept of what the deity actually did. However, there are more vexing religious paradoxes, such as those which have to do with divine foreknowledge and causality in connection with evil, and it can rightly be demanded of an adequate theological story that it escape contradiction.

Not only must the theologian work to ensure that paradox in the strong

---

69. Elliott Mendelson, *Introduction to Mathematical Logic*, 4th ed. (New York: Chapman and Hall, 1997), p. 3.

sense of contradiction not issue from the construal made of the foundational axioms, but the more imaginative and historical elements of the entire narrative must be presented in a way that does not undercut the entire enterprise. The theologian's effort in this direction can have about it an air of studied artificiality. But then, so can the efforts of mathematicians working to handle mathematical paradoxes (Russell's theory of types has the air of artificiality, to say nothing of the Intuitionists' rejection of the law of the excluded middle).

For the theological project to succeed, the system may need to generate new concepts. It is not simply a matter of taking the original "givens" and working with them in some sort of quasi-mechanical or mathematical form. It is possible to get the impression that that is how it works by an insensitive reading of Aquinas, who tells us theology is a science because it rests on axioms received from "the science above theology" that only God possesses. It can look as though, given the divinely revealed teachings, there is little or nothing to do but grind away at the proofs, using Aristotle's syllogistic theory or some modern counterpart. But that would be a grave misreading of Aquinas — and of the reality. For as Aristotle and Aquinas recognized — and has been recognized by many logicians since — there is more to logic and more to systematization than cranking away on the axioms.

So, we say, an inquirer seeking help in identifying or discovering relevant data can look to the integration of various kinds of stories in one or another great theological synthesis. The result of that synthesis can be a wondrous thing. It may satisfy the demand to escape paradox in the sense of contradiction, while honoring mysteries; it may appeal to axioms and justify them by introducing fresh concepts; and it may manage at the same time to blend in complementary, imaginative, and historical stories. And this sort of synthesis may be more than a mere guide in the effort to learn whether a good God has revealed anything to us. The unfolding of the story, along with its unifying power, may itself be just about all an inquirer needs to conclude that the associated revelatory claim is (probably) true.

5 Objection: Revelatory Claims Lack Adequate Explanatory Power

5.1. The Objection

Supranatural theories wrapped in the myths of putative revelations are hopelessly outclassed by science, many say. Earlier, in chapter 1, we argued that the contentions of the "scientific demystifiers" should not stop an agnostic inquirer's project. Science is not disenchanting the world in such a way that there is no room left for complementary supranatural explanations. But it is one thing for there to be room for supranatural explanations and another thing to actually find them. And if there is no good reason to think that at least one powerful supranatural explanation is discoverable, then it would seem our Key Conditional is false.

The contention that there *is* good reason will strike some as incredible. God reminds Job that he was not present when the foundations of the world were laid, and God does not take the occasion to explain how it was done. "Let there be light," which Genesis reports God as saying, is unilluminating about the character of the process. Genesis even gives us daylight before the sun is made. In thousands of languages the genuine causes of things and processes have been revealed by human beings. About none of this, the complaint continues, does the Bible tell us anything better than it tells us about the languages in which creative conceptions find expression. The earliest humans shared a common language, the story of the Tower of Babel reports; but having mastered monumental brick architecture, the arrogant humans built a tower reaching into the heavens. Perceiving that humans could do almost anything if they shared a common language, God put an end to the business and confused their tongues. This is myth, the complaint goes, nothing more than myth, and it is no match for theories about the unity and multiplicity of human languages, theories now expressed in the fundamental language of science.

Furthermore, it may seem, it is quite clear from what revelatory traditions themselves say that we are not going to get explanations: God's ways are not our ways. It makes perfectly good sense for a vision scientist to say that retinoids play an important role in cell metabolism through processes not yet fully understood, because, though those mechanisms are now imperfectly understood, there is a good chance that they will be very well understood in the not-too-distant future. But if the vision scientist were to say that retinoids play an important role, but we need to give up on ever understanding at all how they work, one would wonder why scientists are so confident they play such a role, and are not just accidentally connected to the system.

Many philosophers are fully persuaded: references to first causes or origi- nators or creators or divine designers — appeals to mysterious, supranatural entities, events, properties, and relations — do not do any work. Philip Kitcher aptly expresses this point by titling a section of an essay on design arguments with the question "Where's the beef?"[1] Kitcher writes (in remarks directed against neo-creationist accounts of the world, but quite generalizable):

> I come at last to *the most basic difficulty* with the neo-creo attack, its dim suggestions that the scientific world needs a shot of supernaturalism. . . . How exactly is the appeal to creative design supposed to help?
> . . . we ought to be a little curious about what sort of magic a creative de- sign model might be able to work.[2]

We may imagine Kitcher or some other critic of supranatural explanation continuing: "In the face of complaints about the absence of a causal mecha- nism in creative design models, it can be anticipated that the religious claim will be shrunk to the vacuity that revelation enlightens only with respect to morals. But modern psychiatry, psychology, anthropology, neuroscience, pharmacology, and other sciences tell us worlds more about what makes us tick morally than revelations abounding in fables such as the story of the pri- meval Fall. Even when it comes to ideas where putative revelations speak in- triguingly, the best explanations of the phenomena are to be found elsewhere, as in Kant's vastly superior account[3] of what has been called 'original sin.'"

1. Philip Kitcher, "Born-Again Creationism," in Robert T. Pennock, *Intelligent Design Creationism and Its Critics* (Cambridge, MA: MIT Press, 2001).

2. Kitcher, "Born-Again Creationism," p. 281 (italics added).

3. In Immanuel Kant, *Religion within the Boundaries of Mere Reason*, ed. Allen Wood and George di Giovanni (Cambridge, UK: Cambridge University Press, 1998).

So goes the objection. It would take more than a book to deal with it in a fully satisfactory way, if that is even possible. But in the space we have available here we can at least draw attention to some good reasons for suspecting that it cannot be sustained.

5.2. Prelude to the Illustrations: Knowing "That" Without Knowing "How"

Ideal explanations, as we have seen, are out of reach for human beings. The question is only to what extent deviation from the ideal can occur and still leave us with an acceptable and useful explanation. Ideal friends do not exist any more than ideal explanations do. But a friend in need is a friend indeed, and so are explanations: friends to the mind when there is a need.

Can revelatory explanations play the role of friend to the mind, even though they appeal to substances and processes and functions beyond this world? A revelatory explanation will, of course, at the very least posit a supranatural being (given our stipulated definition of what a revelatory claim is). Beyond this, revelations will point to divine operations whose existence is mysterious: there may be references to gracious influence on the will, to the "real presence" in the Eucharist, to ways in which God does or could draw good out of evil. Revelations are full of mysteries, operations in which the causal mechanisms are not manifest.

Our argument that revelatory explanations can play the role of friend to the mind, though they do not display causal mechanisms, starts with Newton, who thought that his gravitational hypothesis explained not only the motion of planets and comets but "the impenetrability, mobility, and impetus of bodies, and the laws of motion. . . ."[4] His explanation falls short of the ideal in all kinds of ways. Of particular interest is the fact that Newton did not have any idea how what he called "gravity" could work the wonder of moving objects at enormous distances instantaneously. Newton provided a mathematical expression of the inverse law that spells out how bodies will move under certain conditions, but he could only name the power; he could not depict the mechanism by which the power worked its wonders.

Why, then, was Newton's theory acceptable when he proposed it? Because it was better than the alternatives.[5]

4. *Isaac Newton: The Principia*, trans. I. Bernard Choen and Anne Whitmean (Berkeley and Los Angeles: University of California Press, 1999), p. 943.

5. For a modern parallel to what we will be saying about Newton, we could take certain the-

And what were the alternatives?

Descartes's theory of push-and-pull was one; however, Descartes's theory was inconsistent with the data, and Newton's theory was not. Another alternative was to reject Descartes's theory because it did not comport with the data, and to reject Newton's theory as well, on the grounds that Newton's just had too many problems. His most notable problem was positing instantaneous action at great distances, without even a pretense of explaining how causality was exercised. On this second alternative, one could modestly say that neither Descartes's theory nor Newton's was acceptable, and that one simply did not know how to explain the phenomena.

But a number of scientists in Newton's day took another route altogether. In the spirit of latter-day positivism, they wanted to drop all talk of gravity, of postulating a hidden cause without a mechanism; instead, they wanted to speak of mathematical relationships among the phenomena. It is *irresponsible* to postulate an occult force between sun and moon, the one pulling on the other, they said; instead, we should speak of objects moving in accordance with the inverse law. They adopted what we might call a "no-theory theory." Their decision was very different from the modest decision not to accept any one of the theories offered. The no-theory theory is not at all modest: it insists that gravity be rejected simply because a cause is postulated without a causal mechanism.

As it turns out, however, the no-theory theory leads to a destructive, nihilistic conclusion. If one adopts the no-theory theory, there are no grounds for postulating a sun or a moon at all. For sun and moon are substances (or collections of substances); and a substance is postulated to explain why a bunch of properties are bound together. The moon's shape, its rough surface, and its color (or its power to produce a sensation of color) are bound together because they all inhere in the same substance(s). Now the inherence relationship involves causality, and a question arises about the causal relationship: How is it that a substance roots, gets a grip on, the associated properties, some of which are transient and others relatively permanent? We do not

---

oretical developments in quantum mechanics. It is difficult to reconcile quantum mechanics with relativity theory. But it can be done. Certain hidden-variables theories can be rendered empirically adequate and consistent with relativity. There is a price to pay, namely, that all hope is lost of exhibiting the mechanism of producing the phenomena. Still, while that price is steep, it may have to be paid. Jeffrey Barrett argues that while some empirically adequate accounts of relativistic quantum mechanics "provide neither mechanical nor causal explanations for local quantum events. . . . it may simply prove too much to ask for such explanations in relativistic quantum mechanics." Jeffrey Barrett, "Relativistic Quantum Mechanics Through Frame-Dependent Constructions" (2004): 1, forthcoming in *Philosophy of Science,* retrieved Jan. 12, 2006, from <www.socsci.uci.edu/lps/home/fac-staff/faculty/barrett/papers.html>.

know — any more than we know what the causal mechanism is when one body (apparently) pulls on another.

This question about the inherence relationship is in the neighborhood of other questions sometimes raised about substances. But we are not repeating the common contention that substances are unobservable or that they are bare particulars. Rather, we are considering the idea that there is no reason to postulate substances, given that no explanation works unless the mechanism of causality is displayed. For a person is inclined to postulate substances, for instance, in the case of the moon, in order to account for the lunar properties being bundled together: the properties are co-present in an underlying something. But if we say they hang together *because* they are rooted in the same substance, this accords the substance a causal role. The substance sustains the properties, roots them. If no causal role can intelligibly be assigned unless the mechanism is displayed, then either we must display the mechanism of the rooting or admit that the explanation is vacant. But the explanation is not vacant; and yet we cannot display the mechanism. It follows that it is simply not the case that no explanation has been given at all if a mechanism has not been (and perhaps cannot be) displayed.

It might be said that modern physics has gotten rid of substances. Bertrand Russell makes that claim: "Since Einstein, and still more since Heisenberg and Schrödinger, the physical world is no longer regarded as consisting of persistent pieces of matter moving in a three-dimensional space, but as a four-dimensional manifold of events in space-time."[6] Well, maybe, but Einstein himself was not so convinced. In explicit criticism of Russell on this point, Einstein said:

> No matter how much one may admire the acute analysis which Russell has given us in his latest book on *Meaning and Truth*, it still seems to me that even there the spectre of the metaphysical fear has caused some damage. For this fear seems to me, for example, to be the cause for conceiving of the "thing" as a "bundle of qualities," such that the "qualities" are to be taken from the sensory raw-material. . . . Over against that I see no "metaphysical" danger in taking the thing (the object in the sense of physics) as an independent concept into the system together with the proper spatio-temporal structure.[7]

In fact, the danger lies in a different direction. If we take Russell's line, even the self vanishes, for the same sort of reason that substances disappear

6. Bertrand Russell, in *The Philosophy of Bertrand Russell*, ed. Paul Arthur Schilpp (La Salle, IL: Open Court, 1989), p. 701.

7. Albert Einstein, in Schilpp, *The Philosophy of Bertrand Russell*, pp. 289, 291.

on the no-theory theory of Newton's day. Our ordinary conception of self involves thoughts, plans, a sense of agency — and all this crumbles if we cannot say something *roots* and *connects* these things. One could go all the way with Hume in saying that we lack evidence for the existence of a substantival self, and do not possess the cognitive wherewithal to work up even the idea of such a self. But that is a lot to give up, to say the least.

Someone is bound to object that our argument equivocates on "cause." Holding properties together is not something a substance *does,* in the sense in which we ordinarily use that term: a substance does not perform an *action.* True enough. Still, there is a sense in which a substance "does" something: it is causally responsible for something. In the present context, it is enough to find an explanation that invokes *some* kind of cause-explanation, not necessarily an *agent* cause or an explanation based on agent causes. For the original problem was that, where there is no display of mechanism, there seemed to be no explanation. In order for us to handle this problem, it suffices to show that there can be useful causal explanations that do not display a mechanism, and for this purpose, any kind of cause can be cited. Now, while the causality exercised by a substance in rooting its various properties is not efficient causality, it is responsible for the existence and coexistence of the properties. Why do these observable properties go together? "They are all rooted in the same substance." That is an explanation, even though we have no idea how the substance manages to do the rooting.

In sum, embracing the "no-theory theory" is ultimately giving up on moon, sun, and self. And an inquirer quite reasonably holds on to ordinary, deeply ingressed beliefs such as that moon, sun, and self exist. Newton could tell us nothing of the details concerning gravity, nothing to make the causal nexus perspicuous. Yet, though he said, "I do not feign hypotheses," he reflected a good deal on what the nexus might be: How does gravity operate? This quest would surely be pointless unless it was believed that there had to be some mechanism, some way in which bodies affected each other. But some explanation was better than an explanation like Descartes's, which did not fit the data, and better than a no-theory theory (which provides no explanation at all).[8]

---

8. A similar point can be made in connection with mathematics and logic. A mathematician might say that a certain theorem is true and offer a *reductio ad absurdum* (RAA) proof, a sort of proof common in arguments in natural theology. Though some maintain, for various reasons, that such an argument is no proof at all, most accept RAA arguments in mathematics as proofs, believing that they show that a particular proposition *must* be true, given the axioms of the system. Furthermore, even though RAA proofs are indirect and supply no direct insight into why the theorem must be true, into how it flows from the axioms, and even though direct

There is, of course, a limit to how far one can deviate from ideal explanation with regard to identifying a causal nexus. You need to be able to say that there *is* a cause; and you cannot say *that* there is a cause without presupposing at least a tiny bit of "what." When you respond to a "why" question, you are committed to something. You may, for instance, answer some "why" question by saying, "I posit a borogove." You are saying that something you are calling a borogove exists and that it has the power to produce the effect. That is a tiny bit of "what." In most cases, of course, we use a name or description that actually carries with it some information, however minimal. If asked why some person is sleeping in the middle of the day, you might say, "He swallowed a pill with a dormative power." Now that is not much of an explanation; but it is a start. The person was not naturally fatigued, did not inhale ether, and so on. It is less than an ideal explanation, but it is something. To answer the question "Where's the beef?" you only need a few ounces. An inquirer does not have to begin by producing a prize-winning steer.

Return now to the case of explanation involving the divine order. Saying that God is at least in part responsible for an effect is as unexceptionable as Newton's saying that gravity is responsible for an effect — or more generally, as saying that *something* is responsible for an effect, where one has little or no understanding of the mechanism.

Is this the most that can be said? Are we utterly bereft of any fuller idea of supranatural causation? Not at all. We can grasp supranatural causation by comparing it with more familiar forms of causation, making appropriate adjustments.

For example, if there is a creator distinct from the physical universe, distinct from all that is physical, the creator's actions are not going to be physical actions. Therefore, they will not have the properties of physical actions: the actions will not be motions, movements. We can understand that there is such a thing as *motionless activity* by looking within ourselves. Consider the sentence "If Newton was right, Descartes was wrong." We can understand this sentence: it has meaning for us. When we utter this sentence, we produce the first word and then move on to the second, and so forth. By the time we have moved to the second word, the first word is history. But it is altogether otherwise with the thought: we do not think "if," then let that vanish, then think "Newton," and forget about Newton before we get to Descartes. Were we to

---

proofs are much desired, an RAA proof does supply some insight. *Somehow* the axioms make the theorem true; the theorem holds *because* the axioms hold. Similarly, one may think that, though it will forever remain a mystery to us how God works to bring things about in the world, it is plausible to think that it must be so. Demands made on theistic explanation should not be stronger than demands made on scientific and mathematical explanation.

try to proceed in that way, meaning would disintegrate. To grasp a proposition and to see under what conditions it would be true, we have to grasp it as a whole; our understanding of it cannot unfold over time. If we do something when we think, then there is an activity that is not a movement. For movements are divisible: the first part ceases to be when the next part comes into existence. Not so with the "movement" of thought. It is true, of course, that there can be a succession of thoughts. One can think, "If Newton was right, Descartes was wrong; and Newton was right," and so, a moment later, one may think, "Descartes was wrong." Nothing prevents one thought from coming before another.[9] Yet everything stands in the way of one part of a *complete* thought coming before another and marching off into the past before the second part arrives.

Furthermore, our capacity to bring before the mind abstract objects gives us some hint of how there can be a *production,* a creation, without physical action. An action that takes object is a physical action only if the object is in the space-time net, or *is* the space-time net. (If you are going to hammer an object, the object must be somewhere. And it is hard to put a boot on a foot that is not in the space-time net.) But thinking takes an object. And the objects of thought are not in the space-time net. Therefore, thinking is not a wholly physical act: it cannot be physical through and through.[10] Still, we have *produced* the object. We do not produce what it is to be a circle, but we manage to connect with circularity, the property, though circularity is nowhere. So we have some idea of a non-physical action that is productive or creative. It is just not true that we have no idea at all of what God's actions would be like. We have within ourselves intimations of the powers.[11]

9. For discussion of this point, see Peter Geach, *God and the Soul,* 2d ed. (South Bend, IN: St. Augustine's Press, 1969), ch. 3. Our suggestion here coincides with his, except for the fact that Geach says, "The activity of thinking cannot be assigned a position in the physical time-series" (p. 34). It is not necessary to say this, which strikes us as clearly false, in order to hold on to the remainder of the argument. You certainly could have the thought "The cup is about to fall off the table" before the cup actually falls, and after the tea is poured. The main point is not that it cannot be placed in the series but that it is not stretched out within the series.

10. For an extended defense of this claim, see Russell Pannier and Thomas D. Sullivan, "Consciousness and Intentional Awareness of Instantiables," in Alexander Batthyany and Avshalom Elitzur, eds., *Mind and Its Place in the World: Non-reductionist Approaches to the Ontology of Consciousness* (Frankfurt: Ontos Verlag, 2006).

11. Notice that the arguments we have just given are not committed to any sort of dualism. If you are going to consider the arguments, then there comes into view just the kind of action our imagined objector claims to have no idea of. If you understand the terms involved in the debate over dualism, then you understand what it is to conjure up an object through an action that bears no physical relationship to the object. You may deny that it can be done; you may

Granted, a revelatory claim complicates our picture of the world. It postulates at least one extra entity, a world-creator, an entity mysterious in the extreme. But given the various phenomena that are deeply baffling to science (some that we have already discussed and others that we are about to mention in our illustrations), it is not unreasonable to postulate an extra entity to account for the unexplained phenomena. Newton complicated the picture as well. Positivists preferred to talk merely about correlations. But then, as Newton surely saw, all possibility of understanding disappears, and we are left with complete mystery concerning many things. One can reasonably postulate an extra entity to account for a phenomenon even if the source and operation of its power remain forever dark, if on balance the postulated cause is the best explanation, and better than no explanation at all.

This is, in the main, our general response to the question "Where's the beef?" One more thing, however, needs to be taken into account. The objection that there is no beef because the mechanism of divine action is hidden from us makes most sense (though not enough, as we have just argued) in connection with agent causality. But explanations can, of course, also proceed from premises about *ends*. And while it is something of a mystery how ends can be causes of action, they clearly can be, since there are many things that we would not do except for our being motivated to do them by envisioning and adopting an end. In this sense, at least, the envisioned end is a cause of the action. We see some explanations invoking a putative end as more credible than others, even when we may have no idea of how the "mechanism" of envisioning an end leads to action. Thus, for example, we may think that "She wanted to do the community some good" is a better explanation of why someone ran for city council than "She wanted the salary." We can figure out which explanation is best simply by reflecting that the candidate is rich and public-spirited, and the salary is paltry. "Mechanisms" do not enter into the calculation of which is the best explanation. So, when we are thinking about a theistic explanation, we need to consider putative facts about putative ends, as several illustrations will bring out.

All this is rather abstract. We turn, now, to some illustrations.

---

wish to say that thinking just *is* having one itty-bitty thought after another; but the thing you cannot say, if you enter into the argument, is that you have no idea what you are talking about. You do in fact have some idea of what this action would be like, at least with regard to human beings; you are simply denying that an immaterial agent produces such an action.

5.3. Brief Illustrations of the Explanation of Putative Facts

5.3.1. The Role of the Brief Illustrations

We have chosen all our illustrations — the brief beginning illustrations, all of which involve non-moral *explananda,* and the later extended illustrations bearing on morals — to help dispel the common notion that the *explananda* to be taken under consideration when one does natural theology are established facts.

Our brief illustrations touch on the following putative facts:

- A putative scientific fact: humans have a special place in the universe
- A putative fact about originality of doctrine: the beatitudes are original
- A putative fact about resilience of doctrine: the Judaeo-Christian doctrine of omniscience is resilient
- A putative fact about fertility of doctrine: the Judaeo-Christian doctrine of omniscience, as well as the Christian doctrine of the incarnation, are fertile
- A putative fact that is a CUE-fact: consciousness has a function
- A putative fact that is a CUE-fact: humans have libertarian freedom
- A putative fact that is a CUE-fact: some revelatory claims are rationally alluring

Upon reading these brief illustrations, one will quite properly feel that a great deal more must be said about all these issues if anything is to be settled. Yet, to provide no illustrations at all would leave our claim with little concrete justification. Unfortunately, we can hardly go very far with any particular illustrative line of reasoning without creating the impression of giving full-throated endorsement to the illustration itself. All we can do to offset this impression is insist that each illustration would need to be filled out in various ways and at book length to be convincing, and that we are by no means prepared fully to endorse each line of reasoning. Imagine a classicist who is interested in whether there was a Homer arguing that an investigation of the content of the *Iliad* could lead to the unitarian hypothesis, and then sketching a quick case for the claim that the thematic unity in the epic poem is significant. An objector says: "Wait. You have made many controversial claims. You have ignored all sorts of irregularities in the content." However, if the classicist is only saying that an investigation of the *Iliad's* content *might well* lead to the unitarian hypothesis, gesturing in the direction of a case for thematic unity could suffice.

And though the illustrations are necessarily thin, exposing us to a charge of superficiality, our considering more than a few different *explananda* makes possible a sketch of patterns of argument that can be developed in many ways. The patterns are:

- Here is a putative fact probably best explained by an appeal to revelation, thus accrediting the revelation to some degree.
- Here is a collection of putative facts probably best explained by an appeal to revelation, thus accrediting the revelation to some degree.
- Here is a collection of putative facts, at least one of which is probably best explained by an appeal to revelation, thus accrediting the revelation to some degree.

The putative facts may be (but need not be) CUE-facts.

All of our illustrations are intermediate-level illustrations: that is, they involve claims that lie midway between general theistic claims concerning God's existence and very specific claims about particular revelations. Quite possibly, a more thorough intermediate-level investigation than we will carry out here would by itself, without reliance on a particular revelation, suffice to establish that a communication from on high has been received. Still, we do not assert that no particular revelation need be examined in detail. Our claim is only that the illustrations show how the evidence can be accumulated — and how this accumulated evidence might well suffice for some level of success.

If it does prove necessary to examine particular revelations to make a judgment about whether a revelation has been given, the intermediate-level evidence will play an important role as background data. Imagine that a young man who was adopted at birth is looking for possible communications from his biological mother, hoping to find some account of why she gave him up for adoption. He undertakes his search with a background assumption: by and large, mothers love their children, however imperfectly. That gives him a context for reading putative communications from his biological mother. If he is given a letter by the adoption agency and is told that it was written by his biological mother just after he was born, he will have interpretive aids. Knowing that mothers do not typically give up their children for no good reason, he will quite rationally read ambiguous or vague comments in the letter so as to favor the hypothesis that his birth mother really did love him and gave him up for adoption because she loved him. The background information he brings to the search for his birth mother's motives will be crucially important to his discovering the truth of the matter. Similarly, the background information an agnostic inquirer brings to an investigation of the content of particular revelatory claims, and to the investigation of theism it-self, will surely affect outcomes. It can mean the difference between success or failure.

A person defending the thesis that it is possible to arrive at a plausible moral system would at least need to mention, if not endorse, bits and pieces of particular moral teachings. And as it would be foolish for a typical Western defender of anti-skepticism in ethics — a defender of the possibility of a moral system — to dwell on, say, the unfamiliar conceptions of the good life entertained by pre-Zoroastrian aristocratic warriors of Iran, so it would be folly for us to defend the possibility of a revelation by dwelling on unfamiliar elements of regional and world religions. Therefore, except for an occasional glance to one side or the other, we will stick to what we know best, Christianity, with its roots in the Hebrew revelatory tradition.

5.3.2. Brief Illustrations Involving Putative Facts Other than CUE-Facts

A Putative Scientific Fact: Humans Have a Special Place in the Universe
Consider the account in Genesis of the beginning of things. The story — archaic, twice told, and enveloped in myth — is replete with tensions, if not flat-out contradictions. It is difficult to see what, if anything, is to be taken at face value. Yet Jews, Christians, Muslims, and others have understood the story to convey deep, literal truths about God, the world, and the human race. To be counted among these divine teachings is the proposition that human beings occupy a special place within the universe. That is not to say the world was created for us alone. Even so, we occupy a special place. Over the millennia, this assertion has struck countless individuals as true.

However, given what we now know about cosmology, the claim has seemed unsupportable to many moderns. Noble Laureate Richard Feynman points to just this teaching as an illustration of the conflict between science and religion,[12] and Nobel Laureate Steven Weinberg concurs.[13] How can an educated person swallow the idea that the universe was made for us and that we have a special place within it? Once one recognizes the vast size of the universe, its age, and the long development of the mysterious matter within it, Feynman suggests, one comes to think that "the theory that it is

---

12. Richard P. Feynman, *The Meaning of It All: Thoughts of a Citizen-Scientist* (Reading, MA: Helix Books/Perseus Books, 1998), pp. 37ff.

13. See Steven Weinberg's "A Designer Universe?" *The New York Review of Books,* Oct. 21, 1999.

all arranged as a stage for God to watch man's struggle for good and evil seems inadequate."[14]

But it is quite possible to accept the now commonplace facts Feynman points to and yet hold on to the notion that the world was made with us in mind — for at least four reasons.

First, and most obviously, God might have had aims other than or in addition to the production and edification of humankind, aims that would make the universe something more than the "stage" Feynman imagines. Various thinkers have held that a huge universe — indeed, an infinite universe — is needed to display God's infinite majesty.

Second, a good creator might want to provide for creatures a rich and vast environment as an object of reflection. Humans have cognitive powers that are in a sense infinite; it might be eminently reasonable for God to provide a superabundant object for the intellect. Parents want to enrich their children's environment. Humans take great pleasure in discovery (certainly, Feynman does).[15]

Third, since Feynman wrote the above, cosmology has produced a wealth of evidence that must be dealt with by anyone maintaining that the universe was not made with us in mind. It is becoming increasingly evident, for example, that the very vastness Feynman pointed to is required if creatures like us are to exist at all. For a planet like earth to exist, the universe must be big enough (but not too big), cold enough (but not too cold), stable enough (but not too stable), and old enough (but not too old). Thick volumes have been produced detailing the apparent "fine-tuning" of the universe and the planet we live on, the delicate structures and process required for the appearance of complex, intelligent beings like us.

And fourth, there recently has appeared another striking illustration of Newman's "unlooked for correlations found among received truths," a line of reasoning that has received far less attention than have cosmological considerations pertaining to what is required for the emergence and sustaining of human life. The most thorough development of the line of reasoning so far comes out in a work with no hint of its implications in the title: Mark Steiner's *The Applicability of Mathematics as a Philosophical Problem*.[16] Steiner takes as his point of departure the kind of statements made by distinguished physicists such as Eugene Wigner, who speaks of the "unreasonable effectiveness of mathematics in natural science," which is a gift we "neither

14. Feynman, *The Meaning of It All*, p. 39.

15. See, for instance, Feynman, *The Pleasure of Finding Things Out* (Cambridge, MA: Perseus Books, 1999).

16. Mark Steiner, *The Applicability of Mathematics as a Philosophical Problem* (Cambridge, MA: Harvard University Press, 1998).

understand nor deserve."[17] Steiner contends that contemporary physics is anthropocentric inasmuch as it pursues strategies for discovery that make no sense unless it is assumed that human beings have a special place in the overall scheme. Of course, this does not mean that today's physicists consciously proceed on this assumption; indeed, most of them may believe and say quite the opposite. But their practice betrays them. Steiner sees this anthropocentrism most pointedly in the physicists' practice of relying for discovery on mathematical analogies based solely on syntactical considerations. Physicists take their cues from the mere structure of formulas, apart from their meaning. It is as though the rules of chess shed light on the rules of the cosmos, or as if a palindrome, such as DENNIS AND EDNA SINNED, has a better chance of being true because it is spelled the same way frontward and backward.[18] And the physicists' practices succeed often enough (not always, not even for the most part, but often enough), Steiner concludes, to defy understanding within a framework that denies the universe was made for us.

The argument has met with vigorous criticism.[19] Assume that the critics are right, that the phenomena Steiner points to, considered in isolation from all other evidence of a good God, are best explained by some more parsimonious philosophy of mathematics and science than that favored by Steiner. Nevertheless, these phenomena, when conjoined with all the other evidence, might help support the view that the universe was made for us, at least in part.

A Putative Fact About *Originality* of Doctrine: The Beatitudes Are Original

A new teaching appears among a people unprepared to produce anything so daringly different. With varying degrees of justification, originality is claimed on behalf of many religions, including, as we have already noted, Jewish monotheism.[20]

17. Steiner, *The Applicability of Mathematics as a Philosophical Problem,* p. 2.

18. Steiner, *The Applicability of Mathematics as a Philosophical Problem,* pp. 71-72.

19. Peter Simons does not buy it. Yet Simons does grant that at this stage of our knowledge something of the wonder at the regularity of the universe perhaps should remain. Peter Simons, review of *The Applicability of Mathematics as a Philosophical Problem* by Mark Steiner, *British Journal of the Philosophy of Science* 52 (2001): 181-84.

20. W. Gunther Plaut argues that God's voice can be identified in the Torah partly through the uniqueness of the message: "We see the vast distance between the more primitive elements of the Torah and its most sublime and advanced passages; and we marvel that such great progress occurred in a few centuries. . . . No satisfactory explanation has ever been given in terms of climatic, geographical, economic, and political factors for the unique religio-ethical development in Israel. It is thus not unreasonable to discern revelation *within* the historical process." W. Gunther Plaut, ed., *The Torah: A Modern Commentary* (New York: Union of American Hebrew Congregations, 1981), p. xxxvi. The religious development of Israel may not be as unique as Plaut contends. John D.

To take another example, think of the teachings of the Christian beatitudes on how we should live our lives. Blessed are the poor in spirit, the meek, those who mourn, those who hunger and thirst after righteousness, the merciful, the pure in heart, the peacemakers, and those who suffer persecution for righteousness' sake.[21]

These instructions can be seen as novel even by those who do not subscribe to Christian values. One hostile observer, Richard Taylor, speaks in a Nietzschean frame of mind about the rise of Christian values as "the eclipse of ancient ideals" — the ideals of personal excellence and aspiration, of nobility, of elevation above the common person. Taylor laments the inversion of the old values and the advent of a system in which people are judged valuable simply by virtue of their minimal humanity, by virtue of being images of God. With dismay and astonishment, he notes that the new religion has declared "the humble and the meek, that is, the *least* among us, to be the very salt of the earth and already blessed beyond measure."[22] To some degree, the "new" teachings have lost their freshness, partly because they have grown familiar and partly because the teachings have been domesticated by adherents who have managed to reconcile them to the ways of the world. But seen in their original context, the Christian teachings on morality strike many as original. (They are rooted in the originality of what Christians made of Jesus: the ignominiously executed Galilean Jew was, less than twenty years after his crucifixion, said by Christians to be *identical* with God. How did this happen? It is, some scholars suggest, the "basic question of New Testament Christology.")[23]

Of course, claims of originality are contested. Some say that there is little in Christian moral teachings that is innovative, little that departs from Jewish thought of the time. It was John Calvin's view that the Sermon on the Mount was firmly rooted in the Jewish law, and, according to Hans Dieter Betz, "To a surprising degree modern scholarship can confirm Calvin's insights."[24] Others take a diametrically opposed view. Rabbi Meir Y. Solo-

---

Kronen suggests that it is not, writing (in private correspondence): "Zoroaster's Gathas are as sublime as the most sublime parts of the Old Testament, and there were no Iranian Prophets who preceded him. He single-handedly transformed polytheism (which, here and there, contained hints of a nobler type of religion) into a lofty ethical monotheism."

21. See Matt. 5:1-11.

22. Richard Taylor, *Ethics, Faith, and Reason* (Englewood Cliffs, NJ: Prentice-Hall, 1985), p. 8.

23. M. Hengel, "Christological Titles in Early Christianity," in James H. Charlesworth, ed., *The Messiah: Developments in Earliest Judaism and Christianity* (Minneapolis: Fortress Press, 1987), p. 443.

24. Hans Dieter Betz, *The Sermon on the Mount*, ed. Adela Yarbro Collins (Minneapolis: Fortress Press, 1995), p. 17.

veichik maintains that Jesus' mandate to love our enemies is completely new and entirely inconsistent with the Jewish tradition of the time (Soloveichik rejects the mandate).[25]

However we may resolve questions of what is owed to whom, elements of the great theistic religions strike many observers as new at the time of their propagation. It does not follow from the fact that a teaching is novel, that it is true. But originality counts in favor of a teaching's heavenly origin if the teaching appears to be beyond the creative powers of those who proclaim it.

Still, a skeptic might say, do we not have other perfectly good explanations of what may strike us as innovative teaching? Have not anthropologists such as Mircea Eliade explained well enough how primitive peoples arrive at gaudy simulacra of genuine theories? The great questions of life admit of only so many basic answers, and eventually all will be enunciated by one group or another, Eliade suggests. In illustration of Eliade's version of the thesis, Ioan Couliano points to religious teachings regarding the psyche.[26] Given the sense all humans share of a body and something like a three-dimensional mental screen, it will be all but inevitable that speculation will arise about the relationship between the mind or psyche and the body. Once it is hypothesized that the psyche is a different kind of entity from the body, the question of their relationship immediately arises. Only a few major options are available. Either there is a soul or there is not. If there is, then either the soul pre-exists the body or does not. And either it is created or it is not. And so on, and so on. Each possibility will, in time, attract the notice of a group, and many groups will find it appropriate to use sacred language to express the particular possibilities they have seized upon. Some particular possibilities will get glossed with imagery, with mythological re-expression. There is no need, in the view of Eliade and his followers, to invoke divine assistance to account for the originality.

This might be convincing if it were always easy to think up the abstract possibilities. But it is often difficult — sometimes incredibly so. After all, some of the great discoveries in the history of science turn on the recognition of a logical option nobody had noticed.[27] Consider an imaginary archaic revelatory claim about what we now call our solar system. There are just so

25. Meir Y. Soloveichik, "The Virtue of Hate," *First Things* 129 (Feb. 2003): 41-46.

26. Mircea Eliade and Ioan P. Couliano, with Hillary S. Wiesner, *The Eliade Guide to World Religions* (San Francisco: HarperCollins, 1991), pp. 1-7.

27. For example, Einstein's revolutionary special theory of relativity avoided seeming contradictions and absurdities about the independence of the speed of light from the light source by rejecting unquestioned assumptions among physicists concerning the simultaneity of measuring an event from two different points within the same frame. See John Stachel, *Einstein from B to Z* (Boston: Birkhauser, 2002), p. 166.

many logical possibilities regarding the position of the earth within the system. Either it is fixed or not, either at the center or not. If it is not fixed, either it moves about the sun or it does not. And if it does, then either it alone does, or so do some other planets. And if other planets do, either these other planets have satellites or they do not. And if they do, either Jupiter does or it does not. Or again, light travels from these bodies either with finite or infinite speed . . . and so on. But who would think that an archaic revelation hitting on just the right alternatives, the ones depicting what we now know about our solar system, just happened to identify the truth? It is all too strange that the right choices should be made at each choice-point, too strange to be assigned to mere luck. In fact, the mere positing of options is itself illuminating and may be beyond what we think a people should be able to come up with all on their own, even when — perhaps especially when — the fresh options pertain to our all-too-familiar way of life, as in the case of the beatitudes.

A Putative Fact about *Resilience* of Doctrine: The Judaeo-Christian Doctrine of Omniscience Is Resilient   God's providential gaze extends everywhere: "[T]hat which holds all things together knows what is said."[28] God knows whatever is knowable. Versions of the contention can claim backing in the Hebrew, Islamic, and Christian traditions.

But how can God know whatever is knowable? How can God know all true propositions, given the existence of propositions such as "I am making a mess"? In order to know this proposition, it seems necessary to know more than that somebody in such-and-such a place, at such-and-such a time, is making a mess. These neighboring thoughts or propositions do not contain the same information as contained in the thought or proposition that *I* am making a mess.[29]

The critics are right to say that no proposition close to "I am making a mess" adequately represents what I know when I know the proposition. Even so, it is not necessary to say that an omniscient being is an impossibility.[30] And here is the reason: it is *false* that, in order to know what I know, an omniscient being must represent what is known propositionally. Maimonides noticed that the opponents of the Hebrew revelation had a bad habit of making just this as-

28. Wisdom of Solomon 1:7 (NRSV).

29. Among the most persistent and skillful of the opponents of omniscience, Patrick Grim has run an argument in several publications that turns on the claim that no being distinct from me knows what I know in knowing that I am making a mess. See, for instance, Patrick Grim, *The Incomplete Universe: Totality, Knowledge, and Truth* (Cambridge, MA: MIT Press, 1991).

30. For a fuller discussion of this matter, see Thomas D. Sullivan, "Omnipotence, Omniscience, and the Divine Mode of Knowing," *Faith and Philosophy* 8, no. 1 (1991): 21-35.

sumption. Aquinas gives reasons for thinking that the tacit assumption is unwarrantable. Perhaps an omniscient being could know what I know without *representing* the fact, or state of affairs, or event, without forming a representative structure of the kind we often call a "proposition." Is it not likely that a world-creator, a god, the first cause of reality, would have a very different way of representing reality? We humans must put together our thoughts, a bit of this and a bit of that, synthesized into a whole. Might not a superior being grasp things as they are, without using a mode of representation that synthesizes cognitive scraps? One who is born blind might gain a sense of the length of something by synthesizing discrete perceptions of touch. Such a person may have no conception at all of how the whole could sensuously be grasped without the synthesis of separate tactile perceptions. If God's noetic representation is superior not just in what it attains but in its mode of representation, then we should not be surprised by the fact that we have no way of adequately representing what the Omniscient One knows.[31] "For my thoughts are not your thoughts, nor are your ways my ways, says the LORD."[32]

Of course, even if our suggested analysis of "omniscience" is correct, that hardly shows that there is an omniscient being, much less that it was revealed to the Jews that there is.[33] Again, it must be remembered that the argument is not that this or that isolated fact is best explained by assuming that some individual or group has received a true revelation; it is, rather, that there is a combination of facts that may in the end warrant such a conclusion. Some revelatory traditions have the property of expressing natural theological claims that are exceedingly difficult to refute, the ten thousand objections in Aquinas's *Summa* met by ten thousand answers, many successful, and by many more answers outside the *Summa*, equally good or better, ranging throughout a tradition of Abrahamic theology (Hebrew, Christian, and Islamic) that cannot be dismissed without raising the suspicion that bold dismissals are rooted in sheer ignorance of monuments of rationality in the religious traditions.[34]

---

31. The line of thought mentioned in this paragraph can also be developed to respond to objections to omniscience based on time, *"de presenti"* arguments.

32. Isa. 55:8 (NRSV).

33. John D. Kronen informs us that the Nyaya-Vaisesika theory of God's omniscience also holds that God does not know propositionally.

34. Readers unfamiliar with Aquinas's *Summa,* for example, might reflect on the implication of the proposal of logician C. Anthony Anderson that "Alonzo Church be taken to be the denotation of the definite description, 'The most rational man since St. Thomas Aquinas' — a designation which Church himself is said to have reserved for Kurt Gödel." C. Anthony Anderson, "Alonzo Church's Contributions to Philosophy and Intensional Logic," *The Bulletin of Symbolic Logic* 4, no. 2 (1998): 168-69.

A Putative Fact About *Fertility* of Doctrine: The Judaeo-Christian Doctrine of Omniscience and the Christian Doctrine of the Incarnation Are Fertile
An inquirer might find that some particular revelatory claim has been superabundantly fertile, producing a flowering of ideas, of whole systems of thought. The fertility of a doctrine is one more mark of truth, one more thing to be explained.

Critics of religion have pointed often, and not without some justification, to the deleterious consequences of various doctrines taught in the name of God. Overpopulation, famine, wars of aggression, torture, genocide, slavery, oppression of women, abuse of children, destruction of the natural world — all these things and more have been blamed on teachings put forward as divinely revealed. Let us grant that all these things have resulted from teachings proclaimed as divine.

Still, the inquirer must also reckon with the positive consequences of religious doctrines, and in particular with the positive intellectual consequences of revelatory claims. For example, there is more to be learned from the study of revealed teachings on omniscience than that the teachings are resilient. We are led strongly to suspect that there is a lesson for *epistemology* in the traditional notion, defended by Maimonides and Aquinas and articulated in our discussion of "resilience," that, in order to know what I know, an omniscient being need *not* represent what is known propositionally. Here, then, is another fact to be explained: the doctrine of omniscience as embedded in Christianity and developed by natural theologians is *fertile*. Ever since Plato's *Theaetetus*, philosophers have been looking for a definition of knowledge. They have thought that the definition would begin by saying that knowledge is true belief, and then would go on to add something. The proposed definitions invariably meet with serious objection. The above discussion of omniscience suggests that the difficulties may be rooted in the very first part of the definition, the part about belief. It may be entirely accidental to knowledge that it be belief, at least if belief is understood as a propositional attitude. Perhaps what is called for is something like the Aristotelian idea that knowledge is some kind of *identification* with the object known. The revelatory claim that God is omniscient, the insistence that this is so despite well-known problems concerning knowledge of the self (*de se* knowledge), lifts us out of the rut. Indeed, it points us in the direction of a specific solution to the problem of defining knowledge.

For another example of intellectual fertility, consider the doctrine of the incarnation of the Second Person of the Trinity in Jesus.[35] Christianity has historically maintained that the Logos of God assumed a human form, a human

35. One could for the same purpose consider the avatar of Krishna in the *Bhagavad-Gita*.

nature, that the human and divine natures were, without dissolution, realized in one subject, one person. Now it scarcely needs to be said that this doctrine has its difficulties. Maimonides argued that not even a miracle would suffice to overturn the argument that this is impossible. Whether it is possible or not, the doctrine of the incarnation entails something extraordinarily important about the general concept of an essence: contrary to the current conception of essence, it is not to be defined modally. A human nature is an essence. And an essence is typically defined modally, as a collection of necessary attributes. But that is not the way it is conceived in the doctrine of the incarnation, because the Second Person of the Trinity picks up a human nature, and so is not necessarily connected to it. (The point is elaborated in Aquinas.) Thus the doctrine of the incarnation drives in the direction of postulating a hypothesis not easily conceived in abstraction from revelation.[36] And once more, the fertility of the content of a revelatory claim calls for an explanation.

5.3.3. Brief Illustrations Involving CUE-Facts

A CUE-Fact: Consciousness Has a Function   Consciousness appears to be *for* something. That it has a function is often taken as a brute fact. As Jerry Fodor says:

> [I]f it isn't literally true that my wanting is causally responsible for my reaching, and my itching is causally responsible for my scratching . . . if none of that is literally true, then practically everything I believe about anything is false and it's the end of the world.[37]

Even so, we think it must be admitted that while the sheer existence of conscious states is undeniable, the putative fact that conscious states are causally responsible for actions in the world is not. That consciousness not only exists but plays a causal role is best understood as a CUE-fact. We can accept its causal role as a fact if only an explanation is available.

What are the prospects of giving an entirely naturalistic explanation of consciousness? The naturalist may take several lines.

36. It can be done. At least one contemporary analytic philosopher (Kit Fine) has done it; but it is not easy. See Kit Fine, "The Concept of Essence," *Philosophical Perspectives,* vol. 8, ed. James E. Tomberlin (Atascadero, CA: Ridgeview Publishing Company, 1994). See also Michael Gorman, "The Essential and the Accidental," in *Ratio* 18 (2005).

37. Jerry Fodor, "Making Mind Matter More," *Philosophical Topics* 17 (1989); reprinted in *A Theory of Content and Other Essays* (Cambridge, MA: MIT Press, 1990), p. 156.

First, it may be alleged, Charles Darwin and Alfred Russel Wallace showed that living things do not have functions. Yes, one can argue, as Fred Dretske has, that what Darwin and Wallace actually showed was that things could *have* functions without a designer. Dretske points out "that some of these things [organs, processes, and behavior of plants and animal] *have* functions . . . seems evident not only from a common-sense standpoint but also from the practice, if not the explicit avowals, of biologists and botanists."[38] Let us suppose, though, for the sake of the argument, that living things do not have functions: the heart does not beat to circulate blood; it just beats *with the result that* blood circulates, and so forth. Still, the fundamental question remains, since it can be raised without using the Aristotelian or teleological language of "function" or "purpose." For it surely is sensible to ask what survival value consciousness has. That is exactly the kind of question Darwin himself raised. So this first problem is merely verbal.

Second, it may be argued that consciousness has no survival value, that it no more fits us for existence than a multitude of characteristics that biologists see as accidents of the evolutionary process — that is, neither advancing nor hindering reproduction. There probably are some neutral variations, some human characteristics that arose accidentally. Could consciousness be among them? The fascinating phenomenon of "blind sight" seems to suggest that consciousness is not necessary for certain sorts of visual "perception." Some people whose primary visual cortex is badly damaged respond with an accuracy much greater than chance would dictate when given certain visual discrimination tasks and asked to "guess" among several concrete alternatives, though they report that they have no visual experience or consciousness in their "blind" field.[39] Thus it seems possible that we just happen to be conscious, though consciousness serves no role at all in survival.

But the thought rankles. Could one of the most important things in our universe have just *happened?* The commonsense answer is "no," and that is the answer most scientists give as well. In the words of Stephen Palmer:

> The unconscious automaton can, by definition, engage in all of the same evolutionarily useful activities — successfully finding food, shelter, and mates while avoiding cliffs, predators, and falling objects — so it is unclear on what basis consciousness could be evolutionarily selected.
>
> One possibility is that the problem is ill-posed. Perhaps the automaton actually could *not* perform all the tasks that the consciously perceiving or-

38. Fred Dretske, *Explaining Behavior: Reasons in a World of Causes* (Cambridge, MA: MIT Press, 1991), pp. 63-64.

39. Stephen E. Palmer, *Vision Science* (Cambridge, MA: MIT Press, 1999), pp. 633-36.

ganism could. Perhaps consciousness plays some crucial and as-yet-unspecified role in our perceptual abilities.[40]

It might be thought that Palmer is here speculating that

1) It is impossible to produce anything that could do what humans do without producing consciousness (though the consciousness is not *instrumental* to survival).

There is another reading, though, better by far, that construes him as instead tentatively proposing that

2) Conscious organisms survive *in virtue of* being conscious; for that reason it is impossible to produce anything that could do what humans do without producing consciousness.

The first reading would be akin to saying that it is impossible to clench your fist without your fingers heating up, but the survival value of clenching your fist is not tied to the heating of your fingers. On this account it is completely accidental — one might almost say, a sheer miracle — that the right kinds of experiences accompany various activities (e.g., that pleasure accompanies activities that promote reproduction). This is equivalent to the earlier view that consciousness is epiphenomenal, with its attendant difficulties.

The second way of reading Palmer has it that consciousness is not epiphenomenal, and that, though presently no naturalistic theory accounts for its function, some theory will someday succeed. But this is a promissory note, one that there is good reason to refuse to accept.[41]

A reason to refuse is that current efforts by neuroscientists to explain the function of consciousness often begin by raising the problem in a clear form but then burying it when they go on to the solution. In *The Quest for Consciousness: A Neurobiological Approach,* a work John Searle has praised as the best of its kind, Christof Koch devotes an entire chapter to his speculations about the function of consciousness. Koch feels the problem acutely, since in earlier chapters he had emphasized how in a rapid and flawless manner both healthy and brain-damaged humans execute learned, stereotypical behavior. The possibility of all activity being carried out in this zombie-like fashion — Koch entitles one chapter "The Zombie Within" — prompts him to raise the

---

40. Palmer, *Vision Science,* p. 15.

41. See Jaegwon Kim on the difficulties of functionalizing qualia, in his *Physicalism, or Something Near Enough* (Princeton, NJ: Princeton University Press, 2005).

troubling question: "If so much processing can go on in the dark, without any feelings, why is a conscious mental life needed at all? What evolutionary advantage favored conscious brains over brains that are nothing but large bundles of zombie agents?"[42] Koch lists seventeen possibilities. Consciousness might be critical for promoting access to short-term memory, and so on. Yet, as Koch proceeds to focus on one function, "executive summary," he sets the stage by reiterating a point he earlier made in a book with Francis Crick. "Our . . . assumption is based on the broad idea of the biological usefulness of visual awareness *(or, strictly, of its neural correlate)*."[43] Yes indeed, "strictly." Because that is all we get, talk actually about the function of the activities of the neural correlate, not consciousness itself. Contrary to Koch's intentions, his parenthetical remark undercuts the entire project of explaining the function of consciousness. Crick and Koch pose a hard question about consciousness, but then, *sotto voce,* they replace it with a more tractable cousin. While it is often enough proclaimed that in this millennium an answer to the hard questions will be forthcoming, we have as yet not even a hint of what shape a purely physicalistic answer could take.

Here again, a non-naturalistic view of the world has something to offer. It is possible to explain the purpose of consciousness by recognizing the life of the mind as inherently pleasurable and worthy, a gift a supranatural creator might fittingly bestow upon creatures. What is consciousness for? It is for wonder at the starry heavens above and the moral law within. It is a gift that is given in lesser measure to some creatures, but in abundance to that being whose existence, as Kant said, "is not restricted to the conditions and boundaries of this life" but reaches "into the infinite."[44]

A CUE-Fact: Humans Have Libertarian Freedom   Non-naturalism saves libertarian freedom.

That there is such a thing as libertarian freedom is another CUE-fact. It certainly seems to all of us that we can do otherwise than what we do, as is clear from a) internal experience, b) the poverty of the data showing otherwise, c) the presupposition of certain branches of neuroscience that we have libertarian freedom, and d) the concessions of noted *determinists* who admit they cannot shake off the belief that they have libertarian freedom.

About a) and b), far too much has been written to require elaboration

---

42. Christof Koch, *The Quest for Consciousness: A Neurobiological Approach* (Englewood, CO: Roberts and Co., 2004), p. 231.

43. Koch, *The Quest for Consciousness,* p. 233 (italics added).

44. Immanuel Kant, *Critique of Practical Reason,* ed. Mary Gregor (Cambridge, UK: Cambridge University Press, 1997), p. 134 [5:162].

here. Looking within, it surely seems to us that we can do or refrain from doing; and there is little by way of direct evidence showing that this is an illusion. It would be necessary, in order to show that it is an illusion, to predict
human behavior in a great variety of circumstances, and human behavior is
notoriously difficult to predict. Less well appreciated is c), the reliance of
some branches of science on the belief that we can do otherwise than what we
do. Cognitive neuroscience considers physical correlates of voluntary movement. This kind of movement is best defined against the backdrop of the involuntary, which is manifest when there is brain damage. For example, when
there is damage to the subthalamic nucleus, people's arms frequently jerk
around wildly; they are unable to stop the movements. That is the reason why
these movements are called involuntary. As Apostolos Georgopoulos points
out, the best definition of voluntary movement is set against this backdrop.
Voluntary movement is "a movement that *can be suppressed* (or not initiated
at all) *at will*."[45] Should it be doubted that certain movements can be initiated
or suppressed at will, the distinction between the voluntary and involuntary
would be obliterated, and students of the voluntary would have nothing to
study. As for d), the concession of determinists, John Searle stands out:

> [F]or reasons I don't really understand, evolution has given us a form of ex-
> perience of voluntary action where the experience of freedom, that is to say,
> the experience of the sense of alternative possibilities, is built into the very
> structure of conscious, voluntary, intentional human behaviour. For that
> reason, I believe, neither this discussion nor any other will ever convince us
> that our behaviour is unfree.[46]

The supranatural view preserves the beliefs and hopes a grimmer philosophy
would destroy.[47] What we do is, at least sometimes, partly up to us. We can act
or refrain from acting, making our way in the world.

   This CUE-fact that alternative courses of action are open to us differs from
the CUE-fact discussed above — that consciousness plays a role in our lives. It is

---

45. Apostolos P. Georgopoulos, "Voluntary Movement: Computational Principles and Neural Mechanisms," in Michael D. Rugg, ed., *Cognitive Neuroscience* (Cambridge, MA: The MIT
Press, 1997), p. 132.

46. John Searle, *Minds, Brains, and Science* (Cambridge, MA: Harvard University Press,
1984), p. 98.

47. For a detailed account of the grim implications of the rejection of libertarian free will,
see Ted Honderich, *A Theory of Determinism*, Vol. 2: *The Consequences of Determinism* (Oxford:
Clarendon Press, 1988). Determinist Honderich says determinism can be "a black thing" that
can "weigh on our existence like an incubus," as it did for John Stuart Mill and for Honderich
himself (p. 12).

possible to allow the latter and deny the former. This is what most of us do when it comes to at least some animals. These animals are aware of their environment and act on the basis of that awareness, but they are not in a position to choose or refrain from choosing, to act or refrain from acting, to commit one way rather than another. We are, however. Or so we can scarcely help but believe.

The CUE-fact that alternative courses of action are open to us also differs from another CUE-fact with which it is intimately connected and sometimes conflated: the CUE-fact that we are morally responsible for our actions. Indeed, many philosophers have argued that it is only because of the possibility of alternative choices and courses of action that we are morally responsible for anything at all. Jurists have long espoused this idea.[48]

Naturalism appears to exclude freedom to do things other than the things a person actually does. Alternative possibilities are open to us because we are not mere matter in motion. Of course, this supranaturalist hypothesis faces difficulties. But it does seem that only a supranatural view can preserve our sense of full agency, our sense that at least sometimes what we do is up to us. What, after all, is the alternative hypothesis that can explain the fact, if it is a fact, that we can do otherwise than what we do? That it is difficult to imagine another hypothesis is implicit in a condensed criticism of the supranatural hypothesis.

> It has been argued . . . that libertarianism does not give us an explanation of human action. It gives us a blank where an explanation should be. And, one might add, it would take a very odd *something* to fill in the blank. The desired entity — whether called mind, soul, self, agent, or originator — must be sufficiently connected to the past to constitute a continuing locus of personal responsibility, but sufficiently disconnected so that its past does not determine its present. It must be sufficiently connected to the causal chain to be able to interrupt it, but sufficiently disconnected not to get trapped. It must be susceptible to being shaped and maybe governed by motives, threats, punishments, and desires, but not totally controlled by them.[49]

How odd, this something! What fills the blank, particularly if it is supranatural, is indeed strange. Yet we must postulate some such entity if our abil-

---

48. Martin Gardner and Richard Singer cite Oliver Wendell Holmes as representative. Holmes observed in *The Common Law* (1881): "[I]t is felt to be impolitic and unjust to make a man answerable for harm, unless he might have chosen otherwise." See Martin R. Gardner and Richard G. Singer, *Crimes and Punishment: Cases, Materials, and Readings in Criminal Law,* 4th ed. (Newark, NJ: LexisNexis, 2004), p. 334.

49. Roy C. Weatherford, in *The Oxford Companion to Philosophy,* ed. Ted C. Honderich (Oxford: Oxford University Press, 1995), entry on "freedom and determinism," p. 293.

ity to do otherwise is to be preserved. And we should not infer from the mere fact that the blank is filled with an odd entity that there is no such entity. After all, it is not only the *entity* that is odd but the fact conceded on all sides that *we envision alternatives,* even if they are not (despite appearances) really open to us. This envisioning bears on nonexistent objects and states of affairs. You seek the perfect friend, you imagine jumping over thirty feet in the high jump at the next Olympics. Either you consider these nonexistent entities and states of affairs without forming a relationship to them, or you form a relationship. But how strange an envisioning of x without any relationship to x. And if there is a relationship to x, when x is nonexistent, what an odd relationship. It is certainly not a physical relationship, since physical relationships presuppose that *both* related items are in the space-time network. One could opt with Alexius Meinong for there being objects such that there are no such objects; but this is hardly less strange than anything else surrounding familiar yet mysterious intentional mental acts. The intentional was, for Franz Brentano and his followers such as Chisholm, the mark of the mental. But for their medieval predecessors, who took the realm of the supranatural for granted, intentionality was also a mark of the immaterial. The nature of an entity could be inferred from its characteristic operations. That we at least deliberate and thus envision nonexistent alternatives is a given. Strange act, strange subject of the act. What else should we expect?

Libertarian freedom can be explained on a supranatural understanding of the world — and no other.

A CUE-Fact: Some Revelatory Claims Are Rationally Alluring

Revelatory claims are not alluring to everyone. Philosopher Thomas Nagel says:

> . . . I want atheism to be true and am made uneasy by the fact that some of the most intelligent and well-informed people I know are religious believers. It isn't just that I don't believe in God and, naturally, hope that I'm right in my belief. It's that I hope there is no God! I don't want there to be a God; I don't want the universe to be like that.[50]

But even those who, like Nagel, reject revelatory claims as personally unappetizing, acknowledge the claims' unmistakable allure for the vast majority of humankind. One might argue that the content of revelatory claims can ex-

---

50. Thomas Nagel, *The Last Word* (New York: Oxford University Press, 1997), p. 130. Revelatory claims embed explanations of Nagel's anti-authoritarian sentiments, as Russell Pannier notes in his commentary on Nagel in "From a Logical Point of View," *Logos: A Journal of Catholic Thought and Culture* 5, no. 2 (2002): 176.

plain the widely acknowledged psychological fact that revelatory claims are generally alluring. Our focus here, though, is on a related fact, a CUE-fact: some revelatory claims are *rationally* alluring. Contemporary thinkers have perhaps grown sufficiently accustomed to the pessimistic view that there is no goal of human existence not to be struck by the strangeness of the reality, if that is the reality, and by the queer conflict between our actions and our pessimistic conviction, if this is indeed our deepest conviction.

The yearning is there, in most people. Is it rational?

Recall Aristotle's efforts in the *Ethics* to deal with the question of the goal of human existence. Not every choice can be a choice of a means; we cannot choose everything for the sake of something else. The chain of choices always terminates in some end. Aristotle thinks it safe to say that there is one end of all — happiness. His answer in the final book of the *Ethics* to the question "What, then, is happiness (eudaimonia)?" famously celebrates the theoretical life. But Aristotle argues that this blissful life is in a way too high for human beings. Yes, we should strain every fiber of our being to bring what is best in ourselves to bear on the best object, or the best Object. But this form of happiness is obviously subject to limitations of this life. It flickers, and we die. Aristotle, whatever his view of the afterlife, seems to think it is irrational to desire a form of happiness that is out of reach.

Yet Aquinas, always sympathetic to Aristotle as far as the truth allows, parts company with him here. The rational person has every right not to be satisfied.

> But this view also seems unreasonable. For all agree that happiness or bliss is a good of rational or intellectual natures and so wherever such natures truly exist, not by imitation, we should find true bliss and not just an imitation of it. Now human beings don't simply echo understanding (in the way other animals echo reason, imitating planning in some way in their behaviour), but are truly rational and intellectual; so we must believe they can sometimes attain true bliss and not simply an imitation of it; for otherwise the natural desire of their intellectual nature will have no function.[51]

Aquinas's judgment that it is Aristotle who is being unreasonable, and not the ordinary person discontented with the severe limits on human happiness, presupposes the proposition "Nature does nothing in vain." Naïve? In this post-Darwinian era, it surely seems so, and we have no ambition to defend the general proposition. Yet there is something quite remarkable about a be-

---

51. Aquinas, *Commentary on the Sentences*, in Timothy McDermott, ed., *Aquinas: Selected Philosophical Writings* (Oxford: Oxford University Press, 1993), p. 325.

ing so constituted that its natural desires should be for an infinite bliss infinitely beyond its reach, a flightless bird that spends its life straining to fly to
the stars. Could it be that the desire for real bliss is rational after all? And if it
is, do we have any better conception of how it could be than what has been
given to us in the most elevated, most plausible revelations?

Toward the end of his life Aristotle may have been of a mind to concede
all this. He wrote: "The more I am a loner, the more I have become a lover of
myths."[52] The myths, perhaps, promised something beyond the contempla-
tive life he recommended in Book X of the *Ethics*, hinted at the possibility of
divine friendship in a world that completes what is lacking in this world. The
state of bliss promised for the next world is the completion of a series of actions that begin in this world. (If standing in the winner's circle at a race is to
mean anything, one needs actually to have run the race. Jumping into the
winner's circle without participating in the race means nothing.) Religious
doctrines express more articulately, less metaphorically than myth, how this
completion through divine friendship can occur. And they purport to have
epistemic backing for the possibility of such completion, something myths
lack, as Aristotle recognized. Religious doctrines tell us that *in this world*
there can begin a superhuman satisfaction, betokening continuation in a life
beyond.

But how, it might be objected, is divine friendship possible for us, given
the great ontological divide between humans and the divine? Aristotle said
that proximity is required for friendship: friends must dwell together. Can
what is infinite dwell with what is finite, and can what is wholly immaterial
dwell with embodied creatures, even creatures with immaterial minds? Aquinas answers no: human beings cannot, qua humans, be friends with God; we
must be divinized. Divinization requires aid from above. According to the
content of various revelatory claims, God makes the aid available, beginning
in this lifetime. We may meet and commune with God in sacrificial rituals, in
sacraments. We may meet God in the content of revelation. Think of the
friendships, even the loves, that have started through discussions on the
Internet: one *meets* the other in the discourse. We need not see those whom
we love. We may meet God in the person of another human being who has
been transformed by contact with the divine: religious traditions point us to
saints and holy persons, those who call us to a higher way and prove the possibility of another mode of existence, one more demanding and more fulfill-
ing than the Greek conceptions of the good life. Lives of prophets in the wil-

52. Valentinus Rose, *Aristotelis Fragmenta* (Leipzig: B. G. Teubner, 1886), p. 420; fragment
668. Translation (and reference to the source) by Kevin L. Flannery, in private communication.

derness, lives of cloistered religious — these are lives of love. And so, too, the lives of many extraordinary ordinary people.

5.4. An Extended Illustration of the Explanation of Two CUE-Facts

5.4.1. Declarations of Equality and of Inalienable Rights: Two CUE-Facts

Can cherished beliefs about morals be as well explained — and thereby as well secured — on a purely secular basis as on a nonsecular basis? Our aim will not be to propose a definitive response to this question but rather to suggest why pursuing the question further might well lead to the conclusion that some deeply ingressed ethical beliefs can be explained adequately only by appealing to the supranatural, and can best be explained by appealing to a God of the sort described in major revelatory claims. The question will be brought to bear chiefly on two beliefs central to liberal democracies: humans are all in some sense basically equal, and all humans have certain inalienable rights.

According to Thomas Jefferson, these two great principles are "self-evident."[53] But in Jefferson's time critics called the principles "self-evident lies," and even today they are not uniformly accepted. Moreover, the two principles do not comport well with some other widely held beliefs such as that good is to be maximized above all: if good is to be maximized above all, then it is not difficult to think of extreme circumstances in which innocent people would need to be sacrificed to achieve this good. For these and other reasons, many philosophers have become persuaded that both principles are to be discarded. Human life is to be "unsanctified."[54]

With the acids of philosophical reflection threatening to burn holes through the "self-evident" principles, we could just give them up. Should we? Not readily. They not only lie at the core of the philosophy of liberal democracy, but of a wider set of beliefs about conduct necessary to secure the blessings of a human society. Thus the United Nations' Universal Declaration of

53. Jefferson spoke of "unalienable" rights; we take unalienable rights, inalienable rights, and inviolable rights to be the same thing.

54. See, for example, Helga Kuhse and Peter Singer, eds., *Unsanctifying Human Life: Singer on Ethics* (Oxford: Blackwell, 2002). In *Natural Rights and the Right to Choose* (Cambridge, UK: Cambridge University Press, 2002), Hadley Arkes argues powerfully that many Americans in the last thirty years have talked themselves out of the doctrines of equality and natural rights. It is possible to grant Arkes's point while maintaining that many of the same individuals also retain belief in these same fundamental teachings, accepting both yea and nay components of an ideology flexible enough to accommodate contradictories.

Human Rights begins: "Whereas recognition of the inherent dignity and of the equal and inalienable rights of all members of the human family is the foundation of freedom, justice and peace in the world. . . ."[55] Furthermore, ethical theories that deny the two propositions have their own significant problems. For example, consequentialists insist that we are morally bound always to act in such a way as to achieve the greatest balance of satisfaction, on the one hand, over dissatisfaction or suffering, on the other, tallying everyone's prospective state. That sounds good at first, but doubts set in as soon as we consider how we are to estimate consequences, or why the tally should take everyone into account, or why some should be ground up if the anticipated benefits require a nasty deed for the salvation of the many, or why anyone should feel attached to the greatest satisfaction for the greatest number (or some such payoff), or why the requirement to maximize satisfaction should be accepted when, consequentialists' assertions to the contrary notwithstanding, the foundational consequentialist postulate is anything but axiomatic in the sense of evident on its face and no argument comes close to conclusively demonstrating the postulate.

Under the circumstances, it seems best not to regard the precepts about human equality and inalienable rights as Jeffersonian "self-evident" or United Nations–"recognized" facts, but as CUE-facts, propositions whose acceptance is conditional upon explanation. We shall take the claim that all humans are in some sense basically equal as an ontological CUE-fact, and that all humans have certain inalienable rights as a moral CUE-fact.

The two general principles are expressed in many forms. Let us call any expression or interpretation of the first a "declaration of equality," and any expression or interpretation of the second a "declaration of inalienable rights." Our question, then, is this: Can a satisfying, purely secular justification-explanation be given for a significant, purely secular declaration of equality and a significant, purely secular declaration of inalienable rights?

What do we mean by a purely secular declaration? Certainly not a declaration such as Jefferson's. All are "created" equal and are "endowed by their creator" with certain inalienable rights. Mention of a "creator" suggests something transcendent, something beyond the natural. Jefferson himself may have only been thinking of nature, though it is bizarre to think nature has endowed anything with inalienable rights. But the verbal declaration itself,

---

55. Retrieved Jan. 21, 2006, from <http://www.unhchr.ch/udhr/lang/eng.htm>. In this and other "declarations," Jefferson's "self-evident" is avoided. "Recognition" is broad enough to include perception of the self-evident, but also derivation from a deeper set of principles, and mere postulation or contract to secure the envisioned benefits.

whatever Jefferson's private thoughts, is commonly understood to point beyond the natural order — even by secularists. An indication of this is that formal declarations of equality and inalienable rights these days routinely suppress all Jeffersonian references to a creator creating or endowing. The UN declaration simply begins: "Whereas recognition of the inherent dignity . . ." and so forth, leaving it to the reader to guess how this "recognition" is possible without reference to a creator. What may not occur to a reader is that there is no mention in either the Jeffersonian or UN declaration of a soul. A declaration that either mentions or presupposes the existence of immaterial entities, subjects of consciousness somehow attached to bodies, would be resting the case on something supranatural. It is possible to accept souls, little gods, without accepting an infinite God, but we shall here assume that any position on equality and rights that requires souls is less than purely secular. A purely secular declaration and a purely secular justification-explanation will thus make no explicit or implicit reference to the supranatural whatsoever. There is a continuum of the nonsecular: a secular declaration must avoid every point on the continuum, from relatively modest references to immaterial souls, to more venturesome references to a deistic creator-god, to full-throated references to a God of a revelatory claim. The greater the commitment to the supranatural, the more it strengthens our case. But any degree of commitment provides considerable evidence for our position.

What we want to know, then, is whether declarations of equality and inalienable rights can be justified without appeal to the divine. We want to know whether the claims that humans enjoy such equality and rights are true, and whether they can be shown to be true, whether their obtaining can be explained. Of course, we are also interested in whether the doctrines of equality and inalienable rights can serve to justify Western liberal democracies or, for that matter, decent communities that cannot be so depicted. And we would like to know whether it is true that, as the UN's declaration contends, "recognition of the inherent dignity and of the equal and inalienable rights of all members of the human family is the foundation of freedom, justice, and peace in the world." Still, these are not the questions that we are asking here. Our attention at the moment is confined to a topic large enough for a series of books: whether a satisfactory, purely secular argument can be worked out for the two CUE-facts.

Our contention is that the prospects of finding a purely secular justification-explanation of a significant declaration of equality and a significant declaration of inalienable rights are quite poor.

We make this argument with considerable unease. This is in part because we fully recognize that our probe of the matter in the available space can hardly result in more than a suggestion of the difficulties moral systems of great nobility and ingenuity have in establishing an appropriate declaration. Our earlier comments on the necessity and danger of providing illustrations apply in full force here. We have only the very limited aim of exposing more concrete evidence for the suspicion that allegedly secular justification-explanations of fundamental equality and inalienable rights are probably not to be had, and that therefore an inquirer should take seriously the revelatory traditions that speak to these issues. Our discomfort is also rooted in the fact that, like many, we have hoped that religious differences can be put aside as a sane world order is established on the basis of principles that appeal to nothing but transparent principles of right reason.[56] Yet it does not follow from the fact (if it is a fact) that there is no purely secular justification of equality or of inalienable rights, that the existence of equality and of inalienable rights comes to nothing more than an arbitrary divine command, or that reason cannot locate the foundation for rights, for reason can inspect foundations offered in revelations, some of which do not represent the commands of God as arbitrary.[57]

56. Perhaps the hope can be realized in the way John Rawls has suggested, without securing the reasonableness of conferring or recognizing political rights through an underlying universal ethics. (However, see the note on Rawls below.)

57. A few coreligionists acquainted with our line of reasoning have cautioned us that we are contradicting settled Catholic teaching on natural law. Of course, this need be no worry at all for inquirers or believers who reject the authority of Rome. Still, since it is a concern for those who accept that authority and for inquirers who are willing to consider the possibility that the claims of Rome are correct (and since we ourselves believe that they are correct), we will speak briefly to this objection. Should our position on this topic really be inconsistent with settled teaching, as Catholics we would willingly admit that we are wrong. And even if our position does not clearly deviate from Scripture, councils, definitive papal teachings, or the constant teaching of the church, we would still be troubled if a case could be made that we are roaming through a dangerous neighborhood.

But we are not troubled on this account. Yes, Catholic philosophers have often given the world the impression that it is Catholic dogma that reason can discern a bedrock foundation for fundamental rights that is natural (i.e., not supernatural). But in fact there is little or nothing in Catholic teaching that clearly says any such thing. On the contrary, many statements by John Paul II suggest that the truth is the exact opposite. He puts the point in *Veritatis Splendor:*

> Only God, the Supreme Good, constitutes the unshakable foundation and essential condition of morality, and thus of the commandments, particularly those negative commandments which always and in every case prohibit behavior and actions incompatible with the personal dignity of every man. (*The Encyclicals of John Paul II,* ed. J. Michael Miller [Huntington, IN: Our Sunday Visitor, 2001], p. 647, sec. 99.1).

Someone determined to cling to what has passed among intellectuals as Catholicism's constant teaching on natural law no doubt can find creative ways to explain away this and everything else John Paul says about the divine foundation of human dignity and morality. But, without going

Yet does this not leave a defender of equality and rights with next to nothing to say in the public square? What is the defender to do? Reassure everyone that they will see the truth if only they will accept some divine revelation?

This need not be the only thing that a defender can say, though we see no reason — contrary to what some ardent supporters of the separation of church and state maintain — to silence the religious believer, to rule out of order all suggestions that public policy be grounded in religious belief. After all, the founders commonly did just that, as did the civil rights movement. However, the main thing is that, while in the end it may be the case, as we argue, that only divine ordination supports equality and rights, a public argument over these CUE-facts can invoke other reasons for their adoption. How so? Well, consider a parallel from mathematics. Set theory is often seen by mathematicians as fundamental to the whole of mathematics. Thus everything hangs on the truth of the set-theoretical axioms. These axioms, however, are no longer put forward as an adequate set of self-evident truths, the way geometrical axioms were in the time of the Greeks and for ages afterward. As mathematician-logician A. G. Hamilton puts it:

> There are not enough self-evident properties to provide an axiom system which is strong enough. The axiom of choice and the continuum hypothesis are the most celebrated examples of assertions about sets whose acceptability is uncertain. Consequently, we are forced to move away from the conception of axioms as self-evident truths, and to consider set theory axioms as expressing properties of sets which we hope are characteristic and sufficient, and, more importantly, which we *hope* are true.[58]

Thus mathematicians evidently invite each other to go with axioms that are neither self-evident nor, presumably, demonstrable from yet more epistemically fundamental axioms. The argument must be that these axioms will get us what we need to found and unify mathematics, and they are not clearly

---

further into papal declarations, which would be inappropriate in the present context, we conclude with this very brief reflection on the antecedent probability of what the Catholic church would teach on this subject. *Remove* a single proposition, the parallel postulate, from Euclid's set of axioms, and the result is a shrunken "natural geometry" that leaves out many familiar theorems. *Negate* that single proposition and the result, depending on how the postulate is negated, is one or another strange non-Euclidean geometries. Is it really plausible that a dozen propositions about the divine origin and destiny of immortal human beings can be deleted from the set of fundamental assumptions a church makes about ultimate realities without anything of significance happening to its teachings on human rights?

58. A. G. Hamilton, *Numbers, Sets and Axioms: The Apparatus of Mathematics* (Cambridge, UK: Cambridge University Press, 1982), p. 116.

false. A defender of CUE-facts about equality and rights can do the same kind of thing, though for different reasons. This is what the UN does, in effect, in its declaration. Upholding equality and inalienable rights *works*. That is motive enough for espousing the ontological and moral CUE-facts.

5.4.2. *The Search for Secular Foundations for Equality*

It is possible to understand a declaration of equality in a number of ways. It might be understood prescriptively, as the claim that all humans are to be *treated* equally. That is very vague and can be refined in various ways. It might, for instance, mean that public policies should aim at producing a society where people share more equally in wealth or opportunity or education or healthcare. But a declaration of equality may also be understood descriptively, as an ontological assertion, a claim that all humans have a fundamental equality that *underlies* our particular egalitarian aims.

As we have noted above, our eye here will be on this last notion. What we are primarily concerned with in this section is whether there is any reason to think fundamental equality is explainable, and if so, whether it is plausible to believe it can be explained without appeal to the supranatural.

Despite declaring his "truths" to be self-evident, Jefferson himself occasionally gestured in the direction of argument.

> The general spread of the light of science has already laid open to every view the palpable truth that the mass of mankind has not been born, with saddles on their backs, nor a favored few booted and spurred, ready to ride them legitimately, by the grace of god.[59]

No, indeed, the mass of humankind has not been born with saddles. But neither has the mass of horsekind. Nonetheless, Jefferson posed proudly on his horse.

Are there arguments better than this line of reasoning from Jefferson?

It is quite astonishing how little the philosophical community has to offer. As Jeremy Waldron observes, contemporary literature is nearly silent on the question of how egalitarianism might be defended philosophically: nothing

---

59. Letter to Roger C. Weightman, June 24, 1826, written in response to an invitation from the city of Washington to join the citizens for their celebration of the 50th anniversary of American independence. The letter was the last Jefferson ever wrote; it is part of the Jefferson manuscript collection in the Library of Congress. For a facsimile, see <http://www.loc.gov/exhibits/jefferson/images/vc214p1.jpg>.

in Dworkin, "a page or two" from Bernard Williams, Gregory Vlastos, Stanley Benn, and D. A. Lloyd Thomas; a few pages in Rawls's *Theory of Justice*.[60] It is a stunning phenomenon, given the enormous volume written on equality as an aim of policy.

Waldron points us to John Locke for a defense of egalitarianism, suggesting that Locke's mature corpus "is as well-worked-out a theory of basic equality as we have in the canon of political philosophy."[61] Locke's argument begins, it appears, with the contention that humans have a significant range property (a property of being within a certain specified range), namely, that they are capable, to greater and lesser degrees, of grasping the truth that God exists and makes moral demands. And if all humans have this range property, he maintains, then all humans are entitled to equal respect. If this is, indeed, Locke's argument for the claim that all humans are entitled to equal respect, then his moral egalitarianism rests on a theistic ontological premise. As Waldron puts it — and this is the main thesis of his book — Lockean equality "is a conception of equality that makes no sense except in the light of the particular relation between man and God."[62]

Locke's theological justification looks quite shaky when we take his egalitarianism in the strong sense in which he appears to intend it, the sense central to liberal democracies. His nominalism, his refusal to countenance real essences, makes it difficult for him to support the claim that *all* humans have a significant range property. It simply is not the case that all humans can grasp the proposition that God exists and makes moral demands. Babies cannot. The severely retarded cannot. The senile cannot. Locke's waffling on the question of male and female equality is some evidence of the shaky ground he is on. Indeed, it is not clear even that all who possess standard intellectual functions are capable of grasping as true the proposition that God exists. We have already argued that it can be exceedingly difficult for inquiring agnostics to accept that proposition on the basis of traditional natural theology.

In any event, the justification is certainly not secular. Waldron doubts that any purely secular defense is available.[63]

---

60. Jeremy Waldron, *God, Locke, and Equality: Christian Foundations in Locke's Political Thought* (Cambridge, UK: Cambridge University Press, 2002), pp. 2-3.

61. Waldron, *God, Locke, and Equality*, p. 1. Our account, while heavily indebted to Waldron, may at points deviate from his view of Locke.

62. Waldron, *God, Locke, and Equality*, p. 82.

63. Waldron thinks an atheist will be unable to do any better than Locke in grounding egalitarianism: "Someone in denial of or indifferent to the existence of God is not going to be able to come up with anything like the sort of basis for equality that Locke came up with" (Waldron, *God, Locke, and Equality*, p. 81). But Waldron is unclear about why that should be.

The problem for the atheist (which Waldron leaves undeveloped) begins with the need to find an ontological ground for fundamental equality. An atheist will presumably be unwilling to countenance souls. Souls are little divinities; one might just as well countenance immaterial mind of a higher (divine) order. Thus, in locating a range property, the atheist must point to the organization of matter. But organization of matter admits of degrees, and it is exceedingly difficult to answer the question that arises: Why do the differences in degree not count? The notion of a fundamental capacity that even the severely retarded have slips away.

If, on the other hand, one is willing to postulate a soul, one is able to begin to express why it is that humans share a fundamental equality, because human souls possess the same fundamental operational capacities of a high order, displayed or inhibited depending on the disposition of matter. The soul informs or organizes the matter, but it does so in a way that disallows differences in the degree of the human soul, the organizing principle itself. At least that is the view taken by Aristotle (or Aristotle on Aquinas's reading). Now an Aristotelian-Thomistic doctrine of soul will not suffice to ground ontological or moral egalitarianism unless the *significance* of select operational capacities is identified. Revelatory claims can provide a rich sense of the significance of the higher-order capacities. Revelatory claims also give an account of the origin of the soul: it comes to be through a creative act of God.

5.4.3. The Search for Secular Foundations for Inalienable Rights

5.4.3.1. Setting Up the Search

How good are the prospects of finding a purely secular foundation for inalienable rights?

It is sobering to recall that Elizabeth Anscombe, one of the major figures of philosophy in the twentieth century, noted that as philosophers detached themselves from the religious traditions that had nourished philosophy through the centuries, they gradually came to believe less and less in inalienable rights.[64] This should perhaps not be surprising if we are correct that there is no secular foundation for ontological equality. For it is reasonable to suppose that there will be a secular defense of universal individual rights only

---

64. G. E. M. Anscombe, "Modern Moral Philosophy," originally published in 1958, reprinted in *The Collected Philosophical Papers of G. E. M. Anscombe*, Vol. III: *Ethics, Religion and Politics* (Minneapolis: University of Minnesota Press, 1981).

if there is a secular defense of ontological equality. What makes Jefferson's declaration so memorable is (among other things) that he brings equality and inalienable rights together in the way they need to be brought together, his words — if not his thoughts — intimating that equality is the foundation of rights. It does not take much to see why, if one backs off the idea that humans are in some important sense fundamentally equal, it will be impossible to see *all* humans as having inalienable rights. The thought immediately suggests itself that the rights of the underendowed have to be sacrificed in some circumstances to the rights of the more fully endowed, in accord with the idea suggested in Aristotle's *Ethics,* that, as Alan Gewirth puts it, "if x units of some property Q justify that one have x units of some right or duty E, then y units of Q justify that one have y units of E."[65]

Of course, one can say that the consequentialists are correct, and all declarations of inalienable rights are false: there are prima facie rights, but they are all defeasible. Genocide? Terrorism? Why not, if the payoff is right? So one can say. Let us not say that, however, at least not immediately. Let us instead move forward on the assumption that, if there are good explanations for the existence of inalienable rights, we ought to accept the reality of the rights.

The question at present, then, is whether a secular justification-explanation of inalienable rights can be had. We will argue that, *even if* a secular account could be constructed for ontological equality, there would be further problems in providing a secular foundation for inalienable rights.

Willingness to agree that someone has an "inalienable right to x" depends, of course, both on what is meant by an "inalienable right" and what "x" stands for. We need take the analysis no further (for our purposes) than to note an essential connection between a declaration of inalienable rights, and exceptionless precepts of the form "It is always impermissible to do acts of kind K to a human being." If your possession of the inalienable right to x is consistent with its being acceptable for someone intentionally to annihilate, torture, or imprison you, even though you are innocent, that is, have done nothing to deserve that punishment and are not threatening to harm anyone, then your vaunted inalienable right to x, whatever x is, is worthless.[66] There can be *more* to having a right to x than that it is always wrong to do certain kinds of things to you, to act against you. But there is no *less* to

---

65. Alan Gewirth, "The Non-Trivializability of Universalizability," *Australasian Journal of Philosophy* 47, no. 2 (1969): 126.

66. Some philosophers, e.g., Michael J. Perry, hold otherwise. J. L. A. Garcia has commented: "[A]n inviolability that countenances such blatant violations [as Perry countenances] . . . cannot ground any human rights that are worth a damn." *Faith and Philosophy* 19, no. 2 (2002): 260. We stand with Garcia.

having a significant right to x than to be protected from assaults on you with respect to x.[67]

So our original question about a declaration of inalienable rights is to be understood as essentially bound up with exceptionless precepts. More specifically, if there are no exceptionless precepts, then there can be no inalienable rights. What are the prospects of a secular justification-explanation of exceptionless precepts? Prospects are good only if purely secular theoretical considerations can be set out in accord with the following *general* schema or framework:

1-Gen) Necessarily, it is impermissible to do (or fail to do) *such and such.*
2-Gen) Necessarily, all acts *of kind K* include doing *such and such.*
3-Gen) Therefore, necessarily, all acts *of kind K* are impermissible.

Since Anscombe wrote her despairing remarks about the prospects of success for secular undergirding of exceptionless precepts, several attempts have been made to extract from the Judaeo-Christian tradition purely secular principles adequate to ground a declaration of inalienable rights. We will go on to probe two of these that are particularly distinguished, one in the Kantian tradition, the other in the tradition of natural law. Both of these efforts quite consciously attempt to secure — on purely philosophical grounds — what the Judaeo-Christian tradition has taught about these matters.

The task of grounding exceptionless precepts in reason alone is easy if we are thinking of such precepts as "Never do a wrongful act" or "Never murder," where "murder" is understood as "wrongful killing," or "Never torture a cat for the fun of it." Reason can detect that these are exceptionless precepts — at least the first two obviously are — but they are not the kinds of precepts we have in mind. The first two are tautological; the condemnation of the act is packed into the identification of the act. Such tautologies are obviously true, but useless, since it will remain an open question whether the act the agent considers performing falls under the evaluative concept. So, we must understand "acts of kind K" to be specifiable independently of the moral judgment about the act. As for the third example, we allow that it is obviously wrong to torture a cat just for the fun of it — but the obviousness derives from the addition of a bad motive, "just for the fun of it." So, for our purposes we must understand "acts of kind K" to be independent of particular motives.

---

67. Those who think we have all too quickly ruled out utilitarian foundations for rights by linking them in this way to absolute prohibitions can simply treat our inquiry as an investigation of the question whether a secular foundation can be given for exceptionless precepts.

Are we looking in the wrong place for a secular account? Would we not be better advised to attend carefully to attempts by atheists to get the same results? Perhaps, though one should not be particularly hopeful that turning in that direction would pay dividends. Indeed, when one looks around at atheistic accounts of these matters, what one frequently runs into is the sort of thing that is put forward by Kai Nielsen in *Ethics Without God,* where he confronts this charge: "The secularist is surreptitiously drawing on Christian inspiration when he insists that all men should be considered equal and that people's rights must be respected."[68] But, as we had occasion to note in chapter 1, while Nielsen at first maintains that he can produce a purely secular argument for treating people fairly, in the end he concedes that, with respect to torturing and killing the innocent in terrorist acts, "there are circumstances when such violence must be reluctantly assented to or even taken to be something that one, morally speaking, must do."[69]

That atheists so rarely defend an ethics involving exceptionless precepts should tell us something. The natural home for such an ethics is in a theological context. Unsurprisingly, it is religious believers who make the strongest efforts to secure philosophically (that is, without reliance on revelation) exceptionless precepts given in revelation.

5.4.3.2. A Notable Kantian Account

Alan Donagan contends that Kant provides the best foundation for purely philosophical (i.e., secular) reconstruction of the Hebrew-Christian tradition of morality, with its exceptionless precepts. Donagan's neglected *Theory of Morality* carries out this project with great skill and insight. His account snugly fits our secular schematic framework.[70] And while Donagan's interpretations of Kant differ on some points from those of more recent commentators, his reconstruction makes it far easier to see how the Kantian defense of exceptionless precepts covers the very young, the very old, those with mental and emotional afflictions, and the morally wayward.[71]

---

68. Kai Nielsen, *Ethics Without God,* 2d ed. (Buffalo, NY: Prometheus, 1990), p. 123.

69. Nielsen, *Ethics Without God,* p. 132.

70. Indeed, our schema is a generalization of an argument Donagan offers. See Alan Donagan, *The Theory of Morality* (Chicago: The University of Chicago Press, 1977), pp. 67-68. We add modal operators to Donagan's language.

71. With Donagan, more recent Kantian scholarship tends to prefer the second formulation of the categorical imperative over the first, but unlike Donagan, takes "humanity" [*die Menschheit*] not as referring to all human beings, or even the property of being rational. Just what it refers to varies from scholar to scholar, but on many of these interpretations, the prop-

1-Kant) Necessarily, it is impermissible not to respect every human being, oneself and any other, as a rational creature. [Donagan holds, plausibly enough, that this is equivalent to "It is impermissible not to treat every human being as an end and not a mere means." In this context, "creature" is not intended to imply a creator.]

2-Kant) Necessarily, all actions of kind K fail to respect some human being as a rational creature.

3-Kant) Therefore, necessarily, all actions of kind K are impermissible.

The first premise, 1-Kant, is a variant of the second form of Kant's categorical imperative. Donagan's choice of this form of categorical imperative enjoys the enormous advantage of deflecting criticism against Kant that his ethics is purely formal and is blind to human goods.[72]

Is 1-Kant self-evident? If it were, then consequentialism in all of its main forms would be not merely false but self-evidently false. Given that many have thought consequentialist principles are self-evident, it is farfetched to claim that they are self-evidently false. Furthermore, a self-evident proposition has no ground, for there is no proposition or set of propositions from which it can be proved (though there are propositions from which it can be derived). But Kant scholars point to grounds for the categorical imperative. Donagan says:

> [T]he principle of morality *(oberstes praktisches Prinzip)*, according to Kant, is that rational nature exists as an end in itself *(die vernünftige Natur existiert als Zweck an sich selbst)*. From this ground it *obviously* follows that no rational being should ever be used merely as a means. . . .[73]

The claim that rational nature is an end in itself can be taken prescriptively or descriptively. If taken prescriptively, the categorical imperative will follow,

---

erty referred to is not found in every member of the human race. Richard Dean, for example, argues throughout half his book that "humanity" refers to good will, the property of being committed to moral imperatives. See Richard Dean, *The Value of Humanity in Kant's Moral Theory* (Oxford: Clarendon Press, 2006). Dean must then explain how the young, the mentally confused, the morally corrupt, and others are deserving of respect. Donagan's reconstruction situates all humans immediately in the domain of those covered by the categorical imperative, and he thus provides us with a cleaner example of a secular attempt to defend the exceptionless precepts than can be found in more recent Kantian commentary.

72. Donagan does not quite say it, but K is, as it should be, a placeholder for acts that can be depicted without packing into their definition any moral evaluations. It is not merely "wrongful murder" that is wrong, but intentional killing of innocent humans.

73. Donagan, *The Theory of Morality,* p. 229 (italics added).

but only because it is a repetition of the point asserted in the "ground." In that case, the "ground" is not really an epistemic ground; it would beg the question to take it as such. On the other hand, if the ground is taken descriptively, the prescriptive claim does not immediately follow. The difficulty is familiar: you cannot derive a prescription from a description alone.

And even if the categorical imperative did follow either from the ground alone ("humanity is an end in itself") or from the ground plus another quite intuitively evident premise, the ground is not self-evident.[74] One needs an argument for it. Why would it be irrational to refuse to view humanity this way? Donagan tells us that what Kant wrote directly on the subject in the *Groundwork of the Metaphysics of Morals* is "meager." Donagan further observes that, far from being obvious, as Kant thought, the claim that humanity is an end in itself appears false on a natural reading of it. Nothing prevents us from thinking of our existence as pointless. Kant's meaning, Donagan suggests, is better brought out in the thrust of the argument of the *Groundwork*. What is the argument of the *Groundwork?* Donagan offers an inventive reconstruction.[75] But recall that Paul Guyer observes that two centuries of study of the *Groundwork* and many excellent commentaries have not altered the fact that it is a deeply perplexing book. And bafflement is not diminished by going to other of Kant's writings. Since a justification is adequate only if the sequence of reasoning is reasonably transparent, we are left with the well-justified suspicion that no argument in Kant counts as an adequate justification-explanation of exceptionless precepts.

Moreover, despite gray mists surrounding the structure of Kant's thought on the categorical imperative, one strut is visible, a strut that, if it is really load-bearing, guarantees that a nonsecular justification will not be found. For there can be little doubt that Kant finds it necessary to invoke the supranatural. How exactly it fits in is unclear, but he is convinced that it is indispensable. For all the obscurity attending Kant's argument, he appears entirely convinced that the whole practical system depends on the assumption that we are free beings and in some mysterious way transcend the order of the natural, an assumption that eludes the power of theoretical reason to prove. In his

---

74. Though the coherence of the notion of a nonproducible end-in-itself is often called into question, Donagan does defend it at some length; see *The Theory of Morality*, pp. 63-64. So does Paul Guyer; see his *Kant on Freedom, Law, and Happiness* (Cambridge, UK: Cambridge University Press, 2000), pp. 149-50, n. 19. We think the notion is coherent, though we would give a different defense than would either Donagan or Guyer. Kantian Donagan cites Aquinas in making his point. We get a strong whiff of a connection between the two great thinkers on the foundations of morality.

75. Donagan, *The Theory of Morality*, pp. 220-39.

Critique of Practical Reason, Kant raises the question of the origin of duty and answers that it is "nothing other than *personality,* i.e., the freedom and independence of the mechanism of nature in its entirety. . . ."[76] Unless we posit a self that escapes the mechanisms of nature, we cannot grasp the greatness of human dignity, why and how rational creatures are ends in themselves, or grasp why we should cleave to the categorical imperative.[77] The positing of a self that escapes the bounds of nature is but one of the postulates necessary to complete the account of morality. There are others: God and immortality. Exactly why these postulates are needed is, as always with Kant, a subject of scholarly debate. But the posits are there. "Morality," as Kant says, "thus inevitably leads to religion. . . ."[78]

There may be a further difficulty with a secular Kantian justification of inalienable rights. It seems to prove too much: in particular, it seems to forbid suicide, even when suicide appears eminently rational (from a secular vantage point). At least, it forbids suicide if it forbids murder — the intentional killing of the innocent — and it is certainly supposed to forbid murder. It is easy to imagine circumstances where suicide seems rational if there is no God. Killing oneself rather than living a few excruciatingly painful minutes more in a burning building would seem rational, for the choice of nonexistence rather than existence *under these conditions* seems rational. Or imagine that a terrorist with a track record of doing what he says he will do says that, unless you commit suicide in front of a video camera, he will execute you and launch a nuclear missile, but if you comply he will not launch the missile. Why would it be wrong to meet the demand, assuming there is no God?

Unable to accept the consequence that suicide is always wrong, Donagan asserts that suicide in some circumstances is not the kind of act that fails to re-

---

76. Cited by Guyer, *Kant on Freedom, Law, and Happiness,* p. 154 [5:86].

77. Donagan holds that unless humans possess a power as agents that transcends the physical order, unless it is not the case that everything humans do, every event they bring about, is explicable wholly in terms of physical causes, "it is flatly impossible that human beings should be agent-causes, as the conception of them as ends in themselves presupposes." Donagan, *The Theory of Morality,* p. 233.

78. Kant, *Religion within the Boundaries of Mere Reason,* p. 35. It will surely be protested that these Kantian "posits" are only practical. But how a propositional posit manages to be only practical is obscure in the extreme. Kant's troublesome statements on the character of a practical postulate have led at least one distinguished commentator to propose that the relevant propositions do not function as objects of belief but are like images we entertain to arouse ourselves to action. "Here it seems explicitly asserted that to adopt something 'from a practical point of view' is simply to make it effective in the concentration of one's powers in a way demanded by practical reason, and does not imply any cognitive attitude toward the proposition at all." Guyer, *Kant on Freedom, Law, and Happiness,* pp. 363-64.

spect the humanity of a person. Donagan holds on to the Kantian claim 1-Kant, but refuses to see suicide as an instance of kind K in 2-Kant, insisting that "What Kant wrote is only intelligible as expressing the religious conviction that to take one's own life is to repudiate one's existence as a divine creation."[79]

Did Kant understand the implications of Kantian ethics, and in particular the claim at 1-Kant, better than Donagan and other Kantians willing to countenance suicide? As we have said, if suicide is not forbidden, then neither would it always be wrong to kill the innocent. It would be impermissible only under certain circumstances. And one might think that those circumstances would be few. Killing the innocent would be licit only to achieve a great good or avoid a great evil, one might think; or perhaps only if, in addition, the individual to be destroyed consented. Of course, if it is licit without consent, nothing of any substance distinguishes the position from many forms of consequentialism. But on what grounds could consent be insisted on? It is not always morally impermissible to interfere in a person's life, contrary to the individual's will, if that will is irrationally set against the common good. One could simply *assert* that consent is required — but it is not required, say, for marching people off to war. And if a person could commit suicide for the sake of the common good, that opens up the possibility that it would not just be permissible but obligatory. The individual who refused to serve the common good by self-immolation might then be acting as irrationally as the individual who refused to run mortal risks in defense of the nation. In any event, if it is not always wrong to kill the innocent, as it is not if suicide is permissible, the remaining absolute prohibitions are in grave jeopardy.[80]

A thoroughly secular Kantian account of ethics faces a conundrum: on the one hand, it appears that there are circumstances in which suicide is eminently rational; on the other, it appears that to license suicide in these circumstances is also to license acts of killing that strike many people as highly objectionable. Is there some deeper principle to which one might appeal to untie this knot?

5.4.3.3. New Natural-Law Theory

Another distinguished attempt to ground exceptionless precepts, and thereby declarations of inalienable rights, is the system that has grown out of seminal work by Germain Grisez. Though it first gained attention in the mid-1960s

79. Donagan, *The Theory of Morality*, p. 77.

80. See Thomas D. Sullivan, "Assisted Suicide and Assisted Torture," *Logos: A Journal of Catholic Thought and Culture* 2, no. 3 (1999): 77-95.

with Grisez's article on Aquinas's teachings on natural law, it is still often referred to as "new," in part because it remains fresh as it continually unfolds through the exceedingly thoughtful efforts of writers such as John Finnis, Joseph M. Boyle, Jr., Robert P. George, Patrick Lee, and Grisez himself. The theory owes much to Aquinas, and at least some in the group are reluctant to part company with him; but the unfolded theory consciously conflicts with Aquinas on substantive matters, and so it is at most "Thomistic" in a loose sense.[81] The theory has been worked out with considerable ingenuity and deserves the reputation it enjoys as possibly *the* leading natural-law theory. It has many advantages, not the least of which is that it points in the right direction toward exceptionless precepts, and on specific issues, such as the (il)legitimacy of the use of nuclear weapons as a deterrent, offers forceful arguments that deserve to be much better known. Moreover, from the beginning the theory is connected with goods, and therefore does not need to struggle, as do Kantian theories, to connect the right and the good. Many of the standard criticisms brought to bear on the theory appear to lack substance, including the charge that the theory floats in thin air, having no roots in an appreciation of human nature.

How does the theory work?[82] In outline, it takes as self-evident a moral principle the collaborators call the "first principle of morality," which runs:

> In voluntarily acting for human goods and avoiding what is opposed to them, one ought to choose and otherwise will those and only those possibilities whose willing is compatible with integral human fulfillment.[83]

81. Work by Kevin L. Flannery, Anthony J. Lisska, Ralph M. McInerny, and Henry Babcock Veatch may be closer to the main lines of Aquinas's own thinking, and certainly has merit. Nonetheless, considerations of space require us to confine ourselves to the better-known natural-law theory represented by Grisez et al.

82. A major obstacle to setting out even the outline of the theory is that these authors have written together and alone over quite a long period of time, and there seems to be no one place to turn for a definitive statement of the theory. The best-known document is probably John Finnis's *Natural Law and Natural Rights* (Oxford: Clarendon Press, 1979), but it is comparatively early. All things considered, a better overview is available in the later (and neglected) *Nuclear Deterrence, Morality and Realism* (Oxford: Clarendon Press, 1987), by John Finnis, Germain Grisez, and Joseph M. Boyle, Jr. See also John Finnis, *Moral Absolutes: Tradition, Revision, and Truth* (Washington, DC: Catholic University Press, 1988). The fullest account to date is in Germain Grisez, Joseph M. Boyle, Jr., and John Finnis, "Practical Principles, Moral Truth, and Ultimate Ends," *American Journal of Jurisprudence* 32 (1987): 99-151.

83. Finnis, Grisez, and Boyle, *Nuclear Deterrence, Morality and Realism*, p. 283. The first principle of morality is not to be confused with the first principle of practical reasoning: good is to be done and pursued, evil avoided. In the view of Grisez and Finnis, the latter is not a specifically moral principle but a broader principle that governs all kinds of doings.

Although, as its name suggests, this principle roots all morality, it is insuffi-cient to ground *immediately* any specific moral norm, the new natural-law theorists say.[84] To arrive at substantive moral norms, particularly absolute prohibitions, it is necessary to derive intermediate principles from the first or fundamental moral principle. It is from these intermediate principles that substantive moral norms in turn follow. Among these intermediate principles (Grisez calls them "modes of responsibility") are the Golden Rule, the rule of universalizability, and the rule "Do no evil that good may come of it."

Should we slot into 1-Gen (in the secular schema) a version of one of these intermediate principles, we would be following Grisez, Finnis, and Boyle very closely. Yet, in so doing we would also be deflecting attention from a feature of their work that makes it distinctive, a feature that owes much, though not everything, to Aquinas. This is the idea that there exist "basic" hu-man goods, a fact ascertainable by considering our natural inclinations, and that the precepts of the natural law are tied to these goods.[85] These "basic" — that is, non-instrumental — goods include life, knowledge, friendship, and other factors recognizably satisfying our deepest desires. It thus seems best to highlight the fact that the theory requires that a possible filler for 1-Gen be:

> 1-NatLaw) Necessarily, any choice to destroy, damage, or impede some in-stance of a basic good is impermissible (even for an ulterior good end).[86]

Is this built into the "first moral principle," or a consequence of it, or an addi-tional principle of some sort? We have not found a place where these ques-tions are settled. Still, it is evident enough that, were the authors to give up on 1-NatLaw as just formulated, there would be too little left in their theory to defend absolute prohibitions, and thereby inalienable rights.

Is proposition 1-NatLaw self-evident? Not so far as we can see. For one thing, designation of the proposition about integral human fulfillment as "the first moral principle" strongly suggests that other propositions are based on it, including 1-NatLaw — in which case 1-NatLaw is not self-evident. Fur-

---

84. Finnis, Grisez, and Boyle, *Nuclear Deterrence, Morality and Realism*, p. 283.

85. Commenting (in private correspondence) on an earlier wording of our point, Patrick Lee has written: "I would say, they [the basic goods] are grasped in our natural inclinations, since they are not (according to the theory) deduced from propositions about natural inclina-tions." But what is grasped in our natural inclinations are the goods that are in fact basic, not the fact that they are basic.

86. Finnis, Grisez, and Boyle give a formulation only trivially different. Finnis, Grisez, and Boyle, *Nuclear Deterrence, Morality and Realism*, pp. 286-87.

thermore, what we said about the Kantian fundamental principle of morality can be said about the "first principle of morality" of the new natural-law theorists as well: plenty of philosophers have denied it, and if it were self-evident, then consequentialism and utilitarianism would not only be wrong but self-evidently wrong, which they are not. Finnis, Grisez, and Boyle themselves acknowledge that the principle as they state it is "quite opaque."[87] There would appear to be plenty of room for doubt about its self-evidence.

So an argument for it is required. Any such argument is going to run up against the following problem: 1-NatLaw presupposes that the basic goods are not commensurable (if they were, then a lesser good could be sacrificed for a greater good); but prima facie, at least, it looks as though the basic goods *are* commensurable, since we sometimes have no trouble saying to ourselves that, for instance, it would be better not to fiddle while the city burns.[88]

Grisez, Finnis, and Boyle vigorously contest the idea that the basic goods are commensurable.[89] What is their best argument? Assuming, as Boyle has told us, that the most authoritative articulation of the new theory is provided by "Practical Principles, Moral Truth, and Ultimate Ends," the best would seem to be the following pithy argument in that controlling document:

> [I]f they [the basic goods] were commensurable, they would have to be homogeneous with one another or reducible to something prior by which they could be measured. If they were homogenous with one another, they would not constitute diverse categories. If they were reducible to something prior, they would not be primary principles. Thus, they are incommensurable: No basic good considered precisely as such can be meaningfully said to be better than another.[90]

This argument is interesting, but faulty. The initial conditional leaves out an alternative: two basic goods might be commensurable (at least in the sense

87. Finnis, Grisez, and Boyle, *Nuclear Deterrence, Morality and Realism*, p. 283.

88. See Russell Pannier, "Finnis and the Commensurability of Goods," *The New Scholasticism* LXI, no. 4 (1987): 440-61.

89. Does the claim that basic goods are incommensurable function as a premise for the fundamental principle of morality, or is it rather a proposition that must be conjoined to it, or joined to the modes of responsibility to produce the norms, or what? It is unclear to us what answer should be given. No matter what the answer, the proposition that the basic goods cannot be commensurated is essential to the theory.

90. Grisez, Boyle, and Finnis, "Practical Principles, Moral Truth, and Ultimate Ends," p. 110. Patrick Lee, in private correspondence, calls attention to the fact that in some writings the new natural-law theorists prefer to talk about incommensurable choices rather than goods. In the end, we do not see how it matters, since the incommensurability of the choices would be traced back to the incommensurability of the things chosen.

of being *comparable,* which is what counts) and yet neither homogeneous with each other nor reducible to something prior by which they could be measured. God and humans do not belong to the same genus, and are not reducible to something prior. Yet one is incomparably better than the other. It may be that there is no common measure between playing in the sandbox, on the one hand, and searching for a proof of the Poincaré conjecture, on the other — or searching for a lost child. Still, these activities are comparable even if neither homogenous nor reducible to something prior. Aristotle saw clearly that comparisons can be made without reference to any single scale of units of value as he set out an all but completely unknown logic of preferability in Book III of the *Topics.* Comparability is a broader concept than commensurability. At last the topic of comparability is again being analyzed philosophically with great care, though, as Ruth Chang says, it is still in an early stage of investigation.[91] Even so, Chang contends, plausibly, that "there is almost certainly no easy argument for incomparability," and that "[m]any of the existing arguments are *fatally* flawed. . . ."[92] If the basic goods are comparable, though not necessarily commensurable, then the support for 1-NatLaw disintegrates, for we now have no reason to believe that one good cannot be sacrificed for another in those cases in which both cannot be realized.

Furthermore, the "first moral principle" has non-secular presuppositions. As Finnis writes:

> Materialism's denials or determined agnosticism about *soul* and *species* radically misrepresent our experience as choosers. . . . Materialism likewise devastates the case for holding that "by nature all human beings are equal," and that there are human rights and requirements of justice which do not discriminate between male and female, intelligent and dull, race and race, young and old, healthy and infirm.[93]

There we have it, all in one breath, a huge presupposition of the entire theory — freedom rooted in an immaterial entity (a soul?), a metaphysical commitment without which there is available no suitable declaration of inalienable rights.

The new natural-law theorists may also face the problem that their theory proves too much — too much from a secular perspective. For the theorists

---

91. Ruth Chang, ed., *Incommensurability, Incomparability, and Practical Reason* (Cambridge, MA: Harvard University Press, 1997), p. 1.

92. Chang, *Incommensurability, Incomparability, and Practical Reason,* p. 3; see also pp. 1-35.

93. John Finnis, *Aquinas: Moral, Political, and Legal Theory* (Oxford: Oxford University Press, 1998), p. 180.

maintain that their theory forbids suicide, and, as we have already indicated, from a purely secular viewpoint it is difficult to see that position as rational. To recapitulate:

1) If one can be better off dead, then suicide is sometimes permissible (assuming there is no God).
2) One can be better off dead.
3) If suicide is sometimes permissible, then murder is sometimes permissible (assuming there is no God).
4) If murder is sometimes permissible, then no exceptionless precepts hold (assuming there is no God).

A defender of the universal prohibition against suicide drawn to the new natural-law theory might try to escape the difficulty by insisting that a human being cannot be better off dead. After all, if you are dead, you do not exist, and if you do not exist, you can be neither better nor worse off. This much is surely right. Furthermore, Jorge Garcia rightly points out (in the context of discussing euthanasia) that this fact "deprives an argument for euthanasia of a key element, for the harm the mercy killer does to his or her chosen 'beneficiary' can no longer be balanced by the benefit the beneficiary receives in being relieved from pain."[94] But while this does indeed deprive *an* argument for euthanasia (and suicide) — perhaps the most common argument — of a key element, it does not so deprive *every* argument. For an argument can be constructed that makes no use of the concept of being better off dead. Instead, the new argument contemplates two states, that of existing in horrendous conditions just prior to death and that of not existing at all, and declares that while in neither situation is one better off, the second situation is rationally preferable to the first because the first is worse than zero.

Some, including the new natural-law theorists, seem to think either that the comparison cannot be made because a) the two *states of affairs* (burning in agony with the prospect of imminent death, and not existing) are incommensurable, or b) the two *choices* bearing on the states of affairs are incommensurable. But the pre-moral states of affairs certainly seem comparable. So do the choices, just because they bear on the production of the comparable states of affairs. There appears to be little difficulty in comparing the state of affairs of living in flames and not living at all during the same time. The 9-11 victims jumping out of windows had little trouble making the comparison.

94. Jorge Garcia, "Are Some People Better Off Dead? A Reflection," *Logos: A Journal of Catholic Thought and Culture* 2, no. 1 (1999): 71.

As for the choices about life and death, they too seem comparable. The choice that leads to a quick and painless death can be compared with a choice that leads, in the case of illness, to a long and painful dying. It can be argued that the choice to terminate one's own life is morally superior to the choice of bearing with the difficulties of life, but then a comparison is being made between the allegedly incomparable choices. Furthermore, the moral superiority of one choice over another cannot in this context be assumed. For the claim that one choice is better than another is being argued on the basis of the incomparability of the choices. If the natural-law theory forbids taking one's life, even if one would be "better off dead," it must do so for reasons other than maintaining that comparisons cannot be made.

Standing back a bit, then, we find that the problems that first emerged in considering Donagan's Kantian justification also appear in the work of the new natural-law theorists. Often advocates of the system declare that some substitution-instance of 1-Gen in the secular argument-schema is self-evident, when none is. When backing is supplied, explicitly or tacitly, it is often not at all clear how the argument goes. Furthermore, it is often unclear whether the supporting statements for substitution-instances of 1-Gen are true (in particular, new natural-law theories make dubious claims concerning commensurability). Further still, sometimes the filler for 1-Gen tacitly presupposes some degree of the supranatural, a small god in the form of an immaterial soul, or beyond that a full-fledged deity. And finally, purely secular substitutions for 1-Gen prove too much: they condemn certain kinds of acts, notably suicide, that seem quite rational unless the Socratic answer to the question "Why not exit this forlorn world?" is correct: "I am not my own."[95]

5.4.4. Revealed Foundations for Equality and Rights: Preliminary Considerations

Can support for a declaration of equality or a declaration of inalienable rights be provided within the framework of a revelatory tradition? It can — by resting equality and rights on "love precepts" that are set against the backdrop of a supranatural metaphysics.

Fundamental to Jewish and Christian thought are two love precepts. Israel is commanded: "[L]ove the LORD your God with all your heart, and with all your soul, and with all your might,"[96] and "love your neighbor as your-

---

95. As noted, though, rational argument *also* appears to support the impermissibility of suicide: we have a conundrum.

96. Deut. 6:5 (NRSV).

self. . . ."[97] Jesus brings the two commandments together in an answer to a lawyer who has asked what the greatest commandment is.

> He said to him, "You shall love the Lord your God with all your heart, and with all your soul, and with all your mind." This is the greatest and first commandment. And a second is like it: "You shall love your neighbor as yourself." On these two commandments hang all the law and the prophets.[98]

Aquinas's commentary in the *Summa* on the Mosaic Decalogue certainly agrees that the precepts have a foundational role. (The position Aquinas adopts accords well with much that is written in the Hebrew and Christian traditions,[99] but Aquinas sets it out more systematically than do most, so we focus on his account.) The Decalogue contains universally binding precepts, a subset of which are negative. The negative precepts specify things that can never be done to anyone, and thereby underpin — or are identical with — rights. All of the precepts of the Decalogue, Aquinas says, follow from the love precepts, which provide the warrant for and explanation of the entire set; and out of these two love precepts flow, in different ways, all moral precepts, and

---

97. Lev. 19:18 (NRSV).

98. Matt. 22:37-40 (NRSV).

99. Hillel famously responds to a request from a non-Jew to briefly summarize the teaching of Judaism with: "That which is hateful to you, do not do unto others." See "Love of Neighbor," in Geoffrey Wigoder, ed., *The New Encyclopedia of Judaism* (New York: New York University Press, 2002), p. 482. There is no mention of the love of God in Hillel's statement. Nor is there in Paul's statement: "For the whole law is summed up in a single commandment, 'You shall love your neighbor as yourself'" (Gal. 5:14 [NRSV]). Aquinas argues that the commandments to love God and neighbor are mutually implicative, and so the apostle Paul can speak of only one precept because "love of one's neighbor includes love of God, when we love our neighbor for God's sake." *Summa Theologiae* I-II, q. 99, a. 1, ad 2, trans. Fathers of the English Dominican Province (New York: Benziger Bros., 1948).

An issue that calls for clarification is the relationship between what Aquinas says in the texts on the Old Law, which make the love precepts primary, and his discussion of foundational practical principles in the *Summa Theologiae* I-II, q. 94, a. 2. Alan Donagan credits Germain Grisez with giving the only feasible solution to the question: What, for Aquinas, is rock-bottom? Some texts seem to suggest things bottom on the precept "Love your neighbor"; others on "Good is to be done and pursued, and evil avoided." But it seems to us that R. Mary Hayden Lemmons more clearly brings to the fore the primacy of the love precepts (see R. Mary Hayden, "Love and the First Principles of St. Thomas's Natural Law," doctoral dissertation, Center for Thomistic Studies, University of St. Thomas, Houston [1988]). Others who have discussed these questions include Anthony J. Lisska, *Aquinas's Theory of Natural Law: A Reconstruction* (New York: Oxford University Press, 1996), and Kevin L. Flannery, *Acts Amid Precepts: The Aristotelian Logical Structure of Thomas Aquinas's Moral Theory* (Washington, DC: Catholic University of America Press, 2001).

precepts that hold only "for the most part," and the moral and intellectual virtues, and prudential judgment, and the rest of morality as well. Though the language of equality and rights is not used in the Mosaic Decalogue, Aquinas sees the two love precepts as mandating fair and kind treatment of humans, irrespective of their condition, personal or social.[100] To this extent, at least, they mandate equal treatment of all members of the species, and protect all from certain kinds of hostile acts, whatever the consequences, thereby underwriting fundamental or inalienable rights.

A philosophical case can be made for the love precepts' being foundational to all of morality; but for our part, we need only argue that they are fundamental to basic equality and inalienable rights, assuming that there is a good God. Seeing the strength of this argument contributes via IBE to the case that there is a good God, as well as the case that there is a good God who has revealed.

Before presenting our argument that the love precepts are fundamental to basic equality and inalienable rights (in the next section), we find it useful to express the precepts in a way that makes it clear that, if true, they can generate exceptionless precepts, and to sketch the nature of the theory or account we wish to support. Bearing in mind our earlier schema, we could say, using a label intended to refer to the Judaeo-Christian tradition:

1-JC) Necessarily, it is impermissible to will an act (or the omission of an act) incompatible with the love of God and neighbor (i.e., any human being).

To which is joined specifications of the Ks in:

2-JC) Necessarily, to perform an act of kind $K_1, \ldots K_n$ is to will an act incompatible with the love of God and neighbor.

This is still only a framework, since there is much disagreement about the meaning of 1-JC in Judaeo-Christian revelatory traditions, and about what fills out the Ks in 2-JC, even when the meaning of 1-JC is held fixed.

Begin with 1-JC. Does the love of God include an emotional element, or is it constituted essentially by the contemplation of God and the carrying out of the commandments? Is love of one's neighbor to be taken in a restricted sense (e.g., merely the elect Israel) or in an unrestricted sense, applying to all human beings, including those we think of as enemies? In what sense are other

---

100. Aquinas does not hesitate to use rights language; see Finnis's *Aquinas*, pp. 132ff.

humans to be loved "as oneself"? Does this mean that others must be loved to the same degree that one loves oneself? The thirteenth-century Bible commentator and Talmudic scholar Nahmanides took it this way,[101] and so did Kierkegaard in *Works of Love*. Obviously we cannot enter into all these disputes here. But, given our purpose of seeing whether a revelation could furnish reasonable grounds for recognizing fundamental equality and inalienable rights, we read the love precepts as including wholehearted attachment to God and a fixed determination to enhance the lives of others, so far as is consistent with a proper concern for self. By allowing for an "order of charity," as it is sometimes called, reading "as oneself" as "in the same manner as oneself," we are backing away from what Philip Quinn thinks makes Kierkegaard's account of love of neighbor so radical and, presumably, attractive.[102] However, since it is doubtful that loving all indiscriminately, without favoring any, is either possible[103] or wise, and since the undergirding of precepts that honor fundamental equality and rights does not depend on the positing of a universally indiscriminate love, we here assume that the precept to love others is satisfied if one is not indifferent to their welfare and never wills them evil.

Questions also arise with respect to the interpretation of 2-JC. What satisfies the Ks? That is, what kinds of acts are inconsistent with divine and human love? Aquinas thought that all the acts forbidden by the Decalogue are such, and a good number of other kinds of acts as well. He also believed that the negative precepts of the tablet *obviously* follow from the fundamental precepts of love. Some, such as the precept against murder, certainly seem to, at least at first glance. Will there not be cases where it is unclear whether a particular action falls under the concept of willing, or failing to will, an act incompatible with love of God and neighbor? Perhaps. But according to many revelatory claims, of course, it is *revealed* whether or not whole ranges of acts are incompatible with love of God and neighbor. And even leaving that point aside, it is likely to be no less evident that a particular act is incompatible with love of God and neighbor than it is that a particular act impedes some instance of a basic good, or fails to respect some humans as rational beings.

Is this a divine command theory? Not as that expression is ordinarily understood, though our approach involves some elements of a divine command

101. Wigoder, *The New Encyclopedia of Judaism*, p. 482.

102. Philip Quinn, "Divine Command Theory," in Hugh LaFollette, ed., *The Blackwell Guide to Ethical Theory* (Oxford: Blackwell, 2002), p. 58.

103. Contemporaries who read the precept in this radical way often concede that it is impossible to live in accordance with it. See Frances Howard-Snyder, "On These Two Commandments Hang All the Law and the Prophets," *Faith and Philosophy* 22, no. 1 (2005): 3-20.

theory. If one wants a tag for the kind of theory we are proposing, "divine or-dination theory" would be less misleading. Divine command theories come in many shapes and sizes, but they all root the rightness or wrongness of an act directly in divine commands.[104] A divine ordination theory can be set out without any appeal to commands. Note that neither 1-JC nor 2-JC is in the form of a command. They are deontic statements. The statements can be true or false (commands cannot be), and their truth value could depend only on the structure of reality and the place of agents within it (and not on divine commands). Should God structure the world in such a way as to bring into existence rational creatures that stand in certain relationships to each other and to things below and above, at least some of what is permissible or imper-missible would be grounded in these facts,[105] whether or not God adds "Thou shalt" do this or "Thou shalt not" do that to warn recalcitrant rational creatures with deviant inclinations that they had better comply with the de-mands of duty, or, when the demands of duty are less than perspicuous, to in-form us what they are (as, perhaps, in the case of suicide).

With a fundamental order in place, God might choose to add specific commands consistent with the duties that spring from the basic order. Addi-tional obligations would then come into existence. Such obligations would more directly depend on divine volition. The other obligations would do so only inasmuch as the structure of reality is rooted in the divine will. What God could do once the structure is in place is open to debate. As we have noted earlier, we are inclined to think a good, all-powerful, all-knowing God could not create a world like our own without providing for an afterlife, could not, that is, create vulnerable humans, creatures subject to the woes of this world, unable to put down their own insurrections against reason, and des-

---

104. Mention of divine command theory often provokes reactions suggesting that it is thought that a) it is essential to divine command theory that God can command what he wants; b) the recipient of divine commands is bound by them; and perhaps c) that is the only way obli-gations arise. We certainly deny the first of these claims, a, and take b to be true only of com-mands God *could* issue, given that God is all-good. Nutty or awful commands do not bind: no-body is bound by a command to cruelly punish all who do good (if God could issue such a command). We reject c.

Suppose someone who is looking at Frege's work in logic asks: "Is this logical theory a syllo-gistic theory?" And the response is offered: "No, this is a brand-new theory." Now Aristotle's definition of a syllogism coincides basically with the definition of deduction that Frege gives us. Still, nobody describes Frege as doing syllogistic theory: it is too misleading.

We speak of "divine ordination theory" to highlight the undergirding ontology (which frames and limits commands) and to avoid misleading.

105. This is not to say grounded in *only* these facts. Bridge principles connecting the facts and values would be required.

tine them for a merely natural end. If so, that would condition what God could command. Absolute prohibitions could have a place in such an order. The objection "How can you hold on to absolute prohibitions when there are circumstances such that cleaving to the prohibitions will have disastrous consequences?" can be replied to by pointing out that there are no disastrous consequences in the long run if there is a supranatural end such as that promised in major revelatory traditions. But in any event, not just any commands could be given. We certainly have no truck with the notion favored by Ockham and others that, if God were to order us to hate each other, then hatred would be obligatory.

In sum, then, the divine ordination theory put forward here roots morals in metaphysics: acts are permissible, impermissible, and obligatory in virtue of supranatural metaphysics.[106] Permissibility and impermissibility are sometimes a function of a direct command, but what can be commanded in such cases is limited by the metaphysical base that includes the world order God has established and the nature of the divine being who creates.[107]

5.4.5. The Explanatory Power of Revealed Foundations for Ethics

5.4.5.1. Objections to Divine Ordination Theory, and Replies

Before we enumerate advantages of the hypothesis that ethics has a revealed foundation, it will be useful to clear the ground by examining some objections that might be brought against what we have described as "divine ordination theory."

---

106. This basic idea can be found in religious traditions other than the Judaeo-Christian. Saral Jhingran makes a strong case for thinking that it is not accidental that non-theistic Indian schools of thought did not teach any sort of active ethic of love and did nothing to undermine the caste structure, while theistic schools taught against the caste system. She writes: "The Visnu Purana presents the concept of God (Vasudeva) as the all-in-all, and goes on to derive a very high moral code from this vision. According to it, since the Divine Being resides in the hearts of all beings, He is the Object of all sacrifices, worship and even violence, so that if one hurts others, one in fact hurts God Himself." Saral Jhingran, *Aspects of Hindu Morality* (Delhi: Motilal Banarsidass Publishers, 1989), p. 155. We thank John D. Kronen for this reference.

107. The divine ordination theory is not a theory for the believer alone, but for the agnostic inquirer. The inquirer is not invited to consider replacing whatever understanding "impermissible" bears in a secular mind with the conception *forbidden by God*. That is not what the term "impermissible" means in this context. Not all acts that are impermissible are so because they are forbidden, but even those that are, are *thereby* impermissible. That is, they are impermissible because forbidden, not forbidden because forbidden.

Objection: "The Fundamental Precepts of Revealed Ethics Are Not Self-Evident" We have observed that the fundamental assumptions of secular ethical systems are not self-evident. But if that is a problem of secular ethics, is not the lack of self-evidence all the more a problem of revealed ethics?

We must immediately concede that 1-JC — the proposition that, necessarily, it is impermissible to will an act (or the omission of an act) incompatible with the love of God and neighbor — is *not* self-evident.[108] Yet this concession does no harm at all to the position we are defending, for it is unnecessary to found ethics, revealed or secular, on evident first principles. (We did not insist above that secular ethics be founded on self-evident principles; rather, we said that, absent self-evidence, an argument for the principles is required, and such an argument is hard to come by.) The point is obscured by the insistence to the contrary of moralists, both those who eschew absolute prohibitions and those who posit them, such as Kant, Donagan, Grisez, and many others.[109] This is a key point. It is easy to set aside a revealed ethics if a secular system based on self-evident secular foundational principles is available. If all these systems must treat their foundational principles as hypotheses, though, then revealed systems must be given a hearing, provided only that they have something going for them. And they would certainly seem to have more than a little going for them since, as we have seen, secular systems supporting exceptionless precepts echo the teachings of this great tradition.

Does this mean that ethical systems, revealed and secular, just hang in the air as mere speculations? One might think so, since ethical hypotheses could hardly be verified or corroborated in the way scientific hypotheses are — that is, in the crucible of experimentation.

But before drawing the conclusion that all ethical systems must then come to naught, it would be wise to reflect a little on a lesson from the history of mathematics. Early in the history of mathematics it was thought that mathematical knowledge rested on intuitively evident axioms. The curiosity of the consistency of non-Euclidean geometry, and disturbing irregularities in the

---

108. Aquinas says that the love precepts are self-evident either to natural understanding *or to faith*. But the love precepts could be self-evident only if the existence of God were self-evident. And the latter is not, as Aquinas himself points out. That is why he offers demonstrations of God's existence. Some commentators have attempted to make a go of the idea that the love precepts are self-evident. As far as we can see, however, they are going in the wrong direction.

109. The new natural-law theorists write about first principles: "As *first principles*, they cannot be derived from any theoretical knowledge. . . . Thus, they cannot be verified by experience or deduced from any more basic truths through a middle term. They are self-evident." Grisez, Boyle, and Finnis, "Practical Principles, Moral Truth, and Ultimate Ends," p. 106.

foundations of analysis temporarily shook the mathematical community; and after the paradoxes of set theory generated by Burali-Forti, Cantor, and Russell gained attention, a sense of genuine crisis developed. The paradoxes (and other difficulties) led mathematicians to seek to reconstruct the foundations of set theory. Their reconstructions, however, appeared ad hoc. More recently, the foundations of set theory have been reconstructed in a way that seems to blunt the charge that the axioms are ad hoc. Nevertheless, the foundational assumptions suffer from a serious drawback: they cannot pretend to intuitive certainty. Why, then, believe them? Bertrand Russell once argued that the premises of mathematical arguments are believable because their consequences are. This cannot be quite right, because in many cases we cannot see that complex theorems are true. But Russell was on to something many mathematicians now maintain, that the axioms can be justified through inference to the best explanation — though, when it comes to very abstract mathematical propositions, the *explananda* are CUE-facts. Mathematics is now widely viewed as resting on assumptions that are secured via IBE.[110]

There certainly is no good reason to expect more of ethics. If ethical principles need not be self-evident, if they can be treated as hypotheses, then they too can be evaluated in terms of their illuminating power. And if so, then revealed ethics can be evaluated the same way. Revealed ethics may offer the best explanation of the CUE-facts concerning equality and inalienable rights, and may illumine much else.

Judgments about the hypothesis concerning revealed ethics must be made against the backdrop of the complete theory. The theory involves not just an ethics, but also a metaphysics. Now one can try to confine the metaphysics to the natural order entirely. But we have seen that secular ethical systems purporting to yield declarations of equality or inalienable rights in the end appeal to something above nature, if only to freedom (Kant also appeals to God and immortality). And so far as we can see, a supranatural love ethic strong enough to support such declarations must do the same. What that comes to varies with the revelatory tradition. Jesus says, "Why do you ask me about what is good? There is only one who is good. If you wish to enter into life, keep the commandments."[111]

---

110. For a full discussion, see Marcus Giaquinto, *The Search for Certainty* (Oxford: Oxford University Press, 2004).

111. Matt. 19:17 (NRSV). "Life" could here conceivably mean no more than "full earthly existence"; however, because we think handling the problem of evil requires an appeal to an afterlife, we have no interest in defending revelatory claims that do not look beyond the natural human end.

Objections to Divine Command Theory, Applied to Divine Ordination Theory As noted, the theory we have sketched is not a divine command theory, but rather a divine ordination theory. However, it might be thought that some objections raised against divine command theories could (perhaps with slight modification) tell also against our own theory. So we mention five such objections, drawing on Philip Quinn's helpful discussion.[112] The reader might wish to compare our responses to the rather different replies Quinn provides. We take a tack different from his in part because, unlike Quinn, we speak specifically to agnostics. We are suggesting that a divine ordination theory should be considered by an agnostic seeking to determine whether certain ethical CUE-facts hold.[113]

First objection: "If exceptionless precepts hold only because God has commanded that they be obeyed, then one could infer that God exists from the recognition of the truth of some declarations of equality or inalienable rights. This trivializes natural theology." It does so only if there is something wrong with the entire way we are arguing from CUE-facts. There is no trivialization of natural theology if inference to the best explanation is a decent way to argue. And it is.

Second objection: "On the view that exceptionless precepts are undergirded by a divine order, then one could know what is right only by knowing the mind of God, which is impossible." It is not necessary to *know* the truth of moral precepts; it is enough to have good reason to believe that they are true. One way to have good reason to believe that they are true is to have good reason to believe that a revelation has been given to us. And this a person might have, in part at least, by seeing that only a divine order supports common morality's declarations of equality and of inalienable rights. There may be other ways to have good reason to believe that the exceptionless precepts hold. Natural sympathy supports belief in their truth. In this respect, belief in such CUE-facts is not all that different from belief, despite objections from neuroscience and physics to the contrary, that things are colored.

Third objection: "We should be looking for a moral theory that all can accept. Any theory that rests on the content of revelation is bound to be not generally acceptable. In fact, there are vast differences even among believing communities as to the meaning of the love precepts and the kinds of acts that are intrinsically inconsistent with love of God or neighbor." Indeed, we should seek

---

112. Quinn, "Divine Command Theory," pp. 53-73.

113. Quinn comments that his theory "is not, strictly speaking, a divine command theory; it is instead a divine intention theory . . . [which] pictures divine commands as expressing or revealing God's antecedent intentions." Quinn holds that the theory can be "supported from within a monotheistic worldview by a strong cumulative case argument." Quinn, "Divine Command Theory," pp. 57, 71.

to minimize differences. But, given all the work that has been done on the foundations of ethics, it is naïve to think that the disputes will disappear. Christians, Jews, Muslims, and Hindus disagree with others and among themselves about fundamental principles; but then, so do Kantians, natural-law theorists, consequentialists, error theorists, and hosts of others. The charge at issue, that a theory based on revelation of a divine order promotes divisiveness, holds against any theory whatever, as long as none rests on perfectly evident first principles. Furthermore, what we should be looking for is a moral theory that can be accepted by *rational* individuals able to give enough time and thought to the matter, and able to emancipate themselves from whatever is blocking acceptance of truth: that is, what we should be looking for is a rational moral theory. If one is looking for a theory that all can accept while holding on to their present commitments, one is driven to look for a subset of moral principles shared by everyone. Even if some such subset exists, and it is doubtful one does, it is probably too weak to generate much of anything in the moral order.

Fourth objection: "A revealed theory of the foundations of ethics can add nothing to moral theory. The theory amounts to saying that what conforms to the will of God is right. But we cannot know what conforms to the will of God without first knowing what is right." As we have argued, however, one need not know what is right first. One may take fundamental equality and human rights as CUE-facts and then accept them as facts if a good explanation can be found. If a good explanation of a divine order can be found in a revelation, then the truth of the revelation and the moral facts can be accepted *simultaneously.*

Fifth objection: "If the moral ultimately depends on divine commands, then God could command anything and it would be right. The stories in the Bible of God ordering the patriarchs to do immoral things — Abraham to sacrifice Isaac, the Israelites to plunder the Egyptians, Hosea to bed an adulteress — all point toward this conclusion." We are not committed to the idea that anything goes so long as it is commanded by God. Rather, we are committed to the notion that, should a revelation lay down precepts — against the backdrop of a supranatural metaphysics — that make sense of equality and rights and much else in the moral order, that would count in favor of the revelation, properly construed, being true. There are various ways of understanding the stories of the immoralities of the patriarchs that render the putative revelation consistent with the divine order. Aquinas, taking the events as actually commanded by God, gives several.[114] And the possibility remains of seeing at least some of these stories as parables.

---

114. See Patrick Lee, "The Permanence of the Ten Commandments: St. Thomas and His Modern Commentators," *Theological Studies* 42 (1981): 422-43.

5.4.5.2. Advantages of a Revelatory Base

What, then, are the advantages of a revelatory base for declarations of equality and declarations of inalienable rights? There are at least five.

First Advantage   Revealed foundations can provide a fuller, deeper explanation of such declarations, even if the secular explanations that appeal to respect for all and integral human fulfillment are acceptable so far as they go. That is, the revelatory explanation may be closer to the ideal (in ways discussed above). In the sciences some theoretical explanations run deeper than others. The answers to "why?" questions terminate later in the better explanations. Why does gold resist oxidation and corrosion? Because gold has a very strong grip on its outermost electron, the one available for chemical bonding. Why does it have this strong grip on its outermost electron? Because the nucleus of gold has a large positive charge, causing the electrons to move nearly the speed of light, increasing their mass and making them move closer to the nucleus. Why not stop the explanation sooner? Because we have not reached bottom. Chemists' explanations do not go as far as physicists' explanations do — in fact, do not go far enough. The same is true of secular explanations of fundamental equality, inalienable rights, exceptionless precepts, and much else, even if they are correct as far as they go (and we have expressed doubts that they are correct as far as they go): they do not go far enough. Some secular moral precepts, such as "respect all humans as rational beings," may well be true as they stand; but there is a deeper explanation of their truth than secular moral theory can provide. Revealed ethics can ground the maxim that calls for respect of every human being in the strong requirement of love of neighbor, and can further root the love of neighbor in the love of God. The two love precepts, according to the common Judaeo-Christian revelatory tradition, are so intertwined they are mutually inter-derivable. The revelatory explanation is better because it is deeper, more satisfying, and more complete.

The meaning of life, decided over the heads of rational creatures, is found in union with a loving God — eternal union, in some versions of theological ethics. If there is such a thing as fundamental equality, and such a thing as an inalienable right, how are these connected to the meaning or goal of existence? We rightly ask the question. Donagan's Kantian approach leaves the question completely unanswered. Kant himself realized that, without a tie between the right and the good (and indeed ultimate good), agents will lack motivation to act on his specified rational principles of right conduct. Accordingly, Kant postulates "practically" what the theological tradition insists on theoretically. The new natural-law theorists recognize among the basic goods some need to satisfy religious instincts; but they do not integrate into their system an actual commitment to union with God as an end.[115] The secular explanations stop too soon.

The power of the deeper theological explanations is illustrated by the role religious accounts of human dignity and equality played in opposing slavery in America. Secular arguments were given, but they stood in stark contrast to the powerful religious explanation given by the likes of abolitionist William Ellery Channing:

> I come now to what is to my own mind the great argument against seizing and using a man as property. . . . [H]e is a Rational, Moral, Immortal Being, because created in God's image, and therefore in the highest sense his child, because created to unfold godlike faculties, and to govern himself by a Divine Law written on his heart, and republished in God's word.[116]

One cannot treat beings with godlike features as property. These persons are friends of the One to whom we owe our existence and are called to dwell with forever. Loving them as children of the same great family, God forbids treating them as property.

Second Advantage It may be that some secular "foundational" precepts, such as the precept not to attack basic goods (which we labeled 1-NatLaw), simply *are not true* except on some theological condition, perhaps a condition presupposing a good God who provides a compensatory afterlife. That is, perhaps if theism does not hold, there is no reason the norm holds; and if theism does not hold, that partly explains why the norm does not hold. So, where "t" stands for "theism holds," and "n" stands for "the norm holds":

~t [entails & explains] ~n

This presents a situation that is not equivalent to the one we envisioned in describing the first advantage of our approach, the situation in which:

t [entails & explains] n

---

115. The new natural-law theorists say the existence of a first cause of some events is presupposed by their system, but they stop short of working into the set of assumptions from which exceptionless precepts are deduced a proposition to the effect that the goal of human existence is union with God.

116. William Ellery Channing, *Slavery*, 3d ed. (1836), quoted in John Rawls, *Political Liberalism* (New York: Columbia University Press, 1993), p. 249.

A declaration of inalienable rights that builds in an exceptionless precept against intentional killing of innocent human beings (as, we have argued, any satisfactory declaration of inalienable rights must) might not be true unless there is a providential God, a God who has commanded that we not intentionally kill the innocent. Secular systems, it appears, are left with no satisfactory answer to the question "Why should I refrain from committing suicide if I would be better off dead?"; nor an answer to the more general question "Why should I refrain from killing the innocent if the fate of the nation is at stake?"; nor to the still more general question "Why should I not do wrong that a greater good may come of it?" A satisfactory answer to each is possible within a theological tradition. The beginning of the answer is that a great good will come, and come for you, by upholding the exceptionless precepts.

This can only be the beginning of an answer. For there is a difficulty, a serious difficulty, that vexed us earlier. If it is possible for a person to be better off dead, then is it not arbitrary for God to forbid suicide?

We have already argued that, abstracting from the existence of an afterlife, death can seem rationally preferable to life. Why, then, should it be against the love of God or neighbor to commit suicide, or even murder, when from a worldly standpoint some individual (maybe you) would be better off dead, or when it is necessary to save the nation? Is not a divine command against suicide or murder in such circumstances cruel? How, then, could it issue from a good God? The problem can appear even worse in this theological context than it does in the context of Kantian or natural-law theory. For seemingly *God* can choose to take a life, or more precisely, choose to initiate an otherworldly life. People pray to God to bring the gravely afflicted home. The Catholic tradition has it that Mary, the mother of Jesus, was bodily assumed into heaven, lifted by God out of this world. Some may object that the fact is not credible, but nobody claims that, if God did this, then God would have wronged Mary. Now, if God can bring about the death of a human being, could not God bring it about through the commissioned instrumentality of another human? Socrates refused to commit suicide, though he judged that the next world would be better. "I am not my own," he argued; he belonged to the gods. Still, he drank the hemlock, acting as Athens' appointed executioner. Just authority demanded the unjust death of a just man. Could he not have done the same if the Ultimate Authority had told him to close the curtain on his own earthly life? And if God could license or command the slaying of one innocent, then it would seem God could license the slaying of multitudes for the sake of the kingdom. This reasoning brings us to the edge of disaster.

It well may be, however, that God *cannot* license suicide or murder, and that it is not arbitrary at all for God to forbid these things. Perhaps the fact that we are images of God (assuming that is a fact) makes it impermissible not only for us to murder one another, or take our own lives, but also impermissible for God to command it: the relationship we have to God, and thereby to one another, may preclude such directives. Though God is not precluded from taking human life, we may be. Similarly, the relationship Euthyphro had to his father might have made it wrong for him to prosecute his father for murder, even if someone else rightly could have conducted the prosecution. Or, to take a different example, you can sometimes ask another person to apologize for you (if you are on your deathbed, for instance); but to ask someone to apologize on your behalf for a serious wrong, for no other reason than that you do not want to take the time to do it, or are ashamed to do it, is unacceptable. The relationship you have to the person you have wronged blocks the delegation. God is the author of nature and the designer of roles and duties; it may not be possible for God to require us to step out of our assigned positions. And suicide and murder may be impossible without stepping out of position in relationship to God and neighbor. (Of course, even if God could in principle license suicide or murder, there would be problems knowing about the license, because, if one is faced with a seeming mandate from God to kill the innocent, the correct conclusion to draw is almost certainly that one is delusional.)

And there may be other warrants for divine commands against suicide and murder. Christians teach that the burdens of the friends of God are in some utterly mysterious way "completing what is lacking in Christ's afflictions for the sake of his body, that is, the church."[117] If there is a Creator, is it implausible to expect that the ultimate vindication of moral principles is tied to the judgments of that Creator, who alone understands where, when, and how it all ends? There may be reasons, at present deeply mysterious to us, why we must remain at our stations regardless of the cost.

So we deny that it must be arbitrary for God to absolutely prohibit suicide and murder. Since God's prohibition need not be arbitrary, secular ethical precepts can find a secure grounding in the theological love precepts.

Third Advantage A revelatory base for ethics can reconcile the right and the good. This advantage might be seen as a corollary of the preceding advantage, for the power the revelatory base has to reconcile the right and the good is a consequence of its ability to deal with potential personal and social disasters (for instance, circumstances in which one contemplates suicide or the end of

117. Col. 1:24 (NRSV).

the world). Our line of reasoning above concerning suicide supplies the ground for the third premise of the following argument:

1) A foundational principle, such as 1-Kant or 1-NatLaw, is acceptable only if it grounds a system that reconciles the right and the good.
2) It does so only if it can adequately deal with potential personal and social disasters (such as circumstances in which suicide is contemplated).
3) It does that only by appeal to a divinely ordered plan that includes an afterlife.
4) So a foundational principle is acceptable only if it appeals to a divinely ordered plan.

Kantian ethicists and the new natural-law theorists do aspire to reconcile the right and the good. And they do, we have argued, in the end appeal to non-secular aspects of a divinely ordered plan. That they do so in the end constitutes more than a modicum of evidence for the truth of some revelatory claim that explicitly expresses the reliance on a supranatural metaphysics, a divine order. "I am the gate. . . . I came that they may have life, and have it abundantly," Christian Scripture tells us, presenting its version of the claim that the right and the good are indeed compatible.[118]

Fourth Advantage Revealed or theological ethics has a broader scope than does secular ethics. Revealed ethics explains more. Charity — *caritas* — toward God and neighbor is not only the foundation of the precepts 1-Kant and 1-NatLaw, but also, as Aquinas says, "the mother and root of all the virtues."[119] Here the revealed foundation entirely outstrips the competition as an explanation of CUE-facts about the appropriate response to poverty and the call to solidarity with those in need. The revelatory hypothesis explains why we are to reach out in charity to all others, whatever their condition. They are beloved children and images of the one God. "Many contemporary ethical debates have relatively little to say about the wider issues with which discussions of charity were [in earlier times] concerned," Onora O'Neill observes.[120] She astutely puts her finger on two major reasons: general rejection of accounts of the human good adequate to anchor strong connections between human needs and the virtues; and the prominence of theories that

---

118. John 10:9-10 (NRSV).

119. Aquinas, *Summa Theologiae* I-II, q. 62, a. 4.

120. Onora O'Neill, "Charity," in Lawrence C. Becker and Charlotte B. Becker, eds., *Encyclopedia of Ethics* (New York: Routledge, 2001), p. 203.

ground everything in rights, which "can say little about the traditional 'imperfect' duties to which no rights correspond."[121]

It is unsurprising that the postulates of many ethical systems devoid of reference to a loving Creator lack the reach of richer postulate systems that do so refer. If a Creator loves us all and destines us for eternal happiness, can this fact, if it is a fact, be irrelevant to ethics? In mathematics, the removal of an axiom from the set founding the system can result in the set being much diminished in power. It would be remarkable if the same conclusions about the way to conduct ourselves on a journey that leads beyond this life should be justified and well explained on the basis of a drastically reduced set of assumptions that make no mention of the providence of God.[122]

Fifth Advantage   Revealed ethics is more open to verification than is secular ethics. What do we mean by that? We mean that, *because revealed ethics appeals to authority, because it brings in something that is going on outside philosophical ethics, there is a way in which it is the only ethics that is verifiable.* Consider, for instance, the claim that living in accordance with a certain set of precepts (whether purely philosophical or grounded in revealed ethics) might lead to satisfaction of one's deepest desires. How does satisfying one's deepest desires count as verification of the truth of the precepts? Some think that ethics has nothing to do with inclinations. Others disagree. There seems no way to settle the matter without going *outside* the system of philosophical ethics altogether. Revealed ethics, by bringing divine authority into the picture, makes itself more open to verification. For the question whether there is a divine authority is itself a question open to testing and verification. Ethical claims can draw support from various other claims and facts and CUE-facts constituting a revelatory content. One looks outside the system to see whether credibility is lent to what is not by itself an empirical claim. Non-Euclidean geometry, with its strange denial of the parallel postulate and daz-

---

121. O'Neill, "Charity," p. 204; see also O'Neill, *Towards Justice and Virtue: A Constructive Account of Practical Reasoning* (Cambridge, UK: Cambridge University Press, 1996).

122. It is, however, a serious mistake to think that turning to revelation for foundations for ethics means that secular philosophy is anything less than terribly important. Even if equality and inalienable rights cannot be defended through pure philosophy, much else in philosophical ethics may remain in place: almost all of Aristotle's ethics, for instance; perhaps most of Kant, and most of natural-law theory. Furthermore, philosophy uncovers problems with various secular theories (including relativism and utilitarianism). And it goes a good distance in displaying the foundations of ethics, if not as far as theology. And philosophy shows its own limits (our own argument in this book is purely philosophical; it does not rely on revealed premises, but it includes argument that theology is necessary). And philosophy is indispensable in clarifying and adjudicating issues in the testing of revealed ethics.

zling theorems that strain common sense, is rendered more credible as a mathematical system because it works in general relativity theory, which itself is supported by the provable demonstrability of non-Euclidean geometry relative to Euclidean geometry.

One can, of course, take as evidence for, say, the claim that Kantian ethics is true the fact that a great philosopher thought so, and perhaps even draw from Kant's life, or the lives of his disciples, some kind of evidence for the system of duties Kant proclaimed credible on the basis of mere reason alone. Few, though, seem to argue this way for Kantian ethics. But many argue for the truth of revealed ethics because those they most admire live in accord with the higher call of the revealed ethics. The many may well be right.

6 Objection: The Requirement of Faith Invalidates Mainline Revelatory Claims

6.1. The Objection

We have urged an agnostic inquirer to work toward a probable case, an argument with a probability greater than .5 for the claim that a good God has revealed. Could an inquirer who has assembled a case only slightly better than .5 actually be warranted in *believing* that a good God has revealed? Alvin Plantinga speaks to this issue:

> But if my only ground for Christian teaching is its probability with respect to K [background knowledge], and all I know about that probability is that it is greater than .5, then I can't rationally *believe* that teaching. Suppose I know that the coin you are about to toss is loaded. I don't know just how heavily it is loaded, so I don't know what the probability is that it will come up heads, but I do know that this probability is greater than .5. Under those conditions I do not believe that the next toss of this coin will come up heads. (Of course I also don't believe that it will come up *tails;* and I *suspect* that it will come up heads.)[1]

However, Plantinga's example shows, at best, that knowing that the probability of some proposition is greater than .5 is not always sufficient for believing that the proposition is true. It does not follow that it is *never* sufficient. That Plantinga's argument fails does not entail that one is ever warranted in believing a proposition when one knows the evidence supporting it is greater than .5. But the possibility is not foreclosed in the way he

1. Alvin C. Plantinga, *Warranted Christian Belief* (New York: Oxford University Press, 2000), p. 274.

imagines. And we know of no other argument for the conclusion he supports that succeeds.

Nevertheless, the obstacles to warranted assent to a revelatory claim appear formidable. The problem is not just that an inquirer's case may be only slightly better than .5. Beyond this difficulty is the fact that the major revelatory traditions — and many inquirers will deem them the only live options — require not "mere" belief but wholehearted and resolute conviction. The true believer does not pray "Oh God, if there really is a God, save my soul, if I really do have a soul." The true believer prays in the manner of the Hebrews: "Help me, Yahweh my God, save me since you love me." The true believer goes to the flames for belief. And there must be a determination to hold on not only when confronted with bodily persecutions: steadfast allegiance in the face of intellectual difficulties — commitment of mind and heart despite troubling counterevidence — is asked. How can such resolve be respectable in the absence of a judgment that the claim that a good God has revealed is highly likely? Without a nearly irresistible case for belief, it looks like the assent demanded by the three great Abrahamic religions could be justified only if intellectual dishonesty were also justified.

Now unbelievers find many of the virtues held up as ideals by Judaism, Christianity, and Islam attractive, even if they are difficult to rationalize on wholly secular grounds. Universal love, readiness to forgive injuries, and humility are much admired, though the followers of Nietzsche among us scorn the soft dispositions. Other virtues, "monkish virtues" as Hume called them, such as chastity, are more difficult to see as attractive, but one senses that they may be made intelligible in light of the assumption that this world is passing away and we are preparing for another. But it is very different with the so-called virtue of faith. What sense can there be in wholehearted and resolute belief — in the teeth of difficulties — even on the assumption that we are destined for another world? How could a good God demand such apparent fanaticism?

If the faith demanded by leading revelatory traditions is actually not a virtue but a vice, and if one can see this *prior* to careful consideration of the content of revelatory claims, then our Key Conditional is false.

No one has put the worries more vigorously than the nineteenth-century Roman Catholic philosopher of religion W. G. Ward. With Catholicism chiefly in mind, Ward voiced a complaint he saw, and others now see, as applicable to other religions, *mutatis mutandis*. Ward calls this the "chief stronghold of philosophical objectors against the Church":

> Catholics are taught to regard it as a sacred duty that they shall hold, most
> firmly and without a shadow of doubt, the truth of certain marvels which

are alleged to have taken place nineteen centuries ago. As to examining the *evidence* for those truths, the great mass of Catholics are of course philosophically uncultured and simply incompetent to such a task. . . .

. . . I place before him some serious difficulty, which tells against the most central facts of his religion: he had never heard of the difficulty before, and he is not now at all sure that he will be able to answer it. I should have expected, were it not for my knowledge of Catholics, that the confidence of his conviction would be *diminished* by this circumstance; for, plainly, an unanswered difficulty is no slight abatement from the body of proof on which his creed reposes. But he says unblushingly that if he were to study for ten years without seeing how to meet the point I have suggested, his belief in his Church, whose claim of authority he recognizes as divinely authorized, would be in no respect or degree affected by the circumstance. . . .

I have no general prejudice against Catholics; on the contrary, I think many of them possess some first-rate qualities. But while their avowed intellectual maxims are those above recited, I must regard them as external to the pale of intellectual civilization.[2]

Does the requirement of faith — of wholehearted, resolute belief — invalidate mainline revelatory claims?[3]

6.2. Is Faith a Vice?

In order to deal with this problem, we must formulate it more precisely. And to formulate it more precisely, we need a credible version of a proportionality precept. Here is one standard formulation:

It is always wrong not to proportion belief in a proposition to one's evidence for the proposition.

The formulation expresses, at least roughly, a judgment of many. And from John Locke's discussion of "surplusage of assurance," to Bertrand Russell, to Brand Blanchard, the demand to equate belief to the evidence has been repre-

2. William G. Ward, *Essays on the Philosophy of Theism,* vol. 2, ed. Wilfred Ward (London: Kegan Paul, Trench, 1884), pp. 245-46. Ward had already converted to Catholicism when he wrote these words. Influenced by Newman and the Oxford movement, Ward joined the Roman Catholic Church shortly before Newman himself did.

3. Different traditions have different concepts of faith. Some include the troubling idea that belief must be resolute; others do not. By including this idea in our understanding of faith, we make the present project more difficult for ourselves than it would otherwise be.

sented as a challenge to the notion that faith is a virtue. However, this standard proportionality precept is really not plausible enough to be serviceable. We will work our way dialectically toward a revision, taking up a variety of objections to this simple precept.

Some criticisms of it are clearly off the mark. Here are three.

It has been said that proportionality precepts are meaningless because assent does not admit of degrees. Newman insists on this at some length, pointing to the chapter in Locke's *Essay* entitled "Degrees of Assent" as an egregious disavowal of what everyone who assents to anything actually experiences. In response to a follower of Locke, Newman says: "Can there be a better illustration than this passage supplies of what I have been insisting on above, viz. that, in teaching various degrees of assent, we tend to destroy assent, as an act of the mind, altogether?"[4] A person might as well talk of degrees of truth as degrees of assent, Newman tells us: one can no more partially assent to a proposition than partially touch something. But we may simply grant that "assent" means complete adhesion to a proposition (as H. H. Price observes in his Gifford Lectures), acknowledging that in that case one cannot assent by degrees, and then go on to note that there are well-recognized psychological states between being dead certain that something is the case and dead certain that it is not. (One may touch an object lightly, or press firmly, or hit it as hard as possible.) So the problem can be reformulated using some term other than "assent."

And it is sometimes said that proportionality precepts cannot be true because most of our evidence for what we believe is tacit, and so the precepts are impossible to follow.[5] Ward thought Newman's main solution to the problem of faith consisted in making this point. However, this point cannot be sustained. It is true that most of your evidence for, say, the proposition that a particular friend is honest will be implicit. If you tried to make a list of the times your friend has proved honest, the list might be embarrassingly short. Yet you know that there have been thousands of times when your friend has been honest, often involving circumstances where narrow self-interest would dictate dishonesty. Thus it is not impossible for you roughly to proportion your belief to your evidence. Similarly, for more reasons than you can possibly articulate you will be sure that India exists and that England is an island, while you know

---

4. John Henry Cardinal Newman, *An Essay in Aid of a Grammar of Assent* (Notre Dame, IN: University of Notre Dame Press, 1979), p. 147.

5. For a contemporary account along these lines of the problems, as applied to philosophy and science as well as religion, see Peter van Inwagen's helpful discussion in Jeff Jordan and Daniel Howard-Snyder, eds., *Faith, Freedom, and Rationality: Philosophy of Religion Today* (London: Rowman and Littlefield, 1996), pp. 137-53.

that you have little or no implicit evidence for the existence of the latest hypothetical entity posited by physicists trying to explain the superconductivity of certain ceramics. You can, and frequently do — at least roughly — proportion your belief to the evidence you know you have. An objector to proportionality precepts might as well say that the rule "Proportion your spending to your wealth" is impossible to follow because you do not know precisely the sum total of your assets. Granted, holdings cannot be precisely valued, and nobody knows exactly how much change is hidden under the cushions; nevertheless, there is such a thing as failing to live within one's means.

Finally, it is sometimes said that, while there may be a version of a "threshold principle" properly requiring us to believe only on evidence affording a certain level of probability, once we have attained the threshold, the strength of belief is immaterial. George Mavrodes says that "it seems hard to think . . . of how that *strength* of belief, as distinct from the *fact* of belief, could be a defect in my cognitive life."[6] But the defect may be this: belief stronger than warranted may bias the search for truth. Just as there may be no necessary connection between envy and hatred, so there may be no necessary connection between over-belief and woodenheaded rejection of contrary signs; but the first tends to lead to the second. It has been said of Philip II of Spain that no experience of the failure of his policy could shake his belief in its essential excellence. Perhaps, as Mavrodes suggests, strong belief in the face of seeming counterevidence is not a *cognitive* defect; but that does not rule out its being a *moral* defect, a defect of the will, consisting in an insufficient openness to the truth.

Although these three criticisms of the simple proportionality precept fail, it is not exceedingly difficult to find counterexamples to the precept. As Ward observes, if the precept were correct, children who love their parents would be obliged, because of their affection and partiality, to scrutinize their parents' behavior to detect faults. Moreover, the children would be obliged to delay accepting even the most fundamental instructions from their parents until the children had tested them in the light of their own experience. Children surely do not have these obligations. And, though the point may be most obvious with regard to children, neither do adults have the obligation to call to mind for the purpose of scrutiny, constantly and simultaneously, every dispositionally held belief: most of our dispositional beliefs are properly left undisturbed. In any event, we cannot possibly raise to consciousness at once every dispositionally held belief for simultaneous scrutiny. As Newman ob-

6. George Mavrodes, "Belief, Proportionality, and Probability," in Michael Bradie and Kenneth Sayre, eds., *Reason and Decision* (Bowling Green, OH: Applied Philosophy Program, 1982), p. 64.

served in his time, and Plantinga and others in the Reformed tradition have effectively shown in ours, we properly begin by believing many things without any evidence or argument, and we reasonably continue on in life with some such beliefs.

Now it is one thing to say that we properly begin by believing many things without evidence or argument, but it is quite another to say that we properly continue with unwavering belief in the face of genuine difficulties. At one stage in life we were within our epistemic rights to follow our credulity dispositions and believe firmly in Santa Claus, but not now. When we are aware of unanswered objections to a proposition, caution may be incumbent upon us, and we may be obliged to proportion belief to the evidence. At least, proportioning belief may be the thing to do when the objections to the proposition are genuinely troubling. Not every objection meets that condition. Most of us believe that the world exists independently of our minds; but many of us are puzzled by certain skeptical arguments, unable to say exactly where they go wrong and not at all confident that anyone can show the best skeptical arguments to be defective. Yet we are not about to trim our confidence in the world's extra-mental reality just because we are thrown by arcane philosophic considerations. Zeno's paradoxes have vexed mathematicians interested in the concept of the infinite, but they do not trouble most of us, even if we have never heard of the mathematical solutions: people simply know that things move. These considerations can all be accommodated in a revised proportionality precept:

> It is always wrong not to proportion belief in a proposition to one's evidence *when one is aware of unanswered, troubling objections to the proposition, and does not know the proposition to be true.*

And this allows us to formulate a more precise version of the problem of resolute belief, one that does the problem justice:

1) Major revelatory claims include the assertion that God requires resolute belief involving a firmness disproportionate to the evidential warrant for the belief; more specifically, they require firm belief in the face of unanswered, troubling objections, and in the absence of knowledge that the claims at issue are true.
2) It is always wrong not to proportion belief in a proposition to one's evidence when one is aware of unanswered, troubling objections to the proposition, and does not know the proposition to be true.
3) So, major revelatory claims assert that God requires something that is wrong.

6.3. Resolving the Problem of Resolute Belief

6.3.1. Solutions Unworkable for Agnostic Inquirers

6.3.1.1. Are There Concepts of Faith That Do Not Require Resolute Belief?

It is a commonplace that there are many concepts of faith, even in the biblical works shared by Jews and Christians. Might it be that only some of these concepts require disproportioning belief to evidence and dispelling doubts, and that the concepts making the seemingly insane demands can be set aside while others are retained? Indeed, it might even seem an advantage to be able to narrow the search for a true revelation by eliminating all revelatory claims requiring the kind of faith that generates the problem of resolute belief.

Real differences do, of course, exist among concepts of faith; but important differences in understandings of faith often have no bearing on the problem now confronting us. Consider, for instance, Luther's insistence on "justification by faith alone, not by works." Whether faith is both necessary and by itself sufficient for salvation, as Luther held, or not, as Aquinas maintained, is a question that is distinct from the question of whether faith involves confidence in propositions disproportionate to evidence. Luther and Aquinas differ on the former issue but not on the latter. And two religious claimants may differ widely, of course, on *what* must be held without differing at all on the proposition that *whatever* is held is to be most firmly believed despite a lack of compelling evidence. Luther and Zwingli could differ on the Eucharist without differing on the nature of faith with respect to this point.

And some alleged differences among concepts of faith, differences that might be relevant if they existed, may not really exist — not in a form that is to the point. Consider the difference between those who insist that faith is exclusively a matter of trust in God and not a matter of acceptance of propositions, and those who maintain that acceptance of propositions is essential. (The problem of resolute belief cannot arise, not as we have formulated it, if faith does not involve acceptance of propositions.) One authoritative philosophical source tells us that Luther denied that faith is "primarily cognitive," and that while "a person of faith believes that various propositions about God are true . . . those beliefs are subordinate to trust in God, which for Luther is the core of faith." That source gives a different account of faith in Aquinas, for whom faith is said to be "a voluntarily induced belief whose content is a set of propositions revealed authoritatively by God and typically codified in a confessional creed."[7] But despite the differences in emphasis, Luther and Aquinas concur that faith has a bearing on propositions, and it is likely they agree that evidence for the truth of the propositions is less than compelling. Faith is a matter of both trust in God and belief in propositions. Again, Kierkegaard's position is in some respects worlds removed from Aquinas's. Aquinas does not believe the epistemic grounds of the faithful for accepting the propositions of faith are shaky. And many of Kierkegaard's remarks can be interpreted as defending the claim that the epistemic grounds *are* shaky. Yet, for all the differences between the two views, there is agreement on the point of present interest: a believer accepts propositions with a confidence out of proportion to the available evidence.

Fundamental agreement that believers must have confidence that outstrips available evidence is often buried. Some accounts of faith appear to deny that propositions are even at issue. *The Oxford Dictionary of the Jewish Religion* says that biblical accounts present faith as "unwavering truth and confidence in God, rather than assent to theological propositions."[8] But the same source continues: "In due course, however, and in response to a variety of aggressive cultural alternatives, a more self-conscious awareness of faith as belief in the truth of certain ideas and propositions developed."[9] However much a religious community emphasizes that what counts for eternity is attachment to God, it is all but inevitable that it will find itself using language that at least connotes, if not directly expresses, confidence in *teachings*. After all, how can it be made out that an old man with neither property nor progeny trusted God to make him patriarch of a nation without taking him to trust *that* God would do it? As another authoritative source puts it, "The entire structure of beliefs and practices called Judaism rests upon certain cognitive presuppositions, in the absence of which the entire structure collapses."[10] Strings of propositions must be accepted. And the position is to be found in Islamic as well as Jewish and Christian theologies. "The orthodox [Islamic] doctrine on Faith, now generally accepted, is that it is the belief of the heart or mind . . . of the articles of the creed; *the intellectual conviction of the truth,* quite irrespective of the confession of the tongue, or the performance of good works."[11] And in all these the-

7. William E. Mann, "Theological Virtues," in Edward Craig, ed., *Routledge Encyclopedia of Philosophy* (London: Routledge, 1998).

8. See "Faith," in *The Oxford Dictionary of the Jewish Religion*, ed. R. J. Zwi Wereblowsky and Geoffrey Wigoder (New York and Oxford: Oxford University Press, 1997), p. 249.

9. "Faith," *The Oxford Dictionary of the Jewish Religion*, p. 249.

10. "Faith," in *The New Encyclopedia of Judaism*, ed. Geoffrey Wigoder (New York: New York University Press, 2002), p. 269.

11. F. A. Klein, *The Religion of Islam* (London: Curzon Press, 1985), p. 40 (italics added).

ologies it is said time and again that the believer "walks by faith and not by sight": there is a gap between the warrant for belief and the belief itself.[12]

In any event, an agnostic inquirer's own aims likely will make it unnecessary to investigate questions about exactly what the opponents of intellectualized accounts of faith really meant to assert. A philosophically inclined agnostic inquirer who wants an argument for religious belief will not be helped out of the present difficulty by those who say that there are plenty of highly respected representatives of revelatory religions who deny that any truth claims are at issue. For the philosophically inclined agnostic inquirer, it is all about truth claims.

6.3.1.2. Can an Agnostic Deny That Evidence Is Disproportionate to Belief?

Some reflective believers would reject the first premise of the argument expressing the problem of resolute belief — at least insofar as that premise is intended to capture the view of the religious communities to which they belong — on the grounds that faith rests on a superabundance of evidence. That is, they would reject:

1) Major religious communities claim that God requires resolute belief involving a firmness disproportionate to the evidential warrant for the belief; more specifically, they require firm belief in the face of unanswered, troubling objections, and absent knowledge that the claims at issue are true.

On the view of those who think faith rests on superabundant evidence, the faithful may be conscious of various difficulties with belief. But the difficulties are in some sense "academic": they are like the difficulties with Zeno's paradoxes concerning infinity. The vast majority of us *know* that things move,

---

12. In all three of the great Abrahamic religions, noted representatives have resisted the rationalization of the faith. The resistance is often described in ways that suggest that they really are denying that propositions are at issue. It is said, for example, that "[t]he intellectualist school of Saadiah, Baḥya, and Maimonides interpreted 'faith' in the cognitive mode of 'faith that . . .,' a form of intellectual knowledge," while the "[v]oluntarist school of Judah Halevi and Crescas interpreted *emunah* as 'faith in . . .,' a 'trust' which is a total emotional commitment characterized by love and joy." ("Faith," *The New Encyclopedia of Judaism,* p. 270.) But "S believes that p" does not exclude "S's commitment is full of love and joy." Do Judah Halevi and Hasdai Crescas really mean to say that they are committed to no truths at all? It hardly seems likely. And they do not really mean to deny that they are if, when asked whether they trust God to bring about what he promised, they are prepared to say "yes." For they cannot trust God to bring about what he promised if they also deny *that* the promises will be fulfilled.

despite the fact that we cannot pinpoint the problem with Zeno's reasoning; and believers may also *know* that what they believe is true, according to those who hold that faith is supported by superabundant evidence.

Ward himself maintains (though one cannot tell it from the long passage we quoted above) that Catholicism does *not* require assent beyond the evidence. Believers possess a "super-superabundance" of evidence, he says; they are privileged to see ordinary evidence more clearly than others. The believer has "cognizance of various premises which (according to the accumulative method of reasoning) are super-superabundantly sufficient to establish the truth" of Catholicism, and "God, in imparting and upholding the gift of faith, specially illuminates the Catholic's mind, so that he shall give those premmises their due weight, and thus reasonably possess certitude."[13] What are the arguments establishing this certitude? They are familiar arguments offered by natural theologians following the standard ordering protocol for investigating the question of revelation. Begin with the fact that things move. Whatever is moved is moved by another — so there is an unmoved mover. The unmoved mover possesses the attributes of omnipotence, omniscience, and perfect goodness, and hence is God. Being perfectly good, God must be unfailingly truthful. Thus we may have perfect confidence in any revelation from God. Miracles and other evidence compellingly testify to the fact of revelation. At every stage of the way, reason supplies grounds for belief: we get a virtual transmutation of faith into knowledge.

Similarly, Newman speaks of the "illative sense," which gives us certitude about concrete matters through a mode of knowing more personal than what can be captured by "paper logic." Through the illative sense, the mind spontaneously divines some conclusion as inevitable, feels it to be "as good as proved," even though it has not been reached syllogistically. The mind, operating on converging probabilities, can (Newman says) reach certitude about the divinity of Christ in the same way it can about the existence of India: a mountain of implicit evidence backs these propositions.

And one can find in both Roman Catholic and Protestant catechisms the suggestion that the propositions of faith must be secure since they come from God. The Roman habit is to add "who can neither deceive nor be deceived." Calvin puts it this way: "When that which is set before us is acknowledged to be the Word of God, there is no one so deplorably insolent — unless devoid

---

13. William G. Ward, "The Reasonable Basis of Certitude," originally published in 1878, reprinted in Gerald D. McCarthy, ed., *The Ethics of Belief Debate* (Atlanta: Scholars Press, 1986), p. 185.

also both of common sense and of humanity itself — as to dare impugn the credibility of Him who speaks."[14]

But an account of faith that makes it out to rest on a "super-superabundance" of evidence — or even merely a superabundance — will not do for an agnostic. Indeed, it will not do even for Catholics (Ward and Newman were both Catholics), since it is established Catholic teaching that faith is meritorious, and this because faith requires an act of the will. If the evidence were compelling, one would no more need to make an act of the will to believe in the real presence of Christ in the Eucharist than to believe in the real presence of the sun in the sky.[15] Reason plays a role, but, as Aquinas says, the certitude of faith is rooted in the will.[16] And of course, many believers do not see the evidence as rendering all argument on the other side obviously irrational. In any event, *agnostics* most certainly do not see the evidence as super-superabundant.

A related solution to the problem of resolute belief, a solution that also targets the first premise of the argument generating the problem, can be drawn from the writings of Alvin Plantinga. Working from within the Calvinist tradition of "Reformed epistemology," Plantinga has articulated a notion of warrant that might be adopted to defend the claim that revealed truth can be known in a strict sense (though Calvin, like Aquinas, seems to us to hold that faith is knowledge only in a popular sense).[17] God endows us with cogni-

14. John Calvin, *Institutes of the Christian Religion,* John T. McNeill, ed. (Philadelphia: Westminster Press, 1960), I, vi. 1, cited by William J. Abraham, *Canon and Criterion in Christian Theology: From the Fathers to Feminism* (Oxford: Oxford University Press, 2002), p. 132. As we have already had occasion to emphasize, two questions must be held distinct: "Has God spoken to us?" and "If so, can we be certain that what God says is true?" For more on this point in its historical context, see Abraham, *Canon and Criterion,* pp. 111-39, especially pp. 132-34.

15. Ward tries to meet this difficulty by invoking a distinction of Cardinal Franzelin: a truth can be absolutely "certain" without its being "evident." Ward writes: "Where a truth is exhibited as 'evident,' doubt is impossible; as in the instance of a demonstrated mathematical theorem. But where it is exhibited as 'certain' indeed but not as 'evident,' doubt is possible though most unreasonable, and belief therefore laudable" (Ward, "The Reasonable Basis of Certitude," p. 185). This Franzelin-Ward solution is very unsatisfactory. For surely what is praiseworthy about faith is not that one refrains from working up a doubt where it is just barely possible to doubt.

16. See Aquinas, *Disputed Questions on Truth,* q. 14, a. 2.

17. One should not be misled by the practice of Aquinas and other theologians who call faith "knowledge," even "scientific knowledge" *(scientia).* For Aquinas such usages are justified by nothing more than the fact that faith, like knowledge, is very firm true belief. Faith is just a habit of mind by which eternal life exists inchoately in us, making us assent to what is not apparent. *Summa Theologiae* II-II, q. 4, a. 1, corpus. In *Disputed Questions on Truth,* q. 10, a. 12, response to "on the contrary" 6, Aquinas observes that, though faith is in some sense a certain

tive faculties devised in such a way as to achieve true beliefs, Plantinga suggests: when the believer's cognitive capacities are working the way they were designed to work in the kind of environment for which they were designed, a believer's religious beliefs have positive epistemic status. On Plantinga's model, if Christianity is in fact true, we can be warranted in believing that it is true simply by exercising our cognitive capacities in the way they were meant to be exercised. As you look at the starry skies, your mind, operating as God designed it to operate, in the setting for which God designed it, forms the true judgment that God exists. There is no end to knowing Christian doctrine in this way. You need only to hear the Word, accept it, and hold it to the right degree — firmly. There will be no disproportion between the firmness of the belief and the warranting evidence.

Plantinga's approach has several advantages, particularly from the standpoint of those inclined to read Christian Scripture and Calvin as holding that faith is knowledge, literally and non-analogically. For though Plantinga's account of warrant is perhaps narrower than some, it is broader than the stringent definitions of knowledge suggested by the classical foundationalism of Aristotle or Aquinas, which require that the known truth be immediately or derivatively evident. It is thus possible with Plantinga to hold that Christian belief is knowledge without claiming with the Catholics cited above that Christian belief is made certain by super-superabundant evidence displayed as such by the light of grace.

An *agnostic* facing the problem of faith, however, can find no solution to the problem in accounts such as Plantinga's and Ward's. We do not dispute Plantinga's account of *his* epistemic practices (or Ward's account of his illuminated evidence); their accounts may be taken at face value. If someone reports synesthetic perceptions — seeing colors that have sounds or smells — there may not be much to say by way of criticism of the claimed experiences. But, as we observed at the beginning of this book, agnostics believe that they have no such knowledge-conferring experiences and will be prone to doubt that they will ever have them. And even if some believers have the knowledge Plantinga describes, many do not. Many believers (including the present authors) share Plantinga's conviction that the Christian mysteries are true, but do not think that they *know* that Christianity is true. We believe, but we do not find basic religious truths lodged in our epistemic foundations. It might

---

cognition, that certitude is due to a firmness of adhesion rooted in the will, and that since evidence for what is believed is incomplete, "disturbing doubts are able to arise in the believer." ("Et inde est quod de his quae sunt fidei, potest motus dubitationis insurgere in credente" [our translation].)

be said that our conception of knowledge is off base or that our self-understanding is flawed; it might be said that we really do know basic religious truths, though we are unaware of our knowledge. But then we will not *know* that we know that there is a God. Thus we cannot have the confidence required by the view that faith is knowledge. In any event, nonbelievers (along with many believers) will typically resonate more with Kierkegaard than with Plantinga: religion appears filled with paradox, and hardly the sort of thing that strikes one as obvious.

6.3.2. The Core of a Solution for Agnostics

6.3.2.1. The First Stage: Scrutinizing the Proportionality Precept

Thus standard solutions to the problem of resolute belief are inadequate, at least for agnostic inquirers. However, a solution is available to the agnostic.[18] It begins with recognition that the nuanced proportionality precept constituting the second premise of the argument for resolute belief, despite its advantages over less nuanced versions, is false. Again, that precept goes as follows:

2) It is always wrong not to proportion belief in a proposition to one's evidence when one is aware of unanswered, troubling objections to the proposition, and does not know the proposition to be true.

How can the precept's falsity be recognized? Through counterexamples.

A juror who goes into a trial tries to hold fixed a suspended state of judgment until all the testimony and evidence have been presented. Why is that? Because the obligation to discern the truth requires resisting the inclination to pass judgment. Punctilious adherence to even the nuanced proportionality precept operates contrary to the adjudication of truth. And that is not merely

---

18. Earlier versions of our line of argument can be found in Joseph M. Boyle, Jr., J. Hubbard, and Thomas D. Sullivan, "The Reformed Objection to Natural Theology: A Catholic Perspective," *Christian Scholar's Review* XI, no. 3 (1982); Thomas D. Sullivan, "Adequate Evidence for Religious Assent," in A. Kennedy, ed., *Thomistic Papers* IV (Houston: Center for Thomistic Studies, 1988); and Thomas D. Sullivan, "Resolute Belief and the Problem of Objectivity," in Linda Zagzebski, ed., *Rational Faith: Catholic Responses to Reformed Epistemology* (South Bend, IN: University of Notre Dame Press, 1993). We see ourselves as only elaborating a position one can find in Newman, Aquinas, Calvin, and others. The position was obscured — and remains so — by the insistence on the primacy of establishing the existence of a good God through standard natural theology, provoking a different response from the Reformed epistemologists, who see faith as knowledge.

so with respect to court proceedings. If generally followed, the precept would interfere significantly with deliberative processes. This is particularly so with respect to religious matters. Consider Catherine Ward's comments in a letter to Newman:

> Strong convictions I have at times that the Church of Rome is the One true Church — strong yearnings after her blessed teaching of the Holy Sacrament — and then comes the fear, the shrinking from certain doctrines as the teaching of the Evil one, and I am cast back, I cannot say into the English Church, but alas no where — homeless as it were and houseless. . . .[19]

According to even the nuanced proportionality precept, Catherine Ward should be a Catholic one moment and anti-Catholic the next. Whatever one thinks about Catholicism, this cannot be right.

Furthermore, it is possible to have obligations *other than* the obligation to adjudicate the truth, obligations making it reasonable to set aside the nuanced proportionality precept. A friend is slow to accept evidence against our good intentions; no one is a friend who believes in good intentions only to the degree that they are proved. Under certain circumstances we rightly feel that we are obliged to stand by friends when, for example, their integrity is called into question. We do not scrape up every little bit of evidence that calls into question their integrity; we do not open our ears wide for whatever gossip we can catch. If we can, we refuse to dwell on the evidence. If we can. Sometimes we cannot. Sometimes we have other obligations that override the obligations of friendship. And sometimes the evidence is too compelling for us to ignore it. While personal trust is a thing of beauty, it is not blind partiality that makes it beautiful, but a love that sees what others do not see. Truth is the foundation of genuine friendship. But the fact remains that the obligations of friendship show that we have not only the right but the duty, in some circumstances, to hold fixed a conviction that a certain proposition is true ("my friend is a person of integrity"), even though we are aware of troubling and unanswered objections to the proposition, and even though we do not know the proposition to be true. Management of beliefs properly takes place in light of broad goals and obligations.

---

19. Catherine Ward, letter to John Henry Newman, 10 Oct. 1848, in Charles Stephen Dessain, ed., *Letters and Diaries of John Henry Newman*, vol. 12 (London: Thomas Nelson, 1962), p. 289. Newman's response to Ward two days later (p. 289) makes the crucial point: "Reason does not prove that Catholicism is *true*, as it proves that mathematical conclusions are true . . . but it proves that there is a *case* for it so strong that we see we ought to accept it. . . . *You can believe what you will*; the only question is whether your reason tells you that you *ought* to believe. . . ."

Can premise 2 of the argument for resolute belief be modified to avoid these and similar counterexamples? Perhaps. But the qualifications that would need to be built in are very broad indeed, so broad as to render the precept impotent. To wit:

> It is always wrong not to proportion belief in a proposition to one's evidence when one is aware of unanswered, troubling objections to the proposition, and does not know the proposition to be true, *unless proportioning belief violates an overriding obligation (such as the obligation to adjudicate the truth, or trust a friend).*

The problem here is that the question in the first place was whether it is wrong to disproportion belief to the evidence. Virtually the whole weight of this question has been shifted to the clause at the end that warns of the possibility that proportioning belief violates an overriding obligation. An inquirer vexed by the original question is likely to feel virtually clueless about what counts as an overriding obligation. The expanded precept is useless.

In sum, then, the nuanced proportionality precept (i.e., premise 2 of the argument for resolute belief) is false, and it is not obvious how to revise it to make it both true and useful. Acknowledging this is the start of a solution to the problem of resolute belief, setting up a fuller solution that recognizes that a command to believe resolutely may be rational — and so also obedience to such a command.

*6.3.2.2. The Second Stage: Seeing Sense in the
Command to Believe Resolutely*

What could justify resolute belief that something is the case? Even if, as we have just argued, the nuanced proportionality precept does not hold universally, it remains something of a mystery how someone could be *justified* in believing resolutely. How is it possible? The argument/explanation we will be offering in this section turns on a slight development of a quite simple idea. The simple idea is this. In general, if acting to attain some end, e, is obligatory, and means m is indispensable to achieving the end, then m, too, is obligatory. The slight development adds that this holds true if pursuit of end e and means m are merely *deemed to be* obligatory (in the case of the pursuit of e), and *deemed to be* indispensable (in the case of m). In other words, if an individual thinks that the available evidence warrants the judgment that a certain end is obligatory and an action indispensable to the end, then the individual is obliged to act. Now, if this is correct, we can easily see how resolute belief can become obligatory — and hence justified. A person becomes convinced that a revelation is true and that the revelation proclaims union with God obligatory and resolute belief indispensable to this end.

A bit more elaborately:

1) If a person believes that there is a better case for than against some end being obligatory and some act being indispensable for achieving that end, then the act is obligatory (and hence justified) for that person.

2) If a person believes that there is a better case for than against a particular revelatory claim, and understands its central teachings to include the requirement that people are obliged to seek union with God through the act of resolute belief, then that person believes that there is a better case for than against the end of union with God being obligatory, and the act of resolute belief being indispensable for achieving that end.

3) So, if a person believes that there is a better case for than against a particular revelatory claim, and understands its central teachings to include the requirement that people are obliged to seek union with God through the act of resolute belief, then the act of resolute belief is obligatory (and hence justified) for that person.

Let us refer to this as the Argument for Faith.[20]

The second premise is unobjectionable.

And if the first premise does not immediately strike an inquirer as true, examples will suggest its plausibility. Imagine that you believe that you are obliged to give your students fair grades, and you believe that reading their papers is indispensable to giving fair grades; you then have an obligation to read their papers. Or imagine that you are walking past your neighbor's house and, looking over the fence, see what might be the body of an infant floating unattended in a swimming pool. Maybe it is just a doll — you are not sure. But you judge that there is a better case for than against your having an obligation to get a closer look at the pool. Breaking the flimsy lock on the gate is, let us imagine, the only way to get closer. So it is obligatory for you to break the lock; you are justified in doing so.

---

20. Some readers have asked if we are embracing the position of William James in his famous essay "The Will to Believe." We hold with James, and indeed with his opponent W. K. Clifford, that assenting and withholding assent are moral matters. But our position is different from James's inasmuch as James argues no more than that it can be right to believe on "insufficient evidence." That conclusion makes us uncomfortable. We certainly do not argue for it. James does not even directly confront the issue we are concerned with, that of believing wholeheartedly when the evidence for a given proposition is pretty good — better than 50/50 — but not compelling.

Take an example more obviously relevant to an agnostic inquirer's situation. Imagine that you are in an abandoned mine, a mine nobody knows you have entered, and you are suddenly shut off from the entrance by the collapse of the ceiling. The remaining oxygen will last only a short time. As you search in the dark for a way out, you see — or think you see — a line of light passing through a narrow passage, a passage that may lead up and out. And you hear — or think you hear — a voice above calling down to you. You have no conclusive proof, of course, that the passage will not be a dead end, nor proof that, if you try to crawl up through it, you will not get stuck. But you have adequate reason to believe that the end of escape is obligatory and an action — seeking the light and the voice — indispensable to reaching that end. Are you not bound to follow where they lead?

In these examples it is obvious enough that the actors have the ultimate obligations at issue: give fair grades; rescue babies from death; escape death yourself.[21] Now, for an inquirer to hold that there is indeed an obligation to believe some religious proposition resolutely, there must be a belief that the revelatory claim that imposes the obligation is more probable than not. And resolute belief can rationally be perceived as an obligatory means to an indispensable end only if it is plausible that a good God would make such a demand. Divine commands have to be intelligibly connected to some good. Is there any good that could be connected to the command of resolute belief?

It does not follow straightaway that, if we do not see a link between resolute belief and some good, there could not be one. Therefore, even if a person could not think of a good reason for God's requiring faith, it still might be deemed that faith is necessary if evidence in favor of the revelatory claim is sufficiently strong. One of the functions of revelation may be to make known what is good for us, even if — abstracting from revelation — reason does not grasp *why* it is good for us.

However, it *is* possible to think of good reasons why God might require faith. Resolute belief solidifies the bond among persons. If we saw more clearly the things we believe on faith, we would not have to yearn for those things and work alongside others as we attempt to plumb the mysteries of creation and Creator, and ponder the economy of salvation. Even at the human level it makes sense that we would need to strengthen our connections with others. And *a fortiori* at the divine level. Faith is free and willful adher-

21. What if you think there is less than a .5 probability that the object in the pool is a baby, or a less than .5 probability that you will find an escape route from the mine? In both these cases, would you not still be obliged to act? Indeed you would. But that fact does not generate counterexamples to our claim, or render our examples irrelevant to the point at issue. It simply raises other questions.

ence to God; our way of grasping God is via propositions; therefore, steadfast adherence to God could reasonably require steadfast acceptance of propositions relating to God. Should we be ready to let go of the propositional tie to God for less than compelling reasons, we would be ready to let go of God — whom we grasp through propositions — for less than compelling reasons. If we saw more clearly the things we believe on faith, we would not have to willfully attach ourselves to the good. But we see through a glass, darkly. By deliberately cleaving to the good, we lift ourselves up into the realm of the transcendent and become capable of love; and through love we bind ourselves to God and to the people of God. So have religious communities claimed over the centuries. Their claim is not easily refuted.

Return, now, to the nuanced proportionality precept we abandoned as problematic in presenting the first stage of our solution to the problem of resolute belief:

2) It is always wrong not to proportion belief in a proposition to one's evidence when one is aware of unanswered, troubling objections to the proposition, and does not know the proposition to be true.

This proportionality precept is, of course, stronger than the proposition that one must believe on adequate evidence; and, as we have argued, it can be rejected by the rational agnostic inquirer who requires adequate evidence before accepting the proposition that a good God has revealed. The evidence can be *adequate* for the judgment that one is obliged to believe resolutely without being *compelling*. On the other hand, the precept can be read in a way that may appeal to rationalistic agnostic inquirers, and it can be given an interpretation that does not make it inconsistent with the Argument for Faith we have just presented.[22] If a revelatory claim includes a requirement of faith, and an inquirer judges that, all things considered, the claim is somewhat more probable than not, and thus assents to the claim and has (or works to have) wholehearted and resolute belief or faith — is that clearly believing in a way that is disproportionate to the evidence? The "all things considered" judgment that the claim is more probable than not *includes* the (possibly troublesome) fact that the claim embeds a requirement of faith, resolute assent. Again, if, despite this, an inquirer deems the claim probably true and embraces the faith, is that really believing "beyond the evidence"? No — if believing beyond the evidence entails having belief without adequate warrant. Yes — if believing beyond the

---

22. If an inquirer is to commit to 2, some response to the counterexamples we provided above will be needed.

evidence is entailed by wholehearted assent in the absence of compelling evidence. Perhaps the latter take is the more natural one: faith crosses an evidential gap. But the matter is not entirely clear.

Notice that our argument for the rationality of faith has appealed to the *content of revelatory claims*. The content both generates the problem of resolute belief (due to the command to believe resolutely), and helps provide a solution by showing us why the command might make sense. The fact that we can come to see the reasonableness of a command to believe resolutely means that we can acquire additional evidence on behalf of the proposition that a good God has revealed.

And we might acquire similar evidence upon reflecting on other obligations imposed by revelatory claims, obligations that, like the obligation to believe resolutely, require setting aside proportionality precepts. For instance, a revelatory claim may bid us not to judge anyone: not to judge others, not to judge ourselves. Even when we have very strong evidence that some human being is a moral degenerate, we are told to refrain from negative judgments about the person's heart. Here again, we are told to ignore any principle like the nuanced proportionality precept. What sense could there be to the admonition not to judge? It may be necessary to believe that people are better than they appear to be, because it is necessary to believe *oneself* better than one appears to be. And it may be necessary to believe this about oneself because, without that belief, one will be so sunk in despair that it will be impossible to operate as a moral agent. Revelatory claims give us reason to think that we are not in the end lethally infected, not lost causes who have no way to crawl out of the holes we are in. Philosophy can give us no such assurance.[23]

6.3.3. Six Objections to the Solution

First Objection "Different people make positive appraisals of the cases for different religions; so, according to your Argument for Faith, members of dif-

---

23. As Robert Adams indicates, Kant has a hard time with this problem. Adams writes: "The very idea of the divine assistance involved in sanctifying grace is problematic for Kant, however, because of his insistence that anything by virtue of which our lives are to have moral worth must be the work of our own freedom." Adams thinks Kant offers an ingenious solution to the problem, but suggests it is a solution that compromises Kant's conception of the good will because it requires that we "share with God the productive responsibility for what is accredited to us as morally good. . . ." Robert Merrihew Adams, "Introduction," in Immanuel Kant, *Religion within the Boundaries of Mere Reason*, ed. Allen Wood and George di Giovanni (Cambridge, UK: Cambridge University Press, 1998), pp. xxii, xxiii.

ferent religions may be obliged resolutely to believe different things. Furthermore, since an atheist may see resolute atheism as an indispensable means to the obligatory end of truth, for some people even resolute atheism is obligatory. These are intolerable consequences of your Argument for Faith."

They are no such thing. It is no embarrassment to our argument that Hindus, Jews, Christians, Muslims, and others worshiping according to their lights are doing their duty. To the extent that the systems are incompatible, some believers must be wrong in their judgments about what is the case and about what should be done. That no more tells against the proposed ends-means framework than does the fact that physicians could be morally bound to use medications they mistakenly regard as efficacious. Moreover, with respect to worship and activity not obviously pernicious, it is to be expected that a Searcher of Hearts would bless the agents, if not their work.

Is the same to be said even for resolute atheism? Yes, if it is possible that *resolute* disbelief, as opposed to *mere* disbelief, could be seen as a duty. But how could resolute disbelief be seen as a duty? The believer's obligation, we have suggested, is tied to a perceived need to bind oneself to a person. The atheist has no such motive. A religious believer who is asked to justify the conviction that resolute belief or faith is required will point to scriptural or ecclesial statements taken to express God's will. An atheist cannot similarly point to some Bible of Disbelief to justify resolute atheism. An atheist can believe that truth is a necessary end, and that, since God does not exist, disbelief is obligatory. But nothing in this argues *resolute* disbelief. Might an atheist — or even an agnostic — reasonably resolve to hold on to atheism or agnosticism because religion offers temptations that should be resisted, and can be resisted only through sober resolution? Perhaps. Steven Weinberg says:

> It is an almost irresistible temptation to believe with Bede and Edwin that there must be something for us outside the banqueting hall. The honor of resisting this temptation is only a thin substitute for the consolations of religion, but it is not entirely without satisfactions of its own.[24]

But resisting the "temptation" of religion is honorable only if, *after due investigation*, it is judged false. And investigation adequate to underwrite atheism, we have argued, must include serious inquiry into revelatory claims.

Second Objection "According to many major revelatory claims, grace is essential to the act of faith. But the Argument for Faith allows no room for grace."

24. Steven Weinberg, *Dreams of a Final Theory* (New York: Random House, 1994), p. 261.

Why should one think the Argument for Faith allows no room for grace? The reasoning, presumably, would go something like this:

1) Suppose the case for a given revelation is better than the case against.
2) If that is so, it looks like there can be no need for grace, any more than there is a need for grace to recognize or accept the conclusions of other probable arguments.

But the reasoning is flawed.

The problem begins with the statement of the first premise. As we have taken pains to emphasize, it is misleading to speak in the abstract of "the case for" or "the case against" a revelation. What an inquirer should target is *a* case for a revelation that is better than any and all cases against. Framing the issue in terms of a search for *a* case is helpful in dealing with the present objection, because it calls attention to the point that there may be various constructible cases supporting a revelation. There may be as many cases as there are inquirers. And that makes it easy to see a problem with the second premise. Divine assistance may be needed to find, or even simply to recognize that one possesses, relevant evidence. Serious religions make serious demands, and those demands can interfere with obtaining a clear-eyed view of the evidence. As King David needed Nathan's assistance to accurately perceive his dealings with Uriah and Bathsheba, so may an inquirer need the assistance of divine grace.

Furthermore, resolute belief means hanging on in the face of difficulties. Whereas in many nonreligious situations there is no point in clinging to belief when difficulties present themselves, in the case of faith there is a point, and gracious assistance may be needed to resist the temptation to turn away. A nonreligious example can orient us here. Sometimes it is hard to think well of another person, someone who is or has been your friend. You may need help from another human being, someone who can remind you of difficulties in your friend's life, or of the many good things your friend has done for you, or of your own faults and shortcomings. Once the case is laid out, you may see things in a certain light, a light that makes it desirable and possible for you to hold on to your esteem for your friend. Clear-eyed vision of our own faults and shortcomings is particularly difficult without special assistance. And since there is room for help from another human being, is there not room for supranatural aids? Through Scripture and other gracious divine aids we may acquire a more accurate perception of ourselves — and our end.

Third Objection   "Major revelatory claims warn about the sin of doubt. But the Argument for Faith allows room for doubt."

This objection holds only if the Argument for Faith allows room for doubt and uses "doubt" *in the very same sense* operative when major revelatory claims forbid doubt.

Some revelatory claims include requirements for faith that are rightly off-putting. Cultish rules about who cannot be listened to or what cannot be read are highly troubling. If a group that is making a revelatory claim builds into its pronouncement the demand that you believe that the evidence for the revelatory claim is compelling, and you think it is not compelling, that is an insurmountable obstacle (to accepting this particular claim). And the same is true if you are told that you must believe that all objections to the revelatory claim are frivolous, and they obviously are not frivolous. One must investigate on a case-by-case basis whether specific revelatory claims make inappropriate demands with regard to faith.

One can find in Christian literature expressions of the notion that it is wrong even to *think* about objections to religious teachings. However, more sensible and fuller statements about faith can also be located, often in the very same traditions. A group that points to Aquinas's *Summa* as an outstanding representation of its theology can hardly claim that reflecting on objections to the faith is sinful under all circumstances. The *Summa* is a mountain of objections to faith.

Mainline revelatory claims prohibit *nourishing doubt,* and failing to attend to one's own particular weaknesses with regard to matters of religious belief. That is a very different thing from prohibiting the *having* of doubt. Analogies come quickly. We are all obligated to control emotions and passions, and not to nourish inappropriate desires; in governing ourselves, we naturally reckon with our weaknesses. And we are all obligated (it is reasonable to suppose) to think well of our friends, to be slow to judge them harshly. Thus we should not fan the flames of doubt, and if we are particularly tempted to suspicions, we should not listen to gossip, even if we tell ourselves that we are only listening to help protect the innocent.

However, an objector might insist, mainline revelatory claims also require that a believer actually *expel* doubt. That is much stronger than merely forbidding the feeding of doubt. Can the demand to eradicate doubt be made intelligible?

The requirement to expel doubt can be understood in various ways, some of which will be less than appealing to a philosophically inclined agnostic inquirer (or a philosophically inclined believer, for that matter). a) The requirement might mean that one should delete from consciousness, and to the extent possible from subconsciousness, all evidence contrary to the judgment that a good God has revealed. This will not be a live option for most inquirers, and with good reason. b) It might mean that one should deny the force of evidence to the contrary, somehow set one's teeth against the evidence. Again, this understanding will not entice. c) The requirement to expel doubt might be understood as a command to try to talk oneself into saying that one's evidence amounts to knowledge, when in fact it does not amount to knowledge. Again, this is not attractive. d) "Expel doubt" might be understood as enjoining us to work up a feeling of assurance, to try to get ourselves into a particular emotional state. Aquinas's statement that faith is "certain knowledge" *could* be taken to mean this; or it could mean that the will is fixed in cleaving to the good. e) Another interpretation of the requirement to expel doubt is much more appealing than those just mentioned. One might expel doubt by making belief *actual,* making it *occurrent* (not just dispositional). Actualizing belief, keeping it in mind and heart, dispels doubt in this sense: so long as the belief is active, disbelief is impossible. As Aristotle noted, the belief that p is the contrary of the belief that not-p.[25] Since contraries cannot reside in the same subject at the same time, nobody can *occurrently* believe and disbelieve the same proposition. (Of course, it is possible to do so dispositionally. That is, at one and the same time a person can be disposed to believe and to disbelieve the same proposition.) Men and women of strong faith do not just believe dispositionally; they frequently activate their belief by dwelling on the mysteries, by praying, by performing acts of charity, and by guarding belief from attack by things that weaken it, such as sin.[26] Since actualizing belief does not require refusing to look at evidence to the contrary, it is possible to expel doubt and still separate oneself from the cultist, who will never consider evidence that conflicts with belief.

Fourth Objection   "If it is important to attach ourselves to God by firm belief, then God really should have made the evidence utterly compelling, or at the very least, much stronger than it is. Thus firm belief cannot be so important that it is required of us."

Should God have provided compelling evidence?

Well, to begin with, *could* God make the evidence compelling? Imagine God deciding to spell out in the stars messages such as this: "I, God, love you, my creatures on planet Earth, and I command you to love one another." How exactly would this work? Different galaxies for different languages, the basic

---

25. Aristotle, *Metaphysics*, bk. IV, ch. 3, 1005 b21-34.
26. We were reminded of some of these factors by Rev. James Liekhus.

religious truths appearing each night? Should this have started with, say, the advent of the new millennium? Or are we to imagine that it has always been done, from the first moment human beings had written language? What about the people who cannot read? Maybe we need voices, calling down from the heavens — during the day, so we can sleep at night. Any serious attempt to imagine this sort of thing runs into huge problems. How could star-writing, or messages shouted from on high, unmistakably delineate the consequences of accepting or rejecting perfect goodness? It would not be possible. Would a display help, pictures of rewards and punishments to come? It could not accurately portray heaven, at least not if the traditional doctrine is correct and we are incapable of perceiving perfect beatitude in this lifetime. And even the most hellish pictures will not do justice to the pains (physical and spiritual) of wrongdoing. How often would the displays be put before the mind? Occasionally? People might think they were having hallucinations. Anyway, to really understand matters, we would actually have to experience the pains and the ecstasies; but the ecstasies, at least, would necessarily mislead because they could not give us actual beatific experience of the divine essence. So we would get brief flashes of the pains of hell, alternating with misleading pictures of heaven that focus the mind on the wrong object — new sets of evils for theodicists to explain. We would have surrogates, glimpses of alternative worlds, alternating with and profoundly disturbing the course of human life.

The decision about whether to believe is left to us: it is a matter of will. And no matter what kinds of evidence a deity might provide of its existence, no matter how explicit its communications — star-writing, voices from the mountaintops — we would be able to resist belief. Furthermore, a superabundantly convincing revelation from on high would need to tear the veil off mysteries of freedom, sin, satisfaction, and grace. Kant's view on this matter deserves the highest respect. Regarding such mysteries, God did not and could not reveal anything to us, "for we would not *understand* it."[27]

But suppose all this is wrong: suppose that God could make the evidence in this world irresistible, so strong that we would have no real choice but to assent. It is quite easy to think of a reason God would not want to do that. It is the same reason given earlier, one endorsed by Kant: such a revelation would destroy all freedom of action.

Still, God *could* make matters somewhat clearer than they are. God could have prevented humans from attributing to Yahweh, in the Hebrew scriptures, exceedingly dubious mental and moral states. The Qur'an need not

---

27. Immanuel Kant, *Religion within the Boundaries of Mere Reason*, p. 145 [6:144].

have contained "Satanic verses." Christian scriptures could have been purged of anti-Jewish polemics. If God really raised Christ from the dead, nothing would have prevented the Risen One from appearing to more than just his disciples, a tiny fraction of the human race. The list of possibilities could easily be extended by anyone giving the matter a few moments' thought.

It is also, however, possible to imagine having far *less* evidence. We could have been given nothing but the dying echo of the rumor that God, centuries ago, spoke to one man from a burning bush. Why we find ourselves at just the level of knowledge and ignorance that we do is a mystery; but so is it a mystery why we exist at all with our limited powers. But it is not an utterly impenetrable mystery, for we can get some inkling of the advantages of a resolute faith in the midst of obscurities and difficulties, some inkling of what good would be lost if the judgment that a good God has revealed came as easily as, say, the judgment that there are trees that have flowers.

There can be reasons for God's providing a revelation at a particular point in time, as Richard Swinburne has explained at length.[28] That God gives a historical revelation does not mean that God is unfair to the people who live prior to the revelation, no more than do differences in endowments of reason — and hence access to natural theology and historically revealed instruction — mean that God is unfair to those of average ability. Some people are smarter than others; some have more leisure time to puzzle out foundations and implications of moral principles. To demand that it be otherwise is to demand a world without human beings. And the differences may not always cut in the way we might imagine. From those to whom much is given, much is expected. Those who lack time for philosophizing will not be distracted by intellectual puzzles when they make the key decision of what or Whom they will love. Philosophizing is not always advantageous, though for some, including a philosophically inclined agnostic, it will be unavoidable. There is a kind of egalitarianism attaching to the act of faith: in the end, each person who wills to believe does so without compelling evidence. We start where we are. We come together in the act of faith.

Fifth Objection   "The Argument for Faith is an admission ticket to cults. If resolute belief is justified because it is perceived to be an indispensable means to an obligatory end, then as soon as it is so perceived and the act of faith made, it becomes impossible to say that, conceivably, one might be wrong."

On the contrary, the believer can indeed say, "conceivably, I might be

28. See Richard Swinburne, *Revelation: From Metaphor to Analogy* (Oxford: Clarendon Press, 1992), part I.

wrong," provided the proper sense is attached to "conceivably." A believer who does not *know* that a particular claim believed to be true is in fact true surely could in some sense say, "Conceivably, I might be wrong." One might have evidence supporting a belief — indeed, might feel quite confident about it — and yet at the same time grant that evidence forcing a change in belief could come along: "Conceivably, I might be wrong." Similarly, there is no incoherence in saying, "I believe resolutely that this revelatory claim is true, but for all I *know*, the claim may be false."

And it likely will be possible for a believer to imagine (in some sense of "imagine") properly relinquishing trust in a particular revelatory claim the believer accepts. If, for instance, the pope summoned a general council in the appropriate fashion, and the council deliberately rejected a previously defined doctrine such as the Tridentine teaching that the whole substance of the bread is converted into the body of Christ, only the appearance of bread remaining, that would show that the Roman Catholic Church is not the infallible interpreter of the divine message. Resolute belief is certainly consistent with acknowledging this *epistemic* possibility, though the Catholic will be confident that God will not permit the epistemic possibility to actually occur. It is entirely consistent with resolute belief in a particular revelatory claim to say that one would abandon belief if, upon mature reflection, the case for the claim were to prove inferior to the case against it. The key word, of course, is *if*. The faithful believer is confident the condition will not be satisfied. This willingness to change one's mind if the condition should be satisfied is all that can reasonably be asked. It cannot reasonably be demanded that the believer believe it likely that the relevant condition will be realized.

If God in fact reveals some truth to us, we will never succeed in devising a successful argument to show that what has been revealed is false: there is a sense, then, in which human reason cannot judge divine revelation. But nonbelievers and believers alike can certainly make judgments about whether what some human being (or group of humans) alleges that God says can rationally be believed. Locke made the point over three hundred years ago: "God when he makes the prophet does not unmake the man. He leaves all his faculties in the natural state, to enable him to judge of his inspirations, whether they be of *divine* original or no."[29] The virtue of faith does not require holding on to the belief, come what may, that a revelation has been

---

29. John Locke, *Essay Concerning Human Understanding*, bk. 4, ch. 19 ("Of Enthusiasm"); first published in 1690; reprinted in Steven M. Cahn, ed., *Classics of Western Philosophy*, 2d ed. (Indianapolis: Hackett Publishing, 1977), p. 574.

given, if what may come includes the judgment that, after due consideration, the case against the belief is overwhelming. The strongest argument that one is in the grip of a cult is that the propaganda has it that, no matter how powerful the case against the teaching, one is obliged to believe it. Some ecclesial bodies teach that the case against belief will never be overwhelming to one who has not first failed morally, but that does not entail that one must hold on to religious belief even if long and serious consideration of the matter makes the case against it appear overwhelming. Accepting a revelatory claim does not require checking your reason at the door.

Sixth Objection "It is possible for someone to think that the case for a proposition is better than the case against without believing that proposition. But in such a situation one cannot just *will* to believe the proposition. Therefore, the line of reasoning about being *obliged* to adopt faith as an indispensable means to an obligatory end, union with God, does not work."

Cantor said about one of the strange consequences of his work on set theory: "I've proved it, but I don't believe it."

Nevertheless, we *can* bring ourselves to believe various things, if not directly, by a solitary act, then indirectly, by choosing to consider factors that aid belief. The virtue of being teachable is tied to the ability to bring ourselves to believe things. You may choose to believe the best of another person by dwelling on the individual's good qualities and past favors, your own weaknesses, and so on. And when you are confronted with a paradoxical claim (e.g., "there are ascending orders of infinitude") following from a proof you judge to be correct, your studying the proof may bring the desired psychological assent. If an inquirer affirms that the case for some revelatory claim is likely better than the case against it, but does not find the judgment issuing in belief, then the inquirer may choose to review, to dwell on the evidence, thereby achieving a deeper psychological assent.

Simply by striving always to do what is right, to live a moral life, in accordance with conscience, an inquirer lives out a fundamentally important precept of a number of major religious claims, opening the possibility of new data.

You may choose to go farther, adopting more substantive moral principles espoused by religions, principles concerning charity, self-control, compassion, and so on. You may think it is a standoff on philosophical grounds whether Kant or Aquinas is right about the value of compassion. Kant appears to condemn it. He says that it is impossible for a just person to will that there be more evil in the world than there is; and if compassion is suffering *with* somebody, suffering sympathetically, then compassion will increase the evil in the world. In contrast, Aquinas, following Aristotle and Christian Scripture, argues that when a person in pain sees a friend suffering along in compassion, the suffering of the one initially in pain is reduced. Even if there is a standoff philosophically between Kant and Aquinas, an inquirer might choose a side and "enter in." One can test the doctrine about the proper relationship among human beings without being a religious believer. Does showing compassion for other people strengthen the bonds of friendship, make us less focused on power and lusts of all sorts, and better able to pursue a spiritual and blessed life on earth? Try it and see.

While it is sensible for an inquirer wishing to try out the moral life recommended by revelatory claims to start with moral precepts that are naturally appealing, such as the precept to be compassionate, it is possible then to ascend to somewhat more difficult religious counsels. Revelatory traditions the world over insist that there are absolute moral prohibitions, certain things one is not permitted to do, regardless of the consequences. Murder, lying, and blasphemy are typically deemed absolutely unacceptable. And while intentional killing of the innocent — murder — is not something most of us are tempted to engage in directly, lying is another matter. It is not easy to be truthful always, no matter what the consequences. An inquirer may simply decide: I am going to be the kind of person who does not lie. A case can be made that, whether or not there is a God who has told us that we should not lie, the life of truth is the better and higher form of life. So perhaps little is lost by entering into this religious form of life, even if in the end one comes to reject the religions that recommend it. But an inquirer might decide that the life of truth yields a kind of experience that counts as evidence in favor of certain revelatory claims.

At a higher reach than virtues such as compassion and truthfulness will be virtues that have no natural attraction, but rather what might be called supernatural appeal: the counsels of perfection and the exhortations to "monkish virtues" involving mortifications of the flesh. These involve more difficult duties, duties to change the heart. But an inquirer might choose to take them on.

Indeed, an agnostic inquirer can with good reason enter even further into specific religious practices, moving beyond the realm of ethics. Conditional (but nevertheless sincere) prayer is possible: "Oh God, if there is a God, show me the truth of your existence." *If* there is a God, then there is value in such a prayer. Part of the value is that Someone is offered love. It is right and good that a mother sends letters to a son imprisoned in a distant land, not knowing whether the letters will ever be received, not knowing — maybe not even believing — that her son is still alive. An inquirer need not believe that God exists in order to seek, even to attain, some intimacy with the divine. If you are told that the jewel you are examining will appear brilliant and flawless if you move it out of the artificial light and into daylight, the best way to tell whether that is true may be to make the move. Leading religious figures have held that evidence of the truth of revelatory claims, though deriving from many sources, is conveyed through the experience of living it: illumination increases as one prays, reads Scripture, receives sacraments, and performs religious works of mercy.

Imagine that an inquirer undertakes activities of the kind we have described and with increasing conviction comes to affirm the following: "All things considered, the case for this particular revelatory claim is better than the case against it; thus, since the claim includes the requirement of resolute belief, I have an obligation to believe resolutely that this revelatory claim is true." Imagine that the inquirer tries to believe this resolutely, and strives to follow the prescribed religious practices. Still, something seems to be missing. The inquirer acts "as if" the revelatory claim were true, wills to believe, but lacks the *feelings* we expect religious believers to have, the serene and strong confidence, the joy, the inner conviction that it is all true.

Such an inquirer may actually have attained religious belief. Saints tell of a "dark night" in which, after having had a lively faith with sensible experience of God, that experience is withdrawn and they are bereft of the feelings. Most agnostics would be astonished at the way St. Thérèse of Lisieux described her trials of faith as she approached death. In the year she died (1897) she wrote to her mother superior: "When I sing the happiness of Heaven, the eternal possession of God, I feel no joy in this, for I sing simply what *I want to believe*."[30] Years after her death, one of her Carmelite sisters recalled her as saying toward the end of her life: "I do not believe in eternal life, it seems to me that after this mortal life, there is nothing more. I am not able to express to you the darkness in which I am plunged. . . . All has disappeared for me . . . nothing but love remains for me."[31] It is very difficult to say just what (if anything) is required for belief in God and an afterlife beyond acting "as if" they exist and *willing* to believe that they exist. We do not claim that agnostic seekers who hope there is a God — and in some ways act as though there is — have the loving faith of Thérèse of Lisieux. Still, it is conceivable that inquirers who come to decide that there is a probable case for the truth of a revelatory claim,

---

30. *Manuscripts Autobiographiques,* ms. C 7v°, trans. Elizabeth Atkinson.

31. Sister Thérèse of St. Augustine, *Souvenirs of a Holy Friendship,* p. 9, cited in Sainte Thérèse de l'Enfant-Jésus et de la Sainte-Face, *Derniers Entretiens,* Nouvelle Édition du Centenaire, trans. Elizabeth Atkinson (n.p.: Éditions du Cerf, 1992), p. 786.

and who try to attach themselves to it wholeheartedly but think they have not succeeded in believing, misjudge their success.

6.4. Socrates, the "Agnostic's Agnostic"

If Socrates were alive today, would he be a believer in some revelation? Would he find a "vessel of some divine doctrine" and obtain the safe transport through this world imagined by Simmias? Such questions have little or no meaning. Yet reflection on Socrates' attitude toward myth and religion can illuminate the present situation.

"Sing, Goddess," Homer bids the muse at the beginning of the *Iliad*. What was Socrates' attitude toward the "revelations" of Homer, Hesiod, Aeschylus, and Euripides? This was, in part, the question raised at his trial: Socrates was accused of abandoning the gods of the city and introducing his own gods in their place. Rejecting the myths of his day, many scholars tell us, this hero of reason encouraged the young to become freethinkers, questioning everything, constrained only by reason itself. "So Socrates has become the perfect philosophical martyr: he gave up everything else to live the life of philosophical reason, despite all its dangers, and the mob killed him for it."[32] But this picture of the hero of reason is seriously out of focus, particularly insofar as it represents Socrates as irreligious and hostile to revelatory claims. Socrates worshiped much as his fellow Greeks worshiped, it would appear. "Xenophon's Socrates, it seems, never misses a chance to perform a sacrifice. . . ."[33] And Plato's Socrates offers sacrifices, sings hymns to the gods, and keeps a standard collection of ritual objects. Though the poets are wrong about much, there is something right about what they say about the gods, Plato's Socrates thought. Notoriously, he insisted that he had his own daimonion, a divine voice or sign that signaled him when he should refrain from some action. This hero of reason was not a rationalist who, disdaining the absurdities of the Homeric religion and the pantheon of immoral Greek gods, set out to ascertain the meaning of life on the basis of reason and experience alone. There is no getting around the fact that Socrates accepted revelatory claims.

Socrates, an "agnostic's agnostic," a philosopher who believed he was the

---

32. Thomas C. Brickhouse and Nicholas D. Smith, *Plato's Socrates* (Oxford: Oxford University Press, 1994), p. 188. Brickhouse and Smith continue: "The problem with the ordinary representation of this view is that it is based upon a very anachronistic conception of what 'the life of philosophical reason' is taken to be."

33. Brickhouse and Smith, *Plato's Socrates*, p. 182.

wisest of all because he knew that he did not know, accepted the proposition that revelations have been given to us, and he did so *on the basis of their content,* without relying on belief in miracles or, at any rate, relying substantially on them.[34] We do not mean to suggest that he explicitly set out arguments that the gods exist and communicate with human beings (though it seems possible that the historical Socrates constructed or at least reflected on such arguments; the fact that he was deeply religious does not preclude this). Still, even if he did not work up an apologetic, he had reasons for believing that the gods had revealed, reasons tied to the content of the putative revelations. Furthermore, Socrates embraced revelatory claims *wholeheartedly* (and perhaps, though this is much less clear, even *resolutely*). He appears certain that the gods exist, are good, and care for human beings. That certainty governed his whole life. Consider, for instance, how it affects his view of suicide. Socrates says he is owned by the gods and hence cannot take his life. Now if one thinks that passing to the next world is moving from dark to light, a certain nobility might appear to attach to suicide. No, Socrates insists. Suicide is absolutely unacceptable: a mortal cannot dispose of the property of the gods.

Socrates had at least three kinds of content-based evidence for the truth of (some) revelatory claims.

Philosophy itself provided one sort of evidence. Philosophical analysis leads to certain great conclusions about life and death and the migration of souls that coincide with the picture presented in the myths. On love, Plato's Socrates has learned all he knows from the seer Diotima, whose instruction is a high point of the *Symposium.* On death and the afterlife, he can find no better theory than Homer's.[35] Should one become convinced of philosophical theses regarding the goal of human existence, the blessedness of poverty of spirit, the need for human solidarity, the binding force of exceptionless precepts, the unassailable dignity of human life, the meaning of sexuality, the inadequacy of all human remedies for evil within and without oneself — should one, we say, become convinced of theses secular society largely rejects, and should one find that one or another of most revealed religions have taught the doctrines, have proclaimed them in story, in symbol, in theology, and in the lives of devotees — then one has evidence, not much different from the kind that convinced Socrates, for heavenly doctrines he never imagined.

Another kind of content-based evidence is found in Socrates' arguments that the natural gifts of some poets were inadequate to what they produced on

---

34. One might count as a miracle Diotima's holding off of the plague by prayer and see this as partial warrant for the belief that Diotima's discourse on love is more than philosophy.

35. Brickhouse and Smith, *Plato's Socrates,* p. 206.

some occasions. We are told that there is a striking difference between most of the unmemorable work of Tynnichos of Chalcis and the beautiful poem he produced on one auspicious occasion. On that occasion, Socrates says, he must have been divinely inspired.[36] Christians have argued that the story of Jesus was beyond the productive power of the rude Christian community; Muslims have held that the Qur'an must have come from heaven, being too great for the Prophet to have produced without divine assistance. Both Jews and Christians have said much the same about Israel's monotheism.

And yet another kind of evidence for the existence of genuine revelation comes from Socrates' personal experience living under teachings he took to be divine. Socrates not only accepts revelatory claims; he actually *makes* them. He tells the Athenian jurors that the god who speaks through the Delphic oracle gave him his great philosophic commission: Socrates is the god's servant, and a divine gift to the city of Athens. And, he says repeatedly, he has been assisted in his work by a daimonion. Why does Socrates trust this (putatively) divine voice? He does not test its warnings against his own reason prior to acting in accordance with instructions; that is, he does not pause on each occasion on which he hears the voice and reflect on whether he should in this particular instance follow the sign. But he does have confirmation of the wisdom of the choices made under the daimonion's influence — after he makes the choices, that is. For he says that he was never led astray by the daimonion. In hindsight, then, after he has entered into a certain mode of existence in which he subordinates his inclinations to the instructions of the daimonion, he obtains evidence for the trustworthiness of his voice. If you try out a teaching and find yourself satisfied, that is some evidence in its favor. Socrates was pleased by his conduct at his own trial, and in a way by the entire trial itself, despite the death sentence it brought: the trial's satisfying character confirms the daimonion's wisdom in not warning him off his intended course of action.

Did Socrates have *overwhelming* evidence, evidence *proportional* to his deeply held convictions concerning gods? Probably not. So how could he have had such strong convictions, given the less than compelling evidence?

A parallel question can be raised about Socrates' confidence in moral principles. Never harm a single individual or return a wrong, no matter what you may have suffered at the hands of another, Socrates tells Crito as they argue about whether Socrates should escape from prison to avoid execution. How does Socrates know that this principle is binding? He offers no conclusive proof, and his commitment to elenchic investigation makes such proof

36. Plato, *Ion* 534-35.

impossible. Furthermore, it is not a principle universally accepted. People disagree, Socrates tells us, over the principle, and between those who do and those who do not accept the principle there is no common ground.[37] Humankind divides, and the principle we divide over is life-controlling. Socrates declared for it; it guided his life and brought his death. Why did he affirm it? Conscious of the need for decision, aware that failure to act is a form of action, he risks everything on the good. He opts for the good *because the good is inherently desirable and lovable.* This paradigmatic lover of wisdom, this progenitor of a long succession of Western philosophers, closes the evidential gap by his will. He wills the good.

Likewise, we might see Socrates' supreme confidence that there are beneficent gods, gods who communicate with human beings, as opting for the good. He wills to love what is worthy of love; he risks belief on behalf of the good. As Plato's Socrates puts it at the end of the *Phaedo,* after presenting a long and intricate account of the underworld, and noting that things may not be exactly as he has described them: "I think it is fitting for a man to risk the belief — for the risk is a noble one — that this, or something like this, is true . . . and a man should repeat this to himself as if it were an incantation. . . ."[38] And Socrates does not merely incant his beliefs about the afterworld. He sees his life's work as service to the god. How is doing philosophy serving the god? Gregory Vlastos proposes that Socrates intends his relentless dialogue with fellow citizens to help them develop true beliefs necessary to correctly interpret divine communications, messages transmitted through dreams and oracles. We have already suggested that a good God might require resolute belief because such belief requires trust, and trust develops love. Socrates' committed service to the god, which is at the same time service to humankind, strengthens his love of both divine and human persons, and upbuilds their common community.

Is Socrates' certainty that the gods exist, and are good, and vouchsafe revelations, such that it *cannot* be overturned by reason? Does Socrates' trust in his daimonion trump rational argument? Or is it the other way around: Does rational argument trump the daimonion?

Consider the following scenario. From his youth Socrates hears what he takes to be a divine voice. He learns from experience that the voice is trustworthy (he might even learn from experience how to interpret the signs he receives).[39] In his maturity he has a strong, seemingly invincible conviction that

37. See Plato, *Crito* 49d.

38. Plato, *Phaedo* 114d; G. M. A. Grube, trans., *Plato: Five Dialogues* (Indianapolis: Hackett Publishing, 1981), p. 152.

39. Nicholas Smith suggests this possibility in a letter to Gregory Vlastos (Aug. 26, 1989). See

the voice is, in fact, divine. His confidence is so great that, even when he has what appear to be excellent arguments for undertaking a particular course of action, if the daimonion warns him off, he heeds the voice. In one respect, then, faith masters reason. But were the daimonion to begin signaling disapproval of courses of action that Socrates believes reason obviously favors, then Socrates' trust in the voice would waver. If it began not merely warning him away from certain activities, but actually bidding him to do harm, the content of the communication would undermine Socrates' trust. Of course, Socrates believes that this will not happen; he believes the gods would never command what is unjust. Still, he has not been brainwashed by the daimonion; he is not a cultist. If, contrary to his well-founded expectations, he were to begin to receive, in the same uncanny voice that he had heard from childhood, instructions to harm others, he would stop trusting the daimonion; he would allow reason to reign. The content of the communications would undercut their putatively divine origin.

This is an imaginary scenario. We do not claim that the available evidence warrants the judgment that the historical Socrates, or Plato's Socrates, had exactly this understanding of the relationship between reason and faith. Yet it does not seem in broad outline implausible. This picture of how things might have been allows that Socrates could argue from his trust in the daimonion to his trust in the goodness of the philosophical life — and also from his trust in good arguments to his trust in the daimonion. It is a mistake to think that the arguments can go only in one direction.[40]

The lesson to be learned from this first hero of reason, then, is not that

---

the correspondence among Thomas C. Brickhouse, Mark L. McPherran, Nicholas D. Smith, and Gregory Vlastos in "Socrates and His *Daimonion:* Correspondence among the Authors," in Nicholas D. Smith and Paul B. Woodruff, eds., *Reason and Religion in Socratic Philosophy* (Oxford: Oxford University Press, 2000), p. 194. See also Brickhouse and Smith, "Socrates's *Daimonion* and Rationality," in Pierre Desirée and Nicholas D. Smith, eds., *Socrates' Divine Sign: Religion, Practice, and Value in Socratic Philosophy* (Kelowna, BC, Canada: Academic Printing and Publishing, 2005), pp. 43-62.

40. Smith indicates that only one direction is possible, at least by the time Socrates has reached old age: "What is important is that by the time Socrates is an old man, the mere presence of the *daimonion* or a signal from it utterly vitiates and overturns whatever reasons Socrates may have for acting in the way opposed by the *daimonion*. . . . It seems to me that religion trumps elenchus, and is held — if ever the two come into conflict — as a source of greater confidence." Smith and Woodruff, *Reason and Religion in Socratic Philosophy*, pp. 194, 196. We see no reason to be as confident as Smith. What evidence could anybody have for the conditional: "If Socrates were presented with overwhelming evidence discrediting the existence of his daimonion, he would have held on to his belief in it"? Certainly, Socrates is nowhere reported as having said any such thing.

one must rely on philosophy alone, not that there could be no revelation, not that we could never have reason to deem one authentic, albeit refracted through fallible human minds, not that we could never have great confidence in one, despite a lack of conclusive evidence. Rather, the message is that there could well be a revelation that provides instruction about the ways things are in the unseen world, about our duties, about the means available to carry them out. Furthermore, there well could be reason to accept a revelatory claim as authentic, if it is read in a context of story, song, and symbol, against a backdrop of questions answered informally, imaginatively, and sometimes — with high-pitched attention — philosophically, by hearers of a word who adopt, with greater and lesser success, a peculiar mode of being in the world. Making judicious allowance in light of context, and purging from the revelatory claims reports of divine activities that reason cannot tolerate — lies, rapes, and capriciously vengeful deeds of Homeric gods, genocidal edicts from the God of the Pentateuch — the evidence may suggest that a revelation has indeed been given to us. And there well could be reason to accept wholeheartedly a revelatory claim, notwithstanding the less than compelling evidence, if a plausible case for the claim can be made, and one wills to cling to the Good.

Despite the inferior materials with which he worked (no one around today defends a Homeric pantheon), Socrates found evidence in revelatory claims for the existence of good gods. Today we have better materials that appeal to millions the world over: richer revelatory claims that are woven together with time-tested natural theology. We have said that it is meaningless to ask whether, if Socrates were alive today, he would be a believer in some revelation. Still, the hopeful agnostic may find comfort in the idea that this "agnostic's agnostic" did not turn away from revelatory claims with disdain. True, Socrates was innocent of the demystifying explanations of modern science; at the same time, though, he was unacquainted with scientific evidence that lends credence to revelatory claims, such as the considerable empirical evidence for the emergence of the universe from nothing. Certainly, as we have emphasized, human errors streak the time-honored revelatory claims, and one must work to cleanse the doctrine of the errors. But one may push through the error. One may ascend from lower to higher. Homeric conceptions of friendship and love are rightly subsumed and purified by the conception articulated by Plato's Socrates. Socrates' discourse on love, purportedly inspired by Diotima, is perhaps itself surpassed by Ramanuja's commentary on the *Gita* or Paul's first letter to the Corinthians.

Philosophical ways of thinking about God and revelatory claims, congenial to the intellectual master of the Academy's founder, though all too often ignored in the academy itself, support the notion that investigation into one alleged revelation or another could well be worthwhile. Indeed, it may be that the only way to argue persuasively that there is a good God is by allowing into the database the content of revelatory claims. Thus have we argued in our long meditation on the words of Simmias to Socrates — that we must sail through the dangers of life upon a raft of human theories, "unless someone should make that journey safer and less risky upon a firmer vessel of some divine doctrine."

Index

Subentries are sequenced according to the order of their first appearance in the text.

Abraham (of Ur), 128-29, 164, 208, 240, 280, 289, 296n.

Abraham, William, J., 69n., 72n., 83n., 298n.

Adams, J. C., 59

Adams, Marilyn McCord, 50, 128

Adams, Robert Merrihew, 50, 162, 306n.

Aeschylus, 317

Alpher, Ralph, 99

Alston, William P., 7n., 22n., 45, 52, 54

Ameriks, Karl, 28

Anderson, C. Anthony, 240n.

Anscombe, G. E. M. (Elizabeth), 97n., 154-55, 258, 260

Anselm (of Canterbury), 25

Aquinas, Thomas: Plantinga on A./Calvin model, 9; substantial forms and the space-time net, 43; limited afterlife of disembodied minds, 51; natural theology and the order of inquiry, 52-54n., 209; agent theory of action, 107; God drawing good out of evil, 140; contradictory of "God intends that there is no wrongdoing," 145; perfection requires attendant affection for highest objects, 151; end for A. not

same as end for Kant, 151-52; Thomistic standards for world-grading, 163n.; justice presupposes love and mercy, 165n.; Flannery on A., 183n.; "fittingness" arguments and the probability of creation, 194n.; mandates of sexual ethics, 206; systematic integration of revelatory claims, 220-22; God's knowledge is nonpropositional, 240-42; difficulty of refuting some theological claims, 240; A., Church, and Gödel as paragons of rationality, 240; A. v. Aristotle on the human end, 249; possibility of friendship with God, 250; the soul and fundamental equality, 258; deep connection between A. and Kant on morality, 263n.; natural law and the love precepts, 266-74; love precepts and self-evidence, 277n.; immoralities of the patriarchs, 280; charity as "the mother and root" of all virtues, 285; A., Luther, and Kierkegaard on faith, 294-95; certitude of faith rooted in the will, 298; classical foundationalism, 299; and Argument for Faith, 300n.;

40; ideal physics contains no reference to consciousness, 113; on the purpose of the universe, 234; honor to resist temptation to believe in God, 307

Wiesner, Hillary S., 238n.

Wigner, Eugene (E.P.), 111, 235

Wigoder, Geoffrey, 274n.

Wiles, Andrew, 193

Williams, Bernard, 257

Wittgenstein, Ludwig, 30-34, 84

Wolf, F. A., 66-67

Wolterstorff, Nicholas, 69n.

Wood, Allen W., 23n.

Woodruff, Paul B., 320n., 321n.

Wright, N. T., 71

Xenophon, 317

Zaehner, R. C., 203n., 204n.

Zagzebski, Linda, 300n.

Zeno (of Elea), 293, 296-97

Zetzel, James E. G., 66n.

Zoroaster, 236n.

Zwingli, Huldrych, 294